Cultivating California

Revisiting Rural America

Pete Daniel and Mary C. Neth
Series Editors

Mary Neth, *Preserving the Family Farm:*
Women, Community, and the Foundations of Agribusiness
in the Midwest, 1900–1940

Sally McMurry, *Transforming Rural Life:*
Dairying Families and Agricultural Change, 1820–1885

David B. Danbom, *Born in the Country:*
A History of Rural America

David Vaught, *Cultivating California:*
Growers, Specialty Crops, and Labor, 1875–1920

Cultivating California

Growers, Specialty Crops, and Labor, 1875–1920

David Vaught

The Johns Hopkins University Press
Baltimore and London

© 1999 The Johns Hopkins University Press
All rights reserved. Published 1999
Printed in the United States of America on acid-free paper
9 8 7 6 5 4 3 2 1

The Johns Hopkins University Press
2715 North Charles Street
Baltimore, Maryland 21218-4363
www.press.jhu.edu

Library of Congress Cataloging-in-Publication Data will be found
at the end of this book.
A catalog record for this book is available from the British Library.

ISBN 0-8018-6221-3

For Ethel

Contents

Acknowledgments

It is with great pleasure that I express my gratitude to the following individuals and institutions.

My thanks begin with those who made the research possible. I extend my deepest appreciation to the librarians and staffs at the Bancroft Library, University of California, Berkeley; the California State Archives, Sacramento; the California State Library, Sacramento; the Department of Special Collections, Henry Madden Library, California State University, Fresno; the Department of Special Collections, Meriam Library, California State University, Chico; the Hoover Institution Archives, Stanford University; the Placer County Recorder's Office, Auburn; the Northern Regional Library Facility of the University of California (in Richmond); and the Sacramento Archives and Museum Collection Center. Special thanks go to John Skarstad at the Department of Special Collections, University of California Library, Davis; Ellen Harding, California State Library, Sacramento; John Panter and Kelly Hobbs, Fresno City and County Historical Society; and Bill Green, National Archives, Pacific Sierra Region, San Bruno. Fellowships from the National Endowment for the Humanities, the Bancroft Library, and the Humanities Institute, University of California, Davis, and a Faculty Mini-Grant from Texas A&M University provided invaluable support.

I have had the good fortune to work closely with a number of dedicated scholars and teachers. David Brody, my advisor at Davis, challenged me to write clearly, to trust my instincts, and to reach for the highest of standards. My debt to him is incalculable. Morton Rothstein influenced me to think of this project as agricultural, rather than industrial, history. Michael Magliari shared his enthusiasm for California agriculture, read chapter drafts and the entire manuscript with a keen editorial eye, and helped me sharpen my arguments. Jim Rose and Jeff Kolnick shared the twists and turns of this project from the very start, providing friendship, humor, and advice—all equally invaluable. Robert Cherny, William Issel, and Jules Tygiel stimulated my interest in history when I was an undergraduate student at San Francisco State University; their generosity, integrity, and passion for their profession continue to inspire me. Others who graciously offered assistance along the way include Stuart Graybill, James Gregory, Howell Harris, Charles Katz, James Long, Roland Marchand, Alan Olmstead, Ruth Rosen, Richard Schwab, Michael L. Smith, Steven Stoll, and Clarence Walker. Hal Barron read the manuscript for the Johns Hopkins University Press and gave detailed, challenging, and exceedingly helpful comments. Editor Robert J. Brugger's unwavering support motivated me all the more, and copyeditor Nancy Trotic enhanced the quality of the final product substantially. I also am grateful to my colleagues at Texas A&M, especially Robert Calvert and Thomas Dunlap for their careful critiques of the manuscript, Julia Kirk Blackwelder for her support and encouragement, and R. J. Q. Adams and James Rosenheim for their sheer enthusiasm.

I wish to thank the University of California Press for granting permission to reprint material that appeared previously in two articles: "'An Orchardist's Point of View': Harvest Labor Relations on a California Almond Ranch, 1892–1921," *Agricultural History* 69 (Fall 1995): 563–591; and "Factories in the Field Revisited," *Pacific Historical Review* 66 (May 1997): 149–184. Thanks also to Jeff Grice, Cartographics, Texas A&M University, who redrew the maps with patience and precision; and to the A&M history department, which graciously paid him.

Most importantly, I thank my family. My parents, Robert and Marilyn, and my sister, Katherine, never lost confidence in me, even at times when I had myself. Linda Kato's faith in me inspired me to do my best. No one provided more constant companionship than Fergeson, though he was asleep most of the time. Diana, born in the middle of chapter 1, placed this project in proper perspective. Finally, I dedicate this book to my wife, Ethel Kato. She has given more of herself to me than I can ever give back, but that shall not discourage me from trying.

Cultivating California

Introduction

The raisin situation . . . is more than a private business question. The welfare of this whole community is so bound up in the prosperity of the raisin business, and the progress of that business is so dependent on organized and more or less public action, that raisin affairs have always been treated, and properly treated, as public affairs. . . . The raisin industry, in this community, can not be treated, and never has been treated, as "business" in that narrowly private sense.[1]

CHESTER ROWELL, Editor, *Fresno Morning Republican*, 1909

The old-fashioned farmer has been supplanted by a type to which the term can no longer be applied with accuracy. The new farmer is a grower. He is only semi-rural. Often he regards his farm as a business and has it incorporated. He belongs to a number of wealthy produce exchanges; he is a director of several "protective associations." Moreover, he has a hand in state politics. He employs a bookkeeper, and, in sober truth, he looks rather like a banker. He dabbles in publicity and has learned the trick of mob-baiting. He will never be an ally of labor.[2]

CAREY McWILLIAMS, *American Mercury*, 1934

THESE STATEMENTS SUGGEST two dramatically different conceptions of California agriculture. But only one will seem familiar to most scholars, specialists and nonspecialists alike. In the late nineteenth and early twentieth centuries, growers of deciduous and citrus fruits, grapes, vegetables, nuts, and hops helped pioneer the development of California's major "industry" — specialized, market-oriented, and labor-intensive farming. Chester Rowell, Fresno's most prominent political and social reformer, believed that "the welfare of this whole community" depended on the efforts of raisin growers. Like Rowell, Carey McWilliams was a journalist with a strong social conscience and progressive outlook. But McWilliams regarded California's farmers as a polarizing force. He feared their presence in public affairs and, moreover, believed their "business" mentality was the root cause of "rural civil war in California."[3]

When McWilliams published his *American Mercury* article in 1934, he had just begun his "education" in California's farm labor problem. Yet he already depicted the state's specialty crop farms as "factories" and its growers as "industrial agriculturists"—the twin tenets of an argument that he would develop more fully over the next five years.[4] His portrayal has shaped our understanding of agricultural labor relations in California ever since. Indeed, the highest praise a book on the subject can receive is still "belongs on the same shelf as Carey McWilliams's *Factories in the Field.*"[5]

Rowell's insistence not to treat "the raisin industry" as "business" seems puzzling. He did not mean that raisin and other specialty crop growers did not have capitalistic motives. As Rowell well knew, they sold their products to a national (often world) market and strove to turn a profit. But what are we to make of his depiction of the interdependence of specialty crop growers and their communities? We are not well equipped, it turns out, to answer such a question. Our perceptions of these historical actors have been limited to two dimensions: as avid believers in the family farm, or as people devoid of any ideology or culture whatsoever except the desire to cut costs and maximize profits. We have neglected to analyze the growers' worldview with the same rigor and subtlety that has characterized many studies of farmworkers.

The failure to examine growers on their own terms has yielded only a partial understanding of the state's farm labor *relations*—a concept whose plurality is often overlooked. It may well be that the "factories" metaphor works for certain crops at certain times—cotton in the 1930s, for example. But it cannot be applied to all crops at all times, and it generally works less well the further one goes back in time. The diversity of California's agriculture is well known, but the corresponding diversity and complexity of the labor systems that have sustained it remain something of a mystery.

This study seeks to unravel this mystery. It takes as its central focus the origins and development of farm labor relations in California (roughly 1875–1920), but its principal subjects are farmworkers' employers—specialty crop growers. Put another way, it is my objective to reassess the roots of the state's farm labor relations, and it is my contention that those roots are more likely to be found in grower, rather than worker, culture. Was every specialty crop grower like every other specialty crop grower? With respect to their labor systems, recruiting methods, and harvest needs, the size of their farms, and their interactions with their communities, unions, and the state, the answer, this study argues, is no. Growers should not be characterized in monolithic terms, any more than their workers should. They need to be analyzed in the full context of their culture if farm labor relations are to be understood more fully.

This was not how my research began, however. Like many before me, I set out to write a labor history of California specialty crop agriculture with the intention of building upon the "factories" framework. Inspired by the imaginative insights of "new" labor historians (scholars whose starting point is the worker), I intended to analyze farmworkers' experiences from their own perspectives, paying close attention to their language, ethnicity, gender, class loyalties, family networks, and community relations.

But about a year into my research, I stumbled onto something quite striking—the previously unexamined orchard records and lifelong diary of prominent almond grower George Washington Pierce Jr., rich materials housed on my home campus.[6] Pierce proved to be an intriguing subject. A self-proclaimed "horticulturist," he wrote passionately about his crop. He proudly cited the Bible's frequent references to the almond, he stressed the nut's nutritional value, and he marveled at his trees' esthetic appeal—their early, spectacular bloom in particular. With equal fervor and in minute detail, he described the harvesting process he pioneered in his Sacramento Valley orchards at the turn of the century. Pierce also influenced University of California officials to choose his hometown, Davis, as the site for a new agricultural college in 1906; he played a prominent role in the establishment of the California Almond Growers' Exchange in 1910; and he became the marketing cooperative's president in 1913—a position of considerable stature. With his moral, even righteous ideals about horticulture, Pierce hardly seemed like one of McWilliams's farmers who regarded California agriculture, in an often-repeated phrase, as "a business and not a way of life."

Nor did the scale and scope of Pierce's operation seem like a factory. The 132 acres he planted in the early 1890s made Pierce one of the larger almond growers in the state. But his orchards still were much smaller than the average California farm—which was about 400 acres in 1900. That average, though large, was skewed by a relatively small number of huge livestock and wheat ranches. At the turn of the century, according to census figures, roughly a fourth of all California farms covered less than 20 acres, a fourth between 20 and 49 acres, another fourth between 50 and 174, and the remaining fourth 175 or more. Fruit and nut farms in particular averaged well under 100 acres. Even in Pierce's county, Yolo, where grain and stock raising dominated the landscape, two-thirds of all

farms measured under 175 acres, and one-half under 100 acres.[7] Small orchards and vineyards in close proximity to one another, Pierce proclaimed, offered hard-working, community-minded individuals a "pleasant and profitable" alternative to either the isolation of rural life or the
"hustle and bustle" of the modern industrial city.

Still, farm size alone does not define relations of production—in
Pierce's orchards or elsewhere. And indeed, Pierce's horticultural mission to "minister to the needs and pleasures of mankind," as he put it,
bore an Achilles' heel—harvest labor relations. Every almond harvest
presented him with two interconnected problems: recruiting a sufficient
labor force and maintaining a high quality of work. In time, he came to
depend on a Sikh immigrant contractor to provide him with a ready
source of skillful, compliant workers. When that contractor suddenly returned to India, Pierce became so desperate that he tracked him down in
Hong Kong, sent him a steamer ticket to recross the Pacific, and wran-
gled with Angel Island immigration officials for weeks to obtain his release. This intensely personal grower-contractor relationship did not
seem to fit into the "factories" mold, either. Perhaps most striking was
the fact that while Pierce celebrated his horticultural ideal, his labor relations remained a personal, private affair buried in his diary and orchard
records.[8]

With Pierce at the forefront of my mind, I went back and reread all
the standard works.[9] Their emphasis on large-scale farms, unscrupulous
growers, and anti-union grower organizations seemed to have no place
for Pierce and his turn-of-the-century counterparts. How, I began to
ask, had "factories in the field"—a phrase that had long since "passed
into general use"[10]—endured for so long with so little criticism? With
all we now know about California farmworkers, western irrigation crusaders, and farmers from throughout much of the rest of the country,
why do we know so little about "horticulturists" like Pierce?[11]

The answer lies in the powerful impact of the farm labor strife of the
1930s—a decade that would define how McWilliams and his generation
saw their world. A young, disillusioned attorney and journalist in Los
Angeles during the 1920s, McWilliams considered himself more a bo-
hemian intellectual than a radical social critic. But an explosion of farm
labor strikes throughout much of rural California ignited a transformation in McWilliams's political consciousness. In 1933 alone, an estimated
50,000 farmworkers participated in 37 labor disturbances, culminating in
October when 18,000 cotton pickers went on strike throughout the San

Joaquin Valley. While farm laborers joined unions in unprecedented numbers, growers blamed "Communist agitators" for disrupting their harvests and organized statewide associations to protect their crops, often with violent consequences. "The headlines were so insistent, the social drama so intense, I felt compelled to find out what was going on," McWilliams recollected.[12] In May 1935, McWilliams and fellow journalist Herbert Klein embarked on a 12-day tour of the various strike areas. Driving a beat-up 1928 Dodge roadster through Bakersfield, Fresno, Sacramento, and Salinas, they interviewed workers, labor contractors, growers, and government officials and inspected living and working conditions. "I returned to Los Angeles from this trip," McWilliams remembered, "determined to tell the story of migratory farm labor in California and promptly set to work."[13]

McWilliams proceeded to tell, in his words, "a melodramatic history, a story of theft, fraud, violence, and exploitation." Part muckraking exposé and part narrative history, *Factories in the Field* appeared in 1939 and shattered the myth of "the tranquillity of rural California" by tracing the monopolistic character of landownership back to the pre-statehood Mexican land grants. Focusing primarily on the growth of the sugar beet and cotton industries, McWilliams drew sweeping conclusions for all California specialty crops, arguing that large farms producing specialized crops created a factory-like system whose profits depended on a large force of cheap, mobile workers, particularly vulnerable immigrants. "The rudiments of the [farm labor] problem as it exists today," McWilliams asserted, "existed in 1886," the year California growers shipped their first full train of fruit to the East Coast. McWilliams placed the responsibility for this exploitive labor system squarely on the shoulders of nineteenth-century "land grabbers" such as William S. Chapman, Isaac Friedlander, Henry Miller, and Charles Lux. These efficiently organized and politically powerful men, McWilliams argued, were the forefathers of the virulently anti-union Associated Farmers of the 1930s. While McWilliams referred to the members of this group as "farm fascists," they in turn labeled him "Agricultural Pest No. 1 in California, outranking pear blight and boll weevil."[14]

This passionate engagement with his subject brought McWilliams and *Factories* instant acclaim. His sympathy for agricultural workers, utter contempt for "farm industrialists," and dramatic flair gave *Factories* a near-epic tone. The book remained on the best-seller lists for months while McWilliams and Philip Bancroft, vice-president of the Associated

Farmers, debated the issues on the radio and in public meetings. McWilliams had already established himself as a presumed expert. Six months prior to the publication of *Factories* in July 1939, Governor Culbert L. Olson had appointed him to head the Division of Immigration and Housing, a state agency that inspected labor camps. And, along with the nearly simultaneous publication of John Steinbeck's *The Grapes of Wrath*, McWilliams's *Factories* "provided the thrust necessary" to induce the U.S. Senate Committee on Education and Labor (chaired by Senator Robert La Follette Jr. of Wisconsin) to investigate California farm labor disputes. The "excitement, action, controversy, and conflict" generated by the farm labor problem, McWilliams remembered, seemed to have taken on "apocalyptic overtones."[15]

The outbreak of World War II and the subsequent return of agricultural prosperity, however, severely undermined the expectations that *Factories* had helped create. "What some of us had thought would be a climactic phase of the farm labor story turned out to be merely another chapter," McWilliams wrote.[16] Yet his sympathetic engagement with workers and his activist approach have continued to influence critics of California agriculture. In the late 1960s, in particular, a new generation of activist-intellectuals, motivated by a resurgent farm labor movement led by César Chávez, turned to *Factories* for historical guidance and inspiration.[17] One reviewer of the 1971 reprint of *Factories* captured McWilliams's lasting influence: "If there had been no Carey McWilliams back in the latter days of the 1930s, we would have had to invent one. How else to see in economic and historic perspective the long, bitter conflict that raged in California's golden valleys? How else to understand the repeated, insistent demand of farm workers for a decent wage? How else to account for the unyielding anger, the explosive violence with which the growers met the demand? And how else to fit this everlasting fountain of agricultural wealth into a total scheme of state and nation?"[18]

Though lacking McWilliams's crusading style, Paul S. Taylor's contributions to the history of California farm labor have left a pervasive influence as well. At the onset of the farmworker uprisings in the early 1930s, Taylor had already established his scholarly reputation as an economist at the University of California.[19] Throughout the decade, he investigated the violent strikes for several federal and state government agencies. Taylor observed, researched, and wrote about the 1933 cotton strike and many of the other 150 farm labor disturbances of the decade, and he collaborated with his wife, photographer Dorothea Lange, to document in words and images the working and living conditions of migrant workers.[20] These experiences greatly disturbed Taylor and convinced him of the profoundly exploitive nature of California specialty crop agriculture. He was the key expert witness on agricultural labor for the La Follette Committee, which held hearings in San Francisco in 1939. After presenting testimony, several prepared statements, and dozens of graphs and tables of statistics, he asked the defining question of the hearings and of his career: "Can a large farm labor class be reconciled with democracy?"[21]

Taylor's answer differed little from McWilliams's. Indeed, what McWilliams called "factories in the field," Taylor termed "industrialized agriculture." He defined this concept as much by what it did not signify as by its fundamental characteristics:

> Most Americans are accustomed to think of farming as a family enterprise carried on by a "farmer" working beside his sons and an occasional hired man. But the dominant type of enterprise producing from the soil in California is the industrialized farm, specializing in one or two commercial crops and operated by a "grower" who employs gangs of laborers whom he hires and fires as needed. Under this system, which utilizes foremen, gang labor, piece rates, recruiting by labor agents and contractors, the paternalism traditional between farmer and hired man is virtually absent, unemployment is intermittent and severe, milling about from crop to crop is necessary in order to obtain work, the average annual earnings are low despite wage rates which appear high, and opportunity to ascend the agricultural ladder from laborer to tenant to owner is practically closed.[22]

The development of irrigated, intensive, commercial agriculture, Taylor believed, made the typical farmhand obsolete and required instead a "semi-industrialized rural proletariat."[23] While less vociferous than McWilliams, Taylor also blamed the state's large growers and their demand for cheap labor for this undemocratic, nonagrarian rural social structure. He remained committed to the cause of the family farmer, researching and promoting land and water reform for most of his professional career.[24]

"Factories in the field" and "industrialized agriculture," we need to realize, are themselves products of the 1930s. Strongly motivated by immediate concerns, both McWilliams and Taylor reasoned backward from their perceptions of that turbulent decade to formulate their farm labor histories. Their efforts to create a usable past have left us with an inadequate framework for understanding the earlier history of California agriculture. Taylor all but boasted of his presentist approach. "Whatever I worked upon," he said, "whether contemporary agricultural labor or water problems, I've gone quickly to historical sources to find what light they could throw on the problem, and I've *never* been disappointed. Historical sources always have helped and enriched my understanding enormously."[25] He passed this limited historical perspective on to his graduate students—most notably Varden Fuller, Stuart Jamieson, Walter Goldschmidt, and Walter Stein—who themselves went on to expand upon their mentor's conception of industrialized agriculture.[26]

The "industrial" metaphor continues to hold sway even today. California farmworkers have captured the imagination of recent social historians who are driven by the concept of worker agency and by the principle that the past be seen as it actually happened.[27] These scholars have devoted considerable effort to analyzing agricultural laborers in their social, cultural, and ideological contexts, and have done so, for the most part, with originality and empirical freshness. But growers have not been studied with the same historical sensitivity. They remain as McWilliams and Taylor described them over half a century ago—as cost-conscious employers embedded in the "structure of specialized capitalist agriculture"[28] with little apparent culture or agency of their own. Our understanding of California farm labor relations, so well developed on the one side, has suffered from reductionist cultural materialism on the other. This selective analysis of human agency has obscured as much as it has revealed about the history of California agriculture.[29]

It is time for an alternative approach. This study treats "industrialized agriculture" not as doctrine, but as a problem for empirical study. Just how "industrial" were California specialty crop farms of the late nineteenth and early twentieth centuries? What does it even mean to say that farms took on industrial qualities? Taylor's definition for the La Follette Committee offers a precision generally lacking in both his own writings and those of subsequent historians. Taylor himself often bracketed the phrase "industrialized agriculture" in quotation marks, as though its meaning were self-evident. This vague yet readily accepted concept has become so all-encompassing that virtually all agricultural enterprises in California, apart from the "traditional family farm," have been perceived as "industrial." In most accounts, this way of thinking marks the 1880s as "the beginning of the age of agribusiness" in the state.[30]

My interest in grower culture and my dissatisfaction with "industrialized agriculture" notwithstanding, this study remains a history of labor relations. As such, its starting point is the workplace. In this case, however, the shop floor is not a "factory," but a raisin vineyard, a peach orchard, an almond orchard, and a hop field, each with its own peculiar set of properties. The implications of this cannot be overstated. Specialty crop labor relations need to be analyzed in their *agricultural* context. Day after day, year after year, growers confronted problems that would have baffled most contemporary industrialists, including small-scale—but intensive—production, seasonal and environmental pressures, intricate labor systems, distant markets, community relations, and their own cultural idealism and racial ambivalence. Radicalism and unionism, on the other hand, are de-emphasized here. Farmworkers certainly exhibited these tendencies even prior to the 1930s, but previous accounts have exaggerated both their frequency and their significance.

My focus is more on the everyday interplay of growers and workers, growers and their crops, growers themselves, growers and their communities, growers and their marketing cooperatives, and, especially during the 1910s, growers and the state and federal governments. The dynamics of ethnic relations, especially anti-Asian sentiments, and the role of the state are therefore important threads in this analysis. Over time, approximately two generations, these interactions would shape farm labor relations throughout the state. By the end of World War I, "factories in the field" or "industrialized agriculture" would more aptly describe California specialty crop agriculture. A relatively small number of large growers would begin to dominate both politically and in labor relations, and the larger patterns of agriculture that so troubled McWilliams and Taylor would begin to emerge. Just how this historical process played itself out is the central theme of this study.

It was the growers, my empirical odyssey has convinced me, who were the principal dynamic force in this historical process. This book begins, therefore, by examining in detail the language, perceptions, and behavior of California's first generation of raisin, fresh deciduous fruit, almond, and hop growers. They turn out to be fascinating and complex historical actors. Indeed, Chester Rowell's warning not to treat specialty crop agriculture "as 'business' in that narrowly private sense" rings just as true for us today as it did for contemporaries nearly a century ago. Growers were not simply traditionalists devoted to the "mythic resonance of the family farm," to use one historian's apt phrase.[31] Nor were they simply economic men. We should think of them neither as agrarians nor as industrialists, but as horticulturists. In their orchards and vineyards, horticulturists fervently believed they were cultivating not only specialty crops, but California itself. Their mission was to promote both small, virtuous communities *and* economic development. Unabashedly and often with great exuberance, they advanced this horticultural ideal within a framework that blended both agrarian and capitalist perspectives. Ultimately, however, the labor requirements of their crops, market imperatives, and changing political conditions would undermine their glittering dream.

1 "More Than Manufacturing"

The Making of Specialty Crop Culture

THE FRESNO RAISIN HARVEST of 1902 began in late August and lasted five weeks. "Almost perfect conditions" prevailed in the San Joaquin Valley, the *California Fruit Grower* reported, to "insure the choicest product." Spring had come and gone without significant frost, grasshoppers and other pests had inflicted minimal damage, the summer remained hot and clear, and the rains held off until late October, long after the curing process was over.[1] Fresno vineyardists supplied "the people of the country with practically all the raisins that they eat"—70 million pounds in 1902, two-thirds of the state's crop and almost double Spain's output. Just 20 years earlier, the region had seemed "without a solitary shrub or tree," recalled a resident. "A mirage of water in the road ahead was the only relief to the effect of utter barrenness."[2] Now, within a 20-mile radius of the city of Fresno, 3,000 raisin vineyards of 10 to 40 acres, 5,000 miles of irrigation canals and ditches, and several thriving towns decorated the landscape. Fresno, the prestigious *Overland Monthly* proclaimed, had become "the paradise of the industrious man of small means."[3]

Similarly, "horticulture in the foothills of northern California has in twenty years developed into an industry of enormous proportions," wrote Harry E. Butler, a grower-shipper from the Newcastle fruit district of Placer County. In the early 1880s, pioneers such as Butler's father began to convert this region's economy from mining to fruit growing. Canals constructed by gold seekers in the 1850s irrigated small deciduous orchards (averaging 30 acres) by the turn of the century.[4] Newcastle, located 30 miles northeast of Sacramento on the main line of the Southern Pacific Railroad, became the largest single shipping depot for fresh deciduous fruit in California. In 1902, seven companies on "fruit house row" shipped 1,600 carloads (over 20,000 tons) to markets across the continent. Loomis, Penryn, and Auburn—shipping points within six miles of Newcastle—contributed an additional 1,000 carloads. One-third of the state's total output of "green" fruit was grown within five miles of these four towns. From May through October, the Placer fruit belt was "a bustling scene of activity." On peak days, farm wagons by the hundreds transported fruit to the shipping houses. This fragile, perish-

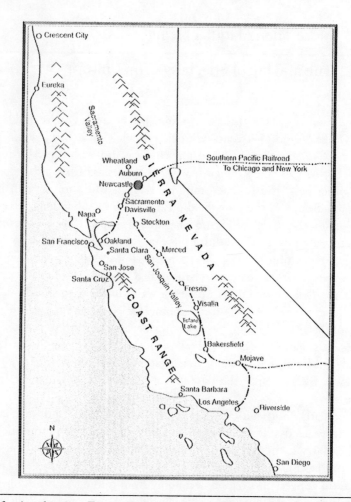

California, showing Fresno, Wheatland, and Davisville, and highlighting Newcastle's favorable shipping location. Based on *Placer County Republican,* October 23, 1913.

able freight would reach midwestern and eastern markets one to three days sooner than would fruit from any other district in the state.[5]

Forty-five miles west down the Southern Pacific tracks, the town of Davisville had become the hub of the state's principal almond district. At the turn of the century, 26 growers owned orchards totaling 1,000 acres bordering Putah Creek in southern Yolo County. In 1902, these growers had their best harvest to date. They produced almost 300 tons of almonds—20 percent of California's total crop, more than any other district. Marketing their crop through the Davisville Almond Growers' Association, the state's "parent almond organization," these 26 growers distributed over $75,000 among themselves that year.[6] Most of these orchardists, including Jacob E. La Rue, James F. Chiles, and George W. Pierce Jr., were also wheat farmers—"agriculturists as well as horticulturists," as the local newspaper put it. Pierce, the association's vice-president, earned over $3,000 from the 14 tons his trees produced in 1902, the first year his almond income surpassed his grain revenue.[7] The success he and other Putah Creek almond growers enjoyed also attracted the attention of the *Overland Monthly*, which described their orchards as "the finest in the world."[8]

For hop growers near the town of Wheatland in southern Yuba County (25 miles northwest of Newcastle, 40 miles northeast of Davisville), the 1902 season also was "a banner one." Hops were rapidly becoming an important crop in California agriculture. Production on the Pacific Coast had surpassed that of New York for the first time in 1893, and by the turn of the century, California had become Oregon's chief competitor.[9] The center of hop culture in the Sacramento Valley, Wheatland produced the largest and best crops of any locality in the state. The soft resin of the Wheatland hop, a product of the Bear River's rich bottomlands, was of great value to British brewers, the crop's principal buyers. D. P. Durst, a physician and one of Wheatland's founders, planted the first hops on the Bear River in 1883.[10] By 1902, his three sons and two other growers, E. Clemons Horst and P. C. Drescher, owned all of Wheatland's hop lands—about 1,200 acres. These three yards produced about 8,000 bales (185 pounds per bale)—15 percent of the state's crop—in that year. "Wheatland has become famous on account of this great industry," declared the *Pacific Rural Press*, the state's leading agricultural journal.[11]

Fresno, Newcastle, Davisville, and Wheatland all had become famous for their crops by the turn of the century. Financiers throughout the world "viewed with amazement the push and energy that is exhibited by the growers of the comparatively new field of industry [in California]," reported a leading New York business journal in 1893.[12] This new field—specialized, market-oriented, and labor-intensive farming—achieved eminence during the last two decades of the nineteenth century. Fruits and nuts in particular made California synonymous with health and prosperity to millions of Americans. By 1900, California farmers produced more than a quarter of all the fruit raised in the United States—including 95 percent of the almonds, walnuts, apricots, and olives and half the plums, prunes, peaches, grapes, and citrus. Fruit growing had become the state's leading industry, generating $28 million at the turn of the century.[13]

These producers referred to themselves, however, neither as farmers nor industrialists, but as horticulturists, orchardists, vineyardists, and growers. Their occupation, they believed, was special. "Horticulture is more than trade—it is more than manufacturing," wrote Edward J. Wickson, editor of the *Pacific Rural Press*, in 1899. "As man develops and improves the plant and shapes its growth to better serve honorable ends, the mental acts react upon the mind itself; it sees new beauties, it discerns new uses, it invents new methods and processes, it perceives new and more refined relations and differences." In mastering the intricacies of their particular crop's culture, these growers believed they were also enriching California's culture. Their horticultural ideal was not only to advance themselves materially, but also to promote economic and social progress in their communities and throughout the state. "The action is horticulture," concluded Wickson, "the reaction is homoculture."[14]

The perception of specialty crop agriculture as "more than manufacturing" stemmed in part from the fact that California manufacturing itself showed little promise. Small local markets, isolation from the population centers of the East Coast and Midwest, a lack of sufficient capital, and a scarcity of iron, coal, and other raw materials retarded industrial expansion into the early twentieth century. Even in San Francisco, which in 1880 had more manufacturing establishments than all the other 24 western cities combined, these restrictions limited industrial development. Manufacturing in California, moreover, was primarily an adjunct of agriculture; San Francisco's leading manufacture in 1900 was the processing of agricultural products. Nor did the first transcontinental railroad (completed in 1869) spur industrial growth in California, as many had anticipated. Instead, the railroad opened up western markets— which Californians had been accustomed to monopolizing—to opportunistic eastern producers.[15] Through the 1920s, neither San Francisco nor any other California city became a major manufacturing center on the order of Pittsburgh or Detroit. The state's economy was rooted in agriculture.

California's natural attributes, while not conducive to manufacturing, were ideal for agriculture. The uniqueness of the state's geology and climate provides for remarkable productivity and diversity. A series of mountain ranges and valleys, created by the westward drift of the North American continent across and above the floor of the Pacific Ocean, divide the state into a number of distinct micro-environments or subregions with their own unique climates, soils, topography, and natural vegetation. These variations enable each subregion to specialize in particular crops—semitropical and temperate-zone fruits, nuts, hops, winter vegetables, cotton, and rice, among others. The Pacific Ocean and two principal mountain chains—the Coast Range on the west and the Sierra Nevada on the east—protect most of the state from extreme temperatures and snow, creating mild winters, rainless summers, and long growing seasons. California encompasses the only region in North America with such superior geographic and climatic assets. In effect, they bestow upon agriculture supply-side advantages that other late-nineteenth-century industries simply did not enjoy.[16]

Yet growers struggled to take advantage of the state's agricultural endowment. "It is almost impossible," observed a contemporary in 1885, "for the younger men and women of California to realize how slowly the horticultural possibilities of this domain of Coast Range, great central valley, and Sierra foothills, were at last revealed."[17] By the bumper harvest of 1902, growers had developed a keen understanding of California's unusual agricultural structure, but only through arduous and expensive experimentation, and by sharing their struggles and triumphs. "In California," Wickson wrote, "equally excellent methods and care may produce perfection in one place and the opposite in another. One who seeks to know California well must undertake to master both its horticultural greatness and littleness."[18] While Wickson was referring to matters of husbandry, his remarks also held the key to understanding specialty crop "homoculture," as he called it: the beliefs, values, symbols, and perceptions growers used to define their world both in and outside their orchards and vineyards are best examined both within the context of their micro-environments and in the aggregate. Four of the more prosperous subregions—Fresno, Newcastle, Davisville, and Wheatland—provide revealing case studies.[19]

FRESNO MAY HAVE BEEN the most unlikely subregion of all to experience agricultural prosperity, especially with raisins as its staple crop. In 1875, according to an early historical sketch, "a more forlorn, dreary, desolate, unpromising-looking place would have been impossible to find.

There was not a single apparent reason for a settlement at this point, and that more than a few hundred people should ever center here seemed an impossibility." Located deep in the interior of the San Joaquin Valley, Fresno was a 10-hour journey from San Francisco by rail and could not be reached by a reliable water route. Nor, as another observer remarked, was there anything "especially attractive in soil or climate above a hundred other places in Northern California." Contemporaries ridiculed the few "sand-lappers" who attempted to reclaim the land for cultivation.[20] Yet in 15 years, the Fresno region had several thriving raisin communities. This metamorphosis could not have occurred without an abundant water supply (the Kings River) and, moreover, without the efforts of land speculators, the Southern Pacific Railroad, and the growers themselves.[21]

Agricultural land settlement in Fresno County took a form different from the individualistic pattern characteristic of nineteenth-century America. When the Central Pacific extended its line into the San Joaquin Valley in the early 1870s, homesteaders did not come there in droves. The public land system did little to attract settlers. Large portions of pre-statehood Mexican land grants remained intact in huge estates covering many thousands of acres. A series of shortsighted state and federal laws effectively conceded California's remaining public lands to wheat barons, cattlemen, and speculators, rather than to small farmers. In the Fresno area, agricultural conditions also contributed to the concentration of landownership. Stock raising in particular proved ideally suited to the area's flat land and sparse population. It required little commitment to improving the land, little experience, and little labor. But the grazing industry demanded landholdings far greater than the 160 acres that federal law allotted to homesteaders—hardly an attraction for prospective settlers.[22] Furthermore, arid conditions made irrigation necessary for more intensive kinds of agriculture. But because California law recognized both prior appropriation and riparian rights, individual water claims often conflicted and could take years to settle in court. An equitable and uniform system of water distribution could be attained only by private means—by an individual or company willing and wealthy enough to purchase a huge block of land, secure its water right, and subdivide it into small irrigation farms. The condemnations by social critics from Henry George to Carey McWilliams notwithstanding, land in the San Joaquin Valley could only be watered by monopolizing it.[23]

Two of California's most notorious land speculators of the late 1860s and 1870s, William Chapman and Isaac Friedlander, were the first to comprehend the obstacles to successful reclamation and settlement. In 1868, four years before the Central Pacific reached Fresno, Chapman and Friedlander organized a syndicate of San Francisco capitalists to purchase 125 sections (80,000 acres) in a nearly solid block surrounding present-day Fresno. That site, they believed, held tremendous agricultural potential: Chapman and two other syndicate members, A. Y. Easterby and Moses J. Church, had successfully cultivated alfalfa and wheat in the area; the close proximity to the Kings River and a high annual rainfall (relative to the western and southern regions of the San Joaquin Valley) ensured an ample water supply; and the railroad would link Fresno to markets across the country. The syndicate proved too promising for its own good; members began selling portions of their interests to outside purchasers, making the original arrangement too cumbersome to manage. In 1873, they dissolved the syndicate and distributed the land among themselves. These men, including Chapman, Easterby, Church, Wendell Easton, and E. B. Perrin, proceeded to organize irrigation companies and subdivide their land into "colonies" — communities of 20-acre farms sustained by a matrix of canals and lateral ditches.[24]

In 1875, Chapman and Bernhard Marks, a frustrated farmer who became one of the state's leading agricultural land salesmen, established the first successful settlement, the Central California Colony. They selected 21 sections of the region's best land, about three miles southwest of the Fresno depot. By August, they had surveyed and leveled six of the sections and divided them into 192 lots of twenty acres each. As their debts mounted, the developers planned for quick and dense settlement. Lots, water rights included, were priced to sell at $1,000 ($100 down, $12.50 per month, and no interest even with delinquent payments). The Fresno Canal and Irrigation Company (incorporated in 1871 by Chapman and Church) built a complete system of canals, laterals, and gates to supply Kings River water to each tract. The developers laid out 23 miles of roads between the lots, lining them with varieties of fruit trees and naming each avenue after its particular fruit. The trees, Marks hoped, "would lend comfort and cheerfulness to the scene, and make the people feel contented. . . . [The] most important thing in founding a colony is to have the people contented."[25] Marks also imported thousands of grapevines from Spain and planted two acres on each tract, and he hired expert farmers to advise agricultural novices.

Nevertheless, the colony attracted only 54 settlers by the end of the

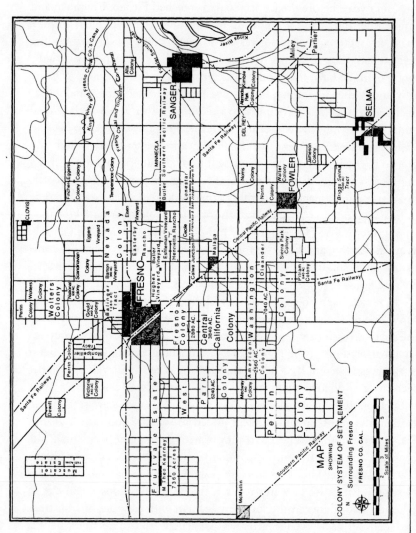

The Fresno colonies, ca. 1900. Based on M. Theo Kearney, *Fresno County, California, and the Evolution of the Fruitvale Estate* (Fresno: by author, 1903), 24.

year. After considering abandoning the scheme, Chapman hired one of his accountants, M. Theo Kearney, to launch an extensive advertising campaign. Kearney promoted the colony in newspapers, pamphlets, and posters throughout the country. His standard pitch began: "Why will you go on year after year planting grain, trusting to the uncertain rainfall, and invariably losing in a dry season the hard-earned savings of several favorable years, when in the CENTRAL CALIFORNIA COLONY, you may secure land and an abundance of water to irrigate it at a moderate price and easy terms of payment?"[26] Kearney's expertise helped save the colony. In the next two years, new settlers purchased the remaining lots and planted vineyards, orchards, and vegetable gardens. They also established a church, a school, a Grange organization, a doctor's office, and even a drama club. This frontier environment had become a self-sufficient community.

The colony founded by Chapman, Marks, and Kearney served as a blueprint for subsequent endeavors. By 1890, 34 similar settlements surrounded Fresno. They varied in area from one to 14 sections and covered over 50,000 acres.[27] Developers provided irrigation, vine cuttings and nursery stock, agricultural guidance, roads, shade trees, and a host of other amenities. Prices and credit terms varied from colony to colony, but competition to attract buyers kept rates reasonable. Most colonists purchased a single 20-acre lot, although some developers sold tracts as large as a quarter section, and on occasion individuals bought more than one standard unit. Kearney himself purchased the Fruit Vale Estate, a 6,720-acre tract centered six miles west of Fresno, and began irrigating and subdividing half of it. Meanwhile, the Southern Pacific did more for the region's growth than merely lay down tracks. Fully aware that its own success was linked to agricultural advancement, the corporation organized free excursion trains from other California cities to Fresno, promoted the benefits of colony life through the popular writings of New York journalist Charles Nordhoff, and established land-development agencies of its own to organize agricultural settlements.[28] The colonies encouraged the development of small towns—Oleander, Malaga, Fowler, and Selma, for example—with schools, churches, dairies, and social clubs. By the turn of the century, colony boundaries had become blurred by further settlement, creating a vast, unbroken region of small farmers. "Continuous rows of vineyards," remarked one observer standing near the Fresno city limits in 1890, extended "as far as we can trace."[29]

The fact that vineyards—mostly raisin vineyards—dominated the landscape tells us much about the settlers and their early experiences. Early on, Chapman, Church, and other developers conceived grapes as primarily ornamental, and anticipated that alfalfa and wheat would be the staple crops. Colonists soon realized, however, that the hot, dry summer days, the cool, moisture-free nights, and the valley's sandy loams produced grapes "of excellent quality . . . clean, large, plump, and juicy."[30] Several bunches, so the legend goes, dried up accidentally in Francis T. Eisen's experimental vineyard in 1875. Marketing them in San Francisco as a "Peruvian importation," Eisen caused an immediate sensation. Settlers discovered that the leading Mediterranean variety of raisin grape— the Muscat—thrived in Fresno's natural environment. And raisin profits averaged $100 to $300 per acre; wheat, in contrast, required 50 acres to clear a similar amount. By the mid-1880s, a "vineyard mania" had swept through the colonies. Production skyrocketed: Fresno growers produced 80,000 pounds of raisins in 1882, 2 million in 1885, and 9.5 million in 1889.[31] Success did not come easily, however. Many settlers, recalled one pioneer's son, at first "hardly knew the difference between a raisin and a prune. . . . The beginning of this enterprise almost looked like a case of 'fools stepping in where angels fear to tread.' I have often wondered at father's nerve."[32]

It took more than nerve, suitable conditions, and developers' amenities to master the intricacies of raisin culture. There was no substitute for practical experience in the vineyards. How far apart to plant the vines? How to mark out a vineyard? How to plant and care for the cuttings? When and how to plow, furrow, graft, prune, pick, and cure? Only after "years of experimenting and study . . . , as well as much money and disappointment to many," wrote contemporary raisin expert Gustav Eisen, did vineyardists find adequate answers to such questions. A. D. Barling's experience is a case in point. Barling rented a lot in the Central Colony in 1882. He and his wife "went to work with a will and set out the land in Muscat cuttings." But in 1885 they lost the entire crop. Conventional wisdom regarded rigorous pruning as essential for large grapes. But Barling noticed that "the vines which were pruned most closely were also those which suffered the most." Without sufficient foliage, it turned out, Barling's grapes had wilted under Fresno's sweltering sun. The following year, he tried more "judicious pruning," and with "great success." His astute observation soon set a new standard for pruning throughout the region, and Barling himself emerged as one of Fresno's most prominent growers.[33]

The empirical nature of raisin growing engendered both pride and a sense of meticulousness. Raisin culture "is eminently made up of details," grower T. C. White explained. "None can be carelessly performed or overlooked." "The more care the better raisins," insisted his neighbor, M. F. Austin. "Too much stress cannot be laid on this work," added Eisen. Proper care, furthermore, not only produced "the essentials of quality and quantity," it also yielded an "esthetic" appeal. A carelessly staked out vineyard, for example, appeared "unsightly," in addition to making plowing and cultivating more difficult. "Crooked rows in a vineyard are the surest signs that the proprietor does not know his business," Eisen wrote. "To the trained horticulturist no sight is more disgusting and inspires less confidence than a vineyard where the rows look as if they were drunk and where the plowman has to pick his way among straggling vines."[34] Eisen, White, Austin, A. B. Butler, Joseph T. Goodman, William Forsyth, Frank H. Ball—these "pioneer vineyardists on the barren plains of the San Joaquin Valley" became icons of raisin culture. The experience, knowledge, and passion they imparted through "essays" and "treatises" published in local newspapers and agricultural periodicals left an enduring legacy. "Their fame," one such journal wrote, "can never be blotted out of the annals of the raisin industry."[35]

The first recipients of that legacy are less well known. Just what type of individual would have pulled up roots and moved to such an unknown, desolate area in response to a promotional pamphlet? Developers targeted a specific "class of people," Marks told an interviewer.[36] While offering numerous inducements, they made it clear that most crops did not produce an immediate positive return. "Get some money first," warned one pamphlet. "Assure yourself of payments. Get the means to live on for two years at least."[37] On the average, in fact, raisins took five years to return a profit. "With the aid of capital," promoters promised, the settler would enjoy the best of both rural and urban worlds. To the farmer dissatisfied with the social isolation of a 160-acre homestead, Fresno offered "near neighbors, a most intelligent community, good schools and ample church accommodations, frequent mails, social pleasures, . . . [and] opportunities to live comfortably and enjoy the benefits of civilization." To "the mechanic, tradesman, clerk, [and] physician" struggling in "life-long drudgery," raisin growing provided "pleasant and profitable employment, . . . health, and the pleasures of a pleasant and happy home."[38] The San Joaquin Valley, wrote Nordhoff, presented "the best opportunity in the world" for those with a small nest egg and "Eastern habits of industry" to attain independence, challenging work, and social fulfillment. For Marks, the "prosperous and industrious people" lured to the colonies left no doubt that "the sceme [sic] was a great success."[39]

A few of those enticed by promotions of "boundless acres of fertile soil with life-giving water" were women. M. F. Austin's Hedge-Row Vineyard, one of the Central California Colony's earliest successes, was "most notable," according to an 1891 history, "from the fact of its having been started . . . by a lady." Minnie Austin, "in company with lady friend, Lucy Hatch," purchased five 20-acre lots along Elm Avenue in 1878 and planted 77 acres of vines. Her contemporaries praised her "New England pluck and energy" and credited her with numerous innovations to Fresno's burgeoning raisin culture. The Hedge-Row Vineyard, however, became most well known for its contributions to Fresno's domestic culture. Drawing upon their "womanly taste and refinement," Austin and Hatch transformed a "paved and dusty wagon road" into a "grand avenue" by bordering their property with a mile-long hedge of pomegranate shrubs. Similarly, their "handsome two-story house"—decorated with gables, porches, galleries, and picture windows—"was of such attractive style and embellishment that the very sight of it gave courage to other settlers." A raisin vineyard, Austin and Hatch seemed to assure their male counterparts, was a place of refuge as well as a place of work and commerce, offering all the Victorian virtues of home, hearth, and domesticity. Raisin growing, however, despite the efforts of Austin and the "many ladies who imitated her," remained a decisively masculine realm. "Mother Nature has favored [Fresno] highly and has given it a wealth that no other district has," wrote a local enthusiast. But it was men, as Eisen wrote, who produced the "strong and vigorous vines" that "made a specialty of the raisin industry." Austin's many publications, in fact, were signed "M. F." to conceal her gender identity. Men, another female vineyardist lamented, clung to "the traditional idea that women knew nothing of affairs."[40]

The promise of community life attracted groups of settlers to Fresno. Kearney, Church, and other promoters traveled to the Midwest, the East Coast, and even Europe to recruit colonists. News of the success of the Central, Washington, and other early colonies provided the best inducement of all. Settlers from Norway, Sweden, Denmark, England, Germany, Portugal, Italy, Turkish Armenia, Russia, China, and Japan came to Fresno during the 1880s and 1890s. Members of these groups tended to settle with relatives or friends from their native countries, and some established separate colonies of their own. The Armenians, Italians, and Portuguese brought their knowledge of viticulture and irrigation agriculture and greatly contributed to the growth of Fresno's raisin industry. Native-born colonists, most of whom migrated from Kansas, Minnesota, Michigan, and other midwestern states, outnumbered the foreign-born by more than two to one. Still, by 1900, Fresno had become one of the more cosmopolitan regions in the country. The colonists' ideal of their new home was captured in the name of an Armenian community—Yettem, meaning the Garden of Eden. They knew well, however, that their fate as irrigation farmers rested on more earthly qualities. "There was never but one Garden of Eden," admitted Wendell Easton, one of three founders of the Washington Colony. "To make success of anything in Fresno County, labor and time are both necessary."[41]

Success in marketing required more than passion and perseverance. Once growers picked and dried their grapes, two distinct processes—packing and selling—remained, and both required the expertise of others. Expensive equipment and facilities well beyond the means of all but a few of the largest growers were needed to prepare the cured grapes for market. To handle that task, 20 packing companies, including Cook & Langley, Griffin & Skelley, and Fresno Home Packing, were established during the 1880s. After purchasing the cured crop outright (in cash) from the growers, these local firms stored the raisins in large sweating houses for several weeks (to equalize the moisture); stemmed, cleaned, graded, and pressed them; and packed them into labeled cartons of 20 pounds. Packers then routed the product through established trade channels, employing the expertise and resources of eastern commission houses. A company such as J. K. Armsby of Chicago, for example, maintained a line of brokers in every major city in the country. The fact that growers consistently received four to seven cents a pound while production quintupled in the late 1880s attests to the commission merchants' skill.[42]

Yet the specter of overproduction loomed. The expansion of bearing raisin vineyards in Fresno County was astounding: there were 16,000 acres by 1890, 39,000 by 1893, and over 50,000 by 1894. But raisins were a luxury crop, used sparingly in holiday desserts; they had yet to find a secure niche in the American diet. In 1889, eastern markets began to flood and prices began to tumble. By November, trading had come to a standstill, and packers were offering growers as little as one cent per pound. Sensing an opportunity to maximize his position in this demoralized market, E. L. Chaddock of the Fresno Home Packing Company offered growers an innovative alternative. He proposed they consign their raisins to his firm, rather than sell them directly. In exchange for 5 percent of the selling price, he would advance them one cent a pound, pack their raisins at cost, and return what was left after selling in the East. Since this advance matched most packers' cash price, growers swamped Chaddock with more business than he could handle. His pooling strategy netted growers three cents per pound, making him "the most popular man in the community." Once other packers employed this "commission system," however, Chaddock lost his competitive advantage. Moreover, production continued to increase geometrically—seven times from 1889 to 1894, to almost 70 million pounds. The nationwide depression of 1893 exacerbated this problem, and the raisin market hit rock bottom, returning growers less than two cents per pound in 1894 and 1895. With limited bargaining power and no alternative to get their fruit to market, growers blamed their economic woes on the commission packers, who remained their scapegoats for years to come.[43]

Growers were beginning to understand they could no longer afford the luxury of simply producing as many raisins as possible. While some pulled out their vines (12,000 acres' worth in 1894 and 1895), others resolved to seize control of the marketing process themselves. Between 1891 and 1897, with prices remaining below the cost of production, growers held dozens of "mass meetings" to assess their predicament. They focused their efforts on preventing price fluctuations and market gluts, on maintaining quality packing, on limiting competition among eastern agents—on anything but the problem of overproduction. Any suggestion of that kind met with immediate resentment. "There is no danger of this," a local paper editorialized, insisting that "the more there is the more demand there will be."[44] Many concluded that their only hope lay in cooperation—in pooling their raisins to fix the price paid by packers and brokers. Though ineffective throughout the early 1890s, the cooperative movement achieved success in 1898 under Kearney's forceful leadership. Prices rose (to as high as six cents per pound in 1899) in conjunction with the establishment of the California Raisin Growers Association (CRGA), prompting its 3,000 members to believe "a revolution has occurred in the California raisin trade." Few realized that higher prices were more the product of a turn-of-the-century economic recovery than of the cooperative's efforts to control the market. That prosperity, in fact, spurred production, which reached pre-depression levels (70 million pounds) by 1902. Not coincidentally, prices again dropped, to three cents.[45]

Though the CRGA disbanded two years later, cooperation restored vineyardists' faith in their way of life — the "contentedness" Bernhard Marks intended 25 years earlier. "Would any of you undertake to argue that the association has not been beneficial and successful with the raisin growers?" T. C. White asked his colleagues in 1900. Few would have so argued. "The figures speak for themselves," an assessor wrote in the *Pacific Rural Press*. Fresno County, by now known as "the raisin capital of the world," had 60,000 acres of raisin grapes in 1902. Twenty-one vineyards contained over 200 acres each, but the great majority belonged to small growers holding 10 to 40 acres. T. J. Alexander, an original settler of the Temperance Colony, for example, garnered 31 tons of raisins from his 11 acres. Marketing his crop through the CRGA, he reaped over $2,800 from his bumper harvest. Just a decade earlier, vineyardists such as Alexander had felt that the disposal of their raisins was "in the hands of strangers, alien to their life and habits." Now, they could read of daily market conditions in San Joaquin Valley newspapers and debate them regularly at "raisin conventions."[46] Cooperation gave growers a sense of control over their economic lives, just as tending their orderly, fruitful vineyards brought a sense of purpose and stability to how they saw their world.

ONE OF WENDELL EASTON'S two Washington Colony associates, Joel Parker Whitney, would find that Placer County fruit growers needed a similar temperament to "realize the possibilities" of their particular micro-environment. When Whitney ventured to California from Massachusetts in 1852, Newcastle was a mining center in one of California's richest gold districts — just 20 miles from Coloma, where James Marshall had made his famous discovery four years earlier. Along with thousands of other gold seekers, Whitney roamed the region's rolling hills and ravines hoping to strike it rich. He made his fortune, however, in sheep raising and fruit growing, not mining. In 1855, Whitney began purchasing pastureland just west of Rocklin, and by 1873 his Spring Valley Ranch contained over 20,000 acres — the largest estate in Placer

County. Just over Boulder Ridge near Penryn, he attempted to establish, in the late 1880s, an agricultural settlement patterned after the Washington Colony.[47] Other miners who had " run out" their claims also turned to agriculture in the 1850s and 1860s. W. J. Wilson and C. M. Silva, for example, started small orchards and gardens near Newcastle in order to sell fresh fruits and vegetables to foothill miners. In 1869, however, Newcastle was still a mining, not an agricultural, region.[48]

The completion of the transcontinental railroad that year seemed to present opportunities for these early fruit growers beyond their wildest dreams. Suddenly the wagons used to haul produce over rocky mountain roads to nearby mining camps could be replaced by the Central Pacific Railroad serving seemingly inexhaustible markets across the country. In less than two years, fruit growers planted almost 50,000 trees in anticipation of a "Green Gold Rush." Silva and Wilson both established shipping houses at Newcastle, the region's principal freight and passenger station. George D. Kellogg and Martin Schnabel, two other miners turned fruit growers, followed suit in the mid-1870s. Yet in 1876, shipments of Newcastle fruit totaled only 50 tons—a substantial beginning, but hardly the bonanza the railroad seemed to have promised. The costs and risks involved for beginning orchardists impeded more extensive horticultural development. Pine forests, manzanita, and chaparral blanketed the land and cost at least $30 per acre to clear. Even after trees were planted, watered, and pruned, they took as long as five years to return a profit and eight to reach full bearing. High freight rates and the decade's sputtering economy made Newcastle residents even more hesitant to start or expand an orchard. Only those local entrepreneurs well stocked with capital from the declining mining industry risked becoming fruit growers.[49]

The few orchards that did get started ranked among the finest in the state, thanks in large part to a legacy from the gold rush. Miners had built an elaborate system of ditches, dams, and reservoirs in the Sierra foothills to supply water to dry digging sites. The Bear River Ditch, constructed in 1852, diverted Bear River water from just north of the town of Colfax across 50 miles of treacherous terrain to Newcastle. From there, a series of small distributing ditches supplied miners in the Newcastle-Penryn area with water for washing the gold-bearing soil. The canal also became the lifeblood of fruit trees. Land with access to the Bear River Ditch produced high yields and fruit of superior quality. As early as 1863, for example, J. R. Nickerson won eight first-place awards at the state fair for his peaches and nectarines. While miners gradually "worked out" their claims, Fred Birdsall, the owner of the ditch company, sought out new customers. In 1878 he offered free water (with no water right required) for five years to new orchardists. Upon maturation in 1885, the trees of these new growers produced 1,500 tons of fruit, triple the amount shipped in 1876.[50]

The Bear River system, however, could irrigate only so much acreage. The small distributing ditches soon proved inadequate to meet the demands of the expanding fruit district. Hydraulic mining along the Bear River near Gold Run (a few miles above where the ditch veered off toward Newcastle) also troubled the growers. "Hydraulickers" washed entire hillsides into the river, which eventually muddied the growers' water supply, rendering it useless for irrigation without treatment. An 1884 federal injunction restricting hydraulic mining solved the latter problem; growers took the former into their own hands.[51] P. W. Butler, N. B. Lardner, A. P. Hall, and other Penryn orchardists clamored for more water and improvements to canals. Whitney and other settlers further south, near Loomis and Rocklin, had no access at all to Bear River water and demanded an extension from the main ditch. Birdsall was reluctant to comply, fearful that the potential water market was considerably smaller than the growers stated. But when 200 orchardists (virtually every one in the county) answered Whitney's and Butler's call for a "Water Convention" in the spring of 1887, Birdsall became convinced. He outbid three other private companies and quelled a small movement for public ownership prompted by the passage of the Wright Irrigation Act in the state legislature that March. Within a year, Birdsall's Bear River Ditch Company upgraded several existing ditches, built three new extensions to serve the Loomis-Rocklin area, constructed reservoirs near Auburn and Loomis, and contracted with the South Yuba Water Company for additional water. The Water Convention promised Placer County a new identity, the *Newcastle News* editorialized. "If she has been a queen among the repositories of mineral wealth, she will be an empress among the fruit-producing regions of the Pacific coast."[52]

Whitney, who served as chairman of the convention, had the most at stake. His Fresno experience led him to believe that a successful colony in Placer County might also spark the entire region's development. He had purchased 1,000 acres of uncleared land near Penryn and Loomis in January of 1887, put up another 1,905 acres from his Rocklin ranch, and convinced Butler and 14 other local landholders to commit an additional

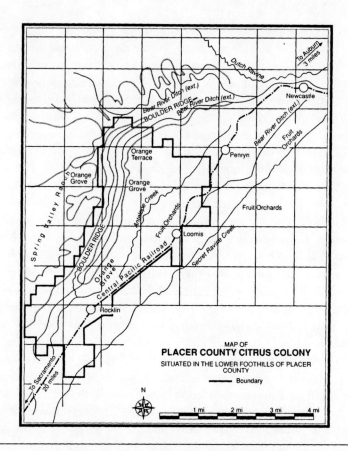

The Placer County Citrus Colony. After the colony's failure in the early 1890s, most of the orange groves were replanted. By the turn of the century, deciduous orchards covered virtually the entire lower fruit belt, shown here, and a good portion of the landscape three to five miles north and west of Newcastle. Based on Placer County Citrus Colony, *Placer County Citrus Colony, in the Lower Foothills of Placer County, California* (San Francisco: Crocker, 1889), 2.

2,260 acres to his project. With the extension of the Bear River system secured, Whitney and his subscribers launched the Placer County Citrus Colony on April 2, 1888.[53] Using the Washington Colony as his model, Whitney traveled to England to recruit settlers and instructed Butler to remain in Penryn and "make a town of it." An estimated 43 British families (218 settlers) arrived to find new roads lined with palm trees, a fruit-shipping house, an "agricultural training college," a weekly newspaper, an elaborate clubhouse, tennis courts, stables, and even a cricket field. "The near future," predicted one of several promotional pamphlets, "will witness for this region a most marvelous advance."[54]

The near future instead brought failure to the colony and resentment from established orchardists. The mid-1890s economic depression and a local outbreak of malaria hampered the colony's development, but Whitney's scheme was doomed from the very start. As one Penryn orchardist later recalled, "From a social standpoint the colony was a huge success, but the agricultural feature was neglected." Whitney's obsession with citrus proved misguided. The orange may have been, in his words, "inviting to the eye, delicious to the palate, . . . [and] suggestive of sunny skies and pleasant lands," but citrus trees did not prosper in the shallow soil and frosty winters of the foothills.[55] Moreover, Whitney had enticed a "well-to-do and higher class of English people" rather than the dissatisfied, ambitious farmer or tradesman lured by Fresno promoters. Butler's son later recalled that the British colonists "expected to pick dollars off the fruit trees." Very few purchased any of the colony's undeveloped land; only acreage already planted to orchards sold in abundance. While newspapers throughout the state focused on the "colorful" social life of the British, local residents complained about fox hunts damaging their orchards and about the colonists' general indifference toward horticulture. Grower-shipper George D. Kellogg, publisher of the *Newcastle News*, admonished the newcomers publicly: "To the man who is looking for fortune without labor, to the man who expects the fertility of the soil to supply all his wants without due effort upon his own part, to the man who desires to live the life of a Silurian wholly upon the 'climate' that surrounds him—to all such, we will say that Placer holds out to him no inducements, and his domicile among us is not solicited."[56] By relying solely on natural processes and conditions and disrespecting the industriousness and expertise horticulture demanded, the colonists were not "man" enough to enter the fruit growers' realm.

In response to the colonists' "negligence," resident growers organized the Placer County Horticultural Society "to promote the science, practice, and interests of fruit growing." In October 1893, orchardists from throughout the region began meeting in Penryn every Saturday for "lectures" on such subjects as "Winter Pruning," "Orchard Planting," and "What to Plant and How." Five elected officers—Whitney, P. W. Butler, Howard E. Parker, George W. Turner, and William B. Gester—along with a 20-member board of directors, served the society. They were determined not to let the colony's failure cast a shadow on their horticultural accomplishments.[57]

Butler delivered one of the first "papers." In precise detail, he shared his knowledge of "the best methods" for "planting and rearing" peaches, cherries, apricots, pears, and berries. He stressed that Placer growers did not have to rely on a single crop; the rich soil and "thermal" climate produced a variety of fruits that stretched the harvest season from May to October. For best results, he emphasized, growers needed first to become "agricultural engineers," for the foothills required extensive terracing before planting. The terraces, 10 to 20 feet broad and four to six feet high, allowed for efficient irrigation, proper drainage, and optimum soil depth. "As I have noticed for some years," he stated, this method "makes a rapid and healthy growth of tree and fruit that . . . fully compensates for the cost of the work" ($30 to $100 an acre). Moreover, he continued, "the terracing gives picturesque beauty to the country, of the highest order known to practical horticulture, thereby creating a value beyond intrinsic comparison." Experience had taught Butler that "certain fruits can be planted and cultivated in a manner to bring sure success to the grower." He also had come to believe that the "higher" aspects of fruit culture required careful cultivation as well. His talk—"highly received" by his audience and published in the *Pacific Rural Press* along with several photographs—captured how Placer orchardists had come to regard their enterprise.[58]

Indeed, even as the Citrus Colony foundered, "practical horticulture" in the Newcastle fruit belt, as the region came to be called, flourished. Trees planted in the early 1880s began bearing fruit in abundance by the end of the decade. Kellogg's orchards, one mile south of Newcastle, typified the average fruit ranch, both in size and in diversity. Kellogg owned 30 acres of several varieties of peaches, and upwards of an acre each of plums, strawberries, pears, cherries, and apricots. Butler's 80-acre ranch, one of the region's largest, contained 50 acres of peaches and smaller amounts of cherries, olives, and berries. A survey of 39 other ranches found they averaged 25 acres, with peaches as their principal crop.[59] In 1888, Newcastle's four shipping houses handled 5,000 tons, more than triple the figure for 1885. Butler and six neighbors established the Penryn Fruit Company in 1886 to meet the growing demand for transportation at the lower end of the belt. This fruit house alone shipped 600 tons in 1889. By 1892, approximately 275 Placer growers had planted over 8,000 acres in fruit, of which 3,500 were in bearing condition. That year, 11 fruit houses (five in Newcastle and two each in Penryn, Loomis, and Auburn) shipped over 10,000 tons of fruit. A decade later, freight agents reported these figures in carloads rather than tonnage—in 1901, shippers transported 1,862 cars of fruit (approximately 24,000 tons).[60] In response to this great increase in output, the *Placer Herald* triumphantly replaced its masthead to read: "Placer County ships more deciduous fruit East than any other county in California."

"Practical horticulture" produced numerous social advantages as well. Newcastle, with a population of 600, erected a new schoolhouse, church, and hotel in 1889. The town already maintained a prosperous business section alongside fruit house row and accommodated "all the fraternal organizations."[61] Growers played the pivotal role in the community's development. Wilson, Silva, Kellogg, and Schnabel, owners of competing shipping houses, organized the town's first fire company and persuaded another dozen orchardists to serve as volunteers. They also led a campaign to implement a special tax to establish the Newcastle school district. Kellogg founded the community's first newspaper, the *Newcastle News*, in 1887, to keep readers abreast of the latest developments in fruit culture and local affairs. At the town's Fourth of July celebrations, growers regularly presided over "literary exercises," reading poetry and the Declaration of Independence to appreciative audiences. The fruit houses served as dance halls during the off-season. And when the county organized a Board of Trade in 1887 to promote the region's commercial interests, Butler, Parker, and Kellogg became its most prominent officers, and orchardists dominated its membership.[62] On a smaller scale, Penryn and Loomis also thrived under the growers' guidance. Kellogg expounded on the region's growing vitality, virility, and allure: "To the man of energy, enterprise, and push, to the man who desires to make a pleasant home where, by industry and frugality, he can become a prosperous tiller of the soil—to such a man we believe we can say truly that Placer County presents more favorable opportunities than any other county in the State."[63]

But this prideful declaration masked an immensely difficult problem. As the *California Fruit Grower* acknowledged in 1890, "Growing [fresh] fruit is one thing, but shipping and marketing it is an entirely different proposition."[64] Fruit growers labored under the same hardship as Fresno vineyardists—their orchards were two to three thousand miles distant from their principal markets. But their fragile, perishable product presented numerous additional dilemmas. It was essential to handle the fruit as little as possible. This required individual growers to pack their own fruit in their orchards—not at a central location, as with raisins. While this reduced local shippers' obligations, the resultant lack of a standardized grade and pack prevented them from pooling their crops. Moreover, time was of the essence with fresh fruit. While with raisins packers could develop an "instinct about knowing when to hold and when to sell,"[65] the ripeness of fresh fruit alone dictated its shipping timetable. Raisins could be stored either at the point of production or at the point of sale to obtain a maximum price, but fresh fruit would spoil if not in the consumer's hands within 10 days after harvest. These requirements demanded special handling and fast transportation, but throughout the late nineteenth century railroads were equipped for neither. Primitive refrigeration technology, high freight rates, and unforeseen delays made for a hazardous seven- to ten-day cross-country journey. "For the fresh fruit shipper there never is and never will be much certainty," lamented Loomis grower William Gester.[66]

Placer shippers and growers, however, turned that uncertainty to their advantage. None of their orchards was more than five miles from a shipping house, and the Newcastle region itself was further east than any other California fruit district. Consequently, fruit could be picked and packed in the morning shade, loaded on a train in the early evening, and transported over the Sierras during the cool of the night, reaching midwestern and eastern destinations in better condition than fruit from other districts, and one to three days sooner. The fact that most of this additional time was spent in the Central Valley's sweltering heat made Placer's location that much more advantageous. Foothill fruit also ripened as much as three weeks earlier than valley fruit, so that Placer shippers had the market virtually to themselves intermittently throughout the summer. By 1890, Newcastle fruits, the *California Fruit Grower* declared, had established a reputation "second to none in the State" among eastern buyers. Not surprisingly, only a few Placer growers chose to ship their crops through the California Fruit Union, the state's first major fresh-fruit marketing cooperative. To join with other growers for the purpose of controlling the market would have negated their geographical advantage.[67]

Growers and shippers depended on each other to uphold the region's reputation. Though skillful horticulturists, most growers knew little of marketing. They left that task to their local shipping houses, which bought the fruit directly from the grower, loaded the freight, and consigned it to commission merchants in Chicago, New York, and a few other large eastern cities. Shippers, in turn, counted on growers for careful orchard work. A shipper, as Kellogg explained, "builds up a trade by knowing that he can rely upon the pick and pack of fruit." A shipper who could sell solely on the basis of his label, and thus remove all doubts of "indiscriminate shipments" from the minds of prospective buyers, held a distinct market advantage. The fact that every Placer shipper throughout the 1880s was a grower himself strengthened this relationship even further. Kellogg, Schnabel, Silva, Wilson, and Butler all regarded themselves as orchardists first, shippers second. "Their interests are identical with that of the other growers," a contemporary noted. This mutual trust had community roots as well. Growers and shippers were business partners, but they also were neighbors, lodge brothers, boosters, and civic leaders. The district's reputation for "being as good a fruit-producing section as there is in the world" rested on the efforts of both.[68]

Newcastle was not an island community, however. Its ever-increasing stature began attracting outsiders during the early 1890s. The Earl Fruit Company and the Porter Brothers' Company established branch offices along Newcastle's fruit house row in 1891 and 1892, respectively, and at Penryn and Loomis as well. At first, locals welcomed these newcomers with open arms. Their presence signified that the Newcastle district was worthy of the country's two most prominent fruit-shipping firms. Kellogg insisted that Earl Fruit's "unparalleled connections in all the principal Eastern cities" would stimulate "new opportunities" for all; and Porter Brothers' arrival generated similar expectations. With production booming, there was more than enough business for the new houses. Furthermore, because Southern Pacific charged by the number of carloads a region could guarantee on a daily basis ($300 per carload for a 10-car train, but double that for fewer than 10), the new firms assured all shippers a reduced rate. In addition, the economic and political leverage that Earl Fruit and Porter Brothers' wielded proved decisive when the railroad lowered its flat rate per car in 1895. The outside firms were also sensitive to local concerns, hiring only fruit belt residents to run their houses. "Their advent into the Newcastle District," the News maintained, "cannot but be of advantage to the whole community."[69]

Market pressures during the mid-1890s, however, jeopardized community unity. Since the late 1880s, shippers had kept competition in check through mutual agreement. Each morning, a committee met in Newcastle, considered quotations from the eastern markets, and set the

prices they would pay Placer growers that day. As long as the market
held firm, both buyers and sellers considered the "Newcastle price" an
"admirable feature of the fruit trade." Shippers avoided outbidding each
other for business, and growers assumed none of the transportation or
marketing risks.[70] But this system could not survive the economic depression that, as one contemporary put it, made for "hard times among
fruit eaters" from 1894 through 1896. Rising production and declining
demand set in motion a near-catastrophic chain of events. Dealers reduced prices to entice retail merchants to buy in greater volume. Shippers in turn cut prices to dealers in their efforts to secure trade. The
smaller shipping houses frequently borrowed from dealers to meet expenses, agreeing in return to consign a specified number of carloads for
the season and to pay a fixed fee (usually $100 per car). The Pullman
strike of July 1894, which shut down the California trade for two weeks,
dealt yet another financial blow to shippers. To ensure a margin of profit,
they lowered the Newcastle price. This left growers with two alterna-
tives: take a flat amount that often did not cover production costs, or
ship on consignment and take full responsibility for risks in shipping
and distributing costs. Either choice often forced them to borrow from
their shipping house just to remain afloat. The largest growers, however,
had one more option. Earl Fruit and Porter Brothers', with their vast resources and "unparalleled connections," offered substantial kickbacks to
growers to secure their business. It was "every man and every house for
himself and the devil for the hindermost," recalled Newcastle grower
Gerald Geraldson. The Newcastle price had now become a symbol of
"a pernicious system."[71]

Geraldson was part of a small but determined group of growers who
took on the system themselves. Denouncing "the injustice that has been
done to the men who have taken the barren and brushy lands and developed them into growing orchards," Newcastle grower W. R. Fountain
called a series of meetings in May and June of 1896 to launch the Placer
County Fruit Growers' Protective Association (PCFGPA). Fountain
and his followers hoped to secure better control of the fruit market and
to bypass the "robber middlemen [whom] Placer County fruit has made
rich." Fountain claimed to have lost $17,000 since becoming a fruit
grower in 1892; and association members, according to the *Placer County
Republican,* were "in 9 cases out of 10 mortgaged . . . and struggling."
The "robber middlemen," however, did not include local shippers, whom
the PCFGPA insisted were "of our class." Earl Fruit and Porter Broth-

ers', on the other hand, "were each put on the gridiron . . . and roasted to a turn." For the next three years, the PCFGA ("Protective" was dropped in 1898) envisioned a "strong, central organization" that would embrace not only Placer orchardists, but fresh deciduous fruit growers throughout northern California. They "could see no good reason," the *News* reported, "why the orchardist should not have a say as to what price his fruit should bring." With "the raisin men of Fresno" as their model, the association members hoped to pool their fruit and even withhold it if necessary. "Better to let it stay on the trees than to pick it for the benefit of others," said Fountain.[72]

Such threats, however, proved idle. "This is an impossibility," *California Fruit Grower* editor B. N. Rowley asserted, citing the packing, shipping, and marketing problems inherent in selling a fragile, perishable crop. "Combination, organization, and co-operation," Rowley added, "may assist in the direction of steady markets and better prices, but cannot be relied upon to fix or maintain prices in direct opposition to the law of supply and demand."[73] Every Placer shipper preferred Rowley's philosophy to Fountain's. They instead had joined the California Fruit Growers' and Shippers' Association (CFGSA) upon its formation in 1895. Rather than selling the fruit itself, this northern California organization intended to rationalize the distribution process. It set up a "bureau of information" to direct fruit to the best markets, sought to expand the market itself, and established auction houses to promote open, competitive buying. This strategy—bolstered by the advent of a lighter, more efficient refrigerator car capable of transporting fruit to more remote markets—proved successful. In 1895, 32 percent of all California fresh fruit flooded Chicago, the central shipping point. By 1899, "new markets in interior places"—Milwaukee, Pittsburgh, and Kansas City, for example—were being exploited, while Chicago's total fell to under 15 percent.[74]

Moreover, prosperity had begun to return to the Placer fruit belt. A revived eastern trade in the summer of 1897 prompted shippers and the Southern Pacific to rebuild Newcastle's fruit house row—replacing individual structures with "one mammoth loading shed" to maximize space along the tracks. In 1899, according to the county recorder, growers paid off $160,000 of mortgages and declared profits ranging as high as $120 per acre. "We are at peace with the world, be its people railroad men, commission merchants, or any other class," wrote Newcastle grower J. M. Francis, one of Fountain's followers. "While it is supposed that all these people have had a good share of the spoils, [growers] have enjoyed a good big slice themselves." Not surprisingly, therefore, when the PCFGA launched its most substantial organizing drive in June of 1899, it drew little interest. Four years earlier, shippers had pleaded with growers to "patronize those who are your neighbors and friends and who stay with you." That trust had been tested, but not broken.[75]

Throughout the turmoil of the 1890s, the Placer County Horticultural Society continued to meet regularly. On a Saturday afternoon in February of 1901, the society held an "animated discussion" at Newcastle's Fraternal Hall. George Kellogg's daughter, Jessie, started the program with "an instrumental selection." Orchardist George Threlkel followed "by giving the growers a talk on 'Spraying of Trees,' relating his [recent] experience. Several other growers also gave their experience which resulted in many points of value being brought out." Threlkel's daughter, Minnie, then "favored the meeting with a vocal solo." The final presentation, by W. R. Fountain, was on a familiar topic—"The Pros and Cons of State Organization." In the discussion that followed, growers objected "to the mingling of Placer County fruit with that of other sections." Pooling their high-quality fruit grown in orchards they had nourished from inception was tantamount "to losing their identity entirely," they insisted.[76] Placer growers had developed a culture all their own. Newcastle, the region's "Fruit Emporium," remained its centerpiece. This mining town that had been in "general dilapidation" just two decades earlier had become "the biggest little city, from a deciduous point of view, in California."[77]

FROM AN ALMOND POINT OF VIEW, Davisville began to prosper in the late 1880s. In this subregion, wheat farmers were the key agents of change. During the 1850s and 1860s, eight midwesterners—James G. Cecil, I. S. Chiles, Charles E. Greene, Hugh M. La Rue, William H. Marden, William W. Montgomery, George W. Pierce, and George H. Swingle—migrated to California and established ranches along Putah Creek ranging in size from 500 to 2,000 acres.[78] Like most contemporary Sacramento Valley farmers, these settlers cultivated wheat, the most easily and profitably produced of frontier crops. Utilizing the latest technology—reapers, headers, threshers, gang plows, combined harvesters—they exploited the valley's virgin soils. Bumper harvests produced 60 to 80 bushels per acre, four to five times the norm for midwestern farms.[79] By 1872 these eight ranchers had helped turn Davisville into an

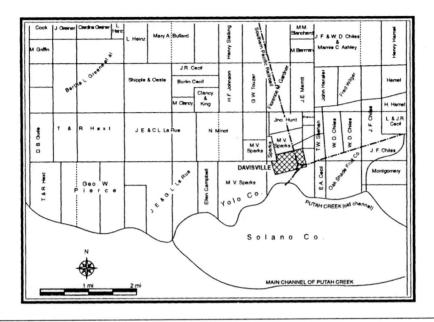

Davisville, Putah Creek, and vicinity, showing the Cecil, Chiles, Greene, La Rue, Montgomery, and Pierce ranches, among others. Based on P. N. Ashley, *Official Map of the County of Yolo, California* (San Francisco: Britton & Rey, 1900).

important wheat center. The town, a major railroad junction following the completion of the Central Pacific, contained eight large grain warehouses and shipped 30,000–40,000 tons of wheat a year to Liverpool and other distant markets. During the mid-1880s, California led the nation in wheat production and became known as "the granary of the world." Yet at the same time, these Putah Creek growers (or their sons) began plowing up small portions of their wheat fields and planting almond orchards. As early as 1890, the *California Fruit Grower* touted Davisville as an "almond district."[80]

The reasons that these Davisville wheat growers began experimenting with almonds challenge conventional explanations for the intensification of California agriculture. There is no doubt the transition occurred. By 1909, California had become one of the world's major fruit, nut, and vegetable producers, yet it imported most of its wheat. Most accounts of this shift emphasize economic factors: in particular, stiffer competition in the world's grain markets; the greater profitability of intensive crops; and the vast markets opened up by the transcontinental railroad.[81] But consider the experience of George W. Pierce Jr. The railroad clearly did not prompt him to begin planting 132 acres of almond trees in 1892; the Southern Pacific had tied Davisville to eastern cities for almost a quarter of a century by then. In 1893, the selling price of his wheat crop fell from $1.20 a bushel to 85 cents—a "ruinous price," in his words. But almond prices also dropped—from 12 cents a pound in 1892 to 7½ cents in 1896, when his trees began bearing.[82] Indeed, between 1870 and 1910, fruit and nut prices declined even more than wheat prices.[83] Growing almonds, furthermore, was known to entail financial risks. As late as 1900, J. K. Armsby, the prominent shipping firm, warned growers that the peculiarities of the almond—its erratic blooming behavior, irregular bearing habits, and strict soil and climate requirements—limited production to "about two good crops out of five."[84]

Nevertheless, almond culture enticed Davisville wheat growers. The almond harvest, starting in mid-August and lasting a month, filled a gap in their yearly cycle between the end of the June wheat harvest and the start of fall plowing. And while almonds can be more temperamental than most orchard fruits, they have certain advantages: the trees take less time to mature (4–5 years), they require minimal pruning, and their product is neither perishable nor fragile. "It is the most easily cared for of any kind of nut or fruit-bearing tree," stated Webster Treat, owner of the Oak Shade Fruit Company in Davisville. Under ideal conditions, another observer remarked, "the almond is a very profitable tree. . . . You can't plant [them] fast enough."[85] Once Hugh M. La Rue and his son Jacob had demonstrated that the bottomlands of Putah Creek appeared favorable to almonds, other Davisville farmers (26 by 1900) quickly followed their lead.[86] Under Treat's guidance, they planted two particular varieties of almonds, the California Nonpareil paper shell and the Ne Plus Ultra soft shell. The smooth and plump kernels these varieties produced, Treat had learned, were favored by eastern consumers and brought nearly double the price of any hard shell.[87]

But almonds were not just another source of income for these wheat growers; they also were intrigued by the cultural rewards horticulture promised to offer. The "Annual Illustrated Number" for 1892 of the *Yolo Weekly Mail* focused upon the "progressive movement" generated by this new form of farming. "In fruit culture," the paper explained, "there is a benign influence, an educating tendency, an elevating discipline not indigenous to other departments of agriculture. . . . There is something in horticulture which quickens the notions and enlarges the ideas, and therefore within its ranks is found a class of people who enrich a community with new blood, new brains, and fresh energy."[88] Putah Creek wheat farmers were ideally suited to become members of this "class of people." The younger Pierce felt just as comfortable at the University Library at Berkeley or the Opera House in San Francisco as he did on his ranch. He was the first graduate of the University of California from the Sacramento Valley (1875) and had intended to become a lawyer before taking over the management of the Davisville ranch following his father's disabling farm accident in the early 1880s. He also served his community as a state assemblyman at the turn of the century and as a charter member of the Davisville Odd Fellows.[89] Hugh M. La Rue, one of the state's more prominent Democrats, held a number of public positions, including state senator, president of the State Agricultural Society, master of the Sacramento Grange, delegate to the second Constitutional Convention in 1879, and regent of the University of California.[90] His son Jacob and second-generation wheat farmers James F. Chiles, Charles E. Greene Jr., and George K. Swingle all commanded respect as community leaders as well: they all graduated from California colleges, participated in Yolo County politics, and claimed membership in prominent social societies.[91] Almond growing offered these men both an intellectual challenge and an opportunity to bring further prestige to their community. It was, in Pierce's words, "both pleasant and profitable."[92]

Though their trees were more "easily cared for" than those bearing fruit, Davisville growers still found great virtue in their new venture. They came to idolize the literal fruits of their profession. Indeed, for Pierce, the almond was an instrument of civility: "As far back as authentic history takes us we read of the Almond. It is frequently referred to in Scripture and has played no small part in ministering to the needs and pleasures of mankind. Its food value is important and its bloom, following closely on the heels of Winter, has probably appealed to the esthetic side of mankind more strongly than has the bloom of any other orchard tree." Such a noble product deserved devotion and attentiveness. "The trees are your partners as well as your property," Pierce maintained. "If you have planted wisely and give it proper care, the tree will do the rest. . . . Too much care cannot be given. . . . A tree that has been neglected, or badly handled . . . will prove poor property."[93] No less than Fresno and Placer growers, Davisville orchardists idealized horticulture and were not shy about expressing themselves. For them, almond growing was not only a commercial endeavor but a nurturing and protective enterprise as well.

When their attention turned to marketing, however, these new orchardists were far less likely to speak in biblical or paternal terms. At first, marketing posed few problems. Growers simply delivered their almonds to the Oak Shade Fruit Company, where J. K. Armsby, Porter Brothers', and other brokerage firms paid "very satisfactory" prices (12–15 cents). But the economic crisis of the mid-1890s exposed the growers' lack of marketing knowledge. Though they tried to generate competition, their informal pooling arrangement was no match for the more sophisticated brokers. "Naturally, we, as a lot of farmers, did not understand the business of inviting bids," Pierce recalled. "We were easily imposed upon. The matter was all fixed before the bidders came to us and they gave us just what they saw fit and afterwards divided the crop among themselves." Davisville growers, though recognized as authorities on almond culture, found themselves at the mercy of collusive middlemen.[94]

Determined to play a more aggressive role in setting the price of their almonds, 15 orchardists (most of whom were still wheat growers as well) met in Davisville in the winter of 1897. Proclaiming that almonds had become "one of the leading industries of this section," they formed the state's first almond cooperative, the Davisville Almond Growers' Association (DAGA), on January 23. They elected Jacob La Rue president and Pierce vice-president; J. W. Anderson, who had managed the Oak Shade Fruit Company, became secretary, DAGA's only paid officer.[95] DAGA members quickly discovered they could increase their bargaining power by storing their almonds in a centralized warehouse, by entertaining bids for the total crop, by rejecting bids deemed "not up to market," and by copyrighting their own brand.[96] Over the next six years, DAGA members took credit for doubling the price of their almonds to 13 cents (disregarding the impact of the expanding economy). Members knew, however, that their association could "never make us complete masters of the market, struggling by itself." La Rue and Pierce, therefore, organized similar associations in Brentwood (Contra Costa County), Capay (Yolo County), and Yuba City (Sutter County), intending ultimately to form a statewide organization. Over the same period, Davisville growers increased their yields almost 50 percent (to over 300 tons, 20 percent of the state's crop), to make their district the leader in production as well as marketing. "The outlook for the almond industry here," proclaimed Secretary Anderson in 1902, "is at the present very encouraging."[97]

For Davisville growers, cooperation brought more than just economic gain. "We had nothing but almonds and a determination to succeed," Pierce recalled. In an era in which middle-class Americans held the "associative impulse" in high esteem, that determination—the desire to be "progressive"—brought the Davisville growers and their community statewide and even national recognition. Indeed, when the *Overland Monthly* proclaimed in 1902 that "this pioneer association" was setting "the standard for the state," it referred not only to improved almond prices, but also to what this band of horticulturists had collectively accomplished.[98]

Most of these new orchardists, it should be emphasized, were wheat growers. For them, almonds and wheat complemented one another. The conventional conception of "wheat versus fruit" portrays them inaccurately. Throughout the Sacramento Valley, in fact, wheat growers—especially those with land along rivers—and fruit growers tended to be one and the same. "Agriculture and horticulture," as the *California Fruit Grower* stated, "go hand in hand in this valley."[99]

HOP CULTURE DID NOT SEEM to fall within the realm of either agriculture or horticulture. Hops shared many of wheat's characteristics: both were classified as a "field crop"; they returned a substantial crop within one year; and they required a variety of specialized, expensive implements. After being "picked" from their vines, hops were dried in kilns —imposing, two-story structures with two wood-burning furnaces occupying the ground floor and numerous heat-distributing metal pipes. In the early 1890s, a wood kiln cost $3,000 to build, while a grower who could afford a more fireproof brick structure paid as much as $10,000. An additional warehouse (the cooling room) and a large baling apparatus powered by horses (the hop press) also were required for market preparation. On the other hand, contemporaries also considered this crop "one of California's agricultural specialties." Hops were even more labor-intensive than orchard and vineyard crops, and required equally sophisticated cultural methods. Throughout the late nineteenth century, growers devised elaborate trellis systems to train their vines, learned the soil and climate requirements for particular varieties, and developed a thorough understanding of planting, pruning, cultivating, harvesting, drying, cooling, and baling.[100] As though unsure themselves of their own identity, hop growers referred to their farms variously as fields, plantations, yards, and even gardens.[101]

The fact that the use of hops was limited to beer brewing distinguished the crop above all else. While the demand for beer varied only slightly from year to year, the production of hops fluctuated wildly. In the world's two principal hop-growing regions, England and Germany, heavy summer rains and/or destructive pests damaged one crop in every three throughout the late nineteenth century.[102] The size of the European crop almost completely determined the so-called hopping rate in California. "If the foreign crops are large, we have low prices; if the foreign crops are short, we have high prices," stated one grower matter-of-factly.[103] But California growers did not accept their fate passively. On at least six different occasions between 1877 and 1900, they organized to try to gain some measure of control of the hopping rate, but to no avail.[104] Such efforts also could not overcome the "tyranny of distance" afflicting the West Coast trade, for English and German breweries were the only worthwhile markets. News about price movements, shipping conditions, and production came from merchant houses in Britain and thus always arrived stale. "There is nothing, so far as my knowledge goes," wrote Sacramento hop expert Daniel Flint, "that grows from the ground that is subject to such extreme fluctuations and uncertainties in regard to price."[105]

Excessively high prices in 1882 enticed D. P. Durst, a Sacramento Valley physician, to try his hand at hop growing. In the 1870s, hop prices ranged from 15 to 45 cents per pound. But because of successive crop failures in England and Germany in 1881 and 1882, the rate jumped to an astronomical $1.10. Suddenly, hops seemed like "gold drops."[106] Durst, a former miner, had practiced medicine in Yuba and Sutter Counties since 1867. In 1876, he purchased 500 acres of bottomland along the Bear River, just south of the town of Wheatland, and began farming alfalfa. Assisted by his eighteen-year-old son, Ralph, he planted 11 acres of hops in 1883. His vines yielded an astounding 1,600 pounds per acre, twice the norm for a first crop. The soil's moisture and the valley's dry heat created near-perfect conditions. The next year, he planted 98 more acres, with similar results. Buyers suddenly descended upon Wheatland in droves to confirm the rumors of Durst's "miraculous" hop fields.[107] But they did not offer him what he anticipated. The "fictitious" price of 1882 had prompted an unparalleled rush to plant hops in California and throughout the world. The market quickly saturated, and prices plummeted to 14 cents by the 1883 harvest. By 1885, California hops sold for just six cents a pound—half the cost of production. The disjuncture between Durst's phenomenal success at raising hops and the market's rude response left him, as he told the local newspaper, "agreeably disappointed." It would also motivate him to become an organizer for three unsuccessful California Hop Growers' Associations.[108]

For a time, it appeared that hop culture might capture the imagination of this farming community. Two other locals with land bordering the Bear River, S. D. Woods and Hugh Roddan, also planted hops in the mid-1880s. Fellow Wheatland residents found these growers' production success "most gratifying as well as astonishing."[109] Durst, Woods, and Roddan were prominent community leaders. All three, for example, led the drive to incorporate the town in 1874, and they helped build the huge levees that protected their town and farms from hydraulic-mining debris.[110] No one else, however, found hops worth the gamble. When the price jumped to 30 cents in the early 1890s, one other farmer, Joseph M. C. Jasper, joined Durst, Woods, and Roddan, but he did not survive the market's inevitable downturn.[111] By 1894, Durst's hop fields covered 350 acres, enough for the *Pacific Rural Press* to crown him "Hop King." The following year, E. Clemons Horst, a young San Francisco hop dealer, purchased a small plot of land further east along the Bear River and within a few years bought out Roddan and Jasper. Not to be outdone, Durst acquired Woods's hop lands. By the turn of the century, Durst and Horst were each cultivating over 500 acres of hops. Both utilized the most up-to-date trellising systems and presses, and both built "the best equipped kilns and curing houses on the Pacific Coast." P. C. Drescher, a Sacramento dealer, provided their only local competition, but he owned fewer than 100 acres. Durst and Horst had effectively divided between them what many considered the most productive hop region in the country.[112]

They did not, however, enhance their community as had raisin, fruit, and almond growers. "Hop culture," wrote editor Wickson in the *Pacific Rural Press*, "is in many respects a pleasant and ought to be a profitable occupation in California." But unlike horticulture, he warned, hop culture was strictly a "business." A grower's long-term success depended first and foremost on his wherewithal to withstand the "spasmodic" market.[113] Most of Wheatland's 1,200 residents identified much more with the grain and dairy industries, either as farmers or as laborers in the

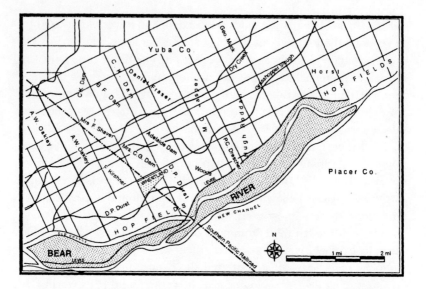

Bear River hop fields, ca. 1895. From information in J. M. Doyle, *Official Map of Yuba County, State of California* (San Francisco: Britton & Rey, 1887), and Leslie B. Crook, *Official Map of Yuba County, California* (San Francisco: Bashford Smith, 1914).

town's large flour mill and creamery. One local history listed 22 "names synonymous with Wheatland's steady growth," and neither Durst nor Horst was among them. Durst, in fact, was revered more for his medical than for his hop-growing expertise. His participation in the failed efforts to sustain a California Hop Growers' Association was an individual, not a community, endeavor. One lifelong Wheatland resident remembered Horst simply as a "city person" whom she had never met face-to-face. A majority of the citizens, moreover, fought for years to make Wheatland a "dry town," and thus found little virtue in hops.[114] Wheatland, in short, had become a community famous for its hops, but it had not become a specialty crop community along the lines of Fresno, Newcastle, and Davisville.

WHAT EXACTLY WAS A SPECIALTY CROP COMMUNITY, THEN? It revolved, its residents knew, around a central dynamic—a specific "class of people" pursuing a "pleasant and profitable" life in micro-environments where water and other natural advantages were abundant. The prevalence of these two phrases in local newspapers, farm journals, popular literature, and personal correspondence strongly suggests that fruit and nut growers perceived themselves as a select social group. In developing their communities into prosperous horticultural regions, these growers stressed hard work, patience, prudence, and cooperation. Their achievements generated an idealism and even an air of haughtiness. "Successful horticulture requires the quick eye, the skilled hand, and the trained intellect," wrote a prominent orchardist. "The mind as well as the hand must be kept ever busy. . . . The fact that success in horticulture depends so largely upon the intelligence of the operator, and that there is a constant need for reaching out, in all its departments, for more knowledge, makes it an exceedingly attractive occupation for persons of some culture. . . . It will be found that our fruit growers are, as a class, men of brains." The benefits of horticulture, this account stressed, extended well beyond the financial. "There is a prosperity that does not appear upon the tax roll and an advancement that can never be estimated in mere dollars and cents. It is this higher prosperity . . . that horticulture is bringing to our state." Horticulture, in short, provided intellectual fulfillment, satisfying work, and cultural advancement.[115]

This was, it should be emphasized, an ideal to which fruit and nut growers aspired. In actuality, horticulture was no more virtuous an undertaking than hop culture, wheat growing, or any other type of farming in California. D. P. Durst struggled just as valiantly to raise hops as George Pierce did to grow wheat, P. W. Butler to produce peaches, and T. C. White to cultivate raisins. Pierce and other Davisville wheat farmers did not undergo any dramatic change in personal values or intelligence upon planting almond trees amid their grain fields. It was wheat farmers like them, after all, who had lobbied the state legislature to establish the California State Agricultural Society in 1854, three decades prior to the state's fruit boom. The society had targeted a largely middle-class, literate membership since its inception. Its publications provided farmers with a wealth of practical information, and its state and county fairs offered lectures and competitions to educate farmers about old and new crops.[116] Since 1871, the *Pacific Rural Press*, the state's leading farm periodical, also had conveyed an image of a state with a progressive rural population and mature institutions. It catered to readers accustomed to taking advice from the printed page and pursued all aspects of agriculture, from grain farming to dairying to fruit growing. Durst, Butler,

White, and Pierce all read the *Pacific Rural Press* regularly and on occasion sent comments and questions to the journal's editor, Edward J. Wickson.[117]

Furthermore, this sort of farmer culture was hardly unique to California. Editors of the *Country Gentleman,* the *American Agriculturist,* the *Rural New Yorker,* and scores of other eastern and midwestern periodicals had been imparting "intelligent, discriminating, agricultural wisdom" (in the words of one Iowa journal) to large numbers of readers since the early nineteenth century.[118] Farmers throughout the northern United States had sought to improve their operations through organized exchanges of information—local newspapers, farm journals, state and county agricultural societies, and fairs. These institutions encouraged farmers to employ the empirical method. "There is no way for making improvements in farming, but by experiments," an agricultural manual advised in 1820. "If the farmer is informed of, or has conceived, a different and better method of culture or management in any branch of farming, he is to test the goodness of that method by experiments; and if these prove successful he may congratulate himself on having performed an act which is serviceable to this country and honorable to himself."[119] The agricultural press became the major vehicle to circulate these discoveries. By mid-century, wrote one historian, "the enterprising farmer was of necessity a book farmer."[120] Moreover, horticulture appears strikingly similar to the agricultural fundamentalism that had shaped northern farmers' attitudes and values since the days of Thomas Jefferson. Viewing the world through the prism of their local communities, northern farmers and California growers alike took great pride in producing their crops, believed in the virtues of rural life even while becoming fully integrated into the market economy, exhibited a strong cooperative bent, and above all regarded themselves not as a separate interest group but as a special class of people responsible for the very well-being of the larger society.[121]

But while eastern periodicals and societies continued to promote "agricultural wisdom," their tenor became increasingly pessimistic. Throughout the second half of the nineteenth century, agricultural writers and orators bemoaned the declining quality of life in northeastern and midwestern farming communities. The "drift to the city" among rural migrants, they lamented, brought about depopulation, depreciation of property values, deteriorating roads, and a waning confidence in rural life in the country's agricultural regions. Farm periodicals became organs for rural reformers to combat out-migration, to chastise those who left, and to criticize their betrayal of the producer ethic. "True courage," wrote the editor of the *Country Gentleman* in 1857, "seems to us to be, not in venturing with the multitude to the farthest lengths of speculation, but in daring to refrain from it when almost everybody else is more or less deeply involved." Dissatisfaction with urban growth and an emerging industrial ethos at the expense of the countryside engendered a defensiveness that pervaded the agricultural press.[122]

In stark contrast, California agricultural periodicals celebrated the progressive role played by the state's farmers. "The men engaged in fruit growing in California are of an entirely different class from those found in the same pursuits elsewhere," the *California Fruit Grower* proclaimed.[123] The difference between the California and the eastern farmer, however, was less a matter of "class" than of context. Whereas eastern agricultural reformers perceived rural society to be stagnant—to be losing its place as the fountainhead of American virtue—California growers saw themselves at the forefront of progress. Agriculture, after all, was the state's leading industry, and no other commercial enterprise brought the state as much prestige. The headline "Blessed Are They Who Live in Fresno" might have seemed anachronistic to most eastern farmers.[124] But in California, one could still be a farmer as well as a cultural leader.

Horticulturists in particular achieved this heightened status—within their communities, and throughout the state as well. "Horticulture is the broad term applied to fruit growing in California, but it covers far more than this one branch of this wide spread industry," explained editor B. N. Rowley in the *California Fruit Grower*. "Horticulture in the fullest sense of the term embraces . . . everything that makes our country bright, beautiful, ornamental and enjoyable. The great stride made in this State in redeeming it from a parched and unproductive waste and making it a land of plenty and great productiveness, is due to horticulture." California's agricultural transformation came as no surprise to Rowley. "As communities grow in wealth, population and intelligence, grain growing gives way to the fruit tree and vine," he reasoned. The editor of an Iowa farm journal who had hoped his state would become "the very paradise of small fruits" would have agreed with Rowley's portrayal of rural evolution. But only California, Rowley pointed out, had "the natural intrinsic advantages [in] soil, climate, and water" to allow the farmer to reach his full potential. Not to grow fruit in California, as another orchardist put it, would have been "a perversion of nature's gifts."[125]

Believing that "fruit growing is a higher order of agriculture," California orchardists and vineyardists eschewed the most sweeping farmer movement of the late nineteenth century, Populism. Among California growers, hard economic times, high freight rates, and dampened expectations during the 1890s did not precipitate a mass protest, as they did throughout much of the South and Midwest. Small wheat growers in isolated rural regions made up the bulk of California's relatively weak Populist movement. The fact that the state's orchardists identified so strongly with their particular specialty crop may have deterred mass organization; and their more favorable relationship with the Southern Pacific left them without a unifying target of protest.[126] But American farmers joined the Farmers' Alliance and the People's Party for reasons deeper than economics alone. For many, social isolation, a beaten self-image, and little means of self-expression made Alliance communities that much more appealing. Populism, most historians agree, engendered within millions of American farmers a "sense of somebodiness."[127] California specialty crop growers, however, did not find that sense lacking.

Instead, they established institutions of their own—local ones such as the Placer County Horticultural Society, as well as the statewide fruit growers' conventions. Over time, horticulturists became dissatisfied with the State Agricultural Society's fairs and publications. Beginning in 1881 (and continuing through 1938), several hundred orchardists and vineyardists from throughout the state convened once or twice a year "for the purpose of consultation and discussion on . . . such subjects as might be introduced for the improvement of the fruit growing interests of California."[128] Over the course of three or four days, participants heard several dozen papers "by the most intelligent and successful fruit growers of the state," and discussed them at length. Each convention covered the latest developments in production and marketing, generally concentrating on the issues most pertinent to the particular meeting site. The proceedings (often including discussions) were published and distributed without cost to thousands of growers, with demand invariably exceeding supply.[129] The conventions established no constitution or bylaws, nor did they specify any qualifications or membership requirements. Grain farmers, hop growers, and other non-horticulturists understood, however, that these assemblies were "the fruit growers' domain"—as were such specialized periodicals as the *California Fruit Grower, Orchard and*

Farm, and the *California Citrograph.* Though often characterized as elite publications, they were widely disseminated and read by people of various means. As forums for sharing individual experiences—successes and failures alike—these conventions and trade journals represented, in the words of one enthusiast, "a degree of progress hitherto unknown" in California.[130]

All but the first two conventions were held "under the auspices" of the State Board of Horticulture, a government institution in name only. Created in 1883, this agency was operated by and for orchardists and vineyardists to "best promote the horticultural industries of the State."[131] The board's primary function concerned a problem growers could not combat effectively by themselves—pests and diseases. Scales, aphids, moths, slugs, worms, grasshoppers, fungi, blights, and viruses—most of these "enemies" were not indigenous but were brought in during the fruit boom's early stages along with the plants they attacked. Pests seemed to afflict or spare orchards randomly, leaving horticulturists in fear.[132] Growers sought out and received state aid, but they did so with ambivalence. Although they at first applauded the board's quarantine rules, they rarely initiated an action under them. As one official explained, "Very few persons were found willing to lodge a complaint against their neighbors, and it was imperative, under the terms of the act, that such a complaint be made before an official examination could take place."[133] The board also sought guidance from "economic entomologists" from the University of California, who began holding Farmers' Institutes in 1892. But growers preferred their own empirical judgment. Home-mixed solutions ("molasses, one part; vinegar two parts; water five parts," for example), though characterized as "lacking," "crude," or simply "wrong" by specialists and historians alike, came from the growers' own experiences and thus were favored over the chemical pesticides academics proposed. "I graduated from the University of Fruit Row," proclaimed George Kellogg, epitomizing horticulturists' distrust of "the professional." Well into the twentieth century, growers rejected "inspections, police work, . . . and guardians" in favor of the "collection and dissemination of information" through their own fruit growers' conventions.[134] They entrusted the progress of their enterprise to no one but themselves.

Spurning university scientists and relying on their own horticultural expertise, growers helped transform American nutritional habits. At mid-century, the nation subsisted on a "crude and scanty diet" consist-

ing mainly of starch, fat, and salt—potatoes, bread, gristly meat, and
"soups and stews of questionable origins." Not only were fruits and vegetables scarce, they also provoked suspicion and fear. Urbanites in particular believed garden and orchard produce caused cholera, dysentery,
and other diseases. But by the turn of the century, the produce market
and the fresh-fruit stand had become fixtures in American cities. The
average early-twentieth-century family, according to one study, devoted
four times more of its total food expenditure to fruits and vegetables
than it had a century earlier.[135] California growers were fully aware that
they had helped transform the nation's diet. "The old prejudices against
fruit are fast passing away," declared a Placer County orchardist. "Fruit
has become a necessity rather than a luxury." Another grower advised
Americans to "eat fruit and shun the doctor." "Ask your doctor if a
pound and a half a day of California fruit will improve your health," a
promotional pamphlet suggested. "If he says, *yes,* he is wise; if he says no
—hardly think it possible—investigate further. You may need a new
doctor." While the nutritional sciences were still in their infancy, most
experts of the time would have endorsed such sentiments.[136]

The fact that such sentiments pervaded promotional literature demonstrates the lofty status fruit growers had attained. As agricultural en-
trepreneurs, community guardians, and nourishers of an entire American generation, these men replaced the gold rusher as California's
cultural symbol. In the closing years of the nineteenth century, Americans thought of California less as a wild mining camp with little to offer
the ordinary farmer or merchant, and more as an exotic, sun-graced land
of limitless opportunity. No other state advertised itself as aggressively as
California to stimulate immigration. And no theme dominated this
campaign as consistently as specialty crop culture. "Most varieties of
booster literature," the definitive study on this subject asserts, "although
issued primarily by urban-oriented persons and organizations, emphasized the state's opportunities for small farmers." Boosters highlighted
what growers themselves took as an article of faith—that horticulture
required great skill and practical knowledge, lured more stable, intelligent persons into rural areas, promoted community pride and cooperation, and created an esthetic appeal. Promoters eagerly exploited the
state's booming horticultural statistics—the ever-increasing numbers of
farms, trees, vines, irrigated acres, and miles of canals—because these
figures allowed them to measure progress in objective, quantitative
terms.[137] It is no wonder orchardists and vineyardists thought of them-

selves as, in the words of a Newcastle grower, "the most enterprising and public-spirited men in the country."[138]

This heightened self-image displayed itself vividly in an exhibition launched in Placer County in 1891. In April, several orchardists, shippers, and merchants met in a Loomis fruit house determined to make Placer County a household word from one end of the nation to the other. "We must get the people in the East to know of and talk about our county before we can expect much addition to our population," the participants agreed. They decided that a demonstration railroad car — "Placer County on Wheels" — would best serve their interests. The Southern Pacific had been constructing display cars for conventions and fairs since the early 1880s, but this was the first known public effort. "'Placer County on Wheels' is a county move, involving the interest and appealing to the pride of everyone in the county," the *Newcastle News* declared. And indeed, dozens of women and men solicited 25-cent subscriptions throughout the county to raise the $20,000 the project required. Their faith in Placer's potential stemmed from the success of the region's fruit growers. Elaborate displays of thousands of peaches, pears, cherries, and oranges donated by local growers and shippers decorated incandescent showcases mounted inside and outside the car. "Placer County on Wheels" launched its yearlong tour in San Francisco on July 15, 1891, then headed east, stopping at every town of 1,000 or more (including Chicago during the Democratic National Convention). Crowds often numbering in the thousands inspected the fruit and collected promotional pamphlets and posters. The project proved quite a spectacle. In the words of one observer, the car resembled "a huge meteor as it whirls from city to city on its tour of education." The fruits displayed, another remarked, "are perfection itself."[139]

Inspired by orchardists, organized and financed by the entire community, and marveled at by thousands of onlookers, "Placer County on Wheels" epitomized the vitality of specialty crop culture at the turn of the century. As leaders of communities defined by their region's particular specialty crop, Fresno, Newcastle, and Davisville growers came to see themselves as guardians of California's culture — in both meanings of the word. The values and beliefs necessary to nurture a healthy and prosperous orchard or vineyard, they believed, also provided a prescription for a healthy and prosperous society. Their tremendous accomplishments in developing California's horticultural empire — esteemed by their communities and outsiders alike — gave these growers a sense of

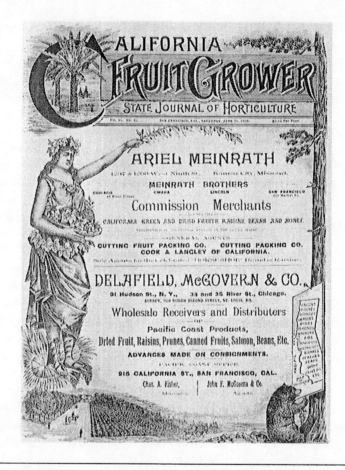

This *California Fruit Grower* cover page (June 21, 1890) vividly portrays the growers' horticultural ideal. Both their social goal of cultivating progressive rural communities and their economic goal of producing fruit for profit are promoted by Pomona, goddess of horticulture, as she reigns over an idyllic orchard and several commission-merchant advertisements. Courtesy of the California History Room, California State Library, Sacramento, California.

self-importance, self-confidence, and empowerment. The horticultural ideal did not extend to Wheatland hop growers, however. Their production success notwithstanding, hops provided neither the sense of community enhancement nor the health value that elevated fruit, nut, and raisin growers to cultural prominence. Ellwood Cooper, president of the State Board of Horticulture, shared Wickson's view that horticulture was "more than manufacturing." "California as a State," he wrote in 1895, "is destined to become one vast fruit orchard. This industry [is] paramount to every other. It will be the controlling interest in State affairs, and will eventually govern the state."[140]

Specialty crop growers believed they could avoid the evils of industrial capitalism without forgoing its economic benefits. They sold their crops to a national market and strove to turn a profit, but, as one grower wrote, did "not hold a death-grip on each dollar with the left hand, until the right hand grasps two in its place."[141] Horticulture was a way of life *and* a business. Its practitioners perceived a strong moral dimension to their brand of capitalism, one that would lift California to new levels of social and economic progress. They drew upon this ideal to define themselves in a time of rapid economic and social change, stressing in particular the nurturing and protective aspects of their enterprise. These expressions made their enterprise appear "natural," even immutable—in stark contrast to western mining and, even more so, to eastern industry. A specialty crop community, they firmly believed, was a virtuous place somewhere between the isolated and self-sufficient Jeffersonian rural order and the market-dominated, impersonal industrial city. It was a place where educated, land-owning families lived on small, orderly, and prosperous orchards or vineyards in close proximity to one another. It thus fostered neighborliness, strong local social, cultural, and political institutions, and economic progress, all in an environment that was esthetically pleasing as well.

Not all aspects of horticulture proved ideal, however. Even in the smallest orchard or vineyard, growers could not harvest their crops without a force of seasonal workers—who generally came from outside their employers' community and often asserted their own economic and cultural agendas. While growers outwardly celebrated their production and marketing accomplishments, labor relations remained a more personal, private affair.

2 "This Bugbear of Labor"

Work and Community Relations

IN EARLY DECEMBER 1902, the Twenty-seventh California Fruit Growers' Convention assembled in San Francisco. Horticulturists from Fresno, Newcastle, Davisville, and specialty crop communities throughout the state filled Pioneer Hall for four days of "spirited sessions." Mayor Eugene Schmitz, State Board of Horticulture president Ellwood Cooper, and University of California president Benjamin Ide Wheeler were featured speakers. "I have never felt prouder of a State than I do at the present time," declared Schmitz, setting the tone for the proceedings. Forty-two papers were read, all but two on familiar topics—recent innovations, marketing and transportation, and pest control. But the two papers on "the Help question . . . proved the most exciting of the sessions. . . . At one time growers all over the hall [were] on their feet asking for recognition by the chair," the horticultural press reported.[1]

"In these conventions," commented Alexander Gordon, a prominent Fresno raisin grower and founder of the Caledonia Colony, "we meet and discuss tree-planting and . . . the tree-planting business, [but] we discuss very little about the labor question and the getting of labor to handle the fruit we raise." Now, however, the labor question could no longer be avoided. When Sacramento Valley orchardist H. P. Stabler declared that an "unprecedented scarcity of orchard help during the past season has been noted in every fruit district of the State," applause filled the hall. No one voiced a dissenting opinion. Two competing solutions dominated the ensuing discussion: induce "intelligent, thrifty, energetic, steady, young white men" from the East and Midwest to California's rural regions, or amend federal immigration laws to admit sufficient numbers of "industrious, patient, docile, and generally reliable" Chinese farm laborers.[2]

Resolutions representing each side passed overwhelmingly, with most growers voting in favor of both. This in itself would not appear out of the ordinary had labor supply been their only concern. But "the scarcity of help" meant different things to different growers. Washington Colony pioneer G. W. Aiken recalled that raisin growers had "depended almost solely upon Chinese labor" 10 years earlier. In retrospect, these contract laborers seemed ideal. "The number of workers were brought to you. . . . No fuss, no trouble." More "Easterners" appealed to Newcastle orchardist George D. Kellogg's community sensibilities. "Why not try this method of getting our own people here to work," he commented. "Let us employ our own people—they make good citizens." Kellogg also reminded fresh-fruit growers of the dangers of "promiscuous and indiscriminate picking, selecting, grading, and packing." But he kept to himself his experience that Chinese and Japanese tenants had proven to be the most conscientious orchard workers. George W. Pierce Jr., in contrast, had hired white itinerant laborers almost exclusively for both his grain and almond harvests until the previous year. He shuddered at the thought of his own encounter with a Japanese contractor when Stabler denounced the "little brown men" who "break their contracts in the height of the fruit season." It was an experience he was determined not to repeat.[3]

Aiken, Kellogg, and Pierce all joined in the chorus of "labor shortage," not realizing just how different their needs really were. In the aggregate, their labor problems appeared to be similar and even a distinctive characteristic of horticulture as a whole. In contrast to the typical factory operation, where commodities are manufactured continuously throughout the year in a controlled environment, orchard and vineyard production is intermittent and dictated by natural forces. Growers required a substantial labor force only at critical points in the production cycle, most notably the harvest. But the number of peak periods and their degree of intensiveness varied from crop to crop. Moreover, the choice of labor system—how many workers to hire, how to pay them, how to secure their labor from task to task and from year to year, what level of skill they required, how much supervision was appropriate—was a subjective one, based as much on social and cultural concerns as on economic factors and environmental conditions.[4] As specialty crop production expanded, growers came to depend on workers "outside" their communities. The increasing presence of these workers exposed a tension within the growers' horticultural ideal—between their economic goal of producing fruit for profit in a highly competitive world market, and their social goals of cultivating a progressive and homogeneous rural community and enriching the state's culture. Sporadic efforts to resolve that tension surfaced at the San Francisco convention, but only in the guise of "labor shortage." Specialty crop growers had not yet developed a means to rationalize the labor market within their own subregions, let alone on a statewide basis.

RATIONALIZING THE LABOR MARKET did not concern the earliest
Fresno settlers. Colonists relied on their "personal attention to the cultivation of the land," as developers had anticipated. "The very success of
any colony," as Bernhard Marks recalled, depended on a system based on
"the family" managing "the details of their lots." The 20-acre tract became the cornerstone of that system, as it was "just large enough and just
small enough to give one industrious man constant employment." But
alfalfa, not raisins, was the colonists' original crop of choice. "No farm,"
stated the *Fresno Weekly Expositor* in 1879, "is considered complete without an alfalfa field. . . . Among the first things that a new settler in the
colonies does is to . . . plant alfalfa." Stockmen competing for grasslands
in the 1870s had just begun to favor this experimental crop as a more intensive, efficient one for beef production. The original idea of the colony
envisioned settlers contributing to the existing grazing industry, but on
a scale that would reduce that industry to a household economy.[5]

As raisins began to supplant alfalfa, colonists reaffirmed the 20-acre
ideal. A vineyard, they believed, was a home as well as a workplace. Collectively, their way of life constituted "a system of ideal homes and communities, where the science of tillage is carried to its greatest perfection,
and where comfort, good taste, and an admirable spirit of helpfulness
and neighborliness abound."[6] At first, such a spirit proved invaluable to
"this comparatively new way of farming." Only entire communities
working together, for example, could protect the young vineyards from
periodic infestations of jackrabbits. These pests, which thrived on the
sudden increase in roots, seeds, and alfalfa, hid in the vineyards, making
it difficult for growers to hunt them. In organized "rabbit drives"—gala
affairs complete with grand marshals, barbecues, and brass bands—hundreds and sometimes thousands of colonists gathered for "the slaughter."
Fanning out in a tight line formation over a three- to four-mile stretch
of countryside, "battalions" of settlers screamed and waved clubs to
frighten the rabbits into a huge V-shaped pen built for the drive. Those
rabbits not killed during the "march" itself were slain inside this enclo-
sure.[7] And with vineyard work itself, young, unmarried men from neighboring lots or towns supplemented family labor when needed. H. Madsen's experience was typical. "I worked a great deal for my neighbors,"
this Fig Avenue resident of the Washington Colony stated, "while gradually getting [my own lot] under cultivation." The fact that vineyards
provided such work fostered both a sense of "community prosperity" and
the notion that "raisins [were] a superior article."[8]

The 20-acre ideal in the Central California Colony (ca. 1880). Courtesy of the California History Room, California State Library, Sacramento, California.

But as the colonies expanded during the 1880s, vineyardists required more than a "spirit of helpfulness and neighborliness." "It has been found that twenty acres of irrigated land is more than one man can handle," acknowledged one observer as early as 1879. A 20-acre vineyard could prosper under the care of a self-sufficient, industrious man and his family "except perhaps during the picking season, when he will need a little help."[9] The number of workers required varied at different points of the production cycle. Beginning in March and extending well into the summer, cultivating (plowing, cross-plowing, weeding, furrowing, sulfuring, and irrigating) was the principal activity. One man with a team (at least two horses) and the proper implements could work 20 acres, but larger vineyards required additional help. The three-week harvest in September was the busiest season. While estimates varied, most colonists employed at least 10 harvesters for every one cultivator. And between January and March, pruning required a substantial workforce as well—roughly one-third that needed for the harvest.[10] Growers and developers believed that "the colony system will in course of time supply our needs." But while Fresno County's population tripled during the decade, to 32,000, raisin production increased more than 100-fold—from 80,000 pounds in 1882 to 9.5 million in 1889. By then, according to one prominent grower's estimate, at least 12,000 temporary workers were needed to harvest and pack raisins from the county's 2,000 vineyards.[11] Even the most zealous Fresno enthusiast no longer linked the self-sufficient family farm to raisin growing.

Newcastle fruit belt orchardists found their labor requirements just as overwhelming. Early on, prospective foothill farmers became embattled settlers when trying to obtain title to land they were attempting to purchase. They were hindered particularly by the federal government's reluctance to declare the land agricultural and thus eligible for sale under preemptive terms ($1.25 per acre). As late as 1878, long after the region's placer mines had ceased to yield gold, the farmer still bore the burden (and cost) of convincing federal authorities his land was valuable only for agriculture. Kellogg, W. J. Wilson, Martin Schnabel, P. W. Butler, and other pioneer orchardists who endured this hardship were not about to limit themselves to a few acres.[12] Butler, for example, purchased 120 acres near Penryn in 1880.[13] But it was more land than he could manage. Though he would become one of the region's more prominent horticulturists, Butler never improved more than two-thirds of his holdings. Most growers, in fact, began on a large scale without realizing just how labor-intensive their operations would become.[14]

An inkling of what lay ahead came early: even before any planting could be done, Newcastle orchardists were confronted with the daunting task of clearing the land. Specialty crop growers in Fresno and most other California regions, as *Pacific Rural Press* editor Edward Wickson wrote in 1891, rarely "had to lift an ax," as their land was "naturally clear for planting." Even where large trees had to be removed, the cost of the work was generally recouped in firewood. In the Placer foothills, however, one paid at least $30 an acre to "subdue the rich wilderness"—to chop down pine and oak trees, remove their stumps, pull up manzanita by the roots, and burn debris. Two men and a team could clear a few acres during the winter, when the ground was wet and soft. But growers were anxious to earn a return on their investment as soon as possible. Additional "muscle and persistence" for this work would always be at a premium.[15] After the land was cleared, leveling, terracing, plowing, harrowing, "laying out" trees (108 per acre), hole and ditch digging, and planting all could be done quickly with teams and minimal manpower at a cost of about eight dollars per acre. Still, Newcastle orchardists knew that their trees would not return a profit until at least the fifth year. The fact that their initial investment ($59 per acre the first year, not including purchase costs) was nearly double that of orchardists in "more favorable conditions of locality" ($34 per acre) added that much more pressure to keep their orchards small.[16]

As their trees matured, additional pressures mounted. Unlike grapevines, peach and other deciduous fruit trees have only one peak season. Trees were pruned to control growth, not to enhance production, and thus required relatively little attention.[17] But the harvest proved far more demanding. Kellogg employed from four to seven workers to tend to his nonharvest needs, but required at least 10 more for just three weeks to pick and pack his 30 acres of peaches. His labor requirements were typical, and, if considered in isolation, not all that unmanageable. But the harvest occurred at the same time for every grower in the region. When some 300,000 peach trees came into bearing virtually all at once during the mid-1880s, orchardists suddenly needed 1,500 harvesters. Such a labor force more than stretched the limits of this sparsely populated region.[18]

Horticulture's small-scale but intensive production confounded Davisville almond growers as well. Most had been managing wheat farms for years, and they conducted their almond operations in much the same way. Early on, the two crops appeared compatible. Even Pierce, whose 132-acre orchard was the region's largest, experienced few labor problems. He plowed, planted, and cultivated his orchard in the early 1890s with the same four to five permanent hands (and occasional extra man or two from town) who tended his wheat.[19] When his almond trees began bearing later in the decade, he easily procured the 10 or so workers he needed for the late-summer harvest. "At this time grain-harvesting is over, and there are usually many men to hire out," as Webster Treat pointed out. By the turn of the century, however, Pierce needed as many as 30 harvesters.[20] His maturing trees almost tripled their yield between 1897 (6 tons) and 1901 (17); and Davisville orchardists together increased production by 50 percent over the same period. Not surprisingly, they began complaining of a labor shortage.[21]

Wheatland hop growers, in contrast, rarely lacked for labor—despite the fact that their enterprise, in E. Clemons Horst's words, was "intensive farming of the highest type."[22] No other specialty crop came even close. The reason lay first in the density of the crop. Vines were planted in rows every seven feet (about 900 per acre), grew 25–30 feet high, and produced 1,800–2,500 pounds per acre. Trained to climb vertically—at first along individual poles, and by the 1890s over 20-foot-high wire trellises—the vines intertwined by harvest time to form an imposing grid of greenish-gold walls and narrow "avenues." The golden hue came from the ripe hops themselves, which are small, sticky "strobiles" resembling fir cones. To produce the best beer flavor, hops needed to be picked and dried without delay. If left on the vines too long—more than about three weeks—they turned red, a sign their moisture content had diminished. Moreover, all the picking during this brief window was done by hand.[23] The demand for pickers, consequently, was extraordinary, even by California specialty crop standards. According to a 1938 study, hops required 23.5 "man-days" per acre to harvest; no other crop needed more than nine. For yards of 500–600 acres, such as Horst's and D. P. Durst's, this meant a labor force of 1,000–1,800, depending on the yield.[24]

How was it that hop growers, despite their crop's extreme seasonality and intensiveness, were able to operate on a so much larger scale than raisin, peach, and almond growers? The answer requires a closer look at the labor process itself. Harvesting fruits and nuts required not only a sufficient labor force, but a quality labor force as well. It was imperative for these growers to hire skilled, experienced workers "who understood the principles involved." Not all crops, however, demanded such careful attention to detail. "The kind of help needed by the individual farmer," as a 1921 farm-management manual put it, "depends on the character of his operations."[25]

The "character" of the hop harvest posed few problems. Once the vines were cut down from the trellis, workers simply pulled the cones off and tossed them into sacks, being careful only to exclude the green leaves. Once or twice a day, "inspectors" appeared in the fields to weigh and record each picker's accumulation before teamsters hauled the hops to the drying kilns. Starting with Durst's first harvest in 1883, Wheatland growers paid their pickers by the hundredweight—one dollar in most years, excluding the 1890s depression (hence the term "dollar hops"). The piece rate gave workers an incentive to work as quickly as possible and to develop picking strategies of their own. Some worked in pairs or foursomes; others competed against one another; and many started well before sunrise hoping the morning dew would tip the scales in their favor. Of equal importance, the piece wage made it unnecessary to distinguish among individuals as to their competence. A typical labor force thus resembled "a conglomerate mass of humanity," as one observer described it. "Men and women of all ages, colors, and conditions mingle in the great annual onslaught," remarked another. Early on, Wheatland growers relied on "citizens of the town," but by the turn of the century, pickers came from throughout northern California, many returning year after year. They were drawn by the relatively easy work, by high wages (as much as $3.50 per day, $1.50 on average), and by the Bear River hops themselves, which they valued for their "plumpness and weightiness." One regular remarked after trying his luck in a Sacramento County yard, "Hell, I can drink more hops in my beer than I can pick [there]."[26]

An altogether different dynamic governed the raisin-production process, however. Persistence and judgment, vineyardists repeatedly stressed, were essential for producing a profitable Muscat raisin. In the late nineteenth and early twentieth centuries, the Muscat — not the Thompson Seedless, which dominates the market today — was the variety of choice. The Muscat was four times the size, plumper, and much stronger and sweeter in flavor. It was "one of the oldest of all known fruits": Spanish missionaries, medieval knights, Shakespeare, and even the Bible itself had "regarded it as wholesome, nourishing, and strengthening."[27] But these "Persian delicacies" contained one serious deficiency — their considerable number of large, hard seeds. Consumers were burdened with the inconvenience of extracting these unpalatable pits. It was imperative, therefore, that Muscats be "produced as handsomely as possible" to attract buyers. They were not sold in bulk, but on the stem, as "Imperial Clusters," "London Layers," and "Dehesa Clusters." Twenty-pound cartons were packed in four layers separated by waxed paper, with the "choicest bunches" selected for the top tier. "Loose" Muscats also were sold, but a vineyard's profit depended on the proportion of "layers" it produced.[28]

"These grapes were picked with care — extreme care," a vineyardist recalled. "They were packed with care, and shipped with care, and they paid. You have to do these things in [this] line of the fruit business."[29] Indeed, "care" was the watchword for just about every vineyard task. Even weeding, a seemingly mundane chore, required scrupulous attention. "Each weed acts like a chimney for the moisture in the soil, which it sucks out to the detriment of the vine and grape," raisin expert Gustav Eisen instructed growers. "No weeds should be allowed to grow in the vineyard." Some of the larger vineyardists employed small numbers of "hoe-ers" year-round for this tedious work, "it being impossible to keep the place free from these pests in any other way."[30] Pruning the vines not only was more intensive, it required even "greater care and judgment," as raisin pioneer T. C. White described. Vines left too long or too short, or with too many or too few spurs, jeopardized not only the quantity produced, but also the size of each bunch, the Muscat's flavor, and the ease with which the bunches would later be picked. While growers exchanged ideas about the best methods, the ultimate responsibility for implementing those methods fell to the worker. As vineyardist Frank Ball stressed, "The *pruner's gauging* must follow, for all vines are not equal."[31]

It was the harvesting process that proved the most intricate of all. Picking commenced in early September when the grapes turned ripe. Those picked too "green" attained neither the size, taste, nor aroma to achieve "cluster" status. Not all grapes ripened at the same time; to "make the best possible raisins out of the grapes," the vines had to be picked over at least three times. The picker determined the ripeness by color or taste or with a saccharimeter (which measured the sweetness of the juice—25 degrees was the desired reading). Pickers used a small, pointed knife to cut the bunches from the vine, and were instructed to leave a small portion of the stem attached. "There is nothing prettier on a bunch of raisins than this broad end of the bunch," wrote Eisen. "It gives an idea of strength and oddity to the raisin cluster, showing the buyer at a glance that it is a cluster which was once solidly attached to the vine . . . , and it invites the purchaser to take hold of it and thus lift the luscious bunch out of the box." The stem served another purpose as well. "The producer must insist on having his grapes handled by the stem at all times," Ball emphasized. "[This] preserves the bloom on the raisins, which is so much admired alike by packers, merchants, and consumers."

Once cut, the grapes were ready for drying. First, the pickers "cleaned" each bunch by removing any leaves, twigs, spiderwebs, or sunburnt grapes. They then placed the bunches on two-by-three-foot metal trays distributed along the mounds between the vineyard rows at the optimum angle for maximum sun. Each vine filled one or two trays with 20 pounds (ultimately six to seven pounds of raisins). In six to eight days, the grapes became about two-thirds dry and were ready to be turned. Two workers accomplished this without handling or damaging the grapes by placing an empty tray on top of the filled one and turning them both over, a task "requiring quite some knack." During the 10- to 14-day drying period, excessive heat (over 110 degrees) or rain could severely damage the crop. To protect the grapes, workers stacked the trays, preferably by the "roof" method: instead of simply placing one tray on top of another, they leaned two piles of trays three to four feet high against each other, creating a roof of sorts that released some of the pressure between the trays and protected the grapes from the rain or sun. Ascertaining when the grapes had dried sufficiently also required considerable expertise. "A perfect raisin should be neither too hard nor too soft," Eisen wrote. "Take a raisin between the thumb and forefinger and roll it gently until softened, when either jelly or water will exude from the stem end," explained White. "If water, it requires further drying." But even on individual bunches, some grapes would be dry enough and others not. Those "destined to make layers" were placed in sweatboxes, wooden structures just large enough to hold a single tray, where they remained another 10 to 30 days to equalize the moisture. Loose raisins received no such treatment; they were "simply dumped" in separate boxes for transport.[32]

Teamsters then delivered both the clusters and loose raisins to the packing house for the final stage of preparation. The loose Muscats were graded and stemmed mechanically — with a crude hand-operated, eight-foot-long cylindrical machine at first, and with a more sophisticated version powered by a 10-horsepower steam engine by the late 1880s. Workers shoveled the stemmed raisins onto inspection tables, where they were cleaned one last time. Inferior raisins were sold in 80-pound sacks, while those of higher quality were packed in 20-, 10-, and 5-pound cartons. Packing "layers" was a quite different process. Once sufficiently moistened in the sweatbox, the clusters were more pliable and could withstand moderate pressure without being damaged. Nevertheless, they could only be graded and packed by hand. On long, narrow tables, workers with "expert fingers" removed them from the sweatboxes, sorted them by quality and appearance (usually by the number of "crowns"), packed all but the top layer in regular rows, "faced" the top layer "as an advertisement for the contents underneath," and finished off the entire process by adorning the carton with an attractive wrapper or label. If workers "exercised the greatest care in all the details of cultivating, picking, curing, and preparation," Eisen's "perfect raisin" was the end result.[33]

The labor process was even more crucial for fresh fruit. Newcastle horticulturists' very enterprise depended on their ability to produce a fragile, perishable fruit "without blemish" for markets two to three thousand miles distant from their orchards. "This, of necessity, carries with it the most careful picking, selecting, grading, and packing," George D. Kellogg maintained. Pickers required "no small amount of skill and experience," A. P. Hall told the Placer County Horticultural Society. "Some with years of practice never acquire the knack of the expert." No fruit demanded more vigilance than the peach. If ripe when picked, the peach would spoil before reaching distant markets. But if picked too green, it not only would be small, but "would never attain good eating qualities." Pickers removed each peach by a slight upward turn or twist, not a jerk from the branch. They then laid the fruit gently into their basket; if dropped "even a few inches," it could bruise and spoil an entire box. As one grower wrote, "From the time the fruit is plucked from the trees it should be handled as carefully as if each was an egg." Packing, done right beneath the trees, required similar expertise. Packers reassessed which peaches were suitable for shipping, wrapped each individual peach, and graded them by size for boxes of 84, 72, 60, or 48. Those not packed "firmly pressed together" would not survive the short wagon trip over foothill roads to the shipping house, let alone the railroad journey across the country. "It matters not how much skill or money has been expended in the production of the fruit," stated the *California Fruit Grower;* "if it is not picked promptly and handled carefully, the business proves a failure."[34]

Almond culture posed few of the problems of fresh fruit or Muscat raisins, especially under the favorable soil and climatic conditions that Putah Creek growers enjoyed. Because of their relatively large size, almond trees needed more space than the average deciduous orchard tree. Growers who planted them the customary 16 to 20 feet apart, rather than 30, ended up having to dig out every other tree. The red spider mite and the peach moth were their most troublesome pests (the former all but destroyed the 1898 crop), but growers learned to keep them under control by spraying homemade sulfur solutions. Otherwise, the trees "beared heavily and regularly," with relatively few complications.[35]

The way of harvesting the crop remained virtually unchanged until the mid-twentieth century.[36] Harvesters worked in crews of five with two canvas sheets (each covering about 40 square feet), several large grain sacks, a 16-foot-long "sled," and one horse. They tacked the sheets to either side of the sled and positioned it between the rows of orchard trees. Almonds were not picked, like peaches; harvesters knocked them from the trees onto the sheets by jarring the branches with 20-foot poles. Once a tree was "knocked," the workers lifted the sheet and emptied the almonds directly into the sled. With two laborers operating on either side of the sled, two rows of trees could be worked simultaneously. While the horse pulled the sled to the next set of trees, the fifth man, usually the crew boss, stood in the sled and sacked the almonds, tied up the sacks, and dumped them off. A teamster then picked them up and hauled them to the packing sheds, where they were hulled, dried, sulfured, and re-sacked for market.[37]

"The process of gathering almonds and preparing them for market is very simple," explained Webster Treat in 1890. The *Pacific Rural Press* concurred: "It requires no experience or practice to harvest the crop, for there is no science needed such as there is in handling fruit." In contrast to a peach picker, an almond knocker needed to employ little finesse in "striking the limbs with sharp blows until all the nuts are shaken off." This "does not injure the tree at all," Treat insisted, "and besides, it hulls a portion of the nuts." Furthermore, the almond's harvest timetable was far more flexible. "The crop may be gathered leisurely. There need be no hurry to gather it within a certain time, like there is for fruit." In fact, the longer the almond remained on the tree, the drier its hull became, making it easier to crack and remove by hand. Ironically, the invention of a mechanical almond huller negated this "advantage." A Read Sure-Pop huller such as the one George W. Pierce Jr. purchased in 1897 could reduce costs by 60 to 80 percent. However, if the hulls had lost too much moisture, the machine would shatter them and, in the process, break the inner shells as well.[38]

As Davisville growers came to identify themselves more as horticulturists than as wheat farmers, their image of the almond harvest changed dramatically. By the turn of the century, the harvest offered an opportunity to display one's resourcefulness and imagination. Knockers, as Pierce told a 1901 Yolo County Farmers' Institute, needed to use "the best of care." "Do not imagine that because you have a pole you must necessarily beat the tree to loosen the nuts," he later instructed growers. "Do not permit it to be abused. . . . Every unnecessary burden placed on the tree draws from vitality that should be expended in production of nuts." Knockers should "gently jar" the trees with "good, tough, springy" poles, preferably sawed from tamarack or fir. Pierce usually operated his huller himself, and with immense satisfaction. It allowed him to participate directly in the harvest and to observe the nut itself, the end result of the horticultural process. "It is your duty," he preached to other grow-

The almond huller that George W. Pierce Jr. operated every harvest, with immense satisfaction. Pierce Family Papers, Department of Special Collections, University of California Library, Davis.

ers, "to make possible the greatest development on the part of the tree." The fact that members of the Davisville Almond Growers' Association regularly "discussed at length . . . the improvement of methods" for gathering their crop suggests that they too had come to believe that almonds deserved the same "proper care and careful handling" as any other California fruit.[39]

Nowhere was this belief more evident than in the wage system horticulturists first employed. To ensure that their workers "exercised the greatest care," they paid a day wage—not a piece rate.[40] This strategy calls into question the logic most scholars have employed to describe California's farm labor market. Piece work, it is generally thought, was the optimum agricultural wage system: it allowed growers to employ virtually any type of labor and to keep costs at a minimum.[41] Vineyardists might have paid their harvesters by the tray, peach orchardists their pickers by the pound, and almond growers their knockers by the tree. But unlike hop growers, they were more concerned with "quality shirking" than "effort shirking." Raisin and peach growers expected each of their workers to meet certain daily standards—25 trays of raisins or 600 pounds of peaches—but feared "neglect" and "recklessness" far more than "a deliberate pace." And while these growers prided themselves on their "thorough management of details," the fact that they depended on their workers to supervise themselves rendered the piece rate even less of a viable option. The incentive wage seemed ideal for almonds, given their durability. But for two generations, Davisville growers had paid both permanent and temporary workers by the day or month. Moreover, the "proper care" they insisted their almonds required reinforced the utility of the day wage in their minds. It gave them a sense of control over the pace and quality of production.[42]

Horticulturists' near-obsessive attention to detail and quality of work stemmed from more than profit concerns alone. Their eloquent descriptions of the labor process expressed their passion and pride for their enterprise. "The culture of the raisin grape, its picking, curing and packing, is pre-eminently the most refined horticultural industry," one grower wrote. "Nothing requires more neatness, more taste, more refinement, or gives more pleasure to the horticulturist than the various labors connected with the vineyard and the packing-house."[43] The members of the Placer County Horticultural Society and the Davisville Almond Growers' Association spoke of their crops in a similar manner. They would not have scoffed at Eisen's impression of the 1889 Fresno harvest:

> The vineyards are full of workers; grape-pickers are stooping by every vine, and are arranging the grapes on small or oblong trays. . . . At every step, we pass teams going in various directions—teams loaded with raisin boxes, teams with raisin trays, teams crowded with raisin pickers hurrying out to the vineyards, teams driven by raisin-growers or colonists generally, who rush to and from town to transact business connected with their one great industry. Everywhere is bustle and life; every one is in a hurry, as the grape-picking has begun. . . . It is a pretty sight, a sight of thrift and intelligence, of enterprise and of success, of wealth and of refinement.[44]

Such enthusiastic exaggeration and self-promotion may sound like rhetorical excess. But horticulturists drew upon the intricacies of the labor process to reinforce their conviction in their way of life. That conviction did not include the self-sufficient family farm. Horticulture's scale of production and labor requirements prevented its practitioners from achieving that ideal, but few expressed any remorse. This did not mean that they had suddenly lost their idealism—nor that their orchards and vineyards had become "factories" in any sense of the word. On the contrary, fruit and nut growers found even deeper meaning in the delicate, "refined" process of preparing their crops for market.

Labor relations, however, proved far more problematic than the labor process itself. Harvesters were temporary workers, hired at the season's beginning and dismissed at its end. No matter how high their wage, their earnings were limited. Few chose to endure the conditions that growers rarely mentioned in their writings and speeches: little, if any, job security; temperatures near 100 degrees; dry and dusty terrain; and, with vineyard work, constant stooping or squatting. Regardless of the skill, experience, or knack required, orchard and vineyard work attracted only those with limited options. For horticulturists, there could have been no greater irony. The labor process they celebrated also posed an inescapable dilemma—recruiting and maintaining a quality workforce. Moreover, the ideal of the contented and prosperous specialty crop community rested upon, by necessity, a poor and largely transient population that horticulture could not benefit for more than a few weeks each year. No other problem, raisin grower T. C. White admitted, was as exasperating as "this bugbear of labor."[45]

Most growers had "a decided race-feeling in behalf of the white men," and hired them early on. They shared the assumption of virtually all nineteenth-century white Americans that nonwhites were inferior. But the vast majority of available whites were transients, like those who had loitered in the streets of the state's rural towns since the 1870s. Refugees from the recurrent depressions of the latter third of the nineteenth century, these itinerants rarely demonstrated the pluck and persistence horticulturists demanded. "It's a common thing for a man to come along, obtain employment, work two or three days, demand his pay and leave, without notice, at a critical time," went the common complaint. From the workers' perspective, however, California's orchards and vineyards offered few rewards, economic or cultural. Their sporadic work habits were an appropriate response to volatile labor market conditions and the nature of itinerant work. Characterized as "pests," "hoboes," and "worthless vagabonds" in local newspapers, some of them may have been

consciously striking back at a social and economic order that both demanded and abhorred their presence.[46]

Their behavior did not deter Davisville orchardists, however. Pierce's
experiences, imparted in his daily journals and account books, are most
revealing. Pierce made little distinction between his regular hands and
his almond harvesters. He referred to them in his journal individually by
first name and collectively as "the boys." He made an effort to engage his
"good men" and punished them (usually by dismissal) for "lying," "in-
toxication," or other forms of insubordination.[47] Hands such as John
Reynolds and John Schmidt earned Pierce's respect and became loyal
workers for years.[48] Pierce's father had treated his ranch workers much
the same way, as had most grain farmers of his generation. Both father
and son recruited temporary workers in the same manner. They made
the five-mile trip to the Davisville train depot, where white itinerant
workers could be found in abundance.[49] The younger Pierce paid his almond harvesters the same wage as his permanent workers, $1.50 a day
without board. Their unsteadiness of employment became quite a nui-
sance, as just one week of journal entries during the 1900 harvest reveals:
" . . . went to town in am for more men, got three. . . . went to town in
pm and got five more men. . . . Four new men came at supper time. . . .
Joe Morgan quit in am. Two others in pm. Went to town at night and
got three new men. . . . Elliot and Warren quit at noon."[50] The harvest
concluded, however, without cause for alarm. In the end, Pierce's almonds—his passion for horticulture notwithstanding—did not require
stable, conscientious workers, only a sufficient number. Moreover, his relationship with his knockers allowed him to maintain at least a veneer of
the paternalism he was used to.

Fresno vineyardists and Newcastle orchardists, on the other hand,
could not tolerate this sort of behavior. They instead turned to another
source of labor, the Chinese. These immigrants had made their presence
felt in California long before the 1880s fruit boom. Pulled by the lure of
"Gold Mountain" and pushed by social and economic turmoil in their
homeland, tens of thousands of Chinese (virtually all men) migrated to
California's mining fields in the 1850s. Though often limited to placer
claims deemed "run out" by previous owners, the Chinese extracted gold
with skill and patience, arousing both the envy and ire of their fellow
miners. When the Central Pacific Railroad began building its transcontinental and subsidiary lines in the 1860s, more than 10,000 Chinese left
the mines to help in the construction. In the following decade, many of

these laborers found employment in the state's burgeoning horticultural regions.[51]

It was the Chinese, in fact, who laid the groundwork for the Fresno colonies. Gangs of Chinese laborers helped build the Fresno Canal, the Centerville Ditch, the Fowler Switch Canal, and the thousands of miles of smaller canals and lateral ditches that linked the colonies to the Kings River. These arteries were upwards of 100 feet wide and 10 feet deep, and were purposely dug through the firmest hardpan to minimize erosion. Chinese laborers also helped build and maintain headgates, flumes, weirs, levees, and other canal structures. Moreover, they helped level the lots, dig holes for the trees that lined the avenues, and plant the initial vines that Bernhard Marks felt were so vital to the colonists' "contentedness." And when the colonists began arriving, Chinese truck gardeners and merchants were among the first to service them.[52]

Chinese immigrants played an equally significant role in the Newcastle region. Harry Butler recalled that fruit growing at first "meant clearing the land," which in turn meant "depending on the Chinese." It was the practice of many orchardists to employ one Chinese worker year-round who could secure additional help when needed. Chinese laborers had cleared approximately 3,000 acres by 1886, 5,000 by 1890, and 8,000 by 1892. Growers relied on the Chinese for terracing, ditch digging, planting, and cultivation as well. White laborers in the region were scarce, and drew higher wages from several nearby granite quarries. Moreover, the Chinese often agreed to cultivate small berry patches between the young nonbearing trees on a share basis, which helped offset some of the growers' expenses.[53]

Chinese immigrants, unlike much of the white population, gravitated toward the opportunities for orchard and vineyard work. They earned $1.00 to $1.25 a day, while white hands generally earned $1.50. Still, it was significantly more than they could earn in China, and more than the average farmworker wage in southern, midwestern, or northeastern states. Chinese orchard and vineyard workers generally started at 6 A.M. and toiled under the blazing sun until 7 P.M., stopping only at noon for a brief meal of rice and vegetables. Growers often interpreted the "willingness" to endure such conditions as "docility." But their principal motivation was their responsibility to their extended families across the Pacific. These workers lived frugally, sometimes setting aside as much as one-third or half their wages, and sent their savings to China.[54]

Their system of labor organization enhanced their value even more.

Where employed in large numbers, Chinese laborers worked in gangs under Chinese foremen. The "China bosses," as they became known to whites, recruited laborers, supervised their work, provided their board, and negotiated their working and wage conditions. The Chinese contractors often were local merchants who had already established both face-to-face relations with prominent whites and contacts with other Chinese merchants in larger cities. The Quong Yuen Long Company in Newcastle and the Sing Long Chung Kan Kee Company in Fresno, for example, could secure large numbers of harvest workers from Sacramento, Stockton, and San Francisco with just a few hours' notice. The system engendered abuses; contractors could demand exorbitant commissions from workers and overcharge for provisions. Most workers, however, recognized that organization was necessary for circumventing language and cultural barriers. And employers marveled at the system's convenience and efficiency.[55]

Horticulturists held the Chinese in high regard for more than their availability, stamina, and organization. These immigrants brought with them a vast agricultural knowledge accumulated by their ancestors over centuries of experience, which they readily adapted to California's environmental conditions. To the delight of small and large growers alike, the Chinese "possessed the intelligence, the discriminating judgment, and the accuracy of sight and touch to carry horticultural work through all its stages." They were preferred, as one grower wrote to the *Pacific Rural Press*, "not because they work cheaper, but because they do the work better and are found more reliable."[56] Newcastle orchardists saw Chinese harvesters as their only viable alternative. "I have never yet been able to get a white man that could pack my fruit and pick my berries in a satisfactory manner," wrote George D. Kellogg in 1886. Kellogg, in fact, had his "China help . . . teach new white help on the ranch how to pick and pack my fruit." If an orchardist had any special harvest concerns—picking out insect-infested fruit, for example—he needed only to "instruct his man" for the entire gang to comply.[57] So esteemed were the Chinese for their skillful vineyard work that they became something of a badge of prestige, especially for smaller growers. "My one Chinaman does all the work with the exception of harvesting and pruning, when I have to have several Chinamen help him," a 20-acre Washington Colony resident boasted to the Fresno Board of Trade in 1887. By that time, the Chinese dominated the labor market in fruit regions throughout the state.[58]

But while their labor was crucial to the developing horticultural economy, the Chinese became only marginal members of horticultural communities. Shortly after Fresno businessmen erected their first tent stores near the Central Pacific depot in 1872, they signed a pledge to neither lease nor sell land on the east side of the tracks to any Chinese merchants. Within a few months, a Chinatown of several hundred people emerged west of the tracks. There they gained some measure of independence and refuge, but as a colony within a colony, racially isolated and culturally insulated. Newcastle and most other fruit settlements also maintained separate Chinese quarters. The ostracism of the Chinese was predetermined by a peculiar ideology afflicting most white Californians. The Chinese were said to be corrupting society, particularly its children, with their obsessive work habits (they worked even on Sundays), strange-sounding language, long hair, mysterious religious practices, peculiar food preferences, fondness for opium, and fetish for daily bathing. Though restricted to their side of the tracks, the Chinese became invaluable community members. In Fresno, for example, they constructed the first courthouse, the first hotel, and the first theater.[59]

For growers, employing the Chinese created a peculiar dilemma. They regarded the Chinese as superior workers, but outside the orchards and vineyards, the Chinese were social outcasts. By hiring Chinese labor, growers risked tarnishing their image as community guardians. Occasional letters to the *Pacific Rural Press* depicting the Chinese as "the ruin of our rising generation" caused particular concern.[60] But growers did not react, as did railroad magnate Charles Crocker and other California industrialists, by publicly denouncing their employees as "the Heathen Chinee"—fit only for backbreaking, mindless work.[61] To do so would have undermined their idyllic notions of orchard and vineyard labor and of horticultural communities in general.

Growers were left with the difficult task of defending their need for Chinese labor without incurring their community's wrath. Increasingly, their approach was simply not to acknowledge the presence of the Chinese, let alone their importance. Eisen's 223-page raisin treatise, for example, alludes to the Chinese only once, as harvesters "willing to do a day's work." In public, growers invariably "expressed themselves directly in favor of white labor," while insisting that "the scarcity of this class has rendered it necessary to employ Chinese." Nor did they take a public position on Chinese exclusion, the most impassioned issue in California politics in the early 1880s.[62] Several Central Valley towns attempted to "get rid of their Chinese" in 1886, often through mob violence. But Newcastle and Fresno growers avoided any uprisings by reassuring their communities that the "natural increase in our [white] population" would, within a generation at most, eliminate the demand for Chinese labor. The limited opposition from these and other communities suggests that growers and nongrowers alike "recognized and acquiesced in the Chinese presence as a [temporary] necessity," as one observer wrote.[63]

That acquiescence, however, gave only the illusion that growers had their labor problems under control. Their labor systems had only begun to evolve by the mid-1880s. As the number of bearing trees and vines continued to multiply year after year, the demand for proficient labor intensified. Realizing this, Chinese, and later Japanese, contractors seized the initiative and gained control of the labor market. The 1890s depression put increased pressure on growers to reassess their labor strategies. Fresno raisin growers reorganized their labor process, experimented with mechanization, and altered their wage system. Newcastle orchardists began employing a different labor system altogether. In the process, however, they grew even more dependent on a labor force of "outsiders," making community relations that much more troublesome.

Ironically, the raisin boom that made Fresno growers famous ultimately undermined the labor relations they had cultivated so carefully. The first signs of this change occurred in packing. Early in the 1880s, T. C. White, A. B. Butler, and a few other large growers packed their own Muscats, as well as those of smaller neighbors, in sheds adjacent to their vineyards. As with cultivating, pruning, and harvesting, they employed Chinese labor almost exclusively.[64] But as production skyrocketed, packing required more capital, more machinery, and more labor. Even the largest grower could no longer "run a set-up of that kind anymore," one prominent packer recalled. Packing, consequently, moved from the vineyard to the city. In Fresno, Oleander, Selma, Fowler, and Malaga, there were 22 packing houses bordering the Southern Pacific tracks by 1888, owned and operated primarily by local and corporate businessmen who were not growers themselves. While the packing process remained mostly the same, these much larger facilities employed as many as 300 to 400 workers at the height of the season. But Chinese workers, while tolerated for "out-of-town work," were "strongly and decidedly opposed" by these new establishments.[65]

As a result, two separate and distinct labor markets emerged. Chinese workers, even after exclusion went into effect in 1882, continued to

dominate vineyard work, earning a day wage and quietly shouldering the
responsibilities for producing the "perfect raisin." Almost 3,000 Chinese
resided in Fresno County in 1890, and an estimated 5,000 more came
from points throughout the state for the harvest.[66] Muscat packing,
though removed from the heat and dust of the vineyard, remained seasonal, low-wage, and exhausting work. With the Chinese unwelcome
and production booming, packing-house operators turned to an "in-
town" labor source—resident white women. As "an encouragement to
the willing and the skillful," a Fresno newspaper recounted, "they were
not offered wages by the day, but by the piece." Packers still relied on the
judgment and proficiency of their workers. But in contrast to the expansive vineyards, the confines of the packing house allowed employers to
use floor supervisors to monitor the quality of each worker's daily output. Employers scaled their wage rate to "the amount a Chinaman usually will do in a day," and summarily dismissed their new workers at season's end.[67] Yet, unlike the Chinese, women packing-house workers were
openly celebrated by the raisin community. "Visit the packing houses," a
promotional pamphlet said, "and see the hundreds of women . . . prepare
luscious raisins." "It takes a girl's nimble fingers to handle the raisins,"
Eisen wrote. "They are patient, and are, in every way, suited for the
work." "The ample supply of feminine labor," the *Pacific Rural Press*
added, "has brought [Fresno] a happy solution to a problem which was
viewed with some apprehension."[68]

The problem of meeting the increased demand for harvest labor
proved more vexing. The abundance of Chinese laborers earlier in the
decade had given growers a false sense of security. A few had tried to
procure African Americans and Native Americans, but to no avail.[69]
"Chinamen seem to be the only help that the raisin grower can depend
upon to harvest his crop," the *California Fruit Grower* reported in July
1889. But now, the journal added, "this class of help have become scarce
and high-priced." Indeed, Chinese contractors had quickly realized their
increased bargaining power. The $1.40 a day they demanded for the 1889
harvest was just a hint of things to come. By 1891, it was the contractors
who were "fixing the wages." Reports emerged of Chinese gangs imposing vineyard "slow downs," "endeavoring to run bluffs," and "manifesting
industrial discontent." Their increased militancy raised the going rate to
$2.00. "I shall never employ a Chinaman on my ranch again, if I can
help it," responded A. D. Barling. "The Chinese must learn they do not
own this community," another strike victim concurred.[70]

The *Fresno Weekly Evening Expositor*, which rarely found the west side of the tracks newsworthy, sent a reporter to Chinatown to investigate. While marveling at the "intelligence," "shrewdness," and "industriousness" of Big Jim, Wing Tai, Sing Woo, Hoy Hop, and other merchants/contractors, the reporter resented the power "the heathen hordes" wielded and demanded more opportunities for "white hands."[71] As the realization of Chinese control of the labor market began to take hold, many Fresno whites expressed similar sentiments. Though still in its initial stages, the economic depression that dominated much of the decade had already brought significant numbers of unemployed industrial workers from western cities to the San Joaquin Valley. The fact that the Chinese commanded high wages while whites roamed the streets in search of work was simply unacceptable. "[Fresno raisin growers] say that the industry cannot flourish without Chinese labor," a particularly bitter resident complained. "If that were true—which it most decidedly is not—I say that it would be better for the industry to go."[72]

Two months prior to the 1892 harvest, 200 growers met in Fresno "to discuss the labor situation." While they agreed that the Chinese "did more and better work," the growers vowed to employ white men, but at a maximum rate of $1.15. With raisin prices tumbling, they hoped not only to accommodate the white job-seeker, but to bring down their escalating wage rates as well. But growers found their white harvesters "utterly unreliable." "Half the white men quit [on the first day], some saying the work did not suit, others that they had a better job," stated one exasperated vineyardist. "Before the second day half the others came for their money. My grapes must be picked; and while I am in favor of giving the Americans a chance, I cannot afford to lose my raisins." The next day, he headed straight to Fresno to "take out a crew of Chinese, . . . whom I can depend on." He most likely paid the contractor's asking price of $1.50. This experience, the *California Fruit Grower* maintained, typified "why vineyardists, though willing to hire white men, cannot afford to do so."[73]

As economic conditions worsened in 1893, growers' resolve to retain Chinese labor raised community hostility to a fever pitch. "The white men who desire to earn a living have for some time been entering quiet protests to vineyardists employing Chinese," newspapers reported on August 15. But on the previous day, as growers prepared for an early harvest, white resentment had exploded. Some 1,000 unemployed men formed an anti-Chinese league, or, as one paper more accurately characterized it, a "raging mob." They seized several wagons of Chinese en route to the harvest and drove a number of gangs out of the vineyards. Late that afternoon, they paraded up and down the streets of Fresno carrying American flags and "shouting for predominance of white labor." As the sun began to set, they started chanting "On to Chinatown" and proceeded west across the tracks, intending to run their nemeses out of the county. Local businessmen managed to prevent a full-scale riot by intervening "on behalf of the white man." Two days later, in a large public meeting, growers agreed to "submit to the teaching of green hands, in order to favor the white men." A 12-man committee established a "citizens' free labor bureau" they hoped would "imitate the efficiency of the Chinese contract." Once again, growers set the going rate for white labor at $1.15, 25 cents below the current Chinese wage. Their "compromise" to preserve community order apparently worked. Although a few relatively mild anti-Chinese activities occurred throughout the region, the harvest concluded with minimal disturbance.[74]

But growers remained dissatisfied. "It is not especially creditable to the white man that he is found inferior to the despised Chinaman as a [raisin] picker, but such is the case," one grower proclaimed matter-of-factly. "The number of [raisin] growers who prefer to employ Chinese over men of their own race, *all other things being equal,* is very few; but the trouble is that other things are not equal," stressed another.[75] In contrast to the "steady and sober" Chinese, white laborers were characterized as "transient cattle bumming through the country, . . . spending every dollar for whisky and beer." In the eyes of nongrowers as well, these workers came to be seen as "vagrants," "bummers," and "nuisances" —"men from everywhere and from nowhere," no longer worthy of community support. The idea of a labor bureau never took hold. Instead, white itinerants were left to congregate around Fresno's courthouse park, where the townspeople stared through them and prospective employers sized them up. They had become, as one self-proclaimed "tramp" professed, "floating help"—as socially invisible and culturally insulated as the Chinese before them.[76]

With the economic recovery in the late 1890s, tensions began to ease. Vineyardists were determined to regain control of the labor market. The fact that California wheat growers had reduced their labor demands with gang plows, combined harvesters, and other equipment did not go unnoticed by raisin men.[77] "I'll bet I can build a machine that will seed raisins," E. L. Chaddock remembered thinking at the time. Packers had toyed with the idea of relieving the consumer from the irksome task of removing Muscat seeds by hand, but their motivation was limited as long as demand held firm. But in 1896, at the ebb of raisin sales and production, they began experimenting with a "seeder" in the hopes of stimulating consumption. The machine consisted of two large rolling pins side by side, one smooth to flatten the raisins out and press the seeds to the surface, the other spiked to punch the seeds out and flick them aside. No one anticipated the new product's popularity with the consumer. In just five years, the seeded Muscat became "the most important branch in the raisin industry," constituting more than half of Fresno's output. This rather simple invention was "a revolutionary step in the raisin industry" —comparable, packers liked to say, "to the effect of the cotton gin."[78]

Vineyard work seemed far removed from any packing-house innovation, and it continued to require immense amounts of labor. But the seeder had eliminated the need for the "perfect raisin." In contrast to "Imperial Clusters," the appeal of seeded Muscats was their convenience, not their appearance. Packed in bulk "in a handy shape [a 12-ounce carton], ready for use, it saves a vast amount of time and trouble," a contemporary remarked.[79] The "extreme care" vineyardists had demanded at every stage of production was no longer of paramount concern. The piece rate, consequently, became a more viable option. Growers had contemplated employing an incentive wage earlier in the decade, but found quality shirking "a difficult thing in practice to regulate." But just one year after the seeder came into prominence, vineyardists began paying harvesters "according to their application," and by the turn of the century, the piece rate had become "almost universal." The benefits for both workers and growers were staggering. Paid 1¾ to 2½ cents per tray, raisin pickers earned as much as $3.00 to $4.00 a day.[80] And whereas a single worker in 1890 harvested 1.3 acres on average over the course of a season, he picked three acres in 1902 and as many as eight by 1908.[81]

Though the piece wage gave workers an incentive to produce at a much higher rate, it did not rid growers of their "bugbear of labor." The new wage system attracted a relatively new source of labor to Fresno whose presence would bewilder vineyardists for years to come. Japanese laborers came to the San Joaquin Valley as early as 1890, but not in significant numbers.[82] In many respects, their immigration pattern resembled that of the Chinese. Mounting economic pressures in Japan prompted many to leave their homes; in its hurry to modernize Japan in the late nineteenth century, the new Meiji regime taxed peasant farmers excessively. Lured by stories of unbounded opportunities for wealth, thousands of these men ventured across the Pacific Ocean hoping to work three to five years and return to Japan with enough money to establish themselves as farmers or businessmen. With their considerable practical experience in intensive farming, they quickly acclimated to Fresno's raisin culture. Their uncomplaining endurance, industry, and self-discipline—all deeply rooted in their religious values, folk traditions, and agricultural experience—endeared them to their employers early on. Through the mid-1890s, the Japanese accepted low wages (as little as 80 cents a day) and appeared just as "docile" as the Chinese had in the previous decade.[83]

Motivated by the desire to make money, the Japanese did not hesitate to assert themselves when conditions turned favorable. By the middle of the 1890s, Chinese exclusion had taken its toll. The Chinese population in Fresno County declined by more than a third, those who remained were becoming older and less active, and harvesters who had migrated from outside the county began settling in Chinese communities (most notably in the Sacramento–San Joaquin Delta).[84] As the economy recovered, the Japanese saw their opportunity. More than 1,000 helped harvest Fresno's raisins in 1897, 4,000 in 1900, and over 5,000 in 1902—well over half the vineyard labor force. They adopted the Chinese contract system and, moreover, took full advantage of the piece rate and the short harvest timetable.[85] Growers were astonished by their speed. As one remarked, they "come bright and early, and work like Trojans, running from vine to vine, scarcely taking time to breathe. Why such haste? Two and a half cents per tray." Japanese contractors knew that the first picking generally produced the most trays, and thus they often sent most of their men to the next job, leaving only a skeleton crew to finish up. This tactic of prolonging the harvest left the grapes more vulnerable to inclement weather, and contractors charged an extra 50 to 75 cents per hour for each man to turn and stack the trays. On other occasions, gangs simply withheld their labor "in the midst of the busy season" and demanded a higher rate. "I cannot control the Japs at all," one grower admitted. Vineyardists made another effort to establish a labor bureau in 1901, but to no avail. Japanese contractors, as the *Fresno Morning Republican* phrased it, had them "on the hip."[86]

By the 1902 fruit growers' convention, raisin growers characterized the harvest as "an emergency that returns annually"—in sharp contrast to Eisen's idyllic description of the 1889 harvest. They were less likely to

Japanese harvesters picking and drying raisins in A. B. Butler's 480-acre vineyard just east of Fresno, ca. 1900. Fresno Historical Society Archives, Fresno.

wax poetic about the labor process than to bemoan "the scarcity of laboring men." "Where is the man with the hoe?" the *Fresno Weekly Democrat* asked nostalgically.[87] Earlier, that man had been Chinese. In the hands of these "industrious, patient, docile, and reliable" workers, the contract system had benefited all concerned. In their yearning for "simpler times," growers now overlooked the "slow downs, bluffs, and industrial discontent," as well as the anti-Chinese violence of the early 1890s. White workers, in contrast, had left few favorable impressions. West Park colonist John S. Dore had tried them recently, but with little satisfaction. "While I needed only about fifty men, I had over two hundred names of laborers on my roll during the season. I had to keep my team continually on the road between the ranch and Fresno taking them to and from town." Fresno raisins had attracted thousands of Japanese harvesters, but growers saw these "erratic creatures" only "as the last resort." Unwilling to accept that fate, conventioneers declared a "scarcity of labor," rectifiable only by a renewed "importation" of Chinese laborers.[88]

Vineyardists' labor relations, though a "serious problem," did not dampen their passion for horticulture. In other sessions on marketing, transportation, and vine disease, they participated enthusiastically. And, as one periodical expressed it, "'Fresno' continues to suggest raisins to vast numbers of people all over the land." But their "Help problem" had exposed an undesirable vulnerability. "Only those who understand the situation can fully sympathize with the vineyardist in his anxiety to get his grapes [harvested]," G. W. Aiken told the convention. Dore, even more defensively, maintained that their "pleasant and profitable" way of life was at stake. "If the time comes that the labor problem is worse than it is now," he confessed, "my vineyard will be for sale."[89]

Newcastle growers faced an equally precarious situation by the turn of the century. They too depended on Asian labor and were confronted with similar community pressures. Differences in settlement, environment, production, and marketing, however, created a "Help problem" in their district that few Fresno vineyardists would have recognized.

The Chinese contract system helped bring prosperity to the New-castle district in the 1880s beyond anyone's expectations. As the fruit belt's reputation soared, so did land values. Vast amounts of foothill land had been available for under $10 per acre in 1880. By 1887, unimproved land within three miles of a shipping house sold for as high as $100 per acre, $300 by 1893. Lots with orchards in full bearing commanded even more. In 1883, one fruit grower sold his 75-acre ranch (with 30 acres improved) less than a mile from the Newcastle depot for $10,000. By the end of the decade, $500 an acre was not unheard of for a comparable transaction. If a sense of community was reinforced by a shared interest in local land values, the "undesirable" Chinese actually enhanced "the public welfare," at least among landowners and aspiring landowners.[90]

But with rising land values came higher tax rates. The total assessed value of all Placer County property more than doubled between 1880 and 1885, and again between 1885 and 1892, a leap attributed mostly to the fruit boom.[91] The county assessor gradually became the orchardist's worst enemy. W. J. Wilson, for example, complained that exaggerated reports of his fruit profits in the local press raised his assessment by $5,000 in 1887. "I don't give any newspaper men any more information about my fruit," he declared the following year. "I don't want another raise in taxes."[92] The "feared Assessor" pressured growers not only to extract the maximum value from their improved land, but also to clear their remaining property for cultivation as soon as possible. But land clearing, they knew firsthand, was just the beginning of a long, expensive process that generated little short-term return. And once the new trees came into bearing, the orchardist would require considerably more harvest workers, making an already delicate operation that much more cumbersome. "The large orchard," Newcastle grower William B. Gester predicted in 1891, "will necessarily be a rare exception."[93]

"The remedy," as Newcastle orchardists began to acknowledge in the mid-1880s, "can be found in the subdivision of the larger tracts."[94] Selling off their undeveloped land in 20- and 40-acre portions, growers reasoned, not only would ease their tax burden, it would also alleviate their social predicament. White families eager to reap the benefits of orchard life could manage "small divisions" without Chinese labor by taking advantage of "the proximity of fellow-laborers." By planting different varieties of peach, pear, cherry, and other fruit trees, they could extend the harvest season from May to October and thus eliminate the desperate need for labor that single-crop orchards imposed. Land clearing would provide additional work to fill in the rest of the year. To promote this vision to prospective orchardists, growers devised several schemes—the English Colony and "Placer County on Wheels" being the most elaborate—and organized an Immigration Society, a Board of Trade, and several real estate companies. The literature they distributed around the country emphasized the benefits of horticulture that growers had discovered for themselves. "The natural home of the peach [is] in the Sierra foothills," declared one particularly zealous pamphleteer. Those "adventurous" enough to respond would enjoy all "the social and moral advantages" this "intelligent and fascinating pursuit" had to offer.[95]

Much of the brief fascination Newcastle growers had with citrus was due to the pressure to subdivide. Prior to the mid-1880s, growers planted orange trees only "for beautifying the garden or lawn." But the orange, as P. W. Butler and other Placer orchardists were well aware, had become "the principal attraction of Southern California," then in the midst of the greatest land boom the state had yet witnessed. Southern California growers and journalists had produced a vast literature depicting the economic and social benefits of citrus culture, complete with illustrations of modest homes engulfed in glistening orange groves backed by snow-capped mountains on the near horizon. "There is a value other than the mere actual profit," Butler admitted, "that [the orange] gives. . . . Their great beauty is fully appreciated when the deciduous trees have lost their foliage." The fact that the navel variety ripened in the winter and thus would further reduce the seasonal drawbacks of orchard life intrigued Newcastle growers even more. There was no reason, they believed, that Newcastle could not become "the Los Angeles of the North," other than lack of effort on their part. Placer growers began planting orange groves alongside their deciduous orchards, distributed even more promotional literature, attended a number of "Citrus Fairs" throughout the state, and declared their district an "orange belt."[96]

But for all their time and effort, growers' endeavors to entice newcomers to the Newcastle district came to very little. From 1887 to 1892, they would welcome only about 80 new settlers into their ranks.[97] One particularly unfortunate incident illustrates why. At the Los Angeles Citrus Fair in December 1887, Butler, Kellogg, W. B. Lardner, and J. F. Madden convinced a large group of skeptical homeseekers to witness for themselves Placer County's "fertility and hospitality." As luck would have it, they stepped off the train in Newcastle to encounter snow not only on the majestic horizon, but at their very feet as well. Half a foot had fallen in the surrounding orange groves.[98] It was just the type of freeze that by its absence had made southern California famous. Placer growers had demonstrated their faith in the horticultural potential of their county and could boast of remarkable growth in production, but the region's natural limitations hindered significant new settlement. Had their visitors stayed longer (they left on the next southbound train), they would have realized, as did the British colonists, that starting an orchard of any kind required "subduing the wilderness"—a "laborious" and expensive task. Newcastle, Penryn, and Loomis, in the end, could not compete with Riverside, Redlands, and Pasadena—or even Fresno, for that matter. Yet, from a historical perspective, Newcastle orchardists' experience should not be overlooked. It has become conventional wisdom among scholars that the availability of Chinese labor gave California specialty crop growers "the incentive to hold on to more of their land than they otherwise would have."[99] Newcastle growers would have preferred to have done quite the contrary.

Landowners were more successful in their efforts to diversify. Peaches continued "to lead all other fruits in popular culture," Butler wrote. Of the county's 325,000 mature fruit trees in 1890, 71 percent bore peaches; 10 years later, peach trees still accounted for 60 percent.[100] But growers also planted many more varieties. The Alexander and the Hale, "the earliest peaches on the market," ripened in late May. Through October, the Crawford, McDevitt's Cling, Foster, Salway, and George's Late ripened "in regular succession." Strawberries were shipped as early as mid-April; cherries and apricots from mid-May to mid-June; plums, pears, and apples from June to October; and olives through the winter. Diversifying decreased the impact of fruit-specific blights, untimely weather, and other natural contingencies, and leveled off the harvest-labor peak from three weeks to several months. But this practice also heightened orchardists' quality-of-work concerns. "Every grower in this section raises from 20 to 40 different varieties and kinds of fruit," grower-shipper J. E. Bergtholdt recalled. "Each variety must be picked at a certain stage of maturity. In order to do this we must have skilled farm labor. . . . Every man must know and understand what he is doing."[101]

As a result, growers became that much more dependent on the Chinese. In the early 1890s, furthermore, an outbreak of malaria in the Newcastle district ensured that the Chinese would be their principal labor source for the time being. Malaria had been epidemic in the region's mining camps during the 1850s and 1860s. The disease's carrier, the anopheles mosquito, thrived in pools of standing water left from the washings. By 1880, the disease appeared to have declined, only to be reinvigorated by the expansion of the Bear River Ditch system later in the decade. Canal and pipe leaks often created swampy conditions that bred the mosquitoes, particularly during the warm summer months. Harvesters, therefore, frequently became victims. Harry Butler recalled seeing numerous white orchard workers lying in rows "with severe chills, . . . stricken with the disease," and added that "the Orientals apparently were not susceptible." Just how epidemic malaria became is not clear, but it could not have come at a worse time. At the peak of the fruit boom, many white orchard workers reportedly fled the region.[102] The Chinese remained and endured the "mosquito's wrath," anticipating that they could profit from changing conditions in Newcastle's orchards.

The labor system fashioned during the 1880s no longer satisfied either workers or employers. Chinese orchard workers were becoming increasingly disgruntled with their fixed day wage. "Very few seem to be trying to save motions or to hurry," one grower reported to the *Pacific Rural Press* in 1891, suggesting that Newcastle harvesters employed the same "slow down" tactics as Fresno raisin pickers. Growers' failure to sell off their uncleared land, the reduced seasonality of their orchards, their increased dependence on skilled harvesters, and the shrinking supply of such workers made the contract system less practical. The same grower offered an alternative. Why not "adopt the tenant system largely prevalent in Eastern States?" he asked. "Employ enough men with families to do all the regular work of the farm. When you need extra men, they will board them for you."[103] Tenancy, this grower believed, offered the landowner a viable alternative to subdivision while securing many of its benefits.

The practice of leasing farmland was not foreign to Newcastle orchardists. Many had migrated from the Midwest, where leasing sections of large frontier estates to relieve land, financial, and labor pressures had been common a generation earlier. And Chinese truck gardeners had leased land in Placer County's mining regions since the 1850s.[104] But prior to the late 1880s, farm tenancy was virtually nonexistent in the Placer fruit belt, though on rare occasions growers too old to manage their orchards had rented them out.[105] Between 1888 and 1894, however, 43 orchardists leased approximately 1,200 acres — all to Chinese tenants.[106] These agreements constituted only the ones filed with the county recorder, and probably represented only a fraction of the total. Harry Butler recalled that leases to Chinese renters tended to be verbal, and a 1922 investigation of California land tenancy estimated that at any given time, only 5 percent of farm leases were by written contract. The "hundred orchards rented to Chinamen" in Placer County reported by the *California Fruit Grower* in 1891 was, perhaps, a more accurate total.[107]

The terms of the lease between John H. Nixon and Ah Tung in 1889 reveal the mutual benefits of such an arrangement. Nixon, originally from Missouri, had purchased 20 acres of land "covered with heavy timber and underbrush" near Loomis in 1858. Over the years, he had cleared 15 acres and planted fruit trees, hiring, like most of his neighbors, Chinese labor. His son, Rudolph, co-managed the farm at the time of the signing of the lease, and also served as secretary of a Newcastle shipping house. Nixon and Tung agreed to a six-year tenure at $1,000 a year ($50 per acre). Nixon showed full confidence in his tenant, allowing him to pay the rent in four installments timed to anticipate harvest peaks ($150 due by June 15, $250 by July 15, $300 by August 15, and $300 by September 15). Tung agreed to "diligently and skillfully cultivate and care for the fruit trees," taking full responsibility for plowing, spraying, picking, packing, and "carrying the crops to market" (presumably to Rudolph's shipping house). Of equal importance, the contract stipulated that Tung would clear the remaining five acres and plant 500 trees (supplied by Nixon) with the same "diligence and skill." The document left implicit Tung's responsibility for all facets of labor management, including costs, suggesting further that the lease merely extended and refined an already existing grower-contractor relationship. Nixon remained in his house on the property, retained his right to oversee all orchard work, and allowed Tung to build himself a "small cabin." Nixon provided the horses, wagons, plows, and spraying equipment, while Tung paid for the more variable inputs, including water and packing materials. For Nixon, the lease secured a guaranteed income, passed on the risks from crop failure and market fluctuations to his tenant, ensured that all his land would be in full bearing by the end of the term, and relieved him of all labor anxieties. In turn, Tung, with limited capital, gained the chance to farm independently (a much-desired status in China), earned all the surplus profits from his skill and hard work, and attained a sense of permanence and stability—the latter emphasized by the fact that it was Tung who requested the lease be filed for record.[108]

Other leases were similar, the terms varying according to the personal needs and preferences of both parties. Most contained a quality-of-work clause, involved land clearing as well as orchard work, covered a tenure long enough to bring new trees to bearing, and specified payment procedures. Some orchardists did not have the personal relationship Nixon apparently shared with Tung. Newcastle grower J. A. Robinson, for example, leased his 80-acre orchard in 1889 to four unfamiliar Chinese men whose reputation for "good workmanlike" conduct was vouched for by the local justice of the peace. Others approached this problem by agreeing to a share-rent arrangement until a mutual trust was established. In all probability, these were at least as prevalent as cash payments, though most went unrecorded. Both share lessor and share lessee could collect with greater assurance—at the fruit house, right at the time of sale—and thus were less inclined to register their agreements at the courthouse. Some cash leases, in contrast, demanded full payment near the beginning of the season. Others anticipated escalating profits from maturing trees and thus stipulated rent increases on a year-by-year basis. And the rent itself varied tremendously, from $25 to $60 an acre. Leases, after all, were the result of bargaining between prospective tenants and owners; they reflected the negotiating ability of both parties.[109]

It did not take long for this new labor system to become a community issue. Hiring the Chinese as wage laborers in the absence of "agreeable whites" was one thing, but leasing land to them for five- and six-year terms was quite another. The fruit belt's very reputation seemed to be at stake, reports in the *Newcastle News* suggested. Chinese tenants were deemed unprincipled and careless horticulturists; they produced "large quantities of inferior fruit" and practiced "dishonest packing." Merchants complained that the Chinese sent "the money received for our fruit crop" across the Pacific rather than spending it in local stores. Others argued that Chinese tenants prevented "a desirable class of white fruit growers from locating among us, . . . a class that will patronize our local tradesmen, read the local papers, help sustain our churches and our schools, and become a portion of our social fabric." Similar criticism came from outside the community. Two San Francisco newspaper editorials that were reprinted in the *News* declared the matter "a crisis." And one prospective homeseeker, first intrigued by "Placer County on Wheels," wrote the *News* after visiting the area that he would never settle in a "Chinese Colony." "The Chinese must go," the *News* proclaimed, "and the sooner they go the better."[110]

Yet the same homeseeker also wrote that "fruit from Placer County was still first choice by a big majority in the markets of New York and Chicago." Therein lay the grower's dilemma. Chinese tenants more than upheld Newcastle's high horticultural standards. But orchard landlords could not retain their market reputation without jeopardizing their status as community guardians. Consider the source that led the assault on Chinese tenants—George D. Kellogg's *Newcastle News*. As the newspaper's publisher, Kellogg felt obligated to circulate current community sentiments. As a grower-shipper, however, he felt equally committed to his region's fruit interests. Kellogg, in fact, extended one of the county's first recorded chattel mortgages to a Chinese tenant orchardist, in December 1892. Ah Sing, who had leased an unspecified number of acres from three Newcastle landowners, received $400, using the fruit he would grow that season as collateral. The advance was repayable on August 15 at 10 percent interest. He agreed further to "carefully tend and take care of the crops, . . . and faithfully and without delay harvest, pack, and deliver the same . . . to the fruit shipping house of George D. Kellogg."[111] Kellogg's confidence in this Chinese horticulturist was just as unmistakable as his desire to beat his competition—but with it came great social risk, as depicted in his own paper.

From an economic standpoint, leasing became more advantageous during the depression years. "Under the circumstances," remarked A. P. Hall at the 1895 fruit growers' convention in Sacramento, "there was really nothing else to do." Placer growers estimated that transportation and marketing costs accounted for 55 percent of their fruit's gross sale value, "leaving only 45 percent for all the costs of production and profits." At that rate, Hall insisted, "the white [grower] cannot make a living." But those who had signed a long-term cash lease avoided this predicament. For Charles H. Kellogg (George's brother), for example, tenancy provided a "bright side of the fruit industry . . . in these hard times." The five-year lease he signed with Ah Youen in October 1894 guaranteed him a $9,000 total cash rental, in addition to the usual improvements to his land. Youen paid the full rent for each of the first three years, and his landlord had "no doubt of [his] ability" to carry out the lease. Both Hall and Kellogg maintained that "the Chinamen, through their industry and persistency, succeed not only in paying their rent, but also get a little profit out of it."[112] However, the fact that George D. Kellogg continued to advance chattel mortgages, and that the Penryn Fruit Company and Schnabel Brothers followed suit in 1897, suggests that Chinese tenant orchardists were as likely to fall into debt as their white counterparts.[113]

The majority of white orchardists continued to rely on contract labor, a system that underwent significant changes itself. As in Fresno, the Chinese were becoming fewer in number, and those who remained preferred to work for their own countrymen. And growers never gave much consideration to reopening the "Tramp question," repeatedly insisting they could not "sacrifice their own interests [for] purely patriotic considerations." Sensing their enhanced bargaining position, many Chinese refused to work any longer for a dollar a day, a stance their employers considered "contrary to the spirit of the times." As one insisted, "It cannot be expected that labor will continue indefinitely to command the same price while all others are dropping." Japanese orchard workers appeared more willing to accept this logic. They came to Newcastle as early as 1891, and by the middle of the decade were employed in significant numbers. They adopted the familiar gang system, worked for as little as 70 cents a day, and demonstrated "much knack in the picking of fruit in a proper manner." As Loomis grower Lee Tudsbury recalled in 1924, "I have no love for a Japanese, but they are certainly good horticulturists."[114]

Had Tudsbury expressed these two sentiments in the mid-1890s, he would have emphasized only the former. Growers, whether leasing or contracting, walked a fine line between their economic and their social concerns. They increasingly denounced the growing presence of Asian workers as a "detriment to our society." One member of the Placer

County Horticultural Society stated, "Chinese have been a curse to California since the first one landed, and the Japs are but a slight improvement." At the same meeting, members discussed at length the importance of "careful handling and packing" for "the value of our fruit." But now, in this discussion, they kept their preference for Asian workers to themselves. The community came to accept this selective line of reasoning. When Hall asked in 1895, "What are the fruit growers to do?" regarding the "Mongolian question," most members of the community responded sympathetically. The *Placer County Republican* suggested they had no choice but to accept the growers' need for Chinese and Japanese labor. "It is now a well known fact," an editorial stated, "that . . . upon the prosperity of the grower depends the prosperity of the grocer, dry goods merchant, blacksmith, harness maker, hardware man, [and] the druggist." Orchardists continued to maintain that they "would gladly employ white men in their orchards, provided they could be assured of as good service as is readily secured from Chinese and Japanese." The possibility —however remote—that growers might eventually be able to profitably employ white laborers had become enough to sustain the community's loyalty.[115]

But not without a price. Growers became increasingly reluctant to air their more immediate labor concerns for fear of community backlash. As the economy began to recover at century's end, Japanese workers demanded higher wages. As in Fresno, these sojourners used their bargaining savvy. They often threatened to "break contracts" at mid-harvest and forced growers to bid against one another, causing wages to climb as high as two dollars a day. Growers had organized themselves on numerous occasions to combat cultural and marketing problems. Though not always successful, these efforts received detailed (and generally favorable) coverage from the local press. But labor issues were different. "Cooperation among all growers is absolutely necessary, . . . for deciding on a scale of wages and sticking to it," a small group of orchardists proclaimed in May 1897 and again in June 1902. But on neither occasion did growers respond. To do so would have called unwanted attention to their desperate need for Asian labor. It was no accident that when Harry Butler published a lengthy article in the *Pacific Rural Press* in 1902 depicting "a bright future for the [Newcastle] horticulturist," he emphasized the region's cultural and marketing advantages, but left out the labor situation entirely.[116]

Here again, leasing proved to be a viable option. It allowed the orchardist to transfer wage and labor-supply problems to the tenant and thus greatly reduce his own exposure to public criticism. Readers of the local press and trade journals would have been unaware that between 1898 and 1902, Placer growers signed 36 agreements with Chinese tenants and another 10 with Japanese tenants.[117] The number of verbal arrangements cannot be determined, but it was no doubt considerable. Most of these probably were one-year share rentals with Japanese contractors, who shared Chinese tenants' desire for independence and stability but did not yet command their landlords' full confidence.[118] Written agreements were a matter of public record, and even verbal ones could not have escaped public knowledge, but neither drew the attention of a community that had learned to turn its back on growers' unsavory labor matters.

Thus, when Kellogg returned from the San Francisco fruit growers' convention in December 1902, Placer growers greeted the plan to recruit white eastern orchard workers with apprehension. At a Farmers' Institute held in the Good Templars Hall in Newcastle the following March, the fruit belt's most prominent growers touched on the issue "briefly and pointedly." They accepted the plan in principle as "a movement in the right direction," but feared that only "the Hobo element" would respond. Even "our best citizens" from the East, one grower mentioned, would be "good, but green, and have to be educated." Moreover, there was no "scarcity of reliable farm help," all agreed. "Notwithstanding the fact that much talk had been heard about shortage of help, there was not a person present who knew of any serious loss of crops from that cause," the *Placer County Republican* reported. Instead, "control of the labor problem" was their main concern. One grower made a sudden, startling admission: "The Jap is a fairly good fellow, but too smart. He is thoroughly organized and takes advantage of the unorganized condition of the growers to demand excessive wages." The others nodded in agreement, but quickly changed the subject. "It seemed as if the discussion was more of a precautionary nature than otherwise," the *Republican* concluded. For the remainder of the two-day session, "the proceedings were of an entertaining and instructive character and were entered into with great zest by those present."[119] Labor, however, had become an issue requiring considerably more discretion.

"Those who have hops are lifted above the troubles which are visiting others," wrote the *Pacific Rural Press* in 1902.[120] Indeed, the pressures that compelled fresh-fruit and Muscat growers to hire Asians did not concern Wheatland hop men. Unwittingly at first, they actually enlarged their labor supply by refusing to hire Chinese workers. D. P. Durst, Hugh Roddan, and S. D. Woods had all employed Chinese as well as white pickers through 1885, claiming they could not afford to turn anyone away. But when a wave of anti-Chinese violence swept through the Sacramento Valley in 1886, Wheatland citizens rebelled. They formed an Anti-Chinese Club, stormed Roddan's ranch and removed his Chinese by force (prior to taking an anti-violence pledge), and instituted a labor and consumer boycott of all businesses hiring "any form of Chinese labor," including the hopyards.[121] Growers "expressed their determination to employ none but whites" in the Sacramento Valley press, but fretted over the loss of a significant labor source. Much to their delight, however, news of the boycott attracted more than enough white pickers to make up the loss. By 1891, the *Four Corners* (edited by Durst's son Murray) declared confidently that "the days for Chinamen in the Wheatland hop-yards is *[sic]* over; every year the crews are made up of a more desirable people."[122]

Hop picking, in fact, increasingly became a white, even middle-class, undertaking. Workers now included "not only the riff-raff of the neighboring towns, but respectable families who seek health and recreation." It even took on "something of a romantic charm," as epitomized by a *Cosmopolitan* reporter's portrayal of the 1893 harvest:

> If your nerves have become supersensitive from the corrosions of city life and you are the victim of ennui, or your liver asserts itself to the prejudice of your digestion, your duties and your friends; in fact, if you have reached the acme of general miserableness, take a vacation among the hop-fields in the gilded early autumn of California. Your days will be made up of dew-exhaled mornings dwindling to the golden point of noon, of afternoons losing their superfluous heat in sunsets flaming the evening summits, and of nights so cordial and sleep-inviting they seem but moments of oblivion.[123]

Growers knew well that the actual work, with or without a Chinese presence, was anything but a "vacation," as the reporter called it. Hop pickers endured excessive dust and pollen, oppressive heat, a contact rash similar to poison oak, the inspector's often unbalanced scale, and even the threat of electrocution from an unexpected storm "taking possession of the wires." Growers were not about to disavow "the picturesque features of hop picking time," however.[124]

As Durst's and Horst's yards increased to over 500 acres each in the

late 1890s, their labor demands grew as well. They adapted with relative
ease, however. Starting in 1897, they began placing advertisements in
Sacramento Valley newspapers and the *Four Corners,* the latter often being reprinted in the *Pacific Rural Press.* The ads appeared a week or two
before the harvest, emphasized the "preference" given to whites, proclaimed the "earliest and best picking in the state," and stated the anticipated piece rate.[125] They began varying the rate as well. Experienced
harvesters knew that as the season advanced, the hops lost moisture and
paid less, and thus these pickers often left early. In 1898, Durst (and later
Horst) countered by offering 80 cents the first week (the previous year's
rate), 85 the second, 95 the third, and $1.00 "the balance." But this made
for muddled advertising. By 1900, they had changed to a set rate (90
cents) with a "Bonus of 10 cents per 100 Pounds" to all who worked
through the harvest. The response was overwhelming; pickers actually
had to be turned away on occasion. To allow them to secure a place,
growers began accepting applications by mail once their ads appeared.[126]

Harvest conditions in 1902 put the system to the test. Durst, Horst,
and P. C. Drescher anticipated a highly successful season. Just one year
earlier, market experts had declared hops a crop whose "days of large
profits . . . are over." Since 1894, prices had rarely exceeded the cost of
production (12 cents per pound). As recently as 1900, hops sold for just
8½ cents, and Durst alone lost a reported $15,000. But the failure of the
1902 European crop (production dropped 52 percent) propelled the California market into one of its manic phases, with prices soaring to 28
cents.[127] Growers knew many weeks in advance that an unusually high
yield seemed likely as well. But a long hot spell in July "forced hops
rapidly" and caught them by surprise. "It will be impossible to secure
sufficient white labor for the season's work," they warned prospective
pickers.[128] Seventy-five Japanese workers arrived at the Durst ranch on
Friday, August 15, when picking commenced. But they were not satisfied
with the wages offered—90 cents plus the 10-cent bonus. On Monday
they demanded a flat dollar rate, which Durst promptly refused to pay.
When 200 white men the next day "followed example and endeavored to
induce others to do likewise," the situation looked grim. "At last accounts a wholesale walkout in all the hop yards is expected," the
Marysville Daily Appeal reported. The first reported Wheatland hop
strike had been launched. But it was "nipped in the bud" by Thursday.
Indeed, just two days after dismissing the malcontents, Durst's system
had attracted so many new applicants that he had to circulate a "no more

pickers required" notice. Neither he nor Horst nor Drescher experienced further trouble. "Peace now reigns," the *Four Corners* declared.[129]

The same could not be said for labor relations in Davisville, however. Asian workers had always been available from nearby Winters or Vacaville, but almond growers had yet to employ them.[130] An early harvest in 1901, however, caught them off guard. Growers, the *Davisville Enterprise* reported on August 15, were "searching every nook and cranny . . . in vain to get white men to do this urgent work and are now driven to the extreme of employing any one they can get, be he white, Chinese, or Jap."[131] Taking heed of these conditions, Asian contractors had already begun to offer their services.

A week earlier, James Chiles had become the first to hire Japanese harvesters through Shi Kubo, a contractor from Sacramento. George W. Pierce decided to follow suit. He drove to Chiles's ranch, met Kubo to discuss terms, and retained one of the Japanese crews. Their agreement called for 11 workers at $1.25 a day. Pierce did not hire them individually, as he had his white workers, and he quickly realized the extent of their collective bargaining power. On just their second day in the orchards, Kubo ordered his workers to withhold their labor and demanded a contract that would double their wage. As Asian fruit pickers typically earned $1.00 a day, Pierce probably felt that his contract with Kubo had been generous, despite the fact that he had paid white harvesters 25 cents more. But labor was scarce, and local growers had been offering as much as $2.50 a day to white workers. Pierce and Kubo were contesting for control of the harvest labor market. But Kubo underestimated the orchardist's resolve. An irate Pierce terminated the contract and informed the *Davisville Enterprise* to warn other orchardists of Kubo's presence.[132]

With no workforce and the harvest in full swing, Pierce drove into town, where, quite unexpectedly, he found his source of labor. In recent weeks, Wing Hai, owner of a Chinese grocery in Davisville, had begun an "Employment Agency" run out of his store on Main Street.[133] Pierce inquired about the availability of almond harvesters the same morning he dismissed the Japanese crew. The following week, 10 Chinese workers Hai had "ordered" from Sacramento arrived in Davisville and began knocking almonds. Pierce also had managed to locate five white workers. He paid both white and Chinese harvesters the same day wage, the $1.25 he had offered the Japanese. The white harvesters, characteristically, proved to have sporadic work habits, but seven of the ten Chinese worked the remaining three weeks of what turned out to be Pierce's

Chinese laborers, contracted through Wing Hai, knocking almonds on the Pierce ranch, ca. 1902. Pierce Family Papers, Department of Special Collections, University of California Library, Davis.

most abundant harvest to date. Pierce contracted with Wing Hai again the following year, with similar results and even higher profits. Increased selling prices, high yields, and a dependable labor force generated for Pierce a gross almond income of $3,000 in 1902, more than triple that of 1897. He even began referring to his Chinese workers as "the boys" in his daily journal.[134]

But when Pierce took the train to San Francisco for the fruit growers' convention that December, Kubo's challenge to his authority was still fresh in his mind. Wing Hai had provided efficient, obedient workers, but Pierce had lost some measure of control over his harvest. Reports of instances of Chinese and Japanese militancy, after all, abounded in the local and agricultural press.[135] During that very harvest, in fact,

another Chinese contractor had coerced Pierce's closest neighbor, Jacob
E. La Rue, into raising his knocking wage.[136] H. P. Stabler's plea to
stimulate the migration of "farmer lads . . . of the Eastern States to . . .
our orchards and vineyards" struck a resounding chord. That winter,
Pierce, his son, and another Davisville almond grower, George Lorenz,
represented "the fruitmen of the State" on a six-week recruiting tour
through Nebraska, Iowa, and Michigan. They presented hundreds of
stereopticon views of "scenic and industrial California" and distributed
100,000 booklets entitled *Grasp This, Your Opportunity*. "Horticulture,"
Pierce emphasized in his 90-minute lectures, "is one of the greatest pursuits of the state. . . . The possibilities are practically unlimited."[137]

Pierce's unbounded optimism masked the harsh reality of labor relations in California horticulture. Wheatland hop growers produced their
crop year after year unburdened by community or quality-of-work concerns. In contrast, horticulturists' mission to, as Pierce phrased it, "minister to the needs and pleasures of mankind"[138] often conflicted with
their desire to turn a profit. Fruits and nuts required seasonal workers
from outside the community who most white Californians felt undermined the very ideals of social progress that growers professed to advance. As self-proclaimed cultural guardians, orchardists and vineyardists found it difficult even to discuss "the labor problem," let alone to
do so with the verve they displayed in all other aspects of their enterprise. Their horticultural ideal gave them a common identity, but it left
the misconception—epitomized by the disjointed debate at the 1902
San Francisco convention—that they all shared the same labor concerns. No one questioned Stabler's assertion that "the slogan of the fruit-
grower is 'Something must be done.'" But growers of different crops
talked past one another, each believing that their particular problem
constituted "God's truth."[139] Labor, consequently, would continue to be
their "bugbear."

3 "Misunderstood and Misrepresented"

Cooperative Marketing and Uncooperative Labor

THE RECRUITING EFFORTS prompted by H. P. Stabler's address proved to be, in one historian's words, "a complete fiasco."[1] In December 1902, *California Fruit Grower* editor B. N. Rowley asked readers to fill out surveys detailing their "prospective needs in the way of labor"—number of harvesters, time of employment, and special skills. Not a single grower responded. "Those most interested in the matter are silent and inactive," Rowley lamented. The response from midwesterners was almost as bleak. Almond growers George W. Pierce Jr. and George Lorenz had embarked on their cross-country lecture tour in early 1903. But a nationwide farm labor shortage and organized labor's efforts to discourage immigration undermined the campaign. Most of the 917 recruits said to have ventured west in the summer of 1903 returned home by December. Recruitment efforts the following year proved equally futile. But few growers voiced any concern. Even those who, like Pierce, preferred whites managed to harvest their crops with a labor force dominated by Asians—and they did so, as State Horticultural Commissioner Ellwood Cooper reported, with "excellent results."[2]

California specialty crop growers prospered during the first decade of the twentieth century. Wheat, once the state's most important crop, still yielded over 36 million bushels at the turn of the century. But by 1910, California had become a net importer, producing only six million bushels. Fruit and nut production rose as dramatically as wheat declined. In 1910, Fresno vineyardists supplied 42,000 tons of raisins, still the vast majority of the state's total; Placer orchardists shipped 2,900 carloads— or 37,000 tons—of fresh deciduous fruit, still about one-third of the state's output; and Davis[3] almond growers produced 738 tons, 22 percent of the state's crop. The total value of the state's fruits and nuts jumped from $28 million in 1900 to $51 million in 1910. Over the course of the decade, California accounted for most of the national expansion in fruit and nut production.[4]

Soaring production required better markets than those of the late 1890s. Growers of several crops now established statewide marketing cooperatives. Managed by salaried executives, these organizations reduced production costs, enforced quality standards, advertised extensively, and

rationalized the distribution process. By competing not solely on the basis of price but with quality control and creative marketing as well, these
professional organizations resembled what historian Alfred D. Chandler
Jr. has termed "modern industrial enterprises." One scholar, in fact, has
employed Chandler's model to argue that these marketing cooperatives
instituted "the corporate reconstruction of California agriculture."[5]

It would be a rush to judgment, however, to conclude that the growers themselves became full-fledged industrialists. To be sure, growers
welcomed the marketing power their cooperatives gave them, even if it
meant ceding individual or local control to self-perpetuating boards of
directors often dominated by merchants, lawyers, and bankers. But they
did so not out of a "commitment to the new capitalism," but to detach
themselves even further from the business end of their enterprise. "Cooperation in the marketing process," as a contemporary journalist put it,
"leaves the grower free to devote all his attention to his trees."[6] Growers
also enjoyed the considerable fame their cooperatives brought to their
communities. That fame reinforced their belief that their ideal of a
"pleasant and profitable" life in horticulture remained intact.

Moreover, labor relations still were decisively not "modern." While
marketing managers prodded growers to improve their product, they left
labor affairs to the individual. "Members of a cooperative association,"
an agricultural economist commented, "often resent having the management discuss production. The management, in their opinion, has been
hired to sell."[7] That resentment stemmed primarily from their harvest-
time troubles. Growers joined forces to secure economies of scale for
selling and distributing their crops, but remained at the mercy of contractors, tenants, and seasonal workers. It is little wonder, therefore, that
they celebrated their cooperatives but took umbrage at the mere mention of their labor problems. That defensiveness, in fact, accounts for
growers' reluctance to respond to Rowley's public survey.

This disjuncture between marketing and labor left growers vulnerable to being "misunderstood and misrepresented," as the *Pacific Rural
Press* put it.[8] Over the course of the decade, it became increasingly difficult for growers to keep labor matters—particularly their preference for
Asian workers—to themselves. Other aspects of their enterprise remained central to the state's booster efforts. "California's future has always been bound up in her [specialty crop] agriculture," declared the
state chamber of commerce in 1910.[9] But on the issue of labor, growers
began to acquire a less flattering reputation. Anti-Asian sentiments in-

creasingly pervaded city and state politics, as reformers, conservatives, unionists, and most leftists hyperbolized the "Yellow Peril" to appeal to voters' racial phobias. In the process, growers' struggle to impose order in their own vineyards and orchards became not only a community issue, but a state, national, and even international one as well. Still cultural guardians in their own minds, they were becoming cultural outcasts in the minds of many others.

FRESNO WAS "perhaps the most discouraged community in the fruit business in California," wrote the *California Fruit Grower* in December 1908. A nationwide financial panic the year before had pushed the raisin market to the brink of disaster. Vineyardists produced 65,000 tons in 1908, an unusually large crop. That, along with a carryover of 30,000 tons from the previous year, all but stifled trade. As in the mid-1890s, packers, who controlled most of the crop following the collapse of the California Raisin Growers' Association (CRGA), refused to buy goods they could not move at a profit. Growers, in turn, blamed packers for "endeavoring to bear the market."[10] The failures of the CRGA and several other pooling efforts earlier in the decade left vineyardists with a sense of impending doom. The raisin culture colonists had nurtured so carefully a generation earlier seemed to be losing its vitality. A few growers continued to believe that market control was the key to rejuvenation. But to succeed, they realized, a cooperative had to incorporate all aspects of raisin culture—not just the desire to turn a profit.

That was the lesson M. Theo Kearney never learned. Though revered for his "masterful business ability," Kearney never achieved his grand ambitions for the CRGA. His "Machiavellian" leadership—as contemporary critics characterized it—was partly to blame. As one of the principal investors in the Fresno colonies, Kearney made a fortune during the 1880s and was regarded by many as the "raisin king." Following the Panic of 1893, however, this title took on a more derogatory meaning. When hundreds of vineyardists who had purchased lots from his Fruit Vale Estate failed to make payments, Kearney foreclosed "with neatness and dispatch." At the same time, he publicized his plan to build for himself a lavish five-story, 13-bedroom, 13-bathroom "Chateau," complete with stained glass windows, formal gardens, Italian-style fountains, and an 11-mile, three-lane boulevard lined with eucalyptus, palm trees, pampas grass, and oleander bushes extending east to Fresno. "It is easy to understand that the circumstances were not likely to make him very popular," a *Saturday Evening Post* writer remarked. Kearney, the writer continued, "had not sought a reputation as a philanthropist. Moreover, he was uncompanionable to the last degree, having no intimates, shunning friendship rather than seeking it. He was brusque in manner, inclined to be irascible. He had persistently refused to have anything to do with the many efforts for co-operation, openly deriding them."[11]

By 1898, however, even Kearney saw organization as a necessity. The foreclosures and prevailing low prices saddled him with over 1,000 acres of unprofitable raisin vineyards. When the CRGA was organized that June, he convinced growers to elect him president. Though widely denounced as a feudal lord in local newspapers, Kearney captivated growers with his formidable oratorical skills and uncanny ability to manipulate their provincial understanding of the trade. "He told the growers they were 'twenty-acre men' who did not have brains enough to run their own business, and that he did," remembered *Fresno Morning Republican* editor Chester Rowell, Kearney's harshest critic. "Strangely enough, this remark was popular. Each grower knew that it was true of all the others." When prices soared to over six cents a pound in 1899, growers' loyalty to Kearney knew no bounds. But when prices collapsed the following year (to three cents—their break-even point, or "living price"), they saw him as he listed himself in city directories—as a "capitalist," unconcerned with the welfare of the raisin community.[12]

The CRGA's failure cannot be pinned on Kearney alone. The seeds of self-destruction were always present. Collectively, all growers stood to benefit from the CRGA's pooling capability. At the same time, an individual grower stood to benefit by selling to a non-association packer or buyer who, with less overhead, could offer a higher price. Kearney called this inherent flaw "holding the umbrella for the outsider," and it frustrated him no end. He knew that once word leaked out that a member had received more for his crop elsewhere, it was only a matter of time before envious neighbors defected as well. This "mischief of the minority," as Kearney called it, repeatedly broke the CRGA's control of the market.[13] Growers required a leap of faith to remain loyal to an association whose benefits could be measured only over the long term.

But Kearney's efforts to secure that trust never succeeded. California law restricted him from the start. It limited growers to two forms of organization: a joint-stock corporation that could control neither the number nor the identity of stockholders; or a cooperative corporation that could restrict its membership but could not sell stock. The repeated failures of attempts to organize earlier in the decade had convinced Kearney that a raisin association needed sufficient capital to fix prices and finance crop advances *and* the power to prevent stock from falling into unfriendly hands. The law, he decided, required a more "creative interpretation." In May 1898, Kearney avoided the limitations of the state's cooperative law and incorporated the CRGA under California's regular incorporation laws with $500,000 in capital stock and under bylaws that restricted shareholding to growers. To join, a grower-shareholder signed a contract agreeing to turn over his crop for three successive years; the association, in turn, sold the crop to the packers, provided that at least 75 percent of the growers committed to the pool. Fresno bankers and packers, the most likely candidates to challenge the plan's legality, fully supported it; both believed that a strong market, regardless of who controlled it, best served their interests as well as those of the growers. Had Kearney remained satisfied with this arrangement, one packer recalled, he "could have built up a powerful association that would have lasted for many years."[14]

But Kearney wanted the CRGA to control not only selling and distribution, but packing as well. "Our experience," he told growers in December 1898, "has convinced me that we cannot blend the interests of the commercial packer with the interests of the grower any more than we can blend oil and water." CRGA members, Kearney well knew, still blamed commission packers for their economic woes earlier in the decade. Following the successful 1899 season, Kearney unveiled a threefold plan to sever this relationship once and for all. First, he proposed that growers sign a supplementary contract (the "yellow slip") that would allow the association to withhold $10 per ton on the next season's crop to finance its own packing operations. Disgruntled packers, Kearney feared, might take the CRGA to court. To circumvent antitrust laws, he suggested that growers lease their vineyards to the CRGA, whose directors, in turn, would pay them 95 percent of the net proceeds as wages for tending their vineyards. As owner of the crop and employer of the growers, the CRGA would not constitute a combination of independent producers and thus could not be accused of restraining trade. Finally, Kearney insisted that the CRGA reincorporate under the less restrictive laws of New Jersey to evade the limitations of California nonstock cooperative law. After all, he told growers, this was the strategy "the Steel trust, and many other corporations, have chosen. . . . What is good enough for them must surely be good enough for us."[15]

Although they very much wanted Kearney for their leader, the vast majority of growers rejected his vision of a "raisin trust." Packers had served as convenient scapegoats in bad times, but they were nonetheless members of the raisin community with whom growers had maintained personal relationships for years. In contrast, Kearney's models—the steel trust and out-of-state corporation law—were anything but familiar. They violated growers' strong and enduring beliefs in the primacy of local control. The notion of giving the CRGA directors control of their crops, their land, and their whole association undermined their very purpose in cooperating. Indeed, Kearney, in Edward Wickson's words, was asking vineyardists to abandon their "wholesome" enterprise for a more "industrial" way of life. Consequently, fewer than half signed their "yellow slips" in 1900. Moreover, they refused to implement the "New Jersey lease" in 1901, they voted Kearney out of office in 1902, and they marketed their crop through the CRGA for the last time in 1903.[16]

Packers, even at the height of Kearney's popularity, never felt particularly threatened by the CRGA. They knew that even had the association been able to finance its operations, it would have taken years to build and equip packing houses, to develop a competitive selling organization, and to establish a name brand. They were confident, E. L. Chaddock recalled, that one way or another, the "Autocrat of the Raisin Industry" would eventually seek their services. Moreover, packers understood that even had CRGA members controlled 100 percent of Fresno's raisins, they still could not have exacted any price they wanted. "The law of supply and demand governs regardless of marketing control," asserted packer Charles Bonner. Because raisins were a luxury crop, the buyer, not the producer, generally fixed the price. And the buyer was interested only during the "holiday months," October through January. Overproduction, vineyardists such as Wylie Giffen were just beginning to realize, would haunt growers until wholesale grocers, bakers, restaurants, and individual consumers "thought it possible to use raisins during the summer months" as well.[17]

Giffen became the chief figure in the movement to organize raisin growers following Kearney's death in 1906. Like his predecessor, Giffen was one of the largest growers in Fresno County. With his purchase of A. B. Butler's vineyard around the turn of the century, he owned approximately 4,200 acres. Smaller vineyardists embraced Giffen as one of their own, however. At the age of 15, he had migrated with his parents from Nebraska to Fowler, where his father started a vineyard in 1889. Giffen pursued the "pleasant and profitable" life the colonies offered, living in a modest residence even after accumulating his vast holdings. He too had been a "half-hearted" CRGA member disillusioned by Kearney's schemes. Cooperation, he believed, was essential, but not at the cost of all that vineyardists valued. To advance "the cause of the raisin grower," he believed, an association needed to be more of a "community project."[18]

But when the CRGA collapsed in 1904, "growers were fed up with cooperative experiments and Associations," as one packer remembered. Several efforts to revive the CRGA between 1904 and 1906 failed, and for the next six years, "free competition was the order of the day."[19] A small group led by Giffen, John Dore, James Madison, and W. R. Nutting continued to promote organization, but in a more conciliatory fashion. To move the huge 1908 holdover crop, they needed to, in Giffen's words, "popularize our chief product, . . . put Fresno on the map, . . . and lift the gloom enshrouding the whole community." They came up with the idea of "Raisin Day," to be celebrated on April 30, 1909, in commemoration of the planting of the first vine in California.[20]

From the outset, Raisin Day "struck a popular chord." A committee of growers and business leaders from throughout the county was organized in February to solicit publicity. "Everyone is to eat a good ration of raisins and do their share in helping the growers to get rid of the goods now in their hands," the committee announced. In less than two months, thousands of Fresnoans contributed over $30,000, about half in raisins from "cash-shy growers." Several men were sent to California cities to persuade grocers, hotel managers, and restaurant owners to "put in good-sized stocks of raisins." They distributed 50,000 lithograph posters of a bountiful bunch of grapes basking in the San Joaquin Valley sun and framed by the message "California Raisin Day—Nature's Prize Recipe." The novelty of the idea carried an appeal that surprised even the most optimistic promoter. Newspapers across the country spread the message "CALIFORNIA RAISIN DAY, APRIL 30th — EAT RAISINS!" The Southern Pacific Railroad provided free publicity by advertising the date in *Sunset Magazine,* by placing a variety of "raisin dishes" on dining cars throughout the Harriman system, and by distributing two million *California Raisins* pamphlets containing recipes and descriptions of the harvesting process. Harvey eating houses from San Francisco to Chicago served complimentary raisin pudding to all diners. There was no better investment, these businesses well understood, than to promote one of California's famous specialty crops. "Every patriotic American," reported the *Overland Monthly,* including "President Taft and all members of Congress," ate "the natural candy" on April 30. The whole country, as one observer remarked, "went raisin crazy."[21]

The craze did not last, however. Raisin Day revelers consumed an estimated 10,000 tons, but, in Giffen's words, "when the celebration was over and we had settled down again to the ordinary routine of life, we found that we had practically as many raisins here as at the beginning of the campaign." In 1909, in fact, raisin prices dropped to 1½ cents per pound, their lowest since 1894. Many growers and businessmen complained they had "thrown their money away." Nonetheless, as Giffen recognized, "some good came from it." For two months, the campaign had generated an enthusiasm throughout the raisin community reminiscent, said many first-generation vineyardists, of the late 1880s. Giffen understood that Raisin Day's success came not from "dollars and cents," but from that rekindled spirit.[22]

Over the next three years, what had begun as a "commercial proposition" evolved into a Fresno institution that would last a quarter century. Committees met year-round planning to "girdle the globe with raisins." Railroads and steamship lines implored passengers to "Eat Raisins April 30th and Every Day," served "Fresno cocktails" (drinks garnished with a raisin instead of an olive), and distributed pamphlets, posters, and recipes by the thousands. On "Post Card Day," San Joaquin Valley residents mailed over 200,000 postcards to friends and family members across the country to "spread the word." A committee persuaded members of the International Association of Bakers to introduce raisin bread to millions of consumers. "If the whole country is not eating raisins on April 30 and many days thereafter," wrote the *California Fruit Grower* in 1910, "it will not be the fault of the Raisin Day boosters." In Fresno itself, Raisin Day became "a festival occasion," as tens of thousands of Californians (including the three gubernatorial candidates in 1910) jammed the downtown area for parades, speeches, music, sporting events, aviation exhibitions, and a glimpse of the Raisin Queen. By all accounts, Raisin Day proved a phenomenal success. Both the 1910 and the 1911 crops were sold with minimal carryover and at a "living price." And the cooperative efforts of growers and nongrowers alike once again

Raisin Day in downtown Fresno, April 30, 1910. Fresno Historical Society Archives, Fresno.

made raisins "a great community enterprise." As one speaker declared in 1912, "Every city can have a Fourth of July celebration or a New Year's celebration, but Fresno alone can have a Raisin Day celebration."[23]

"The psychological moment for organization seemed to have arrived," wrote an early historian. In the past three years, several trial balloons had been launched, to no avail. No plan, it seemed, could overcome the pessimism left over from the Kearney days. But in the fall of 1912, a committee of prominent growers and local businessmen led by Giffen, Nutting, and Madison organized the California Associated Raisin Company (CARC), a "million dollar plan" widely perceived as "the most ambitious attempt yet." The committee embarked on a "whirlwind campaign" to convince growers to finance the company (they asked for $10 per acre, but accepted any amount). Under Madison's direction, dozens of organizers canvassed the state's 4,000 vineyards that winter. They spoke face-to-face with virtually every grower not only in Fresno, but in the 11 other counties that collectively produced about a quarter of the state's crop. Growers' everyday lives would change only for the better, they were promised. They would produce the raisins and the CARC would sell them; the company would buy their raisins in the sweatbox at a guaranteed, uniform price—high enough for a fair profit, but low enough to move the crop; and contracts would not be binding until 75 percent of the growers had signed up. The CARC also agreed to buy the growers' substantial holdover crop from 1912 (the largest crop on record to that time) at a price a full cent higher than the packers offered. But the element that "crystallized public sentiment," as CARC's own historian recounted, was Raisin Day. The Fresno festival's success both that year and earlier, organizers believed, provided growers with tangible evidence of the benefits of cooperation. On March 29, 1913, Giffen contributed the $300 that pushed the campaign over the top, and by Raisin Day, no fewer than 90 percent of the growers had joined. In celebration, Fresno officials declared April 30 a city holiday. Once again, Rowell editorialized, "progress and success are secure." It was a triumph for both "agrarian and commercial interests" alike, the *Overland Monthly* stated.[24]

Though organizers refrained from even mentioning his name, it was something of a triumph for Kearney as well. Unwittingly, growers were embracing a form of cooperation even more "industrial" than Kearney's "raisin trust." Like the CRGA, the CARC was not an agricultural cooperative per se, but a capital stock corporation that intended to control the market at the expense of packers and other "interests hostile to raisin producers." When growers signed up for stock, they also all but signed away their voting power. Stockholders from five geographic districts elected a board of 25 trustees who served seven-year terms. But these trustees then elected a board of seven directors—a "voting trust"—with full power to manage the company's affairs as they saw fit. Of the first directors, all but three (Giffen, Madison, and Nutting) were merchants or attorneys. Under this agreement, the CARC freed itself from the "mass meetings" of Kearney's association, where, as Giffen explained, "the fellow who yelled the loudest got the most attention." The trustees and directors recognized the need for broad-based grower participation, but believed that participation could be effective only within the framework of a powerful, centralized organization. This "benevolent autocracy," Giffen maintained, "is not democratic, but it works." Rising prices during the remainder of the decade would sustain growers' loyalty, even amid dogged opposition to the "raisin monopoly" from packers and state and federal authorities.[25]

Fresh deciduous fruit growers faced an altogether different marketing problem than had raisin growers. Overproduction—or, as Giffen preferred, "underconsumption"—was of little concern. Easterners, particularly those in cities, had learned to eat fruit "as a matter of diet." And it was "our orchardists," the *Sacramento Union* took pride in saying, who had "taught them that fruit is not a luxury, but a necessity." But unlike raisin growers, the state's deciduous fruit growers did not operate in a closed market. "[If] we had our own crop alone to consider the solution would be easier," a prominent grower-shipper explained in 1910, "but California is not the only state with great horticultural interests."[26] Prior to the turn of the century, California orchardists were more concerned with competition among themselves. But it was only a matter of time, prominent Sacramento merchant Harris Weinstock warned them as early as 1886, before growers from outside the state would pose a serious challenge as well.[27]

For peach growers in particular, the time arrived sooner than anticipated. "We are not alone . . . by any means," Newcastle orchardist William B. Gester told the twenty-fifth fruit growers' convention in December 1900. For three years, Gester had traveled across the country to study the major fresh-fruit markets firsthand. Growers in several other states, he found, not only produced in greater abundance, but set a quality standard, both in appearance and taste, that Californians could not meet. "With our great disadvantage of distance," Gester explained, "we are up against a very keen competition, for the Eastern grower permits his fruit to more nearly mature on the tree than we dare to attempt."[28] Census figures corroborate his observations. The number of bearing peach trees in California in 1900 was 7.5 million, a 180 percent increase from 1890. But other states experienced phenomenal expansion as well: Michigan had 8.1 million trees, an increase of 320 percent in the same period; Georgia, 7.7 million (175 percent); Texas, 7.3 million (61 percent). New York, Missouri, Kansas, and Arkansas also provided stiff competition.[29]

California growers and shippers could compensate, Gester insisted, by packing their peaches more attractively, by exploiting new markets, and by keeping closer watch on their eastern competitors—all of which required "systematic organization." A former member of W. R. Fountain's Placer County Fruit Growers' Association, Gester believed that marketing success depended on the efforts of the growers themselves. At his prompting, 75 orchardists from throughout northern California, including 42 from Placer County, met in Sacramento on January 15, 1901, to "combine their interests." Whipped into a near-frenzy by speeches from Kearney, then at the height of his popularity, and A. H. Naftzger, the general manager of the highly successful Southern California Citrus Fruit Exchange, virtually every grower present took the podium to denounce shippers, railroads, eastern agents, and other "enemy middlemen." The next day, they formed the California Fresh Fruit Exchange (CFE—"Fresh" was dropped two years later), declaring organization "is in the air."[30]

Experienced observers, however, were skeptical. "It can easily be killed by cold water," the *Pacific Rural Press* editorialized. Even in Placer County, where high production costs generated considerable interest, organizers faced a tough task. While many orchardists there envied the much-publicized success achieved by orange and raisin growers, they were reluctant to "mix their superior fruit with others." The CFE, consequently, encouraged local autonomy as much as possible. Eschewing Kearney's advice for centralized control, CFE organizers adopted the federated structure that had made Naftzger's citrus association so successful. Each district maintained a separate and distinct account with the main Sacramento office, receiving returns based on its own sales rather than those of the exchange as a whole. When the orange men organized in 1895, viable local associations already existed. But there were no such units among deciduous fruit growers. CFE leaders quickly organized them in Newcastle, Penryn, and Loomis in April 1901, but with little success. The largest, the Newcastle Fruit Growers' Association (NFGA), had only 17 members and shipped just 80 carloads—5 percent of Newcastle's total. The CFE's first annual meeting in December was even less encouraging, as only "a bare quorum" of 23 members attended. A decade later, not much had changed. The NFGA served only 46 growers, and the CFE's volume of business remained minimal (less than 25 percent of the state's crop). "We have been only partially successful," the exchange's general manager admitted. Its federated structure notwithstanding, the CFE, most growers believed, was an impersonal organization whose power emanated from outside their communities.[31]

Far more successful was the California Fruit Distributors (CFD), a capital stock company of independent shippers that essentially took marketing out of growers' hands altogether, much to the relief of most everyone involved. Organized in April 1902, the CFD consisted of essentially the same fruit houses that had joined the California Fruit

Growers' and Shippers' Association (CFGSA) in 1895, and it pursued the same objective—it did not sell the fruit, but acted as a clearinghouse for its members. The CFGSA had not been able to control the competition that raged among its members amid soaring production at the turn of the century. Organized without capital stock, it depended on independent eastern agents for market information. Such an arrangement bred corruption; bribes flowed from retail merchants trying to divert shipments to their cities and from rival shippers seeking to corner the market. The CFD, in contrast, employed its own marketing agents by charging its affiliates $10 per car plus 5 percent of the sales receipts. Contracts obligated CFD managers to monitor and coordinate all shipments "as they shall deem best" and bound them to arbitration when disputes arose.[32] This new system, wrote George D. Kellogg in 1908, "worked splendidly." From 1902 to 1912, the CFD handled 75 to 90 percent of California's shipments, expanded existing markets, opened new ones (28 in 1903 alone), and twice convinced the railroads to reduce cross-country rates. Every Placer shipper, including the NFGA, became members. The CFD, they all agreed—with little dissent from growers—had "rescued the fruit business."[33]

But while this organization tamed the rivalry among California shippers and allowed growers to tend to more local matters, competition with eastern firms intensified. In 1910, Californians produced just under 10 million bushels of peaches, their highest output of the decade, and could now boast that California was "the number one peach state." However, they still produced less than a quarter of the country's total. Led by Georgia and Texas, the 10 southern states produced almost 18 million bushels; and in the Northeast, the crop yielded over 15 million, with New York alone more than doubling its output over the decade. "We now have more rivals among other states than ever before," CFD manager Frank McKevitt told Newcastle growers and shippers in 1909.[34]

The pressure to "meet the eastern peach in its own markets" compelled Californians to "reform" production. Newcastle orchardists introduced padded picking baskets, replaced their "old dead axle wagons" with "springy vehicles," and lobbied the county to maintain better roads —all to minimize "fruit abrasions."[35] Growers made frequent demands for more water, which the South Yuba Water Company—a subsidiary of the Pacific Gas and Electric Company as of 1905—continued to meet to their satisfaction. By 1912, 265 miles of canals, pipelines, and flumes (including a reconstructed Bear River Ditch) delivered water to their orchards.[36] Kellogg became the first shipper to "pre-cool" his fruit, a process "destined to revolutionize the fruit shipping enterprise," as his newspaper declared in 1907. For two years Kellogg, with the help of U.S. Department of Agriculture pomologist G. Harold Powell, searched for a way to reduce the decay of fruit in transit across the country. Cooling and drying the fruit in small ammoniated chambers just prior to shipping, they found, "preserved its natural quality." This innovation not only eliminated the need to re-ice en route to the East, it all but negated the "disadvantage of distance" by allowing the fruit to ripen on the tree. By 1910, every Placer shipping point had its own pre-cooling plant.[37]

The most significant reform of all, however, required self-discipline more than innovation. Competition severely threatened the market reputation cultivated by first-generation Newcastle orchardists. The "fancy prices" eastern buyers offered for the first fruit of the season proved particularly damaging. To get a jump on the market, growers often buried ("stove-piped") unripe fruit in the bottom of the box, a practice shippers overlooked with increasing frequency. But the poor quality of these early shipments did not go undetected. "They arrive East, for the most part, very hard," wrote a Placer County grower who was visiting in New York, "and when they do get soft it is not the ripeness of maturity; they are simply 'tasteless slop,' and no one ever wants them twice."[38] This practice became even more widespread in 1908, just as the market seemed to turn in California's favor. The previous year, peach-yellows disease had destroyed about half the crop in every major region across the country except California. Eager to capitalize on this, growers and shippers flooded the market with carload after carload of fruit "that should never have been permitted to leave California," they later admitted. In 1909, Placer growers produced an estimated 300 carloads of peaches "not fit to eat."[39]

That September, their "orchard decadence" reached the point of embarrassment. Buyers in the Pacific Northwest—a relatively small market, but one that California growers dominated—rejected 60 percent of the fresh peaches shipped to them over the summer. In addition, several boxes to be displayed at the Alaska-Yukon-Pacific Exposition in Seattle arrived "unsalable." When the news reached his office, State Horticultural Commissioner J. W. Jeffrey held "the largest peach growing section in the State" accountable. He called a meeting of growers and shippers for September 29 in Newcastle and declared, "Something has to be done." At the Good Templars Hall that day, Jeffrey presided over what amounted to a mass confession. Over 100 growers and shippers admitted that conditions had become "intolerable." "Horticulture," Jeffrey preached, "is the leading industry in your county and should be considered accordingly." CFD general manager Frank McKevitt spoke more to the point: "It is vital that all fruit shipped from here should be sound and of the best quality. . . . We are fast losing our reputation by sending green and wormy fruit."[40]

To redeem themselves, upwards of 300 growers and shippers attended several "mass meetings" over the next two months. At McKevitt's suggestion, a "committee of fifteen" composed of eight growers and seven shippers was elected on November 22 to devise a "process of standardization." They drew up a formal set of rules for packing all the region's crops—peaches, cherries, plums, apricots, and pears. All boxes were to be of uniform size and reinforced around the corners. Packs were to be "neat," "uniform," and graded by size, and to consist only of "fully matured and carefully picked" fruit on the bottom layer as well as the top. No box without an official stamp of approval was to leave the county. To enforce these standards, the committee appointed George D. Kellogg, Harry E. Butler, H. H. Bowman, Charles Darlson, and W. Tudsbury—"the five most well-known men in the county"—to a board of inspection. They, in turn, hired a "corps of independent inspectors" whose job it was to reject outright any box delivered to a shipping house not packed to standard. By April, all nine shipping firms and the vast majority of the growers in the county had agreed to the plan. They assessed themselves a quarter of a cent per box to defray expenses and gave themselves a name—the Placer County Growers and Shippers Association (PCGSA).[41]

By the end of the 1910 season, standardization had become a movement all its own. "Great progress has been made," McKevitt proclaimed in the CFD's annual report. Throughout the summer, buyers paid as much as double the previous year's prices for peaches and plums. Standardization restored "our reputation for superior fruit in the eastern markets," Kellogg told the thirty-eighth fruit growers' convention in December. "There is more than the direct financial gain to it," Butler pointed out. "A silver thread of 'Get together' sentiment runs through it all." The PCGSA renewed its 1910 agreement on November 22 of every year for the next four years with "a jubilee meeting and a banquet" to "commemorate the anniversary of the inception of the movement." Additional "mass meetings" were called on a regular basis, not only to discuss policy and procedure, but to celebrate—for all the community to see—the return of Placer fruit "to the front rank where it belongs."[42] As in the late 1880s and early 1890s, local newspapers published article after article promoting the "pleasant and profitable"—and now also "progressive"—way of life that standardization had revitalized. It was as though this "home of the peach," as Kellogg characterized it, had been given the opportunity to start afresh.[43]

Meanwhile, similar developments were taking place in Davisville, which growers there called "the home of the almond" with equal fervor. They could support their claim with an abundance of evidence: their almonds won a gold medal at the St. Louis World's Fair in 1905; they routinely took home blue ribbons from the California State Fair; they were the state's top-producing region almost every year; and their marketing cooperative, the Davisville Almond Growers' Association (DAGA), was "the parent body which blazed the way" for others. From 1902 to 1909, DAGA officers George W. Pierce Jr., Jacob La Rue, and J. W. Anderson helped organize eight similar associations in the Sacramento Valley—at Yuba City, Live Oak, Fair Oaks, Orangevale, Antelope, Capay, Oakley, and Lodi. Cooperation brought these growers considerable recognition at the state fair and other public venues. Before long, members of every association began to assert that "their own crops were of a superior quality."[44]

More than just a friendly rivalry ensued, however. Competition among the various almond communities played right into the hands of the wholesale buyers who bid for their crops every summer. They were able to keep prices low by playing each association off the others—just as they had done with individual growers before the advent of local pools. On the average, growers received 8 to 10 cents a pound for their crop between 1898 and 1909. Each year, however, one or two associations were paid as much as 14 cents—validating, in their members' minds, the superiority of their particular district. Only the best-informed association leaders, such as Pierce and B. F. Walton of Yuba City, knew that California almonds sold for an average of 30 cents a pound on the retail market over the same period of time. But the brokers' strategy undermined any effort to secure "the price the market warrants." DAGA members, for example, received 10¾ cents for their almonds in 1903—at least a full cent more than any other association—and voted against their own officers' recommendation to sell in conjunction with their Oakley and Yuba City counterparts. In the long run, as Pierce recalled, such displays of community "pretension" left all growers "surely and safely in the hands of the enemy."[45]

Ultimately, it took an almond novice to bring the associations together. John P. Dargitz had kept the books for a railroad line in Chicago, practiced medicine in New York, taught school in New Mexico, and, after 1896, served as pastor for a number of northern California congregations. His introduction to horticulture came in 1906, when he helped establish a Christian colony on 800 acres in San Joaquin County near Lodi.[46] Dargitz became enamored with the almond's "sensitivity," "unparalleled beauty," and biblical heritage. But he was appalled both by the speculative nature of the almond trade and by the lack of faith among many growers to take matters into their own hands. In 1908, Dargitz embarked on a personal crusade through the state's almond districts to preach the virtues of organization. "More than four thousand years ago Jacob made use of the almond in his efforts to achieve commercial success," he told growers. "We may get lots of pleasure and satisfaction out of our orchards in producing a beautiful bloom and a splendid crop, but . . . we must also be able to make a net profit." Dargitz assured growers that their own associations already demonstrated the value of cooperation. Just as each local had reduced competition among individual growers, so too would a central body create "harmony" among the individual associations. Dargitz's evangelical tone and "practical sense" proved especially effective on the heels of a 1908 bumper crop whose proceeds barely covered production costs. On May 6, 1910, representatives elected from each of the nine associations met in Sacramento determined "to steady the market through cooperation." The next day, they incorporated the California Almond Growers' Exchange (CAGE).[47]

CAGE founders were careful to reassure growers that "the central" would in no way infringe upon the "local." "It is not our purpose to create a trust," Dargitz insisted. "All matters of purely local interest will be handled by the local association." Each association retained its own bylaws and officers, continued to "promulgate advanced ideas" on production, stored the region's almonds in a warehouse "convenient to all members," and sold their crops "on their own merit." Every sack shipped east bore the names of both the local and the exchange. If anything, the exchange's organizational structure increased the local's importance, the *California Fruit Grower* maintained. Each association elected one of its own members to serve on the board of directors, which in turn elected officers to carry out the central's "sole function"—selling the crop. President Walton, Vice-President Pierce, and Manager Dargitz were the first to be "entrusted" with the locals' almonds.[48]

But while CAGE officials were sensitive to growers' fears, they well understood that an increasingly centralized marketplace demanded a more centralized approach. Its rhetoric notwithstanding, CAGE actually took control of the crop away from the locals and, by the end of its first year of operation, placed it in the hands of a single, non-elected individual — the manager. Dargitz and the other directors continued to promote cooperation, organizing locals in Banning, Concord, Colusa, and Orland by 1911 and doubling the number of charter associations by 1914.[49] Selling the crop, however, required an understanding of the trade that even the most knowledgeable grower simply did not have. As manager, Dargitz assumed the responsibility, but early on he recognized the need for someone with a better "grasp of the field and situation." He hired a sales manager, Thaddeus C. Tucker, who had worked for three years both in the Chicago office of the California Fruit Growers' Exchange (citrus) and with the California Fruit Exchange in San Francisco. Though CAGE bylaws made him responsible to the board of directors, Tucker took charge from the moment he took office. He assumed Dargitz's title of manager two years later and ran the exchange with an iron hand for the next 25 years.[50]

Tucker's job was straightforward but hardly simple: secure a fair profit for growers and move the crop without carryover. To get a jump on the market, he set an "opening price" in early September, about halfway through the harvest. His estimation could make or break the exchange. On the one hand, the price had to be significantly higher than the status quo to retain the growers' loyalty; on the other, it had to be low enough to stabilize the market. Moreover, growers had become accustomed to receiving advances of up to 50 percent from eastern brokers. The exchange paid those advances as well, though at first with loans secured by the directors' personal notes. CAGE was a "non-profit cooperative institution" with no capital of its own, and banks did not consider almonds sacked in a warehouse collateral. "Only a properly managed cooperative . . . that could maintain the market . . . was considered a safe risk from the banker's point of view," a director recalled.[51] Tucker left nothing to chance in his efforts to establish the exchange's reputation. Every spring and summer, he toured the major eastern markets, conferring with hundreds of contacts to determine "the most willing price" consumers would pay. On the supply side, he estimated the size of each crop by surveying growers early every summer. By the end of the decade, Tucker would establish a hierarchy of departments run by mid-level managers to perform these tasks. But throughout his tenure, he remained, as one director stated, "the heart of the business."[52]

The business proved enormously successful. Between 1910 and 1914, CAGE expanded its membership from 230 to 900, inspired an almond boom that increased the total number of acres in the state from 11,000 to 35,000, gained control of 80 percent of the crop, advanced prices from 12 to 18 cents, and secured "first rate credit." By 1915, the exchange was selling to over 1,000 wholesalers in every major market across the country.[53] To what extent CAGE policies accounted for this success is difficult to determine. Agricultural prices in general had been climbing gradually throughout the United States since the turn of the century, and the period is often referred to as "the golden age of American agriculture." From 1895 to 1915, the index of agricultural prices nearly doubled, from 55.9 to 103.2.[54] More-experienced businessmen would not have predicted that a new organization would perform so well so quickly. But almond growers expected instant success, and they indeed attained it. "The outlook is most gratifying," a Davisville grower stated. And why should he have believed otherwise? The exchange had lived up to Dargitz's ideal. It allowed growers to pursue "the pleasure and satisfaction of [their] orchards," to retain their sense of community, and to receive a fair price— all without involving themselves directly "in the business."[55]

Growers were not the only ones to benefit from the California Almond Growers' Exchange, the California Fruit Distributors, the California Associated Raisin Company, and other joint marketing ventures. These organizations reinforced what boosters had been stressing since the 1880s: horticulture made California special. After San Francisco's devastating earthquake in April 1906, growers' accomplishments were emphasized even more—not only to lure prospective homeseekers, but to boost the morale of Californians themselves. In 1909, several groups combined to "advertise the state's resources" through a single body—a state chamber of commerce, which they called the California Development Board. The board's literature emphasized one objective over all others: to attract "a population that will settle in our fertile valleys and till the soil." Its annual reports, designed to entice "the best people from all over the world," contained full-page photographs of almond orchards in bloom, bunches of ripe raisin grapes, and expansive orange groves; a myriad of production statistics; and extensive articles on climate, irrigation, and horticulture—"the dominant industry in California."[56] Even the board's most ambitious promotion—the Panama-Pacific International Exposition, held in 1915 to demonstrate the triumph of San Francisco's renewed spirit—drew much of its inspiration from another "great movement": Fresno's Raisin Day, as board vice-president and manager Robert Newton Lynch suggested in 1912.[57]

THERE WAS A WHOLE OTHER SIDE to specialty crop agriculture that the California Development Board did not mention, let alone promote. While growers marketed their crops with increasing sophistication, labor remained their "bugbear." Scholars, as boosters before them did, have treated these two dominant facets of growers' lives as separate. In large part, marketing has been the domain of agricultural economists, while labor has been studied by historians of the working class. Collectively, they have left the impression that marketing and labor were two distinct agricultural worlds occupied by two distinct sets of historical actors. But orchardists and vineyardists occupied only one world, of course, and in it they experienced both marketing triumphs and labor struggles. This is revealed, with special clarity, through the trials and tribulations of George W. Pierce Jr.

As a CAGE officer and successful almond grower, Pierce stood as a symbol in the boosters' rhetoric. But he was also an active booster himself. He applied the same ingenuity exhibited in his almond affairs to several public ventures. He participated in regional and state organizations such as the Sacramento Valley Development Association, the California Promotion Committee, and the California Development Board —"always hammering industriously on some proposition for the benefit and advancement of his section," the *Davis Enterprise* boasted. It was Pierce who "made certain" that the section of the Lincoln Highway between Sacramento and San Francisco passed through Davis.[58] And it was largely through Pierce's efforts that University of California officials chose Davis as the site for a new agricultural college in April 1906. Taking advantage of his status as an influential alumnus, Pierce drafted the original proposal to locate the State Farm at Davisville, arranged for the sale of a fertile tract of land and secured a contract for its water rights, personally chauffeured university president Benjamin Ide Wheeler on a full-day tour of Yolo County, and conducted a successful one-man publicity campaign to convince Governor George C. Pardee of Davisville's advantages. Two years later, Pierce explained to a gathering of influential growers the supreme importance of the State Farm: "The College of Agriculture is more necessary to the state than the school of medicine, law or theology. If we lived a more natural life in the fresh air, we could get along without medicine. If we had no lawyers, we might get along with justice. If we had no theology, we could get along with religion. But we could not live at all without an adequate supply of food, and for that we are dependent upon an intelligent system of agriculture." "If I am anything," Pierce asserted in 1914, "I am a booster."[59]

These were the words of a supremely confident individual—a prime example, it seemed, of the "intelligence, industry and moral worth" California had to offer.[60] Pierce's public image received yet another boost in 1913 when his fellow almond growers elected him CAGE president— the pinnacle of achievement in his profession. Yet for all his success, Pierce, like all experienced horticulturists, knew that every harvest held the potential for disaster. As CAGE's principal spokesman, he extolled the virtues of both the almond and cooperation. But labor was a topic conspicuous by its absence. Pierce typically offered prospective growers only one brief suggestion: "Be ready for the harvest and have a crew of gatherers in proportion to your acreage."[61] Labor contractors, Shi Kubo had taught Pierce in 1901, dictated whether the recruiting process was really as easy as Pierce's statement implied. Yet their services remained essential. Though Pierce would not have admitted it, his image as cultural guardian depended on a relationship he neither controlled nor celebrated.

Pierce thought he had put his labor problems behind him when he contracted with Wing Hai in 1903 for the third straight year.[62] But when he met with Hai again just prior to the 1904 harvest, the Davisville grocer informed him that no Chinese were available. In all likelihood, those who had knocked almonds for Pierce and his neighbors in previous years had found more satisfying work in Chinese communities in the nearby Sacramento–San Joaquin Delta. Undaunted, Pierce devised a scheme to avenge his previous encounter with Kubo. He sold his entire crop for $250 to the Japanese contractor, who agreed to gather, hull, and sack the almonds and deliver them to the DAGA warehouse in exchange for the remaining proceeds. There were, however, no remaining proceeds, as the entire crop netted just $185.[63] Pierce had known his orchards would produce a poor crop. In early March, a "fearful rain and windstorm," in his words, had swept through northern California, wreaking havoc in the region's fruit and nut orchards. Statewide, the 1904 almond crop was only 25 percent of the previous year's output, and Pierce's trees yielded only three-quarters of a ton. Conditions improved little over the next three years, the result of late frosts and an infestation of red spider mites.[64] But Pierce continued to cut his losses by securing favorable agreements with unsuspecting Japanese contractors. In 1907, for example, J. Tanaka agreed to harvest the crop for a half share, a potentially lucrative proposition during a bountiful harvest but a disaster during an off year. Indeed, while Pierce earned nearly $600 for merely signing the contract, Tanaka, after expenses, cleared only $3.39.[65] Japanese contractors in Fresno and other specialty crop regions had already become legendary among growers for their "tricky" bargaining tactics. Pierce's actions, however, revealed that he could be just as tricky.

Harvest conditions once again changed dramatically in 1908. The combination of a dry early spring and the absence of mites (growers had learned to dust their trees with sulfur) produced the largest crop of almonds ever for Pierce and the DAGA. Pierce's 31 tons of almonds—nearly double his previously highest yield, in 1901—grossed almost $6,000, five times the total for 1907. At the same time, a national recession provided growers with a measure of relief with respect to labor, as the *Pacific Rural Press* explained:

> There is one piece of good luck which often comes to California farmers, and that is that whenever they become much alarmed lest their labor supply be short for some coming crop, time brings a solution of the difficulty: either the crop is so short that few men are needed, or some other business slacks up and sends a lot of labor afloat and it blows itself into the rural districts. So now there is a good fruit crop to handle, but we do not hear that there is shortage of help.[66]

Sikhs, immigrants from the Punjab region of northwest India, constituted the labor that "blew itself" into Davisville orchards in the summer of 1908. Religious and political reformers opposed to the caste system and other practices they considered corrupt, Sikhs began immigrating to the Pacific Coast earlier in the decade to escape poverty and British colonialism. Deemed undesirable by the residents of British Columbia, they had filtered down into northern California by 1907, where they found work on the railroads or in lumber mills. Because most Sikhs came from agricultural backgrounds, they gravitated toward the opportunities for orchard work the 1908 bumper crop presented. The popular press labeled them "outcasts," as virtually all of them were males with long hair, beards, and white turbans.[67] For growers such as Pierce, however, they proved indispensable as harvest workers.

In the spring of 1907, four Sikhs had presented themselves to Pierce and offered their services as farmhands. Attracted by their willingness to work for $1.25 a day and by their strong, robust physiques, Pierce hired them to dig irrigation ditches, saw and stack wood, shovel and haul manure, and perform various other mundane chores. Their wages compared favorably with those for other forms of day labor during the recession and greatly exceeded the 10 to 15 cents a day typically earned in India.[68] Two of them, Mousha Singh and Bogosin Singh, returned the following winter. Gradually gaining Pierce's confidence, they began performing tasks demanding more skill, such as pruning, irrigating, and harrowing. The Sikhs found much of this work familiar, as agricultural conditions in the Sacramento Valley closely resembled those of the Punjab. With the huge almond harvest approaching, Pierce rejected a Japanese contractor's offer and asked Mousha and Bogosin to recruit a gang of Sikh harvesters—or "Hindoos," as he and other growers called them, oblivious to the fact that these were committed dissenters from Hinduism.[69]

They did not disappoint him. The two Sikhs linked Pierce to a network of "chain employment" that provided him with a ready source of harvest labor. In early August, Mousha and Bogosin contacted Shaam Singh, a contractor based in nearby Vacaville, who recruited 30 workers for the monthlong harvest at $1.25 a day. With Mousha, Bogosin, Shaam, and one of his white permanent ranch hands as gang bosses, Pierce oversaw the operation of four sleds with as many as six workers per sled knocking almonds. He then resumed his position at the almond huller with the assistance of six additional Sikhs in the packing sheds. He also implemented a new wage strategy that assured greater obedience within his harvest labor force. Whereas he previously had advanced Chinese and Japanese contractors irregular amounts of cash to cover their labor, board, and other immediate costs, he now provided board for his workers, deducted that expense from their total wages, and paid a final settlement to the contractor at the conclusion of the harvest. This strategy shifted the burden of securing a worker's loyalty from Pierce to the contractor. Now, if a harvester quit early, the contractor was responsible for that harvester's costs and lost labor.[70] Mousha, Bogosin, and Shaam restored Pierce's sense of paternalism in providing an abundance of skillful, compliant workers to harvest his most profitable crop of almonds to date.

Not surprisingly, Pierce acted to maintain this arrangement, with Mousha becoming the linchpin for its success. Pierce hired him as one of his permanent field workers, and then depended on Mousha's ties to the Sikh community in northern California to procure an adequate labor force for the almond season. In 1909, a below-average year, Mousha himself assumed the role of contractor, recruiting 10 workers, probably from the large Sikh community in Yuba City, 50 miles north of Davis.[71] By the following year, the positive reputation Mousha had built for the Pierce orchards began to pay dividends. Fifteen unrecruited Sikhs arrived in Davis in early August seeking work as almond harvesters, and Mousha secured another 15 who had applied for work at the Murray and Ready Employment Agency in Sacramento.[72] A similar pattern of harvest employment continued through 1916, as Sikh laborers—either on their own, through private employment agencies, or through a contractor—journeyed to the Pierce ranch every August expecting to find work. Pierce rewarded his workers' loyalty and further enhanced his favorable reputation by raising their wages (to $1.75 in 1910 and $2.00 in 1913), by building them a bunkhouse and kitchen, and by procuring them further employment with his neighbor almond growers. His own faith in Mousha—epitomized by Mousha's sharing the duty of operating the almond huller in 1913—became the focal point for the entire harvest process.[73]

In December 1913, Mousha unexpectedly quit his job on the Pierce ranch and returned to India, perhaps to participate in a rebellion against the British in his homeland.[74] The Sikh referral network he had established, however, remained in place, now managed by three of his contacts, Indar Singh, Kalla Singh, and Anokh Singh. From 1914 to 1916, Indar and Kalla worked as permanent employees for Pierce, served as gang bosses during the almond harvest, and acted as Pierce's liaison to Anokh, a labor contractor based in Isleton in the Sacramento–San Joaquin Delta. Every Christmas, Anokh sent Pierce a crate of celery, a display of allegiance symbolizing the mutual accord underlying this arrangement. Labor relations on the Pierce ranch appeared to have stabilized. Just one year later, however, in 1917, "Hindu insubordination"—as Pierce described it—would disrupt that harmony once again.[75]

Pierce's preference for Sikh over Japanese workers stemmed from more than personal experience alone. Between 1905 and 1913, the "Japanese question" dominated California politics. Because the vast majority of early Japanese immigrants worked in the state's rural districts, they were more ignored than persecuted by most white Californians — in sharp contrast to the anti-Chinese movement led by Denis Kearney's Workingmen's Party in the 1870s and 1880s. But as their numbers began to multiply after the turn of the century, more and more Japanese migrated to the city, especially during the off-season. There they became the victims of a growing uneasiness about Japan's military prowess, punctuated by Admiral Togo's stunning defeat of the Russian navy in the spring of 1905. The *San Francisco Chronicle* ignited the anti-Japanese fervor with a series of sensational articles warning that "the brown stream of Japanese immigration" would soon become a "raging torrent." In May, delegates from 67 union locals formed the Asiatic Exclusion League, whose diatribes made those of the *Chronicle* seem tame in comparison. The league's first order of business was to convince the San Francisco Board of Education to combat the "Yellow Peril" by segregating the city's 93 Japanese schoolchildren. A full-scale diplomatic crisis was averted only when President Theodore Roosevelt worked out the "Gentlemen's Agreement" in March 1907, whereby Japan agreed to deny passports to laborers wishing to emigrate to America. The agitation continued, however. In 1909, conservative Republican state legislators appropriated $10,000 for what was intended as an anti-Japanese investigation, only to be taken aback when State Labor Commissioner John D. MacKenzie reported that the state's "specialized agricultural industries" could not survive without Japanese labor. Progressives then seized the initiative by proposing a number of exclusion bills and by passing the Alien Land Law in 1913. "Anti-Japanese sentiment," one historian has written, "was practically unanimous."[76]

Excluded from that sentiment were Fresno vineyardists, Newcastle orchardists, and other specialty crop growers who had become dependent on Japanese labor. Prior to 1905, the growing presence of Japanese workers had created a sensitive community issue, but one that growers had managed to keep under control. Circumstances beyond their control, however, seemingly overnight turned their orchards and vineyards into targets of public condemnation. By 1908, anti-Japanese agitation had attracted the attention of the U.S. Immigration Commission, created by Congress the year before to temper demands for restricting "new" immigrants from southeastern Europe. Several groups of social scientists studied labor conditions in 12 California specialty crop districts and, as more than 1,000 pages of reports reveal, came away in awe of the labor-market power of a "new" immigrant from across the Pacific Ocean.[77]

Conditions in Fresno were particularly striking. "The grip of the Japanese upon the farmers in harvest time is unmistakable," these investigators concluded after surveying the region's raisin vineyards in September 1908. In just three weeks, an estimated 10,000 pickers—double the labor force of 1902—harvested the region's 50,000 acres. While pickers' "racial composition" varied considerably, over two-thirds were Japanese. Piece work seemed to defy the notion of "cheap labor." At a rate as high as 3¼ cents per tray, pickers earned from three to seven dollars for a 14-hour day. Moreover, it was the Japanese contractors, not the growers, who controlled wages. Contractors met among themselves in advance of each season to set rates, recruit pickers, and arrange for their accommodations in boardinghouses throughout the county. The most powerful contractors were Koichi Kamikawa of Fresno and J. Kawamoto of Selma. Every grower, it seemed, had "done business" with one of these two merchants at one time or another. In 1908, Japanese contractors organized the California Contractors Association to prevent underbidding and to discipline "corrupt" practitioners of their trade. The contract system, in short, had become formally institutionalized.[78]

Growers' failure to form a counter-organization at first baffled the investigators, especially in light of their repeated efforts to join together for marketing purposes. No less than a third of the vineyardists interviewed "complained of strikes by Japanese to compel them to pay higher wages." One grower's experience proved particularly illuminating. Prior to the harvest, this prominent vineyardist entered into an agreement with a well-known, respected Japanese merchant—perhaps even Kamikawa himself—who guaranteed the contract with a "considerable" deposit. Just as the grapes ripened, however, the contractor reneged on his terms, forfeited his deposit, and demanded a higher rate. The grower acceded with little hesitation. Experience had taught him that contractors rarely infringed on each other's territory. There was little chance, he knew, of securing "even a single Japanese to pick his grapes." Gradually, the investigators came to sympathize with the growers. After observing firsthand the pressures of the harvest timetable, weather contingencies, the sheer demand for laborers, and the contractors' immense power, they too came to the conclusion that "no remedy" existed.[79]

Another group of Immigration Commission investigators discovered the following year that "the Japanese . . . have come into control of the majority of the orchards of the Newcastle district." There, however, the principal means was not "the boss system." At the turn of the century, only a minority of growers had found leasing to their liking. But by 1909, tenants farmed over 90 percent of the region's 11,500 acres of bearing fruit trees. Japanese immigrants controlled 60 percent, Chinese 15 percent, Portuguese and Italians another 15 percent, and "Americans" the remaining 10 percent.[80] Growers' initial rationale for leasing had not changed: tenants cleared their land, shared the risks from crop failure and market fluctuations, allowed for crop diversification, and provided the skilled labor necessary to pick and pack fresh deciduous fruit. But two additional developments, only one of which the investigators fully understood, transformed this region's labor system in the span of about five years.

Shippers' interests proved decisive. Although the California Fruit Distributors held competition for eastern markets in check, competition for the growers' business remained keen. In the 1890s, the local shipping houses of George D. Kellogg, the Penryn Fruit Company, and Schnabel Brothers began extending chattel mortgages to tenants on the condition that the borrower deliver his fruit to the lender. But the Producers' Fruit Company, a new Chicago firm (incorporated in 1896) that established houses in Loomis, Newcastle, and Auburn at the end of the decade, was even more creative. At first, the company struggled to gain a foothold, shipping just one carload in 1899. To secure more business, Producers' began paying growers "bonuses" under the table after agreeing to buy fruit only at the Newcastle price. The firm also began to lease orchards itself. Agents paid a cash rent to the landowner and then sublet the orchards to Japanese or, to a lesser extent, Chinese tenants.[81] Prior to the 1900 harvest, Producers' registered 24 such agreements at the county courthouse, and a total of 83 by the end of 1905. Other shippers saw no choice but to follow suit. The Penryn Fruit Company, for example, leased at least 25 orchards between 1901 and 1905.[82] Landowners gradually realized their leverage. By renting their ranches and reserving the right to name the shipper, they could instigate bidding wars for their crops. The trend snowballed. By the time the commission investigators arrived in 1909, "most of the orchards, berry patches, and gardens [were] leased, and chiefly to Asiatics."[83]

Investigators noted rather matter-of-factly that more than half the Japanese tenants were married, "their wives having migrated to the area recently in most cases." But they failed to recognize the significance of this "sociological consideration." Just four years earlier, a *Sacramento Bee* reporter had observed that "little brown men [were] crowding out white laborers and getting hold of ranches." Only on the rarest of occasions had a woman been seen among them. For Japanese tenants, who were no less dependent on seasonal workers than their white landlords had been, the Gentlemen's Agreement made it imperative to seek other sources of labor. While the agreement prohibited the emigration of laborers to America, it did allow residents' relatives to come, assuming they were of "sound financial status and moral character." Tenants wasted no time. Those with families sent for them, and many without arranged for "picture brides." The labor these women and children provided proved invaluable. They worked "as good as the men," a Penryn landowner later remarked. During the harvest, Japanese families astonished their landlords by working 16-hour days, seven days a week. A family of four operating 20 acres "could do most of the work themselves." When pressed, families either helped each other or sought assistance "from their association."[84] By 1909, two chapters of the Japanese Association of America, organized in 1900 to protect the rights of Japanese immigrants, served the Newcastle fruit belt. The Gentlemen's Agreement had entrusted the association with the task of verifying the "character" of prospective immigrants. At the local level, however, one of its more crucial functions was to link tenant farmers to labor markets in Sacramento and other large communities.[85]

But the irony went even deeper. The Gentlemen's Agreement, it turned out, actually fortified not only the tenant system, but the Japanese community itself. In 1907 and 1908, the acreage controlled by the Japanese in Placer County quadrupled, according to Immigration Commission investigators.[86] Penryn, the site of Joel Parker Whitney's failed Citrus Colony, became a magnet for Japanese immigrants. "The Japanese have cleared nearly all the places around here," one of the few remaining Englishmen stated. "People wouldn't have ranches if not for the Japs." Japanese tenants employed "a spirit of cooperation" to secure almost total control of Penryn's orchards. Indeed, landlords who mistreated tenants, or landowners who refused to rent their orchards, found it virtually impossible to procure an adequate labor force. By 1915, 60 of the 68 ranches within a two-mile radius of Penryn were rented—55 to Japanese tenants or sub-tenants. At peak times, it was "a common occurrence to see twenty fruit wagons lined up at the fruit house with a

Newcastle's "fruit house row," ca. 1908. Note that many of the drivers entrusted with delivering the fragile fruit are Japanese. Courtesy of the California History Room, California State Library, Sacramento, California.

Japanese driver on each wagon," an observer remarked. Moreover, "Jap Town" had become a thriving community, with its own Buddhist church, school, and commercial district. "This portion of the town shows much more prosperity than does the American portion," the same observer continued. "There are four grocery stores in the town, two owned by Americans and two by Japanese. One of the Americans has a one-horse delivery wagon, the other has no delivery wagon at all, while both of the Japanese have motor trucks in which to deliver their goods."[87] The Japanese community had changed dramatically, from one dominated by sojourners to one made up of stable family units. Whitney's dream—a colony of families prospering from the fruits of their labor—had come true, except for the fact that Penryn had become a center of Japanese settlement.

Or had it? Despite their overwhelming presence, the Japanese remained virtually invisible to local whites. Tenancy had become an institutionalized feature of horticulture, landowners acknowledged. "But to say that our orchards are going out of the control of their owners, is ridiculous," Harry Butler wrote to the *Sacramento Bee* in 1911. Leases, Butler explained, were simply labor agreements adapted to the "peculiar features" of the foothills. "Formerly the Japanese worked by the day, but this was gradually changed a number of years ago to payment to one boss of a share of the crop." The vast majority of landlords, he insisted, supervised the "picking and packing" and continued to control the marketing of the crop. Moreover, he claimed, most leases covered just one year, renewable only at the landowner's option.[88]

But Butler knew otherwise. He and the Penryn Fruit Company, which he managed, together leased dozens of orchards to Japanese tenants for cash rents and multiyear tenures. These terms provided tenants such as O. Furukawa and K. Matsunami with stronger work incentives. While a share renter could claim only a fraction (usually half) of the residual profits, those paying a fixed rate received the full benefit from their skill and hard work. And a long-term contract (three to five years, generally) helped offset the risks of crop failure or market fluctuation. These terms also demonstrated landowners' supreme confidence in the Japanese. Long tenures generally were the result of intense personal loyalty between landlord and tenant. Moreover, landlords relied almost exclusively on their tenants to supervise themselves and the labor they hired. Butler, in fact, employed just one man to "motor from one ranch to another."[89] Butler felt it necessary to stretch the truth to defend the integrity of his fellow horticulturists, who, he emphasized, operated "the finest deciduous orchards in California." His letter came in response to an attack on his region's labor system by the *Sacramento Bee,* perhaps the most anti-Japanese newspaper in the state. In Butler's defense, the *Pacific Rural Press* praised Newcastle orchardists for their "practical methods," and maintained that under the circumstances, "the Oriental seems the only way to proceed."[90]

The most significant aspect of Butler's long letter was the fact that he responded at all. Only very rarely did growers air their labor concerns so openly. "There is in some quarters," the *Pacific Rural Press* explained, "a disposition [among nongrowers] to be misled by prejudice to such an extent that great injustice is done." Beginning in 1903, growers insisted upon "keeping their discussions to marketing" at their annual conventions. "We know how to grow fruit," they asserted, "so the great problem for us to now solve is how to dispose of it."[91] But in December 1907, the

labor issue burst to the forefront when two prominent orchardists—
John P. Irish of Antioch and George H. Hecke of Woodland—spoke at
the Marysville convention. The Gentlemen's Agreement, they feared,
"extended the [Chinese] exclusion policy to the Japanese." And without
Asian labor, a "crippling" shortage seemed imminent. "What is the
Pacific Coast producer to do?" asked Hecke. That question should concern all Californians, Irish insisted: "The harvesting and marketing of
our crops . . . lie at the foundation of California's prosperity." Both ac-
cused the Asiatic Exclusion League of "theorizing" where it didn't be-
long—particularly with its erroneous contention that Asian labor was
"cheap" and therefore a threat to urban workers. Referring to the San
Francisco union leaders who dominated the Exclusion League, Irish demanded to know why labor should "be permitted to dictate to politicians
of California what their policy shall be toward the rural producer.
Has the rural producer no rights which Tveitmoe and Furuseth and
McCarthy and Cornelius and Casey are bound to respect?" Irish and
Hecke pleaded with growers to convince their congressmen to modify
the Chinese Exclusion Act. Though they interrupted the two papers repeatedly with applause, growers retreated into silence upon leaving the
convention hall. The state's major newspapers and labor journals "misunderstood and misrepresented" their intentions, the *Pacific Rural Press*
maintained, and "berated them as unAmerican and disloyal." Growers
would not address "the Japanese question" in convention again until
World War I.[92]

The papers by Irish and Hecke caught the attention of an obscure
group as well. A letter to the *Pacific Rural Press* stated that growers could
get "plenty of cheap white labor" by contacting the Industrial Workers of
the World (IWW) in San Francisco. "We do not know anything about
this organization," the editor warned readers.[93] Just three years later, almost every Californian would recognize the Wobblies for their inflam-
matory anti-capitalist rhetoric and "free speech fights." In the lore of
California farm labor history, Fresno has become synonymous with one
such battle. In the spring of 1910, Wobblies took to Fresno's streets determined to organize San Joaquin Valley "wage slaves" into their "One
Big Union." Led by famed "hobo agitator" Frank Little, soapboxers attacked the "master class," preached the virtues of industrial unionism,
and prophesied that a final general strike would bring about a workers'
paradise. When local authorities began making arrests, hundreds of
Wobblies from throughout the West "bummed" their way to Fresno and

overloaded the jails. Police terror and vigilantism raged for several months, finally ending the following March in a compromise allowing for limited free speech. The IWW "victory" made the front page of newspapers throughout the country.[94]

Historians have debated that victory's significance ever since. Some have claimed the Fresno fight "enhanced the prestige of the IWW among agricultural workers,"[95] while others have insisted it "left behind no effective labor organization."[96] Few, however, have questioned the underlying assumption that the region's "unorganized, overworked, and underpaid fruit pickers" desired IWW intervention.[97] Lumber, railroad, construction, and other casual workers made up the bulk of Fresno's Local 66. Fruit pickers—particularly the 7,000 Japanese who harvested the county's raisins—were conspicuous by their absence. It was not that the IWW, unlike virtually every other American labor organization, refused to organize Asians. To the contrary, Wobblies repeatedly expressed their admiration, even envy, for Japanese harvesters' solidarity, "job tactics," and ability to "stick it to the boss."[98] But this was precisely why the IWW held so little appeal for the Japanese. They already labored in de facto collective bargaining units with considerable power. Evidence of class divisions and resistance to capitalist values among the Japanese does exist. Vineyard workers, for example, organized a Fresno Labor League in August 1908 to protect their interests against abusive contractors. Japanese socialists took over the league's newspaper and even held a joint rally with Fresno Wobblies on one occasion. But the league disbanded within a year.[99] Indeed, such behavior was exceptional. Most Japanese immigrants considered themselves neither "cheap labor" nor "wage slaves," and in fact exhibited a strong work ethic and a desire to climb the agricultural ladder from laborer to tenant to landowner.[100]

Growers, on the other hand, welcomed outside intervention—not from the IWW, but from the American Federation of Labor (AFL). Between 1908 and 1911, Andrew Furuseth, Paul Scharrenberg, and other prominent San Francisco unionists organized a Migratory Labor League with the expressed purpose of eliminating surplus urban labor that they regarded as a potential source of strikebreakers.[101] Growers saw the league as an organization of white workers with the potential to displace the Japanese contract system. Prior to the 1911 harvest, M. F. Tarpey, one of Fresno's largest growers, agreed to employ several hundred Greek harvesters provided by the league. "There is something peculiarly appropriate in having Greek labor presented to California farmers to do work in a land which has often been spoken of as the Greece of the West," the *Fresno Morning Republican* editorialized, capturing growers' sentiments. The timing of the experiment coincided with AFL president Samuel Gompers's statewide speaking tour, which included a stop in Fresno on September 18. A week into the harvest, however, Tarpey found the Greeks "unfamiliar with the work and unsatisfactory," and he quickly replaced them with Japanese. League organizers promptly placed their recruits with several other growers, but they too "followed Tarpey's example and employed Japanese instead." It cost the AFL over $4,000 to learn that the raisin harvest was not ripe for unionization.[102]

Neither the IWW nor the AFL left even a trace in the Newcastle district. The dominance of Japanese tenants there discouraged labor leaders. To landowners, however, the Japanese tenants themselves "acted like a union."[103] Furthermore, much to the growers' dismay, the standardization movement ended up empowering the Japanese even more. It was one thing to adopt formal picking and packing rules, hire inspectors, and form an association. But it was quite another, growers and shippers found, to persuade at least 320 Japanese tenants to "follow the same standard." On February 7, 1910, 250 Japanese tenants convened at the Good Templars Hall in Newcastle at the request of the Placer County Growers and Shippers Association. The meeting was neither advertised nor reported on by the local press, and only two whites — county horticultural commissioner H. H. Bowman and PCGSA representative George D. Kellogg — attended. Through an interpreter, Bowman and Kellogg explained the situation. Inspectors would not accept "inferior" fruit the upcoming season, they announced. Several "leading Japanese" then spent the better part of the afternoon lecturing on "the best methods of spraying, picking, packing, and shipping fruit."[104] Before adjourning, they formed their own "protective association" to enforce the new rules. As indicated by the subsequent season's overwhelming success, the Japanese delivered their fruit "up to standard." Their protective association, however, also encouraged militancy. Reports surfaced that summer of Japanese "jumping" their leases, demanding cash rents and other more favorable terms, and boycotting uncooperative growers. "Trouble has reached a crisis," the *Placer County Republican* warned. The *Pacific Rural Press* blamed the "exorbitant" demands on a "Japanese labor union," not realizing that standardization had had the effect of institutionalizing Japanese power in the fruit belt.[105]

Standardization epitomized the dual image growers seemed to pro-

ject. On the one hand, it was representative of the marketing prowess
growers of deciduous fruit, raisins, and almonds had achieved through
organization. "United action," a prominent national magazine reported,
gave these orchardists and vineyardists the means to master "the business of growing Quality fruit."[106] On the other hand, standardization
contributed to a shift in the balance of power that clearly favored contractors and tenants. It may seem to us that growers were living a contradiction. How, for example, could Penryn orchardist David Griffith
publish a booster article in 1911 claiming "fruit growing is destined to be
the ultimate glory of California," while having leased 125 acres of bearing peach trees to Asian tenants since 1901? How could the *Placer
County Republican* promote the Penryn district as a "haven of prosperity,
fruit and wealth" when the Japanese strongly influenced not only the orchards but the whole community?[107] When pressed, growers argued that
the Japanese presence was only temporary—that the opening of the
Panama Canal in 1915 would bring an abundance of white workers to
their orchards and vineyards.[108] In truth, however, growers could not rec-
oncile their labor problems with the fame their marketing cooperatives
and horticultural accomplishments had brought them. "We are confronted by a condition, not a theory," they often replied in defense of
their contracting and leasing practices.[109] Thus far, however, that condition had not deflated the rhetoric of wonder that they and others so often employed to describe their enterprise.

There were indications, however, that "the labor question" had
pierced their reputation. Chester Rowell's ambivalence toward growers
is a case in point. There was no bigger booster of raisin growers than the
progressive editor of the *Fresno Morning Republican*. Rowell genuinely
believed that "the welfare of the whole community" depended on their
efforts. Since the Kearney days, he had devoted column after column to
promoting their interests. But Rowell, as an organizer of the Lincoln-
Roosevelt League and, later, as Governor Hiram Johnson's most trusted
advisor, was also the principal progressive spokesman for Japanese exclusion. "There is no right way to solve a race problem except to stop it
before it begins," he wrote in 1909.[110] When State Labor Commissioner
John D. MacKenzie issued his report the following year declaring the
necessity of Japanese labor to California specialty crop agriculture (using
Fresno raisins as a prominent example), Rowell wrote a blistering editorial reprinted in numerous newspapers throughout the state. "If the fruit
industry of California can not permanently exist except on a basis of

servile labor," he concluded, "then it is better that the fruit industry be destroyed than that imported servile labor be made a permanent part of our population and a permanent element in our industrial system."[111]

Growers across the state were stunned. Neither the report itself nor Rowell's condemnation provoked a public reaction from them. Much to the growers' chagrin, the report disclosed the unspoken conflict within their horticultural ideal. As Rowell put it, "According to [the] 'labor' commission, California can not raise both fruit and American civilization, and as the fruit is the more important, we must sacrifice the civilization." Orchardists and vineyardists did not publicly deny Rowell's logic, even though his references to "coolie servility" and "the Orientalization of California" clearly offended them.[112] They were not about to accept the editorial's full implications, however. Echoes of Raisin Day and "Get together" sentiment, after all, continued to reverberate throughout their communities and beyond.

State legislators, however, shared Rowell's disgust with MacKenzie's unwelcome conclusion. They unanimously disapproved the MacKenzie report and never released it in full to the press.[113] Once again, growers felt "misunderstood and misrepresented," this time by the state legislature. But growers had always been skeptical of state interference in their concerns—labor or otherwise. Throughout the late nineteenth and early twentieth centuries, state and federal government officials, in turn, seemed content for the most part to let growers resolve their problems on their own. A complex organization of state and county agencies had been built up for purposes of agricultural service, regulation, and education, but these were regarded as the growers' own agencies that they managed themselves.[114] The nature of the relationship between growers and the state would take a dramatic turn in August 1913, the result of an uprising on the Durst hop ranch to which few vineyardists or orchardists gave a second thought at the time.

4 "The Intrusion of a Third Party"

Growers and the Progressive State

IN THE HISTORY of California agriculture, no farm has gained more notoriety than the Durst hop ranch at Wheatland. The uprising there on August 3, 1913, seemed to display all the elements of "factory farming." Ralph Durst, the quintessential land baron, hired hundreds of migratory harvesters, paid them a piece rate, and provided wretched working and living conditions. Two members of the Industrial Workers of the World were imprisoned for inciting a brief rebellion that resulted in the death of two county officials and two pickers. Of most significance, perhaps, University of California labor economist Carleton Parker investigated the highly publicized incident and wrote a detailed report for the California Commission of Immigration and Housing and the U.S. Commission on Industrial Relations. The report's status as a state and federal government document seems to have legitimized beyond question Parker's assertion that Wheatland embodied "the state's great migratory labor problem."[1] "In the lurid illumination which the fires of the riot cast forth, the ugly facts about the condition of farm labor in California were, for the first time, thoroughly exposed," wrote journalist and social critic Carey McWilliams. The La Follette Committee, investigating farm labor disputes in California, agreed that Parker's report was "required reading" for an understanding of "the character of the working and living conditions among the migratory agricultural workers, the nature of the relationship between them and their employers, and the resulting widespread unrest which constantly threatened to flare into revolt."[2] A multitude of subsequent scholars have accepted Parker's portrayal of the conditions at Wheatland as representative or typical of California specialty crop agriculture.[3]

But Parker and those who have relied on his report have given us a simplistic and misleading portrayal not only of the Wheatland incident itself, but of farm labor relations throughout early-twentieth-century California. The diverse labor systems used by specialty crop growers in Newcastle, Davis, Fresno, and other regions defy the notion that Wheatland was a microcosm of California agriculture. Just four years earlier, U.S. Immigration Commission investigators had been struck by "the variations in the conditions in different localities," not by any particular "pattern."[4] While Wheatland might be seen as a precursor of the farm factories of the 1930s, the 1913 incident, when examined in the context of its own time, seems rather to be an exceptional case. Parker's report, from the standpoint of California agriculture of that era, is still historically significant, but for dramatically different reasons than those typically given by historians. Indeed, his report actually tells us more about grower-state relations than it does about grower-laborer relations. As growers would discover in time, the behavior of the Progressive state was often at odds with how they saw their world.

Prior to the 1910s, neither the state nor the federal government followed a coherent farm labor policy. State and national promoters of arid land reclamation felt that the Wright Act (1887), the Newlands Reclamation Act (1902), and other irrigation legislation offered a solution to the "labor problem" by encouraging the subdivision of baronial wheat and livestock estates into family farms. But farm labor reform was more a by-product of their crusade to restore republican values in the face of industrialization than the focus of the legislation itself.[5] State and federal investigatory commissions produced valuable socioeconomic data, but their recommendations for legislative solutions rarely overcame partisan politics—as demonstrated by the suppression of Labor Commissioner John D. MacKenzie's 1909 report on the Japanese in California agriculture, and by the Immigration Commission's final determination to limit the admission of Japanese and other "new" immigrants.[6] Growers themselves were not averse to using the government for their own purposes. Through the State Horticultural Commission in particular, they exchanged production and marketing information, organized their conventions, and secured tougher regulatory and quarantine legislation. For the most part, however, growers remained wary of the state. Their horticultural ideal demanded nothing less. "The man who owns an orchard [or] a vineyard is the most independent being on earth," they insisted.[7]

The expanding authority of the Progressive state during the Hiram Johnson administration (1911–17) provided both social reformers and growers with new institutional means of expression. That expression, however, was by no means uniform. While reformers seized their opportunities, growers shied away from confrontation. Horticulture had long been the very essence of prosperity in California. But changing political conditions demanded a new style of political behavior. Like all major economic interests, horticulture now needed to organize if its practitioners were to advance their cause. But only a few marketing leaders sensed this. The widespread reluctance to engage in interest-group politics compounded the disarray of grower-state relations. That disarray, in turn, produced an incoherent, disjointed, and often contradictory state farm labor policy that was expressed by a growing hodgepodge of agencies and legislation—most notably new government commissions, the 1913 Alien Land Law, the University of California College of Agriculture, state-sanctioned land colonization, and a short-lived Farmers' Protective League. These developments affected labor relations in Fresno, Newcastle, Davis, and other specialty crop communities only peripherally at first. But they would prove crucial in shaping farm labor policy during the "crisis" of World War I.

THE LABOR SYSTEM FASHIONED BY D. P. Durst in the late 1880s had continued to serve him well. His three sons, Ralph, Murray, and Jonathan, took over the management of the hop ranch in 1903 and became co-owners in 1910, upon their father's death. Wheatland's reputation for lucrative picking and the Durst brothers' clever advertising regularly attracted more than enough harvesters. Depending on the crop's anticipated yield, they accepted between 1,500 and 2,500 applications. The Dursts provided neither railroad fare nor board, but they allowed pickers to camp on their land without charge, rented tents for 75 cents a week, and permitted local merchants to furnish board at "reasonable" rates. Hundreds of "regulars"—men, women, and often entire families—returned year after year.[8]

Prices continued to fluctuate at the whim of the European market. In 1906, for example, low yields overseas prompted Pacific Coast prices to soar to 40 cents per pound. That year, the Dursts shipped 34 carloads and grossed over $200,000.[9] But in the following two years, the inevitable rush to plant more hops and a heavy German crop swamped the market, causing prices to fall to as low as four cents—well below the cost of production. Hop growing was "not a poor man's game," the *Sacramento Union* reaffirmed. Only those "who can afford to watch and wait for the market to go up" survived. The Dursts not only watched and waited, they planted an additional 140 acres. They knew that prices were bound to soar once again—which they did, to 26 cents in 1912. By then, their 642 acres constituted, by their own estimation, "the largest individual hop yard in the world."[10]

They were not without competition, however. Just a mile east up the Bear River, E. Clemons Horst operated 500 acres of his own. But Horst owned six additional hopyards in the Sacramento Valley, two more in Oregon, and another two in British Columbia. The E. Clemons Horst Company controlled 20 percent of the California crop and 10 percent of the entire Pacific Coast crop. While the Dursts grossed an average of $160,000 a year between 1903 and 1912, Horst's company made over $1 million.[11] At harvest time, however, the Dursts held a slight edge. While they often turned pickers away, recruiting a sufficient labor force became "a perpetual headache" for Horst's Wheatland supervisors. Like the Dursts, they advertised for whites only, paid a piece rate, and provided suitable accommodations. But Horst's hops tended to ripen 10 days to two weeks before the Dursts'. At mid-harvest, when the hops began to lose their moisture, Horst's best pickers invariably abandoned his yard for the Dursts'. Subsequent arrivals saw no need to walk the extra mile to Horst's fields when the Dursts' were only a few hundred yards from the Wheatland depot. As a result, Horst had to, as he put it, "fill up with Orientals" to finish each harvest, a "solution" that discouraged white pickers all the more.[12] The Horst ranch also had the misfortune of experiencing a series of fires in 1905, which cost the company over $75,000. Fires in the hot hop kilns were one of the risks of the trade, but Horst, in his frustration, blamed the most damaging one on careless or disgruntled workers dropping matches into their sacks.[13]

Horst could no longer tolerate this state of affairs. He set out to devise what other growers had only dreamed about for years—a hop-picking machine. Early in 1906, he hired a mechanical engineer from Germany and one of his own Wheatland supervisors to launch the experiment. Two years and over a quarter of a million dollars later, they succeeded. Their invention was the size of a small house (75 feet long, 12 feet wide, and 15 feet high) and consisted of a series of revolving iron drums, steel "fingers," and conveyor belts driven by a steam engine. Field workers now needed only to cut down the vines, haul them off, and feed them directly into the machine. One machine, it was promised, would do the work of 25 men and, by picking the hops at their ripest, ensure a higher quality. Horst was so eager to try it out that he spent several thousand dollars to send two men and the mechanical picker to the Southern Hemisphere—Tasmania—for the March 1908 hop harvest. Upon their return, an additional 56 machines were constructed under

E. Clemons Horst hop field, Wheatland. Courtesy of the California History Room, California State Library, Sacramento, California.

the supervision of several Stanford University mechanical engineering students in time for the August harvest. "They will revolutionize the industry," the *California Fruit Grower* trumpeted.[14]

But there were still several kinks to be worked out. The machines "wasted as much hops as they picked," allowed too many leaves to pass through, and constantly broke down. "The hop picking machine," the *Pacific Rural Press* editorialized, "has gone to meet the cotton picking machine." Horst was not about to give up, however, and he ordered his engineers to improve their design. As a precaution, he advertised for a full force of pickers for the 1909 harvest. Over 2,000 arrived at his Perkins ranch along the American River near Sacramento, only to be told that the picking would be done by the "perfected machines." Several hundred "Horst regulars" responded angrily. They seized the teams and wagons, threatened to sabotage the machines, and declared a "general strike" on all Horst's Sacramento Valley yards. With his harvests on the line, Horst agreed to use a combination of hand and machine picking—but for the last time.[15]

Indeed, the next year, Horst fully mechanized—and with remarkable results. The 1910 model picked 25 bales of hops in one day, while it took even the most experienced worker a week to pick just two bales. Moreover, the machine picked "cleaner," with less waste, and, as the *Pacific Rural Press* stated, "without the danger of labor troubles with which hand picking is so seriously menaced." To ensure the safety of his machines, Horst kept them "carefully guarded night and day." At his Wheatland ranch, one machine and a force of 100 men did the work of 2,000 harvesters, at one-third the cost and in half the time. "I have never seen any work done by hand that begins to equal it," observed an official sent by the U.S. Bureau of Plant Industry. By 1912, the E. Clemons Horst Company had planted another 1,000 acres in the Sacramento Valley, with visions of expanding worldwide. Horst himself liked nothing better than to drive parties of East Coast and British brewers through his fields to showcase his "modern system of hop-picking machinery."[16]

The Durst brothers, on the other hand, were in no mood to celebrate. Seemingly overnight, they found themselves competing against a machine whose efficiency they could not hope to match. Unwilling to invest the $40,000 it cost Horst to develop and construct just one machine, the Dursts approached the 1913 harvest in their usual manner, except to emphasize the need for "clean picking" in their advertisements. Toward the end of July, they realized that their hops were going to ripen a full two weeks early, the result of an unusually hot summer. On Tuesday, July 29, pickers began to arrive just as the Dursts were scrambling to prepare for them.[17] No one could have anticipated what would ensue over the course of the next few days.

"An unusually large number of people showed up," Ralph Durst recalled a few months later. Many might have come expecting to find work at Horst's. But the surplus of workers resulted primarily from the severe economic downturn just starting in California. Although historians have underestimated the impact of the 1913–15 depression, many

Hop-picking machines in operation on the E. Clemons Horst ranch, Wheatland, ca. 1913. Courtesy of the California History Room, California State Library, Sacramento, California.

contemporaries have left vivid descriptions of its devastation. In the
summer of 1913, an estimated 75,000 workers lost their jobs in San Francisco and Los Angeles alone. Soup kitchens, breadlines, and emergency
shelters became commonplace even in smaller Central Valley cities such
as Sacramento, Stockton, and Marysville. Many middle-class reformers,
in fact, for the first time acknowledged unemployment as a "problem,"
rather than the result of individual failure.[18] Durst's advertisement, consequently, drew the attention of "a different class of people"—construction workers, miners, lumbermen, and unskilled urban workers, who
normally "did not care to work in agriculture." No one knew just how
many had actually arrived at Wheatland by Sunday—estimates ranged
from two to three thousand—but the "considerable congestion" at the
ranch was apparent to all. The Dursts had not deliberately tried to attract an oversupply of harvest labor, but they made no effort to turn
pickers away—not even some 200 Japanese, as had been their custom.
Their best means of competing against the speed and quality of production of Horst's machine, they felt, was a larger workforce.[19]

    "Smelling a good fight," a number of IWW members (estimates
range from 30 to 100) were among the crowd. Most of them belonged to
Local 71 in Sacramento, and some were veterans of "free speech fights"
in Fresno, San Diego, or Spokane, Washington. Their presence was not

part of a drive to organize agricultural workers, for no such drive existed at that time. The IWW in California had instead focused on loggers, construction workers, and unskilled urban workers (recent immigrants from southeastern Europe, in particular)—whose presence at Wheatland that year presented a "unique opportunity," as one Wobbly recalled.[20] The IWW came with a specific purpose—to instigate a strike. By Friday, they had set up a headquarters (or "Bull pen," as they called it), organized "committees from each nationality" to facilitate communication, and begun agitating for a higher piece rate. Richard "Blackie" Ford, a boilermaker from Stockton, and Herman Suhr, a self-described "blanket-stiff" steeped in German socialism, appeared to be the leaders. They sent at least nine telegrams from Wheatland to IWW locals in Sacramento, Stockton, San Francisco, Oakland, Fresno, and San Pedro relaying their progress and requesting additional speakers and money.[21] The surplus of pickers and the unexpectedly early harvest gave the Wobblies more fuel for the fire. The Dursts, by their own admission, were caught unprepared. To the dismay of their regulars in particular, their camp lacked sufficient sanitation facilities, water, food concessions, and even space for camping. Temperatures exceeding 100 degrees each day compounded the pickers' discomfort. By Saturday night a mass protest seemed imminent. "Twenty-five hundred hop pickers to strike at Durst ranch," Ford wired the *San Francisco Bulletin*. "Strike conducted by IWW. Send reporter to take news."[22]

The *Bulletin* reporter found news, but of a strike derailed. On Sunday morning at about ten o'clock, a committee of several dozen pickers, led by Ford, presented Ralph Durst with a detailed list of demands. Though taken aback by the workers' assertiveness, Durst agreed to build more toilets, provide more garbage cans, send additional water trucks into the fields, and even instruct his foremen to enforce "clean picking" less stringently. He in fact acceded to every demand but one, a wage increase to $1.25 per 100 pounds picked. "Dollar hops" had prevailed throughout California for 30 years, he insisted, and no one had complained about the Dursts' 10-cent bonus system since its implementation in 1902. The committee seemed satisfied. But Durst, fearing Ford's apparent sway among the pickers, demanded that he take the first train out of Wheatland. Ford's allies rallied to his defense, and a brief outburst of shouting and pushing ensued. The committee left all the more determined to go through with the strike, and Durst left all the more determined to have Ford arrested. Later that afternoon, in the company of the district attorney and two sheriff's deputies, Durst came looking for the Wobbly leader. A gathering of about 300 angry pickers blocked their automobile just as it reached the camp's dance platform. One deputy, attempting to lend emphasis to an order to disperse, fired a shot into the air. Rather than sobering the crowd, the shot set off a brief but furious battle. Approximately 20 shots were fired, and four men lay slain: the district attorney, a deputy sheriff, and two pickers. Everyone fled the area. By the time six companies of National Guardsmen dispatched by Governor Hiram Johnson arrived the next morning, the Durst ranch was nearly vacant — except for the *Bulletin* reporter, now joined by dozens of other newsmen.[23]

Their reports set in motion a sensationalization of the incident that has lasted to this day. "Militia Is Mobilized to Quell IWW Riot," read the *Los Angeles Times* headline. "Officers Slain in Fierce Riot at Wheatland," blared the *San Francisco Chronicle.*[24] It was the deaths of the county officials and the IWW's presence that made Wheatland a cause célèbre. Otherwise, the incident would have been no more newsworthy than the first Wheatland strike in 1902 or the 1909 Horst strike. Over the next several months, and especially during the trial of Ford and Suhr the following January, a series of "generally uncontested facts" emerged concerning that fateful Sunday, "facts" that have shaped accounts ever since. Not taken into consideration, however, were the Dursts' long-established labor system, Horst's hop-picking machine, the early harvest, and the depression — which strongly suggest that something other than "typical working and living conditions" prevailed in 1913.[25] The poor conditions, it should be noted, did not deter a sufficient number of pickers from returning and finishing the harvest by August 20 — "the strongest evidence," the Dursts later asserted, "of the underlying and mutual confidence between our people and ourselves."[26] The conditions on the Durst ranch have reached such legendary proportions that the IWW's intentions have been all but forgotten. "Wheatland was not a strike," Carey McWilliams asserted, "but a spontaneous revolt" against "revolting conditions." Few have questioned his assessment. "Three days was not much time to agitate effectively among 2800 workers of diverse nationalities, religions, and languages," another historian has argued. But to ascribe the events of August 3 solely to "the exceedingly irritating and intolerable conditions" disregards the incident's considerable complexity.[27]

This fixation on what one scholar has termed Wheatland's "repressive landscape" stems from three sources, two of which can be traced rather easily.[28] Austin Lewis, the prominent Bay Area Socialist attorney who represented Ford and Suhr, did everything he could to distance his clients from the IWW. At every opportunity during the trial, he launched into detailed descriptions of the "unspeakably vile and insufferable conditions," vividly depicting such scenes as women waiting in line for "fly-infested" toilets. The Wheatland riot was "a spontaneous reaction" to cruel and dehumanizing camp and field conditions, he told the jury, not a product of Ford's and Suhr's agitation.[29] American Federation of Labor leaders shared Lewis's assessment, albeit with different motives. The largest donations to Ford's and Suhr's defense fund came not from the Wobblies, but from unions affiliated with the California State Federation of Labor. This was not, however, an expression of sympathy toward the IWW. The AFL, in fact, all but disregarded their rival's role at Wheatland. When none other than AFL president Samuel Gompers editorialized on "the horrors that made life in one California hop-pickers' camp a veritable hell," he was participating in a campaign to enhance the AFL's tarnished image by stealing the Wobblies' thunder.[30]

The third and by far most influential source is Carleton Parker's report for the California Commission of Immigration and Housing (CCIH) and the U.S. Commission on Industrial Relations (USCIR). Parker, the CCIH's executive secretary, concluded that the Dursts had unconscionably evaded "the question of social responsibility." He described both their bonus system and their "unusual standard of cleanliness" for picking as newly implemented means of "industrial" exploitation. He decried "the absolute want of garbage disposal." The water supply not only was inadequate, but "had an alkali taste" as well. The food and lemonade that was sold there made many pickers ill. The "moral conditions" of the camp were "notoriously lax." The "aliens" in particular "had, as a rule, unclean personal and camp habits, exposed themselves at the pumps in washing, and were indecently careless in the presence of women and children." The toilets were "the most vicious abuse" of all, Parker emphasized.

> They were used indiscriminately by Hindus, Japanese, negroes, whites, women and children. By the end of the second day the seats, scantlings and floors were covered by a semi-liquid mass of filth. The stench, under the great heat, became so nauseating that many instances of vomiting have been recorded. Lines of 15 to 20 women and children frequently formed awaiting

their turns. . . . I have heard of instances of women humiliating themselves
before passing men. Children were seen about the camp in unspeakably
filthy condition, since it was not possible for them to use any toilet without
befouling themselves. . . . Many of the campers soon refused to use the toilets and began using the fields in the near neighborhood of the tents.[31]

Parker's attention to such conditions reflected his own moral and
academic concerns. An assistant professor of economics at Berkeley,
trained at Harvard and the University of Heidelberg, Parker was a
prototype of the modern social engineer, who, in the words of one historian, "brought scientific wisdom down from the ivory tower and set it
to work for the man in the street." Like other youthfully confident and
enthusiastic "social diagnosticians" of the Progressive era, Parker believed that humans were creatures of their environment. The problems
confronting industrial society, therefore, could be remedied by creating a
more harmonious social and physical setting in which workers would
not have to assert their dignity through strikes, violence, or other "radical means." The Dursts and other employers, he concluded, "must learn
that unbearable aggravating living conditions inoculate the minds of the
otherwise peaceful workers with the germs of bitterness and violence."[32]

But there was more to Parker's report than philosophy. Institutional
and political imperatives of the Progressive state shaped the CCIH's
Wheatland investigation in decisive ways. In California, political reformers greatly expanded the state government's administrative infra-
structure during Hiram Johnson's tenure as governor by creating or re-
organizing a number of state commissions. Established in September
1913, the CCIH, by the design of its founder and president, Simon Lubin, investigated immigration problems that were anticipated with the
opening of the Panama Canal in 1915.[33] But the CCIH abruptly
switched its focus to migrant laborers already in the state in the wake of
the Wheatland incident. Lubin's commission, which had received only
half of the $50,000 appropriation he had originally recommended, com-
peted fiercely with other state agencies for a larger slice of the state's ex-
penditures—in particular, the Industrial Welfare Commission, the Industrial Accident Commission, the Bureau of Labor Statistics, and the
Board of Health. The latter, Lubin quipped, did little other than "opening and closing bottles of mustard and sweet pickles." Lubin knew that
state legislators were more likely to fund agencies that had public support, so he jumped at the opportunity that USCIR representative Har-

ris Weinstock (who happened to be his uncle) offered him on January 10, 1914, to co-investigate the Wheatland incident, with Parker in charge. Indeed, throughout his 10-year reign as CCIH president, Lubin's paramount concern was, in his words, "to put our Commission on the map."[34]

Parker's first draft attempted to do just that. Several popular periodicals reprinted his exposé, which earned praise for the CCIH from sympathetic middle-class readers throughout the country.[35] Moreover, Parker's line of reasoning opened the door for an expanded role for the CCIH. The most serious consequence of the Dursts' negligence, Parker intimated, was a stronger IWW. "We can't agitate in the country unless things are rotten enough to bring the crowd along," he quoted one Wobbly as saying. For Parker, the "cure" was self-explanatory: "it is to clean up the housing and wage problem of the seasonal worker," a task requiring "the intrusion of a third party." The CCIH, he wrote to Governor Johnson, was just the agency "to insure a decent standard of comfort . . . and take away the argument and talking weapon of the agitator."[36]

But Parker's references to the IWW touched a deep nerve in Johnson. "Nothing that could be done by us will either prevent [IWW] agitation or meet with the approval of their sympathizers," the governor responded.[37] His previous experience with the Wobblies in San Diego had been a political disaster. When a group of vigilantes and local police resorted to violence to prevent several hundred Wobblies from protesting an anti–free speech ordinance in 1912, Johnson sent Harris Weinstock to San Diego to investigate the controversy. Johnson's actions, by his own admission, "mortally offended the so-called good citizenship" of southern California. Because none of the vigilantes were prosecuted, those favoring the free-speech fighters "took offense" with him as well. "I did what was perfectly obvious to me," he confided to *San Francisco Bulletin* editor Fremont Older, "but won no advocates and created many enemies." Johnson "preserved for all time the record of the situation in San Diego" and vowed never to become entangled in an IWW affair again.[38] Indeed, his quick response to the Wheatland incident—to send out troops and ask questions later—revealed his desire to thwart what he regarded as a potential political crisis.

Thrusting the issue of the IWW back to the forefront turned into a public relations blunder as well. Parker repeatedly ignored Lubin's pleas to "dress up" the CCIH's findings. The "orgies of publicity" Lubin desired sensationalized the investigation in a manner Parker found both distasteful and "unscientific." To Lubin's dismay, Parker displayed a penchant for referring to himself before the press as a USCIR, rather than a CCIH, agent. "This playing second fiddle to the Federal Commission," Lubin scolded him, "doesn't make me mighty happy."[39] Parker's Wheatland report made Lubin even less happy. In early February, without Lubin's permission, he sent a preliminary copy to Frank P. Walsh, the USCIR chairman. Walsh released the report to the press on February 8 —before Lubin or the other commissioners had even read it.[40] Both Lubin and Johnson were furious. "Old Guard" Republican newspapers had a field day with Parker's implicit defense of the IWW. The progressives "deliberately attempted to create sympathy for riotous murderers," editorialized the *San Francisco Chronicle*. "It [would be] wise for your whole Commission to understand exactly what was contemplated in [Parker's] investigations," Johnson wired Lubin in response. Though Lubin took full responsibility for the unauthorized publication of the report, he reprimanded Parker for "upsetting our programs" with his "radical and obstructionist resolutions."[41]

Lubin knew that his hopes for the commission would be in jeopardy should the IWW become the overriding issue of the Wheatland investigation. On February 12, he received help from an unexpected source, E. Clemons Horst. A newspaper article expressing the CCIH's reform plans had caught Horst's eye. "We are in hearty accord with any movement to cure the evils of harvest labor camps," he wrote Lubin. He then requested immediate information "so that we may make the necessary arrangements on all of our ranches to fully comply with the Commission's requirements."[42] Horst's support was just what the CCIH needed to stem the tide of bad publicity, Lubin believed. "Regardless of the sincerity of the writer or the motive behind his letter," he wrote to *Fresno Morning Republican* editor Chester Rowell, "I think that this experience alone . . . gives us the . . . power to clean up the disreputable housing situation in this State." He now urged Rowell and other progressive editors to "exploit" Parker's report "as another feather in the cap of the administration."[43] The *California Outlook* published it in full, and added, "Great ranch owners have asked the Commission to lay down standards of sanitation and housing to which they may comply." Lubin's opportunism apparently reassured Johnson. In late February, Parker had a "grand talk" with the governor. "Nothing was even the matter," Parker reassured Lubin. "[Johnson] endorsed the report and its publicity. We are advised to get out into the state and get publicity for our propaganda."[44]

That spring, the CCIH embarked on a campaign "to clean up the labor camps." The commission was constrained, however, by its limited administrative capacity. Lubin could hire only five to seven "sanitary engineers" to inspect over 900 camps throughout the state. Farm labor camps were not easily accessible and often could be reached only on horseback. Inspectors admitted to being unable to locate many of them, and instead focused most of their attention on construction, lumber, mining, and railroad camps. Moreover, many farmers—Newcastle orchardists, Fresno vineyardists, and Davis almond growers, for example—did not maintain camps as such and thus did not fall under the CCIH's jurisdiction.[45] Although Parker expressed concern for "fruit farm labor groups," the CCIH developed its reform strategy almost exclusively around hops. Under Parker's direction, in fact, the commission transformed the Durst ranch into a "model camp," complete with new outhouses, showers, fly-screened dining tents, sleeping quarters, and garbage incinerators—all described in minute detail in a 54-page publication, *Advisory Pamphlet on Camp Sanitation.*[46] It was as though the sheer volume of facts, figures, photographs, and technical drawings were to compensate for the CCIH's bureaucratic deficiencies.

Publicity continued to be Lubin's chief concern. He sent copies of the *Advisory Pamphlet* to 225 California newspapers, many of which reprinted photographs of latrines, garbage-disposal sites, and other normally unnewsworthy items.[47] He also had Parker rewrite and recirculate his Wheatland report. The second draft opened with several new paragraphs declaring "a new and momentous labor epoch," promising a "new and vigorous analysis," and outlining a "careful method of investigation." Parker also described the "gruesome" conditions on the Durst ranch in even greater detail.[48] Lubin's approach paid large dividends. By July, Governor Johnson, while campaigning for reelection in San Francisco, proclaimed that the CCIH had created "a revolution in the housing conditions of the migratory and seasonal worker." Not incidentally, the following year, the legislature expanded the commission's enforcement powers and increased its appropriation by 20 percent.[49]

On only one occasion did Lubin's efforts backfire. On June 1, 1914, he spoke before the forty-fourth fruit growers' convention at Davis on the state's future labor supply and population. He stressed the necessity of "good working conditions" for "efficient labor," insisted that immigrants arriving via the Panama Canal "will not go out to the farms unless conditions . . . are made attractive," and highlighted his talk with before and after slides of the Durst model camp. In his concluding remarks, he strongly intimated that the farm labor market would remain "thoroughly disorganized" without the CCIH's assistance.[50] Many in the audience found the presentation insulting. The Dursts' problems, fruit growers felt, did not concern them. Indeed, the Wheatland incident had generated very little response from horticulturists throughout the state. Their particular labor systems—though not "modern," in Lubin's view—provided stability and regularity that discouraged IWW organizers and, in their minds, negated any need for state intervention.[51] Fruit growers' preference for Asian workers, though unspoken, distanced them from the CCIH even more. With its focus on hops and white itinerant workers, the commission all but ignored California's most abundant source of agricultural labor.[52]

Parker, who by his own admission lacked "politic or diplomatic skill," never did master the subtleties of public relations. He continued to divert attention to the USCIR (which held hearings in San Francisco in August) and to ignore the recommendations of several CCIH commissioners. On September 30, Lubin asked for his resignation.[53] Before leaving, however, Parker wrote yet a third draft of his Wheatland report —an abridged and more restrained version of the second—at Johnson's request.[54] The fact that scholars have relied primarily on this draft is ironic for more than Parker's impending downfall. Wheatland's notoriety for exposing "the pathology of labor relations in industrialized agriculture,"[55] it turns out, was more a reflection of what Lubin *hoped* would result from the CCIH's investigation than of the incident's actual, and considerably less dramatic, impact.

Eventually, Wheatland would undermine even Lubin's enthusiasm. The IWW waged a fierce campaign to free Ford and Suhr, preaching (though rarely practicing) "arson, sabotage, and assassination," as the governor put it.[56] At first, this provided the CCIH with a chance to promote itself even more. Lubin, for example, claimed there was "no doubt that the model camp was a factor in frustrating" the Wobblies' boycott of the Wheatland hop harvest in August 1914.[57] But as the IWW escalated its "direct action" in 1915 and 1916, Johnson became convinced that state suppression was the only answer. He turned to the CCIH, the only state agency with IWW expertise, for assistance. In response, the commission changed its focus from reform to repression. Investigators— many of them Parker's former students from Berkeley—were sent to "hobo" among the Wobblies with the intent of obstructing their activities. When the IWW "reign of terror" extended into 1917, the CCIH joined forces with the U.S. Department of Justice in a massive crackdown.[58] Federal suppression of the IWW, however, diminished the CCIH's institutional vitality. The Wobblies had helped put Lubin's commission "on the map," but had also steered it far away from its original mission. With the IWW no longer a threat, the CCIH became largely irrelevant. Lubin finally resigned in 1923, unable to obtain even a modest appropriation from the State Board of Control.[59]

The CCIH's tortuous tenure reflects the disorder of grower-state relations in Progressive-era California. Even in the commission's heyday, its farm labor policy was out of sync with farm labor relations in specialty crop regions throughout the state. This disjuncture manifested itself in other reaches of grower-state relations as well. In the give-and-take of state intervention and grower response, growers' sense of isolation—of being "misunderstood and misrepresented"—became ever more pervasive. In the process, their credibility as cultural guardians diminished all the more.

Finessing the issue of Asian labor became increasingly difficult for growers. Just when the commotion over the MacKenzie report seemed to have subsided, the "Japanese question" burst onto the political scene once again in 1913. The same legislature that created the CCIH to assimilate European immigrants focused most of its energies on a discriminatory bill aimed at Japanese farmers and farm laborers—the so-called Alien Land Law.[60] Since 1909, Democrats, Republicans, Progressives, and even Socialists had proposed numerous bills to restrict Japanese landownership. The not-so-hidden objective was exclusion— "to limit their presence by curtailing the privileges which they may enjoy here," in the words of State Attorney General Ulysses S. Webb. The authors of these bills were trying to get around federal intervention, but Presidents Theodore Roosevelt and William Howard Taft, fearful of diplomatic repercussions, effectively blocked every one of their efforts. When Woodrow Wilson, an avid exclusionist, took office in 1913, optimism abounded among "anti-Asiatics." As many as a dozen alien land bills were introduced when the legislature convened in Sacramento that March. At stake, declared State Senator Ernest S. Birdsall, was "the permanent welfare of the citizens of the great State of California."[61]

Birdsall was the author of what proved to be the decisive measure. He was also one of the Newcastle district's preeminent horticulturists. The 60 acres of peach, plum, and cherry trees he owned just outside of

Auburn had been planted by his father in the 1870s. The name Fred Birdsall, locals were fond of saying, "will ever be connected with the history of irrigation in Placer County." It was the elder Birdsall who, in the early 1880s, upgraded and enlarged the Bear River mining ditch to furnish water to the entire fruit belt. His son attended the University of California and tried his luck in the San Francisco business world in the late 1890s. But in 1900, he returned to Auburn to take over his father's ranch. He entered state politics in 1907, but divided his time evenly between the capital and his orchards. Like most Placer County horticulturists by 1913, Birdsall leased to a Japanese family. The region's development, he told an investigator in 1916, "would not have been possible otherwise."[62]

It seems odd, therefore, that Birdsall would introduce such blatantly anti-Japanese legislation. His strongest supporters in the Senate and Assembly were also from rural districts where Japanese were conspicuous. Numerous growers from nearby Newcastle, Florin, and the Sacramento Delta testified in behalf of the Birdsall Bill. Some no doubt feared Japanese competition. "The real prejudice against the Japanese," wrote Carey McWilliams, "dates from the time when they began to be small owners, rather than farm laborers." But as numerous contemporaries pointed out, Japanese landownership was not extensive in 1913. According to county assessors, the Japanese owned just 331 farms in California, totaling 12,726 acres. A considerable number of the purchases were made that year, prompted by the threat of the act itself.[63] Growers lobbied for Birdsall's bill because it expressly authorized Japanese tenancy. Indeed, they were more concerned with preserving their lease arrangements than with restricting ownership.

It was the issue of leasing, in fact, on which the debate in the legislature turned. Two proposals moved to the forefront early on. The first not only prohibited Japanese landownership, it also declared null and void all "contracts, agreements, and leases" made with Asian immigrants. The other simply moved to postpone the action until after 1915, when the Panama-Pacific Exposition was to be held in San Francisco. Speeches reminding legislators of their obligation to avoid a diplomatic crisis with Japan were given considerable emphasis by a weeklong visit from Wilson's secretary of state, William Jennings Bryan. Seeking compromise, legislators replaced all references to the Japanese with the euphemism "aliens ineligible to citizenship." But the bill still did not have enough votes. Birdsall then suggested a clause permitting leasing for periods not exceeding three years. Legislators from rural districts in particular rallied around this amendment. It allowed them to join the chorus of anti-Japanese agitation without depriving constituents of their tenants. Others felt compelled to accept the amendment to secure any land legislation at all. It passed by votes of 35 to 2 in the Senate and 72 to 3 in the Assembly.[64]

Most Californians believed, with Governor Johnson, that the Alien Land Law had "laid [to rest] the ghost of the Japanese question."[65] The campaign had served as a general expression of "anti-Asiatic" feelings. As a result, however, growers had left the distinct impression that they were anti-Japanese as well. The governor himself misread their intentions. "These farmers," he wrote to Theodore Roosevelt in an account of the bill's enactment, "insisted that an alien land bill was absolutely essential for their protection, and necessary for the future welfare of California."[66] What the growers were expressing was not anti-Japanese sentiment so much as relief. For Newcastle growers, for example, the bill kept both their labor system and their horticultural ideal intact. Early that summer, they held a "mass meeting" to assure their tenants that the bill would not affect them, and to reassure themselves of their region's "deciduous preeminence." The three-year lease limitation posed a potential threat, for it was too short to bring most fruit trees to bearing. In some districts, the Japanese circumvented the law by leasing land in the name of their children or in partnership with whites. But in Newcastle, landlords and tenants simply ignored the law without resorting to evasive means. Leases as long as 10 years were not uncommon, though they were rarely recorded at the courthouse. County officials simply looked the other way. "When a community is predominantly favorable to this type of labor," a contemporary observed, "infringements usually pass unnoticed."[67] Growers who relied on Japanese labor hoped that other Californians would look the other way as well.

But this was not the vision of rural community life that in recent years had captured the imagination of reformers in California and across the country. Theodore Roosevelt's famed Country Life Commission had kindled a national movement to revitalize rural institutions as a means of slowing the cityward population drift. This could only be accomplished, disciple Thomas F. Hunt told California fruit growers in 1912, by restoring "proper economic, social, moral, and spiritual ideals." Hunt was a former colleague of the commission's chairman, Liberty Hyde Bailey, dean of the College of Agriculture at Cornell University. A few weeks earlier, Hunt himself had been appointed dean of the College of Agriculture at the University of California. His "immediate duty," as he saw it, was, "through research and education, to make the agriculture of California more prosperous." Though Hunt never mentioned the Japanese, his intentions were clear. The time had come, he announced, to reaffirm "the doctrine of the Anglo-Saxon race." He called for growers to "humanize their labor supply" by renouncing their current "offscourings" in favor of their own "intelligent, thrifty, moral countrymen."[68]

The social and economic welfare of rural California, Hunt believed, demanded a greater commitment from the state — the University of California in particular. As the state's land grant institution of higher education, the University of California had been disseminating agricultural research through Experiment Station bulletins, Farmers' Institutes, correspondence courses, and demonstration trains for half a century.[69] The return on this substantial investment, however, had been disappointing. Growers preferred to advance their agricultural knowledge through their own institutions. Even when they accepted university assistance, they did so with ambivalence. Newcastle growers, for example, expressed their appreciation for the "good professors" who eradicated the peach worm (1902), pear blight (1906), and malaria (1910) from their district by continually scoffing at any "theory or doctrine promulgated from a scholastic source."[70] Hunt, however, convinced Governor Johnson of the "vital importance of promoting agricultural welfare" and secured a substantial appropriation from the state legislature. The new Agricultural Building at Berkeley that he dedicated in the fall of 1912 stood as a symbol of his resolve.[71]

The federal government provided an additional boost. Influenced by the groundswell of support for rural reform, Congress passed the Smith-Lever Act in May 1914. While previous agricultural-education efforts had been essentially passive, the Smith-Lever Act emphasized "in-the-field practical learning" to bring the resources of land grant colleges directly to the farm. The county agents, or farm advisors, were the key figures. Their tasks were to identify farmers willing to cooperate, demonstrate new skills or innovations, and then retreat into the background to allow neighbors to take part on their own. Gradually, legislators presumed, community members would come to trust their agent and then volunteer their assistance by forming a "farm bureau"—what one agent described as "a sort of giant experiment station with several hundred community observers who hold monthly caucuses to compare results."

Hunt was so anxious to get started that he did not wait for the passage of the national act. On July 1, 1913, he hired Cornell graduate Bertram H. Crocheron to organize California's "farm advisor movement." Within three years, 24 counties, with matching funds from the U.S. Department of Agriculture and the state legislature, had established farm bureaus. But it was Crocheron and Hunt who managed the program's day-to-day affairs from their Berkeley offices.[72]

Initially, they achieved considerable success. Yolo County's experience was typical. Businessmen, bankers, politicians, and farm leaders were eager to participate. They supported a resolution to allocate $2,000 a year for three years to pay the farm advisor's expenses—office space, supplies, a Model T Ford, and enough gasoline to get him around the county. On March 14, 1914, in response to Crocheron's challenge to "promote their own advancement," 300 "leading residents" gathered at the town of Yolo for the county's first Farm Bureau Picnic. George W. Pierce Jr. was chosen chairman of the day, and several other Davis almond growers also attended. Crocheron and Hunt spoke with eloquence on the day's topic, "Knowledge + Economy = Efficiency." A local brass band, the warm spring sun, and the opportunity to "leave the farm for a little while" gave the festivities "a holiday aura," a University Farm student observed. Over the next three years, Yolo County farm families met monthly at different locations to attend lectures and demonstrations on such topics as weed control, home canning, and "good roads"; to form 4-H clubs; and, of equal importance, to socialize.[73] Orchardists and vineyardists from Placer, Fresno, and other counties throughout the state participated in similar activities early on. They were flattered by the fact that Hunt and Crocheron believed that California's prosperity depended on their efforts. "At the time the plan of farm advice was adopted," one recalled, "I thought it was a good thing."[74]

It was not long, however, before the novelty of the meetings began to wear off. Growers resented the implication that they did not know how to farm. Much of the literature on "orchard management" distributed by farm advisors offered very little that they themselves had not mastered years earlier. Pamphlets often employed a condescending tone as well. "You must study this organization of picking to get sound fruit with highest economy," one instructed in typical fashion. The fact that such literature generally assumed the presence of white, compliant harvest workers drew the ire of those who had struggled for years with Asian contractors and tenants.[75] Moreover, growers suspected that the university wanted them to produce more to drive down prices. Cooperative leaders in particular believed that if anything, growers were too efficient at what they did. Farm advisors emphasized "production—production —production," a prominent pear grower recalled, but paid no attention to "the dollars and cents" of marketing. Once discredited, even those farm advisors with relevant information found it difficult to garner fruit growers' support. Not surprisingly, grain growers, livestock ranchers, and dairy farmers found the farm bureaus more to their liking.[76]

But Hunt was hardly discouraged by fruit growers' lack of interest. The influx of immigrants expected with the opening of the Panama Canal, he believed, offered the College of Agriculture an even better opportunity to reach its full potential. The timing seemed perfect. Just as Japanese exclusion appeared imminent, tens of thousands of European immigrants were expected to pour through the Golden Gate. Hunt envisioned them not as laborers, but as 10- and 20-acre farmers living in small, thriving agricultural communities up and down the Central Valley. Land colonization, while ambitious, could succeed if carried out through the university's rational, scientific means, Hunt believed.[77] The problem, as he saw it, was competition with several private "back to the land" organizations and other state agencies with the same vision. The Bureau of Labor Statistics, the Industrial Welfare Commission, and the CCIH all proposed land-settlement programs of their own. None matched the boldness of Hunt's, however. If agriculture was the key to assimilation, he reasoned, then immigrants should be received not in San Francisco, but at the University Farm in Davis.[78]

In the end, the key impetus for land colonization came not from the College of Agriculture or other state agencies, but from Hiram Johnson's struggle with the unemployment problem. The Wheatland incident had raised his awareness of the depression's disruptive potential, but it was a personal experience that spurred him to action. On New Year's Day, 1914, upwards of 5,000 men and women marched to the governor's home on Telegraph Hill in San Francisco, where they stayed for two hours demanding to know "what the state was going to do about giving them work." Visibly shaken, Johnson expressed sorrow for their plight but "regretted he could do nothing for them." Front-page photographs of the scene the next morning embarrassed him all the more.[79] Over the next three months, he asked dozens of reformers "to write their views or to confer with the particular commissions upon the subject."[80]

In April, Hunt played his trump card. In the company of university president David P. Barrows, he introduced Elwood Mead, a recent addition to the Berkeley faculty, to the governor. A recognized authority in irrigation engineering, Mead had just returned from Victoria, Australia, where he had served as chairman of the State Rivers and Water Supply Commission since 1907. While supervising the reclamation and settlement of 32 irrigation projects, Mead became enamored with planned colonization. In Victoria, the state purchased the land, constructed irrigation systems, planted crops, built roads, and laid out towns, all before settlers were invited to the project. Mead's experience convinced him that the U.S. government had neglected its social responsibilities. American rural life, he believed, could be rejuvenated through state planning — if managed by the country's best minds. The "Australia method," Mead stressed to Johnson, could also put California's unemployed back to work.[81] Johnson was intrigued by the idea of "state farms," but insisted on sounding out public opinion before committing himself to a course of action. On May 8, Mead outlined his colonization plan to the Commonwealth Club of California, the state's most prestigious reform organization, which in turn recommended that the state undertake its own study. The legislature, as if by reflex, created yet another commission, and appointed Mead its chair. For Hunt, this new State Commission on Land Colonization and Rural Credits marked a clear victory. Its success, as Johnson put it, depended on "the technical education, the virility, and the high character of University men."[82]

Several prominent progressives, including Chester Rowell and Harris Weinstock, served on the commission, but the College of Agriculture largely conducted its affairs. Under Mead's direction, the commission's task, ostensibly, was to determine whether rural conditions necessitated a constitutional amendment that would allow the state to offer low-interest, long-term loans to farmers ("rural credit," as it became known). But Mead left nothing to chance. In September and October of 1915, the commission held public hearings in Sacramento, Willows, Stockton, San Francisco, Fresno, Los Angeles, and El Centro. The locations themselves, as well as those who testified, were chosen with a specific purpose — to paint a bleak picture of rural California. Scores of bankers, real estate brokers, public officials, merchants, newspaper editors, and struggling landowners took the opportunity to air pent-up grievances. Private land companies tended to fail, the overwhelming majority stated, because they speculated, mismanaged irrigation projects, offered limited credit, provided no agricultural guidance, and in general attracted a "poor quality of settler." Mead also hired dozens of graduate students, faculty members, and farm advisors as "special investigators" to survey an additional 32 "typical sections" throughout California. Hundreds of settlers answered questionnaires about the economic and social conditions of their farms and communities. The commission's plan promised to pay political dividends, Rowell assured Johnson, for at the very least, it "would appeal to the popular imagination."[83]

The overall response to the public hearings confirmed Rowell's assessment, but a small, vocal opposition made itself heard. Some of the more conservative Commonwealth Club members defended the successful private land companies that the commission had somehow missed, and stressed the inherent inefficiency of government.[84] The loudest and most sustained protests came from prominent fruit growers. Charles Teague, the state's leading lemon producer, declared that banks already gave growers too much credit, which only added to chronic overproduction and marketing problems. Moreover, the commission's very existence clearly disturbed Teague. Settlement should be left to private means, not to state bureaucrats, he insisted. For proof, he stated matter-of-factly, one needed to look no further than raisin growers' overwhelming success in Fresno. "Where Mr. Mead can find a man who has lost a dollar through his purchase there," Teague promised, "I will give Mr. Mead a hundred dollars—provided that he will give me ten dollars where I find him a success."[85] John P. Irish called the plan "bottle feeding the producer" and asked Weinstock, "Would you want the state as an overlord in your business?"[86] And editor Howard C. Rowley assailed the commission on a weekly basis in his column in *California Fruit News*. Its objectives, he warned, were "definitely paternal and practically socialistic," and as such could only result in a shirking of hard work, individual responsibility, and community spirit—that is, everything that horticulturists valued.[87]

Weinstock fiercely defended the commission, but he sympathized with growers' marketing concerns. He had long maintained that "the prosperity of the State depends upon the prosperity of the fruit industry."[88] Since the 1880s, he had frequently participated in fruit grower conventions, and he had helped organize many of the state's first cooperatives. The hearings convinced him that state-assisted settlement required state-assisted marketing. Only months earlier, Johnson had appointed Weinstock State Market Director, an office created to establish free public markets in order to lower prices on fish, dairy, and farm products for urban consumers. But when it became clear to Weinstock that the state should take a more active role in marketing, he recast the market director's duties. With the help of attorney Aaron Sapiro, he set out to organize the state's producers. And with Johnson's backing, he managed to "legalize his course of action" within the year. Nonetheless, his about-face raised a storm of protest from a number of retail and consumer groups. And once again, bitter criticisms of "the state butting in" arose from leading growers. On this point, Weinstock sided with Mead. "Paternalism which creates opportunity for industry and thrift, awakens hope, arouses ambition, and strengthens belief in the brotherhood of man," they agreed, "is altogether good in its influence on character and on the prosperity of the State."[89]

Mead and Weinstock found fewer reasons to celebrate the findings of the commission's "special investigators." Questionnaires, statements, and summary reports did not always confirm their expectations. This posed quite a dilemma for students such as T. G. Chamberlain, whose assignment was the Newcastle district. Mead's young protégé interviewed 77 fruit belt landowners, including every resident within two miles of the Penryn depot, and pieced together a remarkable understanding of the region's complex production, labor, and marketing systems. He found little sentiment for reform, however. To his surprise, many of those questioned—including George D. Kellogg, Harry Butler, Senator Birdsall, and W. R. Fountain—praised their Japanese tenants for their responsibility, sobriety, cleanliness, and, most of all, "horticultural aptitude." "Taken as a whole," he wrote to his immediate supervisor, "fruit ranch owners are making money and lots of it, just as are the Japanese." In his official report, however, Chamberlain took pains to satisfy his mentor. The final section, entitled "Conditions from a Social Standpoint," argued that Penryn had been "a better town" prior to Japanese tenancy. What he deemed "conclusive proof of the need for a sound policy of land settlement" actually stemmed from a few selected statements by landowners. This was the only section, however, from which Mead quoted in commission publications.[90]

Despite the opposition and strained evidence, Mead prevailed. In January 1917, the legislature enacted a bill prepared by the Commonwealth Club making "the state itself an active participant . . . in stimulating the right kind of settlement of our large agricultural areas."[91] The final hurdle involved convincing Johnson of the bill's utility for "the underdog." But Rowell assured him that by "diverting more capable men" from cities to the countryside, land colonization would "automatically solve the problem of the unemployed."[92] The bill included almost all of Mead's treasured ideas, and in fact followed very closely the 1909 Australian law he had helped write. Mead's only disappointment was the $260,000 appropriation—enough for only one "demonstration." Everything seemed to be in place for the "new and better civilization" planned for the Durham Colony in the northern Sacramento Valley. "We have Dean Hunt to teach the farmers what to produce and how to produce it; Elwood Mead to get them the means of doing so; and Harris Weinstock to organize them for the disposal of their product," declared Rowell. Growers—especially those of long standing—felt otherwise, however. Mead's pet project, as one recalled, "was not in the hands of practical men who knew farming." Like Joel Parker Whitney's Placer County Citrus Colony a generation earlier, Durham, they seemed to know, was destined to fail.[93]

Active opposition to Mead's plan was limited primarily to the state's more prominent growers and marketing leaders. But the time had already come, many realized, for orchardists and vineyardists throughout the state to assert themselves en masse. The very vitality of specialty crop culture was at stake, and growers needed to make their voice heard in the halls of the state capitol. What growers seemed to need more than anything was an issue that would spur them to action. For a time, it appeared that an initiative on the November 1914 ballot would do just that.

From the day a Socialist assemblyman from Los Angeles proposed the "universal eight-hour law," in early January 1914, growers complained loudly. "Oh, how our grandfathers would laugh at us if they should know [we] are forced to seriously consider such a thing for farm labor," one remarked. It was well known that fruit growers were seldom "prime factors in the directing of politics." But at the fruit growers' convention in Davis that June, an entire day was devoted to the initiative. "Of all the subjects which stirred up earnest, vigorous concern and arm-waving oratory, the proposed 8-hour amendment took the lead," reported the *Pacific Rural Press*. With a unanimous vote, growers formed a Farmers' Protective League to campaign against the proposition. It was "the first time in the history of California that the agriculturists have been united," claimed the *Farmers' News*, the league's monthly organ.[94]

Many of the state's cooperative leaders, including Pierce, Teague, George H. Hecke, Frank B. McKevitt, and George B. Cutter, took charge. They took advantage of the network of local marketing associations already in place to organize a series of league branches. Over 100 Placer County orchardists, for example, assembled at Newcastle's Good Templars Hall on July 10, 1914. After a number of speeches, George D. Kellogg, Harry Butler, and J. E. Bergtholdt called for the approval of the league's "Ten Telling Points." The eight-hour law, they asserted, would "kill the industry" by increasing production costs by as much as 75 percent, by decreasing production itself, and by simply ignoring the "laws of nature" that governed the harvest season. "We can't have an eight-hour day because we can't have eight-hour fruit," one orchardist exclaimed. In less than two months, the league declared a membership of "many thousands" from 20 different counties. On November 3, the initiative suffered a resounding defeat. Every county in the state voted against it—most of them by a greater than two-to-one margin. It was an indication, declared the *Farmers' News*, of what growers "can accomplish when they make up their minds to pull together."[95]

Actually, the initiative had few backers from the very start. The state's Socialist Party, whose popularity was in serious decline, provided the only concerted support for it. All summer long, growers and Socialists traded barbs through their various organs, but few others expressed much interest at all.[96] The California State Federation of Labor backed the measure, but with little enthusiasm. Unlike national leaders, California unionists often embraced an expanded state role to improve workers' lives. But in July, American Federation of Labor president Samuel Gompers publicly denounced any legal limitation of the workday that did not stem from unions' "own initiative, power, and influence." While Gompers's edict garnered front-page headlines in the *Farmers' News*, the state's labor leaders acquiesced by simply ignoring the measure.[97] Commonwealth Club members agreed that any such law ought to exclude growers, who were "in a different category from most other industries." Even the state's chamber of commerce, the California Development Board, opposed the proposition as being too stringent. And the state attorney general went on record as saying that the initiative most likely was unconstitutional anyway.[98]

Nonetheless, league organizers believed they had the makings of a viable interest group. Here was a chance, they thought, to finally convince growers to assert themselves in the modern political order. Even the labor unions, McKevitt pointed out, "protect themselves against inimical legislative measures." Pierce set the tone early on in the campaign. "California fruit growers, the impetus is on you," he exclaimed. "Do you realize your position? Marshal your forces as a unit . . . and arouse your community." On September 12, the league made its broader intentions known by organizing on a permanent basis.[99] Over the next few months, it advocated for a new State Board of Agriculture, a reformed initiative law, lower taxes, and stricter quarantine regulations. But to the question posed by the *Farmers' News*, "What'll you do about it, Mr. Farmer?" growers remained silent. By April 1915, the journal was lamenting the league's drastic drop in membership. No other issue seemed to galvanize growers like the eight-hour law. It had allowed them to vent their frustrations on a labor issue without fear of public condemnation. The *Farmers' News* even tried sensationalism, using fear of the IWW; but to no avail. "Where is your interest?" the journal began to plead in 1916. But by then, the glory months of the campaign against the eight-hour day had been all but forgotten.[100]

The abrupt rise and fall of the Farmers' Protective League revealed more than growers' reluctance to take on the Progressive state. Early on, league leaders took the opportunity to reassert their horticultural ideal. "California occupies a unique position," stated Pierce on June 2, 1914, at the Davis convention. "Through years of patient study and experimenting, the adaptability of our soil and climate to the production of an almost endless variety of fruit has been established beyond question. Intelligent planting coupled with expert care have brought the fruit output to such proportions that fruit is both abundant and cheap. Rich and poor alike revel in its enjoyment. The abundance, variety and excellence of our fruits have made California famous." But the language that resonated so deeply in the late nineteenth century now sounded increasingly hollow to nongrowers. Hecke, the speaker who followed Pierce, unintentionally hinted at why. "Wherever agriculture flourishes, cities are rapidly building, for prosperous farming communities create prosperous trade and commerce," Hecke began. California had indeed "passed through a remarkable period of industrial development" since the turn of the century. Horticulture continued to be an important aspect of the state's economy, but it was no longer "more than manufacturing." With each passing year, oil, tourism, motion pictures, and other burgeoning industries stole some of its luster.[101]

Moreover, the Progressive state harbored a different, and often negative, image of horticulture. Labor-camp reform, "anti-Asiatic" legislation, "country life," and land colonization now filled the pages of the state's newspapers. In sharp contrast, growers found their own sentiments increasingly confined to their own journals. Their marginalization, Pierce and Hecke were just beginning to realize, had become "the farmers' burden."[102] The horticultural ideal that had shaped growers' lives for two generations seemed to be misunderstood, contested, or even rejected by Progressive-era Californians, and poorly served by the Progressive state. Growers continued to believe that the values required to nurture a healthy and prosperous orchard or vineyard remained crucial to the health and prosperity of California. But that message, it now appeared, would not be heard without political organization — something their very instincts told them to avoid. The world war that engulfed America in 1917 and 1918 would present growers with an opportunity to recapture their prominence, but in the end would seal their fate as outsiders.

Labor Relations Reach a Watershed

ON THE AFTERNOON of June 2, 1916, 90 Italian immigrant vine pruners employed by Wylie M. Giffen in Fresno County waged a brief strike. They were no longer satisfied with the $1.50 for an 11-hour day that they had earned the previous year. "The present cost of living is such that a man can hardly exist on that," one insisted. Giffen raised their pay to $2.00 with little objection. Everything else about the raisin industry, he knew, was in his favor. For two years, the European war had brought Mediterranean imports to a halt. With the market all to themselves, Fresno vineyardists had already sold their entire 1915 crop—"the first time in memory," Giffen later remarked, that there had been no carry-over. The 77 percent of growers who belonged to the California Associated Raisin Company received four cents a pound, the highest price in 10 years. Not since the "raisin boom" of the 1880s had expanded production coincided "in such harmony" with increased prices.[1]

The incident on the Giffen ranch was a harbinger of things to come. For farmers across the nation, slaughter and destruction across the Atlantic proved to be an economic blessing. European orders for American goods in 1915 and 1916 all but erased the effects of two years of depression. Wheat, sugar, cotton, and meat were in greatest demand, but California orchardists and vineyardists also benefited from the revived economy. Prices and production of most of the state's specialty crops rose steadily after 1914, and then sharply accelerated when the United States entered the war in April 1917. For four straight years, growers congratulated themselves on having "their best season ever."[2] Farmworkers sought to capitalize as well. The war tightened up the labor market in California by stimulating overseas and domestic demand for agricultural products and by ending mass immigration from Europe through the Panama Canal before it ever got started. With their labor in greater demand than ever before, farmworkers engaged in, as one federal official put it, "more or less continuous trouble and agitation." Though most job actions were small in scale and rarely reported, growers were well aware that their workers were every bit as restive and militant as their industrial counterparts across America.[3]

High consumer prices and strike fever eventually prompted state intervention. By the summer of 1916, it had become apparent not only that the war would last for some time, but that food would be critical to its outcome. Production needed to be stimulated, prices stabilized, conservation emphasized, and labor disturbances minimized. In California, proposals for how to proceed proliferated. By one official's estimate, "dozens and dozens" of state, federal, and private agencies were "rustling facts and evidence" by the fall of 1918 to solve the state's "farm problem."[4] The U.S. Food Administration for California (CFA) was created in August 1917 to coordinate these multiple bureaucracies. Led by Ralph P. Merritt, a 34-year-old protégé of Food Administrator Herbert Hoover, the CFA achieved considerable success—except in labor relations. From the start, wartime labor policy lacked uniformity and consistency, as state and federal officials fought for control of their self-defined turf. As late as November 9, 1918—two days before the armistice—government officials and leading growers were still scrambling to formulate a coherent, centralized plan.

Although the war exposed the administrative weaknesses of the state, it had an extraordinary impact on grower-state and grower-laborer relations. In the struggle over the making of farm labor policy, the role of government in growers' affairs assumed a new significance, and growers' own voice in state affairs acquired greater clarity and power. All means of persuasion—under the ubiquitous slogan "Food Will Win the War"—were used to encourage growers to increase production at "fixed" prices. At first, this call for sacrifice appealed to growers' horticultural ideal—to their sense of producing specialty crops for the greater good. They would have agreed with the in-house historian of the Food Administration who wrote that the agency "created a public psychology favorable to almost everything [it] asked."[5] In the process, however, growers' labor problems, despite all their earlier efforts, again became a public issue. Their demands for more workers—"imported" Chinese in particular—affected the "public psychology" far more than their voluntary agreements with the government to limit wartime profits. Though no comprehensive solution to the labor problem had been discovered by war's end, growers had learned a critical lesson: they alone appreciated the virtues of horticulture, but with government assistance, they could attain just about anything they wanted.

THE INCIDENT on the Giffen Ranch also reflected several recent changes in raisin production. As late as 1913, Japanese workers had constituted at least 75 percent of the labor force. Contractors held a firm grip on the labor market, and growers continued to value Japanese expertise and endurance. But during the depression, thousands of unemployed workers—many of them immigrants from southeastern Europe—came to Fresno to work in the vineyards. "It was found upon trial," one grower stated, "that the belief that only the wiry Japanese could succeed at picking grapes is erroneous, and that white labor is quite equal to the task." When the piece rate dropped from 3 cents per tray to as low as 2¼ cents, many Japanese workers fled to the Sacramento–San Joaquin Delta, Newcastle, and other specialty crop regions where their skill was still valued. Pruning, however, continued to demand "men who understand the principles involved." During the war, the Thompson Seedless emerged as the most popular variety. Because it was less sticky than the seeded Muscat, the Thompson Seedless could be packed in small containers using machinery. But its more fragile vines required even greater attention. To ensure the growth of new fruit canes every year, the vines needed to be pruned, trellised, suckered, sprouted, and topped—not only in the winter, but again in June. The fact that growers were "maximizing care of their vineyards" in order to increase production during the war years put an even higher premium on this process. By the summer of 1916, a new source of "skillful hands" was supplementing the Japanese. In the eyes of growers such as Giffen, Italian immigrants, drawing upon their "viticultural backgrounds," had become "supreme in the art of pruning."[6]

Much to the growers' chagrin, they also proved quite adept at asserting themselves. In late November, several weeks prior to the winter pruning season, some 250 Italian vineyard workers held a series of meetings at Columbus Hall in Fresno. After much discussion concerning the increased costs of food and clothing, they formed the Laborers' Friendly Aid Society. Through the local press, the society informed growers that current conditions were no longer acceptable, and demanded $2.50 for an eight-hour day. Such boldness attracted the attention of local union activists. Ludwick Keller, an American Federation of Labor organizer in Fresno for 14 years, and Pete McEvoy, secretary of Industrial Workers of the World Local 66, both offered their services to the society. It was Keller who successfully wooed the Italians. The following week, 400 charter members formed the Agricultural Workers Union (AWU), elected five Italian officers, and affiliated with the Fresno Labor Council.[7]

By January 15, 1917, over 2,000 pruners had joined their ranks. A "full-scale strike is underway," announced the *Fresno Morning Republi-*

can. Several smaller growers, anxious to get their pruning done, acceded to union demands. "They are far-sighted enough to see that it is for their best interests to allow the pruners the conditions they ask," Keller proclaimed. Such optimism proved short-lived, however. Keller found himself negotiating not only with growers, but also with the Japanese, who still constituted about half the labor force. Koichi Kamikawa, still the most powerful contractor in the San Joaquin Valley, saw little reason to trust the AWU. The AFL, after all, had been openly hostile to Japanese immigrants for years. The fact that union leaders were now excluding Japanese contractors from the organizing process added insult to injury. Any chance of conciliation vanished on February 8, when fifty strikers armed with revolvers and knives stormed a large vineyard near Clovis and seized the pruning shears from a Japanese gang. Kamikawa shrewdly turned the incident to his advantage. He convinced numerous growers to hire Japanese pruners at terms approaching those of the union's— $2.50 for a nine-hour day.[8]

In the minds of "the leading growers of the county," the strike had gone far enough. On February 11, Wylie Giffen, M. F. Tarpey, James Madison, W. Flanders Setchel, S. Parker Frisselle, and a dozen others met at the Fresno courthouse. Within an hour, a federal judge "familiar with the grapemen" had issued an injunction against all vineyard picketers. The plaintiffs then called a "mass meeting" for February 13. In the spirit of 25 years of cooperative marketing efforts, over 1,000 vineyardists filled Fresno's municipal auditorium to hear prominent members of the California Associated Raisin Company (CARC) address the "pruning crisis." They were well aware of the significance of their actions. "There is no use disguising the fact that the acute labor situation has brought to a head the necessity of an organization," declared Giffen in his opening statement. By a unanimous vote, those in attendance founded the Valley Fruit Growers Association (VFGA)—raisin growers' first attempt to organize for labor management purposes. They patterned their labor association after their marketing association. Members covered costs in proportion to their holdings (at the rate of five cents per acre), elected officers on a one-vote-per-person basis, and vested all other powers in an executive committee of 15. "Just as the growers of this district have demonstrated through the agency of the California Associated Raisin Company their ability to successfully market their own products," wrote Setchel, "so through the agency of the Valley Fruit Growers' Association will they demonstrate their ability to handle their own labor problems."[9]

The VFGA more than lived up to the expectations of Setchel, the organization's first president. In meetings held at CARC's Fresno offices, the executive committee planned its course of action. On February 16, Giffen announced that all negotiations with the AWU would cease immediately. Later that day, the VFGA set a "standard wage," leaving the number of hours worked per day up to individual members but insisting that pruners receive "exactly 22½ cents an hour"—the prevailing rate prior to the strike for a 10-hour day. Shunning the AWU's threats of a boycott, the committee established an employment bureau in downtown Fresno on February 21 "to bring vineyardists and workers together." The bureau never had to open its doors, however. By the end of the month, workers by the hundreds broke ranks with the AWU. "Every vine," the *Fresno Morning Republican* reported, was pruned "through the regular channels." In protest, the Fresno Labor Council withdrew from the Raisin Day parade in April, but few growers seemed to care. By then, the VFGA had 3,300 members representing nearly 400,000 acres throughout the San Joaquin Valley.[10]

Japanese contractors also yielded to the VFGA's terms. The executive committee's ultimate objective, in fact, was to free the raisin community of Japanese control. "It is our purpose," Setchel made clear, "to use white workers to the fullest possible degree." He promised to conduct recruiting campaigns throughout the country to "attract here workers of a superior type." Setchel sympathized with vineyardists who still depended on Japanese workers, and the presence of these workers in itself caused him little concern. But he could no longer tolerate the power they had wielded for so long. "It is time for the grower to cease his customary insistence upon any one nationality of pruner or other farm worker," he said. By disassociating themselves from the Japanese, Setchel knew, vineyardists would also raise their standing "in the eyes of the community." The VFGA, in short, offered members an opportunity to reassert their cultural, as well as economic, authority.[11]

The Valley Fruit Growers Association, it should be emphasized, was a unique institution at the time. It evolved as a result of not only increased production, but also a series of changes in the labor process and the labor market specific to raisins. Elsewhere in the early stages of the war, growers responded to new marketing challenges, but remained essentially unorganized when it came to labor.

In Newcastle, times were "so good," a local paper reported in August 1916, that California shippers were "not able to supply the East with more than 75 per cent of the fruit they want." This unprecedented demand put standardization to the test. Newcastle's successful movement earlier in the decade had prompted orchardists from other fresh deciduous fruit districts to pursue "the fundamental principles of uniformity, quality, and maturity" as well. It soon became apparent, however, that voluntary efforts alone would not prevent those desiring quick profits from deluging markets with inferior products. Members of the Placer County Growers and Shippers Association, horrified that eastern buyers were "losing confidence in all California fruit," searched for a legal means of enforcement. In the spring of 1915, Harry Butler drew up a bill in his Penryn office, secured the backing of Frank B. McKevitt and other prominent growers and shippers, and lobbied it through the state legislature. The new law did not make standardization compulsory, for orchardists were equally fearful of "overregulation." It simply codified the Newcastle system of inspection and certification and imposed fines for "deviations." It was a victory, Butler proclaimed, for "conscientious growers everywhere."[12]

The war stimulated a new way of almond marketing. Prior to 1915, California and southern European growers maintained almost entirely separate markets in the United States. The California Almond Growers' Exchange sold 95 percent of its crop "in the shell," while 80 percent of the European imports were "meats." For years, East Coast confectioners had found the shelled Jordan almond from Spain to be "in a class by itself." Its kernel was large, plump, and uniform in shape, and could be coated smoothly with candy. Californians, despite numerous attempts, had been unable to cultivate the Jordan successfully on a large scale. Moreover, its hard shell had to be cracked by hand, an expense only European growers, with significantly lower labor and transportation costs, could bear. The decline in European imports at the start of the war offered CAGE a chance to gain a share of the shelled market. Drawing from its considerable "surplus fund," the exchange sent investigators to Spain to study "European methods," developed machinery to shell the California Nonpareil, and constructed its own shelling plant opposite its central warehouse in Sacramento in the spring of 1915. Though it would take several years for confectioners to switch to the soft-shelled and, by most accounts, inferior substitute, CAGE members considered the new facility "a monument to their loyalty and business forethought." The future, concluded president George W. Pierce Jr., "is full of hope."[13]

Unlike Fresno vineyardists, Newcastle and Davis growers saw no reason to alter their labor relations. In Placer County, the vast majority of growers left the harvest in the hands of their tenants. On rare occasions, Asian renters were fined for violating the standardization law. But they were far better known for, as Butler put it, their "skillful and scientific picking and packing." The fact that significant numbers of Japanese farmworkers from Fresno now found Newcastle more to their liking kept the supply of harvest labor plentiful.[14] Rumblings of a labor shortage could be heard in Davis, however. No one knew better than Pierce that "skyrocketing production" increased competition for harvesters. When he had not heard from his trustworthy contractor, Anokh Singh, five days before the 1916 harvest, Pierce anxiously drove 30 miles to Isleton, where he found his contractor at work for an asparagus company. Pierce convinced Anokh to bring his gang to Davis, but only after raising wages from $1.75 to $2.00. Jacob E. La Rue, J. W. Anderson, and several other neighbors who also counted on Anokh's services breathed a collective sigh of relief.[15]

That relief would prove short-lived, not only for Pierce and his neighbors, but for specialty crop growers around the state. Indeed, the year 1917 proved much more trying. "Almost overnight," recalled CAGE manager Thaddeus C. Tucker, "producers experienced the change from peace to war activities."[16] That change both exhilarated and terrified them. On the one hand, growers achieved a level of prestige in the eyes of the public comparable to that which they had enjoyed at the turn of the century. President Woodrow Wilson, in fact, made patriotism and food production synonymous in an address immediately following the April 6 declaration of war: "We must supply abundant food not only for ourselves and for our armies and our seamen, but also for a large part of the nations with whom we have now made common cause, in whose support and by whose sides we shall be fighting. . . . The farmers who devote their thought and their energy to this will be serving the country and conducting the fight for peace and freedom just as truly as the men on the battlefields and in the trenches."[17] The fact that fruits and nuts were not, in Pierce's words, "in the class of necessary food requirements with wheat, beans, and sugar" did not diminish growers' enthusiasm. Like most Americans, they believed the United States had entered "the greatest war history has ever known"; and, with their customary exuberance for their enterprise, they regarded their contribution to "the fight to the finish between autocracy and democracy" as decisive. Their more immediate experiences, on the other hand, brought them back to earth. Warnings about a potential labor shortage and the need for as many as 100,000 additional harvesters were heard throughout the state.[18]

Similar cries from the 1902 and 1907 fruit grower conventions had gone virtually unnoticed. But with Wilson's call to patriotism, there was no shortage of agencies ready and willing to tackle the "farm labor problem." On April 27, the California Development Board devoted its entire annual convention to the issue. "The consensus of opinion" among those who attended, reported the *California Fruit News*, "was that all necessary factors to increasing food production are more or less easily possible of being provided except that most important need—labor."[19] The Sacramento Valley Development Board held its own labor conference in Stockton in early May to "devise a means of getting information and action."[20] The Commonwealth Club held a series of meetings on the theme "How Can Members Help Win the War?"[21] The State Commission of Horticulture launched a "food-producing campaign," stressing "more planting and better cultivation" in dozens of new publications.[22] The state labor commissioner claimed that public employment bureaus could furnish farmers "with all the labor they need." State Market Director Harris Weinstock promised to oversee developments "with the keenest interest."[23] And California Commission of Immigration and Housing president Simon Lubin insisted that improved sanitary conditions in the state's labor camps would "remedy the situation." Each believed that their particular agency was "in a better position to analyze conditions than is any other," in Lubin's words.[24]

It was left to the State Council of Defense to somehow coordinate these competing interests. Organized in early April 1917 to address "all problems of state preparedness," the council regarded a "potential loss of crops in California" as its most pressing issue. At its first meeting, just two days after the declaration of war, William D. Stephens, in one of his first acts as governor, created the Committee on Resources and Food Supply and named University of California president Benjamin Ide Wheeler its chair. Neither the timing nor the appointment was accidental. Back in February, before Stephens took office, Wheeler and Dean Thomas Hunt of the College of Agriculture had offered the governor-elect "all the resources of the University" should the United States enter the war. And in mid-March, Hunt presented Stephens with a complete survey of the College of Agriculture faculty detailing its "readiness for national service." While other agencies struggled just to convince the budget-minded Stephens to retain their appropriation, the University of California already had his full confidence.[25]

From April 10 to May 31, the Committee on Resources and Food Supply, with Hunt presiding, met on the Berkeley campus eight times. Though held under the auspices of the Council of Defense, the conferences were little more than College of Agriculture faculty meetings.[26] The committee's first course of action was to survey the state's labor conditions. Not surprisingly, Hunt relied on in-house personnel. Farm advisors from 17 counties sent out 28,000 stamped postcard questionnaires asking growers to estimate their labor needs for the 1917 harvest. When fewer than 12 percent of the growers returned their cards, and only one-fourth of these requested state assistance, the committee members concluded that "the farm labor need has doubtless been overestimated."[27] After conferring with CCIH executive secretary George Bell, they became even more convinced that potential labor shortages could be prevented by recruitment of "sources of labor not heretofore used." Some 4,000 workers from Sacramento Valley hop ranches "like that of Ralph Durst," Bell told Hunt, could easily be rerouted to "wherever needed . . . by making proper arrangements in advance."[28]

With this objective, the committee organized the State Farm Labor Bureau, with funding provided by the Council of Defense, the College of Agriculture, and the U.S. Department of Agriculture. Hunt named as its head Richard L. Adams, an assistant professor of agronomy who had been one of the more zealous investigators for both Hunt's farm-bureau program and Elwood Mead's land-colonization commission. Assisted by colleagues Bertram H. Crocheron and William T. Clarke, Adams mobilized the county farm advisors "to secure farm labor for the express purpose of winning the war." They focused their efforts on women, high school students, and Boy Scouts, but excluded Asians—for "patriotic reasons," as Hunt put it.[29]

In the meantime, many of the state's leading growers were making plans of their own. The Farmers' Protective League, though only a shell of its former self since the campaign against the eight-hour day, sent out a call to every cooperative marketing association in the state. Several dozen delegates met in Sacramento on May 11 and unanimously denounced the College of Agriculture's notion that an adequate labor force existed for the coming harvest season. Harking back to Wilson's appeal, they reaffirmed their "patriotic spirit to make a supreme effort for maximum output of foods," but insisted that "such a thing cannot be done without more labor of the right kind." All agreed to meet again in San Francisco on May 21 and 22 to discuss how to proceed.[30] By then, the Council of Defense's farm labor plan had become public knowledge. The more than 100 growers from 49 counties who reconvened at the Palace Hotel agreed it was time "to take matters into our own hands." They cheered when CAGE president George W. Pierce Jr. declared, "The poet's 'Man With the Hoe' needs now a brother poem entitled 'The Hoe Without the Man.'" In a manner reminiscent of the reaction to H. P. Stabler's 1902 convention address, growers of different crops offered a variety of opinions as to who "the Man" should be. Sugar beet growers from southern California called for Mexican immigrants, several others favored "importing" white workers from nearby states, and about half—mostly fruit growers—felt that only Asian workers could meet their needs. When the Chinese Consolidated Benevolent Association ("Chinese Six Companies") of San Francisco offered to supply 100,000 "experienced farm laborers" for the duration of the war, most horticulturists believed their troubles were over. After changing their name to the California Association of Practical Farmers, the delegates confidently made arrangements to present their agenda to the Council of Defense.[31]

A joint conference with the council's Committee on Resources and Food Supply was scheduled for 3 P.M. on May 31 at the University of California's Agricultural Building in Berkeley. But, much to the growers' chagrin, the issue was decided in the interim. On May 29, Congress announced that "under no circumstances" would the Chinese Exclusion Act be amended to relieve California growers' labor anxieties. No one was more relieved than Hunt. An hour before the conference, he met with Crocheron, Clarke, and three other committee members in Wheeler's office to put the finishing touches on their "labor program." Before departing, they sent a telegram to every senator and congressman from California thanking them for their "interpretation of the immigration law" and asking them for "sufficient appropriation" for "our county agent and farm bureau system." The eight "practical farmer" delegates were beside themselves when Hunt walked in and announced the committee's intentions. Just how, with the draft and "increased opportunities for industrial work," would growers find enough harvesters to answer "the President's call"? one asked incredulously. "The class of workers" targeted by the committee, they warned, were "not used to farm work. . . .

It will take four women or high school boys to equal one man." The committee's postcard questionnaires provoked the loudest response. No grower dared "bind themselves" to specific numbers or wage rates that far in advance of the harvest, one tried to explain. Another claimed that the survey had been "a waste of energy" in his district, where white men had not worked for 25 years. Not one grower expressed even a hint of confidence in their county farm bureaus. By the end of the conference, it was clear to the growers that they would have to "handle their employment problem on their own."[32]

The conference merely confirmed what some growers already suspected: the Council of Defense—and, by extension, the government itself—had all along had no intention of helping them. "There is nothing clearer or surer than the fact that there is no adequate supply of suitable farm labor," the normally stoic *Pacific Rural Press* complained. Why, in this time of "national emergency," had "those in authority" not listened? Why, "as soon as the first note was sounded that help must come from the outside," was "the political muffler put on all the way from Sacramento to Washington"? Disillusionment burned inside "many a grower." But a few cooperative leaders knew that growers themselves bore a share of the blame. "We are the most important factor in the present struggle," Pierce stressed throughout the May meetings. Without stronger organization, "our side of the farming problems will never get adequate Governmental consideration."[33]

One of the more incensed growers at the Berkeley conference was Valley Fruit Growers Association president W. Flanders Setchel. By all indications, he told Hunt, the Fresno raisin crop promised to be the largest on record. But the harvest would require 20,000 workers, a total well beyond the reach of the county farm agent or the VFGA's own employment bureau. In actuality, neither Hunt nor Setchel had much experience recruiting labor. It had been labor contractors, after all, who had provided this service over the years. But neither cared to admit his ignorance. While Setchel had hoped for state assistance, Hunt looked for guidance from the VFGA, whose exploits the previous year had been well publicized.[34]

On June 6, A. H. Naftzger, vice-chairman of the Council of Defense, journeyed to Fresno to get a firsthand look. He spoke with VFGA officers, who reiterated Setchel's assertion that "home labor" would not suffice. It was at that point that Setchel inquired about Mexican labor. Just two weeks earlier, the U.S. Department of Labor had agreed to exempt Mexican immigrants from the head tax and literacy restrictions of the 1917 immigration act in order to allow them to harvest crops near the border. Both sides were intrigued by the idea, but nothing came of it. Naftzger learned that the mass of bureaucratic procedures required to procure 10,000 Mexican workers—including convincing the railroads to guarantee special rates—could not be surmounted in two months' time, and the VFGA incurred the wrath of local labor and business leaders for "inviting such a menace to our community."[35] Though discouraged, the growers remained determined to save the season's crop. Through late July, they continued to recruit members by the hundreds into their ranks, met with numerous community leaders to "urge them as a patriotic duty to cooperate with the growers," established a piece rate for the harvest of three cents a tray—a 30 percent increase over the previous year—and prepared to reopen their labor bureau.[36]

No one anticipated the announcement that came on August 6. A few days earlier, a member of CARC's board of directors had departed for Washington, D.C., on what he described as "a lark." But a series of fortuitous encounters prompted a decision by the U.S. Army to include Thompson Seedless raisins on its ration list.[37] With their crop now an "official war food," vineyardists' fortunes changed dramatically. The State Council of Defense and the State Labor Commission worked at a fever pitch to avoid what government officials now called "a critical labor crisis [in] raisin-grape picking." On August 23, a "state labor bureau" opened in downtown Fresno to bolster the growers' own recruiting efforts. With government funding and influence, the VFGA advertised its high piece rate in newspapers throughout the state, set up labor camps with the approval of the CCIH, and conducted "raisin classes" to teach novice pickers the tricks of the trade. The "raisin drive" attracted more than enough labor, and the harvest proved enormously successful. "It is a result," the *Fresno Morning Republican* editorialized, "on which all are to be congratulated." The state labor commissioner was more to the point. "The Fresno office showed the wisdom of getting closer to the farmer," he wrote.[38]

That "wisdom" did not manifest itself elsewhere, however, as Pierce's experience demonstrates. Anticipating his largest almond harvest to date, Pierce once again drove to Isleton in mid-July looking for Anokh Singh. "Does not look encouraging," he wrote in his daily journal after their discussion. Though Pierce did not realize it at the time, Anokh had decided to take his crew to Fresno. He simply could not pass up what he had heard over the Sikh grapevine—that raisin pickers could make as much as $7.00 to $12.00 a day.[39] Pierce turned to his "permanent" hands Indar Singh and Kalla Singh, but through mid-August, neither managed to procure enough harvesters at the $2.00 wage their employer offered. With his almonds "ripe and ready," Pierce heeded the advice circulated by the Council of Defense. On August 18, he applied for help at the "State Employment Office" that Farm Labor Agent Richard L. Adams had just opened in Sacramento. The office supplied him with 30 Sikh workers at a set rate of 30 cents an hour, 11 hours a day. But after just one week of knocking almonds, Pierce's new harvesters, fully aware of their optimal bargaining position, demanded an extra nickel an hour —which Pierce, in his own words, "had to pay."[40]

Even with the high wage (now almost double that of the previous year), it was the Sikh workers who bore the brunt of the wartime inflation, rather than their employer. In 1916, the laborer who worked every day of Pierce's harvest earned $42. In 1917, despite the wage increase, he netted just $45. The reason lay in the worker's expenses: a sack of flour purchased at the Davis grocery, for example, cost 40 cents in 1916, but $3.35 in 1917. And while Pierce's labor costs doubled between the two harvests, his real almond income increased substantially, though not enough to satisfy him. Indeed, what Pierce termed "Hindu insubordination" bruised his paternal ego as much as inflation robbed his pocketbook—a transgression he intended to rectify.[41] Publicly, he would continue to preach the necessity of grower organization; privately, he would spend much of the off-season trying to secure the services of the one man he felt could ensure order in his orchards—Mousha Singh.

Meanwhile, the state was failing to "get closer to the farmer" in other specialty crop districts. Throughout the summer, Naftzger, Hunt, and other Council of Defense officers boasted that California was having its "greatest farming year ever." Growers readily acknowledged the record gains in production—even with "nonessential" crops such as fresh deciduous fruit. "We are honest enough to say," a Newcastle orchardist told the press, "that prices we are getting are criminal." Yet despite Hunt's assurance that "Professor Adams has the situation well in hand," growers grew increasingly apprehensive about the labor supply. "Not only is there an actual shortage of dependable labor," insisted grower-shipper Frank B. McKevitt, "but wages have been exorbitant." Even in Japanese-dominated districts such as Newcastle, growers or their tenants "had no choice but to acquiesce" to harvesters' demands for $5.00 and, in some cases, even $10.00 a day. Massive production and price increases more than offset those wages. "But what of the future?" growers asked. Prices, they feared, would return to normal levels far more rapidly than wages, whether or not the war ended soon. Moreover, growers had little faith that the state would step in on their behalf after the war. "Uncle Sam has an acute case of farmlaboritis," quipped the *Pacific Rural Press.* Adams had offered nothing but "high school boys," and his labor bureaus were merely "an opportunity for academicians to fondle sociological ideals." By the end of the 1917 season, the council had done little but confirm growers' deep-seated resentment against "theorists endeavoring to manage their affairs for them."[42]

Growers were not the only critics of the Council of Defense. Chester Rowell, Hiram Johnson—now a U.S. senator—*Sacramento Bee* editor V. S. McClatchy, State Board of Control head John Francis Neylan, and many other prominent Californians had come to regard the council as "an extravagant organization without any power." Relying on it "for a solution to the State labor problem," wrote McClatchy, was "like leaning on a broken reed."[43] Throughout the nation, in fact, the system of federal and state "advisory" food-control programs had fallen into a state of confusion. Skyrocketing inflation and unprecedented labor strife confirmed the worst fears of numerous prominent businessmen and top government officials. They agreed with Herbert Hoover that agriculture needed to be treated as "a munitions industry." By the summer of 1917, Woodrow Wilson thought so as well. The president placed Hoover in charge of the U.S. Food Administration, an agency given sweeping powers of economic control. Hoover anticipated that government management of the prices and distribution of food would not sit well with the American public. He proceeded to conceal his dictatorial powers with an enormous propaganda campaign conducted from state, county, and municipal offices. "Wheatless Mondays," "Meatless Tuesdays," and other "patriotic sacrifices" stirred up emotions and encouraged citizens to monitor each other's behavior—while at the same time insulating them from the government's more serious endeavors.[44]

In late July, Hoover appointed Ralph P. Merritt State Food Administrator for California. He was only 34 years old and, as the press was fond of saying, "he looks even younger." His age and looks notwithstanding, those who were unhappy with the Council of Defense welcomed Merritt with open arms. They agreed wholeheartedly with his assessment that "present conditions in this State indicate an overproduction of words and a famine in results." A self-described "dispassionate ambassador of the State," Merritt set out to "coordinate the efforts of organizations with the policies of Mr. Hoover."[45] He was hardly a detached observer of recent events, however. Hoover had chosen him, in fact, because of his "ties with the various activities in the State." Since graduating from the University of California in 1907, Merritt had been President Wheeler's personal secretary, a ranch foreman and general manager for the Miller and Lux cattle company, comptroller for the University of California, co-manager of the Kearney vineyard in Fresno, the state's Director for Military Registration at the start of the war, and a member of the Council of Defense. Merritt's "proven executive ability," his "earnestness for his new job," and, above all, his ability to appeal to both "academic high brows" and "cow punchers," as one admirer put it, gave the immediate impression that the California Food Administration (CFA) meant business.[46]

Merritt's first chance to prove himself came less than 24 hours after his appointment. During the last week of July, an estimated 1,800 workers walked off their jobs at several San Jose, Oakland, and San Francisco canneries. They hoped to secure both higher wages and recognition for their union, the Toilers of the World, an American Federation of Labor affiliate organized in May. Most were Italian immigrants, and many of them had participated in the Fresno pruners' strike the previous winter. It was the height of the season, and tensions were running high. It did not help that local newspapers, because of the union's suggestive name, linked the strikers to the IWW. Several battles between picketers and local police or federal troops produced considerable bloodshed and several deaths. Exasperated, Governor Stephens wired Merritt on July 26 requesting his help. Hoover himself had already expressed his concern that the strike "threatened the production of goods crucial to the war effort." The next day, Merritt and Harris Weinstock arrived in San Jose to mediate an agreement. They impressed upon the cannery owners the fact that the cost of living had increased 125 percent in less than a year, and convinced union officials that work stoppages had serious "unpatriotic implications." By August 1, a settlement was reached that raised wages substantially. The press hailed the food administrator's efforts, but the incident planted uncertainty in Merritt's own mind. "The seriousness of the situation can hardly be over-estimated," he wrote to Hoover. "Unless we can solve the labor problem, it is useless for us to undertake the reduction in food prices or to even discuss the problems of distribution."[47]

Growers in particular viewed Merritt's actions in San Jose with optimism. "During the past season," wrote California Association of Practical Farmers president D. O. Lively, "we have been stung on getting any assistance whatever in the labor situation." But Merritt's intervention in the cannery strike put them "in a more agreeable state of mind."[48] The "publicity campaign" Merritt launched immediately upon his return to his San Francisco office raised growers' spirits even higher. To impart the "patriotic importance" of voluntary rationing, the Food Administration "educated" the public through newspapers, magazines, billboards, motion pictures, churches, and schools. Newspapers in particular, with the notable exception of the *Los Angeles Times,* eagerly printed everything sent to them. By October, Merritt had 140 daily and 410 weekly papers at his disposal. CFA propaganda glorified growers' contribution to the war effort. Consumers were urged to "Eat less wheat, meat and sugar to save for the army and our allies" and, by the same token, to "Eat more fruits and vegetables." County farm advisors distributed hundreds of pamphlets and news releases reminiscent of the booster literature of the 1880s. "Food Will Win the War," "Orchards for Victory," "Victory Will be Won in the Fields," and other "lines of propaganda" revitalized growers' image as cultural guardians.[49]

Thus, when 100 of the state's "leading growers" assembled at the Palace Hotel in San Francisco on October 5, 1917, at Merritt's request, hopes were high. It was Merritt's stated intention to "wipe the slate clean" and get to the bottom of "the very vital subject of labor." All in attendance were given the opportunity to vent their frustrations, with the understanding that Merritt would then "convey their suggestions to Mr. Hoover." Grower after grower took the floor to complain of labor shortages, high wages, and crop losses—except for three raisin growers from Fresno County who "had not much trouble from lack of labor." Before adjourning, a small majority voted in favor of "bringing more Asiatics to California." When Merritt left for Washington "as their messenger" two days later, growers once again thought their problems were over. "With our natural resources, we could feed the whole American army if given the necessary labor," one stated confidently.[50]

Once again, however, that confidence would be betrayed. The San Francisco meeting turned out to be little more than CFA propaganda.

Merritt took the growers' concerns seriously, but he had become convinced that they could solve their labor problems on their own. That had been his experience, after all, as co-manager of the Kearney vineyard, a position he shared with VFGA organizer S. Parker Frisselle. When M. Theo Kearney died in 1906, he left his entire estate to the University of California. The vineyard continued to be operated as a commercial enterprise under the supervision of Ralph Frisselle, Kearney's longtime general manager. His son Parker took over in 1912. When Merritt became university comptroller in 1913 (and thus manager of all university property), he and Frisselle became "the closest of friends." After the cannery strike, Frisselle convinced Merritt that "our little Labor Association" provided a model for growers throughout the state.[51] Moreover, Merritt hardly came to growers with a "clean slate." The CFA sought only to "give new direction to," not to replace, existing agencies. Merritt's advisory council, in fact, consisted primarily of heads of state agencies and Council of Defense members; and the CFA's Agricultural Production Board, which conducted the October 5 meeting, was chaired by none other than Dean Thomas Hunt. Three days before that meeting, Merritt and his advisors had come to the conclusion that most growers "were in the habit of looking at things either through a microscope or a telescope." "I intend to show Mr. Hoover," Merritt stated, "that California can get along under the war emergency and produce her share of food products regardless of the present conditions."[52]

In Washington, Merritt and Hoover plotted a familiar course of action. Upon Merritt's return to San Francisco in early November, the CFA, as had the Council of Defense before it, created a Committee on Farm Labor—this time under the auspices of the CFA's Agricultural Production Board, but again under Hunt's direction. Seeking to "estimate the probable labor needs of the next crop year," the committee again assigned farm advisors to survey individual growers, again received a minimal response, and again concluded that "the current supply would be sufficient if more intelligently distributed."[53]

Growers were simply dumbfounded. "There seems to be a lack of understanding or a lack of appreciation," lamented those attending the fiftieth fruit growers' convention in Sacramento in late November. Orchardists and vineyardists packed the Senate chamber of the state capitol to discuss, in the words of the chairman, "one of the most important questions that has ever confronted us." For the first time, conventioneers devoted an entire day to "the labor question." Emotions ran high. "This republic has assumed an appalling responsibility," proclaimed John P. Irish at the decisive point in the afternoon discussion. "Our country is at war, and unless we win that war, we lose our liberty and are humiliated forever. To win we must produce food." As the tension mounted, Irish asked the question everyone was waiting for: "Where is the labor to come from? Where is the available supply?" The majority answered in one word—China. Just prior to sitting down to a meatless and wheatless dinner, the growers unanimously adopted a resolution. Their "war measure" called upon the federal government to "permit the introduction of sufficient Chinese or other farm labor to so increase our food production as to assist the United States in discharging its obligation to feed our Allies and their armies and prevent them from being starved into surrender."[54]

Many present no doubt took the resolution literally. For many older growers in particular, it had become something of a tradition to invoke the myth that only the "patient, plodding, and uncomplaining" Chinese could satisfy their needs. The turmoil so many had experienced during the past season made that myth all the more alluring. Others, however, had conceded months ago that Chinese labor was a "dead issue." Irish, Pierce, McKevitt, George Hecke, and Charles Teague, among others, regarded the resolution as a means to another end. They saw how the discussion had whipped the audience into a frenzy. Perhaps the loudest cheer of all came when Irish denounced "the agricultural department of the state University [for assuming] the right and the authority to dictate to the farmers in this state the kind and sort of labor that they need to do their work." Here was an issue, it appeared, that might finally transform growers' political consciousness. "The time has arrived," declared Teague, "that we need to make our needs known." Pierce posed the challenge even more directly. "We, as farmers, are not organized," he stated just before the resolution reached the floor. "We ought to be heard. We as producers ought to be heard."[55]

And heard they were. Headlines such as "Fruit Growers Want Chinese Labor" blared across newspapers throughout the state the next day. The horticultural press reported the events with pride, especially Irish's "fling at the University of California."[56] Most other editors found the growers' actions regrettable, however. The *Fresno Morning Republican* stated flatly that "the importation of the Chinese labor desired is physically, politically, and legally impossible." "Farm agitators" were scolded for diverting attention away from the efforts of "the state and national governments," who now were "attacking the problem with seriousness and resourcefulness." The *San Francisco Chronicle* found the notion of shipping 100,000 Chinese across the Pacific a farce. "We might as well import beans raised in Manchuria as to import Chinese to raise beans in California," it stated. Neither paper, it should be noted, objected to the idea on moral grounds. It was the presence of more "Chinese coolies" in the state, not the act of importing additional labor, that they found appalling. Convention leaders had taken a calculated risk. For them, the clause assigning a "committee of nine" to represent "the fruit-growing interests in California . . . before the federal Government and other authorities" was, in State Horticultural Commissioner Hecke's words, the "most important" part of the labor resolution. That clause was obtained, they knew, at the expense of considerable public ridicule.[57]

On December 12, Hecke, after consulting with Pierce, appointed the nine members of the fruit growers' own Committee on Labor. All were representatives of "leading horticultural organizations," including the California Fruit Distributors (McKevitt), CAGE (Pierce), and CARC (George Roeding). "No better committee could be selected at this time that would be more sure of getting results," Hecke told the press. He did not tell the press that a paper Merritt had presented at the convention influenced his decisions. While Merritt sidestepped the labor question, he spoke straight to the point on marketing and distribution. The CFA, he told the growers, was about to exercise "powers the likes of which this country has never seen." In order to curb inflation and "get the food to the consumer," the CFA planned to regulate each and every process "between production and retail." Where growers were concerned, this would involve setting "reasonable selling prices" for their crops, a task the established cooperatives could "greatly facilitate." Their marketing expertise, Committee on Labor members believed, just might provide them considerable leverage down the line.[58]

The growers' Committee on Labor met in Sacramento on December 17. "No progress can be made," members decided very quickly, "in any plan to import Chinese labor." The only "practical solution" to the potential labor shortage in the coming year, they concluded, was Mexican labor. That evening, they called on the governor to discuss their concerns. How, they asked, could growers become more directly involved in farm labor policy? What would it take to convince the federal government to remove "all obstacles to the importation of Mexican labor"? Stephens was moved by their earnestness. It just so happened, he informed them, that he was due at a Council of Defense meeting in San Francisco the next afternoon. When Stephens informed council members of the growers' intentions, he received a favorable response.[59] Over the next two months, the growers' labor committee attended several Council of Defense meetings and attained exactly what it wanted. The council sent a special committee to Washington "to take up matters with the Department of Immigration," and, on February 26, 1918, created yet another committee on farm labor. This one, for the first time, included growers. "Practical farmers are so seldom a part in the various subdivisions of our government from top to bottom," observed the *California Fruit News*. "This is a definite step in the direction of accomplishing something."[60]

If the growers on the Council of Defense's new labor committee were suspicious of how easily things had progressed, as they later intimated, they were right.[61] The council, they learned only too late, had all but lost whatever real authority it had ever had. The Food Administration's Agricultural Production Board had assumed command of farm labor policy. Indeed, while growers were meeting with the Council of Defense, Dean Hunt was in Washington receiving strict instructions from the U.S. Department of Agriculture regarding "the machinery by which farm labor operations will be run." "The real problem before us," a USDA official stressed, "is not to find laborers in China or Timbuctoo to do our work but to do it ourselves." The plan Hunt presented to the Agricultural Production Board was nearly identical to that carried out the year before by the Council of Defense. "The mobilization of every laboring man, woman, and child in California will be undertaken," Hunt proposed. Schools would end early and start late, a "Women's Land Army" would recruit "soldiers" by the thousands, state employment agencies would be "utilized to the fullest extent," and the state farm labor agent would "act as a clearing-house of information." This time, however, Hunt had the backing of the Food Administration, which conducted a "mass campaign" to publicize "California's huge farm army." Posters, pamphlets, newspapers, and several "war convocations" implored patriotic citizens to "drop what you are doing and report for farm work."[62]

Growers remained skeptical. "The University of California authorities," they feared, "seemed to have absorbed the Federal Government's labor views and are suggesting largely academic remedies." The Council of Defense's new farm labor committee met several times in March and

Editorial cartoon supporting the California Food Administration's solution to the "farm labor problem" of 1918. *Sacramento Bee*, June 3, 1918.

April to develop an agenda of its own. Other than passing several resolutions favoring "patriotic production" and "the importation of Mexican labor," little was accomplished. Readers of the state's newspapers, in fact, continued to learn more about growers' "Coolie infatuation," than about their work on the council's labor committee. The *California Fruit News*, while not wishing to appear unpatriotic, saw no choice but to blame the Food Administration. "With all due respect to Dean Hunt of the University of California and those other learned men who have spent weeks and months theoretically solving the labor problem of the State," an editorial maintained, "the growers are finding they are as far away today from a solution of the labor problem as when they started a year ago."[63]

While the Food Administration paid little attention to growers' labor suggestions, it sought their cooperation in controlling prices. In fact, many of those serving on the council's labor committee—Pierce, McKevitt, and Giffen among them—represented their respective marketing organizations in price-fixing negotiations. While Merritt had the legal power to enforce whatever restrictions he felt were "in the interests of the United States," agreements between growers and the federal government were carried out "on a voluntary basis." In February, Merritt appointed his friend S. Parker Frisselle to oversee negotiations "with the fruit men." Through July, marketing-cooperative leaders filed through Frisselle's San Francisco office. The standard contract they signed indicated that they had little choice but to submit to this "patriotic" procedure: "We, the undersigned producers," it began, "being in full sympathy with the purposes of our Government for the successful prosecution of the war, desire to offer our fullest service and co-operation to the United States Food Administrator, . . . and hereby pledge ourselves to fixing a maximum price . . ."[64]

By mid-April, it had become clear to most growers that they were carrying more than their share of the burden. Their frustrations burst forth with an address Pierce delivered to the Commonwealth Club in San Francisco. The fact that Pierce followed Richard L. Adams in the program made "Farm Labor from an Orchardist's Point of View" all the more poignant. "California orchards and their products have done much to advertise and develop our state," Pierce began. "Horticulture here has at all times received substantial recognition. Its development has placed us at the head of the list." But nobody seemed to appreciate the sacrifice growers were making, Pierce maintained. "The government orders [us] to produce crops, sets a price for them, and compels delivery, . . . and we do not complain." He then expressed indignation toward those who opposed the growers' pleas to import more laborers: "At times when conditions seem to be near the breaking point, some department, bureau, or commission takes up the farm labor problem and with more or less camouflage announces that something is about to be done to relieve the situation. Resolutions galore are adopted. Statistics are sought over ground worn bare by previous seekers, trying to find out something that everybody already knows. Learned professors theorize and designing politicians manipulate." The fact that these critics refused to listen to the growers' appeals confounded Pierce. "Gentlemen," he declared, "you sit down here and ask whether there is a shortage of labor. Get out and try to run a farm and you will find out. It does exist and it will exist, and unless we get more labor, we are not going to produce the amount our Government demands; we are not going to produce our quota of the amount that is necessary to win the war."[65]

Pierce's anger stemmed from more than government neglect. This leading proponent of grower organization and grower-state cooperation remained obsessed with his own labor problems. At the time of his Commonwealth Club address, his efforts to bring Mousha Singh back to his Davis orchards had reached an impasse. Back in the fall of 1917, Pierce had located his former contractor in Hong Kong and quickly sent him a steamship ticket to recross the Pacific. But he received an unexpected telegram on February 26 from the Angel Island Immigration Station on San Francisco Bay. Federal authorities had detained Mousha in compliance with the immigration bill Congress had passed in January that barred immigrants from India. Upon visiting Mousha on Angel Island, Pierce realized the gravity of the situation. On the advice of two CAGE attorneys, he made a formal appeal for Mousha's release, wrote several letters to Anthony Caminetti, the federal commissioner general of immigration, and visited Mousha on Angel Island several times. He finally agreed to serve as Mousha's legal guardian after the Sikh was released on a six-month bond pending a final decision on his case. After four months of detainment, Mousha left Angel Island on June 27 and was back at work on the Pierce ranch on June 29. And just as Pierce had expected, Mousha secured a labor force of 25 Sikhs to harvest almonds in August. Pierce made no effort to consult his neighbors or other CAGE members on wage rates. The peace of mind he had finally secured was well worth the 40 cents an hour his workers demanded.[66]

Pierce's reliance on individual initiative was becoming less the norm, however. Growers around the state instead looked to the Valley Fruit Growers Association for direction. The raisin growers' labor bureau achieved remarkable success in its second year of operation. From February through October of 1918, President Setchel kept vineyardists informed of the VFGA's "systematic recruitment efforts" through his regular column in the CARC's monthly organ, the *Sun-Maid Herald*. The "small army of pickers" that invaded the San Joaquin Valley proved indispensable when a storm hit late in the harvest. Without the "abundance of workers" to stack the trays, Frisselle wrote to Merritt, "the crop might have been lost."[67] Other labor bureaus began "springing up elsewhere," Setchel reported with satisfaction. By July, fruit growers in Sutter, Solano, Napa, Contra Costa, Santa Clara, and Yuba Counties were organizing "along the lines of the Valley Growers Association." With equal determination, members of each group vowed to "take labor matters into our own hands." They received considerable help from their local farm advisors. Indeed, most of the labor associations grew out of farm bureau meetings. Growers had long avoided farm advisors' educational lectures and demonstrations, but when the subject turned to labor, farm bureaus began to attract their attention.[68]

It did not take long, however, for growers to realize the "danger of competition," as Setchel put it. In addition to their own associations, by the spring of 1918 there were 20 permanent state employment bureaus throughout California, 40 "emergency agencies," 28 Women's Land Army "units," 50 "divisions" of the Boys' Working Reserve (supervised by the Young Men's Christian Association), and at least 53 "federal labor offices" opened by the U.S. Department of Labor in May.[69] But they operated with an almost complete lack of coordination. This became abundantly clear to the 30 growers who gathered to hear Setchel's address entitled "Our Experience in Organizing the Farmers" in the Commonwealth Club chambers in San Francisco on May 15. As Pierce sat in the audience listening, it suddenly dawned on him what had happened during the previous harvest. "The reports of 10 and 12 dollars a day rapidly spread among the laborers," he stated during the ensuing discussion. "I was one of the victims of the Fresno organization." The other growers rallied to Pierce's defense. "We have simply been bidding one section against another," they realized.[70] Setchel returned to Fresno and took up the matter with Frisselle and several San Joaquin Valley county farm advisors. They came to the conclusion that "cooperation between the orchardists and the vineyardists" needed to be pursued. The idea of a statewide farm bureau federation had taken root.[71]

But it was too late in the season to organize the cooperation envisioned by Pierce, Setchel, and Frisselle. The only way to ensure a successful harvest, the growers on the Council of Defense's labor committee continued to insist, was to "open the flood gates" to Mexican labor. By June, State Farm Labor Agent Richard L. Adams had reached the same conclusion. "The complaints of farmers . . . were too loud and too numerous to be merely ignored," he later admitted.[72] In the preceding months, Adams had employed "the importation of labor" only as rhetoric. It had been his practice when speaking to growers to list all of Dean Hunt's suggestions, then at the end dangle "the possibility of getting Mexican labor."[73] A study his office conducted in February and March predicted a farm labor shortage for the coming 1918 harvest season of as many as 12,000 workers. At first Adams advised "better utilization of our available supplies," but he had begun to doubt whether that would be enough. He sent John P. Dargitz, the founder of CAGE and now the secretary of the Council of Defense's labor committee, to Mexico to confer with immigration authorities. When Dargitz wired him on June 1 that "labor can be secured in large numbers," Adams began to plan in earnest.[74] But the federal government was still not convinced that California faced a "war crisis." The Department of Labor sent Adams a seven-page circular detailing "regulations regarding admission of agricultural laborers," and the War Department refused to "facilitate matters"—except in southern California, where sugar beet growers, under close supervision, "imported" several thousand Mexican harvesters. Through July, Adams reported to growers that "details are being worked out." But with the peak of the harvest season fast approaching, he knew he had run out of time.[75]

Adams had learned all too well how slowly the wheels of government bureaucracy turned. "The present time is none too early to formulate plans for the 1919 season's labor needs," he told a Council of Defense meeting on October 23.[76] Adams already had a clear plan in mind. Since August, he and State Horticultural Commissioner George Hecke had received hundreds of complaints from growers throughout the state of "scarce and exorbitantly-priced labor." The labor shortage would have been even more critical, many wrote, had inclement weather not reduced their crops. Higher selling prices normally would have compensated for such losses, but most growers were locked into agreements with the Food Administration.[77] Just a year earlier, Adams would have dismissed such statements as hyperbole, but now they confirmed his own worst fears. He was convinced that Mexican labor was the answer, but he knew that that would never come about without a more concerted effort. The first step was to "bring all interested parties together" for a farm labor conference in November. Throughout the month preceding this conference, Adams stressed "the seriousness of the matter" to Council of Defense members, convinced the Food Administration to give the event plenty of advance publicity, and personally invited delegates from the state's "key farm organizations" to attend.[78]

Under the auspices of the State Council of Defense and the U.S. Department of Agriculture, the conference was held in San Francisco on November 8 and 9. Nearly 100 participants debated "farm problems and requirements for the coming year." Most left the meeting believing that no "practical amelioration" would come from their efforts. A resolution to import Chinese labor was quickly voted down; growers declared that "poaching labor from one another" had to be stopped; all were in agreement that "governmental labor-agency machinery was more or less duplicated and confused"; and "no consensus of opinion whatsoever" was reached on the Mexican labor issue. In short, growers and government officials rehashed familiar problems, but proposed few new answers.[79]

But in comparison with similar conferences held in April 1917, remarkable changes had taken place. Though the debate over the farm labor problem remained unresolved, a fundamental shift had occurred in grower-state relations. Prior to the war, all but a few leaders of cooperatives shared a considerable skepticism of the government. The ensuing labor crisis, however, forced growers to organize themselves to pressure the state in order to protect their interests. They defended their demands for special treatment by touting their horticultural expertise as indispensable for winning the war. In the process, they expressed themselves publicly on an issue they had previously discussed only among themselves, if at all. Farm labor relations, in fact, had become a controversial public issue, though in a way that seemed to confirm growers' earlier fears. Indeed, Adams's conference was front-page news — but all the headlines focused on the Chinese labor resolution.

It was the conference's final resolution that proved to be the most significant. Participants appointed "an executive committee of three" — Adams, Dargitz, and cooperative leader (and pear grower) Frank T. Swett — to "carry on the work started here."[80] When the armistice was declared just two days later, it appeared that the conference's work had been for naught. But the committee members were still resolved to advance grower-state relations. Their efforts would prove successful a year later. At the fifty-second fruit growers' convention, held in Chico in November 1919, Swett, Dargitz, and Adams helped create an Agricultural Legislative Committee. "The progress of horticulture," the *California Fruit News* proclaimed, had reached a critical third stage. Fruit grower conventions, the journal recounted, began in the 1880s "with considera-

tions of cultural problems." Then, in the early twentieth century, marketing became the chief concern. Now, growers had finally turned their
attention to "legislative and political activity."[81]

Its sense of historical inevitability notwithstanding, the *California
Fruit News* understood that a watershed had been reached. Under the
leadership of Charles Teague and S. Parker Frisselle, the Agricultural
Legislative Committee—in sharp contrast to the Farmers' Protective
League before the war—exerted considerable influence over all phases
of farm legislation in the 1920s. Frisselle embodied the new grower-state
relationship. His experiences with the Kearney vineyard, the VFGA,
and the Food Administration, he maintained, stimulated both his "farm
conscience" and his "Government conscience." Thus motivated, he
would become perhaps the single most influential figure in California
farm labor policy through the 1930s, particularly as a proponent of Mexican immigration.[82]

Mexican immigration, in turn, contributed significantly to growers'
newfound political boldness. Despite the fact that the government never
developed a definitive farm labor policy during the war, an estimated
30,000 Mexican laborers entered California between 1917 and 1920—the
vast majority of whom failed to register with authorities. Fleeing the political and economic chaos of the Mexican Revolution and lured by
wartime labor shortages and high wages, Mexican immigrants crossed
the border hoping to start life afresh. Instead of returning at the conclusion of the sugar beet harvest, thousands of laborers headed north in
search of more work. The VFGA estimated that as many as 2,000 Mexican workers picked raisins in 1918 and 1919, and reports of Mexicans
"invading" the Sacramento Valley became common. By 1925 they were,
in the words of a U.S. Labor Department official, a "fixed institution"
throughout California, constituting three-quarters of the state's farm labor force. Their presence left the impression that growers' wartime pleas
to the government had been answered.[83]

The impact of Mexican immigration on labor relations was even
more striking. It can be seen vividly in Pierce's experience. Before the
1919 harvest, Mousha Singh obtained permanent admission to the
United States, on the grounds that he had acquired a residence in California prior to the passage of the 1917 immigration act. Once again, he
gathered together a workforce of 28 Sikhs as the August harvest approached. This time, however, the harvesters upset the customary order
of Pierce's orchards. After two weeks of knocking almonds, a "threat-

ened strike materialized," as Pierce recounted in his journal. His workers had discovered that higher wages awaited them in the orchards of
two of Pierce's neighbors, who began offering a piece rate (50 cents a
tree). After Mousha unsuccessfully attempted to find replacements,
Pierce became frantic. More than half of his largest crop of almonds to
date remained on the trees. Seeking help, he drove to two nearby
ranches, but to no avail. Finally, he journeyed 25 miles to Vacaville, leaving word at two groceries that work could be found in his orchards. The
next day, as Pierce explained in his journal, "One Spaniard came in auto
to look at orchard and equipment. He decided to come with crew to
knock almonds at 50c per hour."[84]

Unlike all previous harvesters Pierce had employed, Mexicans usually labored as members of a family unit—"big and little, male and female," as Pierce put it. He tried to pay his new workers a day wage, just
as he had every year for more than a quarter century, but with a slight
change—50 cents per hour for men, 40 cents for women and children.
Foreshadowing the militancy Mexican harvest workers would display in
the late 1920s and 1930s, Pierce's laborers demanded to be paid by the
tree. Reluctantly, Pierce complied. By 1921, he not only paid Mexican
harvesters 80 cents per tree, he also contracted "for [the] entire work—
knocking, hulling, drying, sacking, and piling." This altered wage system
persisted for the remaining 10 years of Pierce's life.[85]

The war and the influx of Mexican workers transformed the central
dynamic of labor relations in Pierce's orchards. In order to secure and
maintain an adequate harvest labor force, Pierce abdicated his prized
post at the almond huller and relinquished his role as supervisor of his
"boys." Pierce no longer served as guardian over his harvest. He now believed that the state and federal governments would ensure a sufficient
labor supply; and he now maintained an impersonal, rather than a paternal, relationship with the Mexican families who harvested his almonds. His horticultural ideal no longer seemed to play an essential role
in his harvest labor relations. Almond growing, it appeared, had become
more a business than a way of life for Pierce. His operation now had
more in common with the "industrialized agriculture" that Paul S. Taylor would describe to the La Follette Committee in 1939 than it did with
the specialty crop culture that had so enticed him in the early 1890s.

That transformation was reflected further in the increasing importance of the labor bureau in growers' lives. Pierce himself often consulted
Sacramento Valley bureaus when Mexican contractors could not meet

his needs.[86] In Fresno and the surrounding counties, the Valley Fruit Growers Association continued to serve thousands of members after the war. Its board of directors, including S. Parker Frisselle and Wylie M. Giffen, fixed wages, recruited workers, and distributed them to San Joaquin Valley growers—not only raisin growers but, by 1921, peach, fig, prune, apricot, alfalfa, and especially cotton growers. Out of nowhere, cotton became "white gold" in the San Joaquin Valley in the 1920s. By the 1925 season, the crop's labor intensiveness overwhelmed the VFGA. That year an estimated 40,000 workers were needed to harvest raisins and other fruits, and another 12,000 to pick cotton—thousands more than the VFGA had handled before. The resulting competition for workers, accompanied by higher wages, careless picking, and delays, cost all San Joaquin Valley growers an estimated $2 million.[87]

Under Frisselle's leadership, growers founded a new organization, the Agricultural Labor Bureau of the San Joaquin Valley, in April 1926. Financed by several county farm bureaus, chambers of commerce, and marketing cooperatives, the bureau was an immediate success. By developing strong working relations with local, state, and federal government officials, the bureau recruited approximately 50,000 workers every year for the remainder of the decade, the vast majority of whom were Mexican. Their presence, Frisselle told the 1927 fruit growers' convention, "solves for us our agricultural difficulties. . . . I think there is no doubt but we have sufficient labor here now to handle the crops we are growing today."[88] Nor was there much doubt about the waning of an earlier horticulturist ethic. Since the boom of the 1880s, labor relations had represented the crucial and problematic juncture between growers' self-conception as horticulturists responsible to their communities and their need to turn a profit in highly commercialized enterprises that relied on the labor of ethnic outsiders. Without a pang of conscience, growers now turned to translocal institutions and organizations, including the state, to control their "bugbear" of labor.

Nonetheless, specialty crop growers' heightened self-image remained intact. Their sense of the grandeur of their enterprise that had once made them California's cultural guardians could still be heard in their public and political rhetoric—though with a noticeably defensive tone. "Are not we, the food producers of America, the ones who hold the key to the situation?" Pierce asked his fellow growers at the 1920 fruit growers' convention in Fresno. "When the agricultural people of the State of California get together as they ought to get together . . . we can get anything we want." Pierce spoke on behalf of the Agricultural Legislative Committee, already the most powerful grower lobby to that time. During the 1930s, this organization would form an even more powerful relationship with the Associated Farmers and the California Farm Bureau Federation to battle farmworkers and their unions.[89] By then, the world that pioneer orchardists and vineyardists had envisioned seemed all but forgotten.

Conclusion

THE QUESTION REMAINS whether or not those who followed California's first two generations of specialty crop growers betrayed the values of those pioneers by acting like "farm fascists" in the 1930s. To put it another way, just how abrupt and thorough were the changes in California specialty crop agriculture following World War I? What do today's growers have in common, if anything, with their turn-of-the-century counterparts? A comprehensive and systematic response would require another full-length treatment, but some telling insights can be suggested here. It would seem appropriate to take a final tour through Fresno, Newcastle, Davis, and Wheatland.

In the raisin industry, remarkably little has changed since the end of World War I. Ninety-five percent of the country's (and half the world's) production still occurs within a 60-mile radius of the city of Fresno. Over 5,000 growers now produce an average of 350,000 tons of raisins per year—almost all of them Thompson Seedless. Following the 1980s agricultural depression, demand rocketed to record levels, thanks in large part to a series of award-winning television commercials featuring Sun-Maid raisins dancing to the tune of "I Heard It through the Grapevine." In the early 1990s, growers sold their crops through 21 different packing companies, with Sun-Maid—the California Associated Raisin Company's successor—garnering the largest market share. Production remains small in scale, with vineyards averaging about 50 acres. These "family farmers," as they are often called, employ at least 50,000 workers every harvest. Indeed, of the 250 crops now grown in the San Joaquin Valley, raisins are still the most labor-intensive. The vast majority of pickers are hired through contractors and paid a piece wage, and 98 percent are Mexican immigrants. This system of labor has worked so well that growers have shown little interest in mechanizing. Labor can still be their "bugbear," however. A late-September storm in 1994 left growers scrambling to find enough workers to stack trays before the raisins rotted. It also left them scrambling to defend their politics. Sun-Maid had just donated almost $1 million to the reelection campaign of Republican governor Pete Wilson, a campaign centered on a ballot measure calling for immigration restrictions (Proposition 187). "Let's face it," one grower admitted. "Fifty percent of the agricultural work force in this valley is illegal. We'd sink economically without them."[1]

The Newcastle fruit belt, in contrast, no longer exists. During World War I, the region's landowners were conspicuous by their absence from the farm labor debate. Harry Butler's most significant contribution, in fact, was to write a history of Placer County's War Exemption Board.[2] The Japanese Association of America was simply better organized to provide labor than the multitude of government and grower committees. Local secretaries mobilized Japanese workers so efficiently that communities such as Newcastle, Penryn, and Loomis rarely lacked for labor.[3] By 1920, Japanese farmers leased or owned over 14,000 of the region's 18,000 acres of orchard land. For the next two decades, they continued to thrive, producing between 1,500 and 2,500 carloads of fruit every year —despite another alien land law, severe immigration restrictions, and the Great Depression. They did not survive World War II, however. In January 1942, Placer County Japanese were "evacuated" to internment camps, and most did not return. Their orchards never recovered. When Newcastle's Japantown was leveled to make way for Highway 40 in 1958, it was a symbol of the end of the region's fruit era. Today, Interstate 80 swings within 100 yards of "fruit house row," but few drivers passing through Sacramento's sprawling "rural suburbia" will recognize its significance. The abandoned shipping houses, an occasional ornamental peach tree, and the towering palm trees that still line the roads through the old citrus colony are all that is left of this once prominent fruit district.[4]

Almond trees still bloom early every spring along Putah Creek near Davis. But the nut is no longer a major crop in southern Yolo County. On the Pierce ranch, for example, alfalfa has become the staple. Yet California still produces all of the country's almonds, the bulk of them now being grown in the San Joaquin Valley. With over 360,000 bearing and nonbearing acres (almost 10 times more than in 1920), almonds are the largest of all California tree crops and are second only to grapes among all fruits and nuts. Like Sun-Maid, Blue Diamond Almond Growers has spurred demand through advertising. Decreased labor costs have also accounted for the nut's soaring production. The harvest is now fully mechanized. In place of "knockers," small motorized "shakers" grab the trees and vibrate them until the nuts fall to the ground, where vacuum carts sweep them up. The "proper care and careful handling" prescribed by George W. Pierce Jr. at the turn of the century, it would seem, are no longer of much concern.[5]

These contrasting developments suggest that it is no longer enough to examine California agriculture subregion by subregion. To fully understand growers, specialty crops, and labor in the modern era requires a different starting point. In the wake of World War I, growers' primary frame of reference shifted away from their local communities to a variety of impersonal, centralized institutions. A growing number of statewide cooperatives marketed their crops with increasing sophistication. The county labor bureaus that began during the war proliferated in the early 1920s, consolidated regionally in the latter part of the decade, and became the driving force behind the anti-union Associated Farmers in the 1930s. Most growers, Richard L. Adams told the La Follette Committee in 1939, remained "strongly individualistic" and thus hesitant to "combine for the purpose of setting wage rates." But they no longer hesitated to reap the benefits of pressure-group politics. When it appeared that Congress would restrict the immigration of Mexican farmworkers in 1926, for example, growers knew they could rely on the California Farm Bureau Federation to protect their interests in Washington. Regional and statewide chambers of commerce still boosted specialty crop agriculture with a great deal of pride, but their efforts were now as much confrontational as promotional. To prevent rebellious workers from distorting their idealistic image of California, they helped finance labor bureaus, the Associated Farmers, and other grower organizations. In short, an altogether new type of grower seems to have emerged in the 1920s and 1930s whose outlook on life and labor was captured in 1926 by George P. Clements, the manager of the Agricultural Department of the Los Angeles Chamber of Commerce: "The old fashioned hired man is a thing of the past. There is no place for him, and the farmer who does not wake up to the realization that there is a caste in labor on the farm is sharing too much of his dollar with labor. . . . California requires fluid labor. We are not husbandmen. We are not farmers. We are producing a product to sell."[6]

Historians have cited that very quotation over and over again to characterize California specialty crop growers from the 1880s to the present. Such a portrayal, this study has argued, is particularly problematic for the period before the 1930s. But just how deep-seated *were* growers' earlier values? When all is said and done, was their horticultural mission to "minister to the needs and pleasures of mankind" superficial? Have the Farm Bureau and other organizations become growers' "political guardians" in the modern economic order at the expense of growers' earlier cultural prominence?[7]

Not if we listen to Victor Davis Hanson, a fifth-generation raisin and plum grower in Fresno County. Hanson lives in a world that still has much in common with an earlier time. His very language and attitudes reflect those of his grandfather and his grandfather's grandfather, who purchased the family's Selma farm in 1878 at the start of the raisin boom. Hanson unabashedly compares his triumphs and struggles to those of the ancient Greeks and Romans. He describes raisin and fruit cultivation with considerable passion and in minute detail, as though he were delivering a paper at a late-nineteenth-century fruit growers' convention. His anger toward the "company brokerage men" during the "raisin holocaust" of the early 1980s recalls his ancestors' disdain for the "dreaded middlemen" of the 1890s. Similarly, his disparagement of "university tinkerers" knows no bounds, though Hanson himself teaches Greek and Latin at the nearby state college when raisins and plums fall below their "living price." When the subject turns to labor, Hanson becomes defensive and blames "the union, the government, and the immigration explosion in Mexico" for compounding the problem. Above all, he asserts —with no hint of sentimentality—that fruit growers such as he are "different, vastly different, from almost all other types of citizens," and indeed embody the very essence of Western culture. That moral responsibility, he concludes, compels him to keep farming, though sheer economics often dictate otherwise. The horticultural ideal, it would seem, remains very much alive.[8]

Finally, what has become of hops, the crop that has played such a key role in California's agricultural history? Hops are now all but extinct in the state. Production reached a peak between 1912 and 1916, but plummeted thereafter. During World War I, when hops were in low demand, both Ralph Durst and E. Clemons Horst replanted their fields with beans, potatoes, and vegetables and used their kilns as drying sheds.[9] Horst in particular was so enthusiastic that Ralph Merritt, Dean Hunt, and even Herbert Hoover came to regard him as "a pest."[10] At war's end, both Durst and Horst replanted hops with the expectation that European trade would boom, and Durst even purchased several hop-picking machines. Prohibition caught them completely by surprise. In the early 1920s, hop growers throughout northern California plowed up two-thirds of their acreage. Though Horst made a successful transition to the dry and canned fruit business, Durst never recovered. He died in 1938, bitter and deeply in debt. Today, the only reminders of what was once the "Hop Growing Capital of the World" are four medieval-looking kilns peeking out of a cornfield and a stone monument on the edge of the town of Wheatland marking the site of the 1913 "hop riot . . . initiated by the I. W. W. Labor Movement."[11]

Two years before Durst's death, Carey McWilliams read Carleton Parker's description of that riot for the first time. He was struck by the similarities to "recent agricultural labor disturbances" and became convinced that Wheatland was the central event in California's agricultural history. McWilliams sought to create a usable past to explain his disturbing present, but at the cost of trying to see the past as it actually happened. That cost was considerable. An earlier way of life that Edward Wickson called specialty crop "homoculture" was lost to us—and along with it the roots of "the problem of farm labor" that McWilliams so passionately wanted to understand.[12]

Notes

Introduction

1. Chester Rowell to W. M. Giffen, December 10, 1909, box 1, Chester Rowell Correspondence and Papers, Bancroft Library, University of California, Berkeley.

2. Carey McWilliams, "The Farmers Get Tough," *American Mercury* 33 (October 1934): 245.

3. Greg Critser, "The Political Rebellion of Carey McWilliams," *UCLA Historical Journal* 4 (1983): 46–48; McWilliams, "The Farmers Get Tough," 241; Miles C. Everett, "Chester Harvey Rowell, Pragmatic Humanist and California Progressive" (Ph.D. diss., University of California, Berkeley, 1966).

4. Carey McWilliams, *The Education of Carey McWilliams* (New York: Simon & Schuster, 1978), 64–81; McWilliams, *Factories in the Field: The Story of Migratory Farm Labor in California* (Boston: Little, Brown, 1939).

5. See the dust jacket of Devra Weber's *Dark Sweat, White Gold: California Farm Workers, Cotton, and the New Deal* (Berkeley: University of California Press, 1994).

6. Pierce Family Papers and George W. Pierce Jr., Daily Journals, 1890–1930, Department of Special Collections, University of California Library, Davis.

7. On farm size, see Victoria Alice Saker, "Benevolent Monopoly: The Legal Transformation of Agricultural Cooperation, 1890–1943" (Ph.D. diss., University of California, Berkeley, 1990), 169–175.

8. David Vaught, "'An Orchardist's Point of View': Harvest Labor Relations on a California Almond Ranch, 1892–1921," *Agricultural History* 69 (Fall 1995): 563–591.

9. McWilliams, *Factories in the Field;* Levi Varden Fuller, "The Supply of Agricultural Labor as a Factor in the Evolution of Farm Organization in California" (Ph.D. diss., University of California, Berkeley, 1939); Paul S. Taylor, "Foundations of California Rural Society," *California Historical Society Quarterly* 24 (1945): 193–228; Lloyd H. Fisher, *The Harvest Labor Market in California* (Cambridge: Harvard University Press, 1953); Cletus E. Daniel, *Bitter Harvest: A History of California Farmworkers, 1870–1941* (Ithaca: Cornell University Press, 1981); Linda C. Majka and Theo J. Majka, *Farm Workers, Agribusiness, and the State* (Philadelphia: Temple University Press, 1982).

10. Walter J. Stein, *California and the Dust Bowl Migration* (Westport, Conn.: Greenwood Press, 1973), 65.

11. There is a rich literature on early promoters of modern irrigation in California, but see especially Donald J. Pisani, *From the Family Farm to Agribusiness: The Irrigation Crusade in California and the West, 1850–1931* (Berkeley: University of California Press, 1984). The "new" rural history, with its emphasis on farmer culture, has not yet made its way to California. It is little wonder, therefore, that the state's specialty crop growers receive scant attention in David B. Danbom's recent survey, *Born in the Country: A History of Rural America* (Baltimore: Johns Hopkins University Press, 1995).

12. McWilliams, *The Education of Carey McWilliams*, 64–81; Carey McWilliams, "Honorable in All Things" (Oral History Program of the University of California, Los Angeles, 1982), 50–53, 65–66; Greg Critser, "The Making of a Cultural Rebel: Carey McWilliams, 1924–1930," *Pacific Historical Review* 55 (May 1986): 226–255.

13. Critser, "The Political Rebellion of Carey McWilliams," 49–52; McWilliams, *The Education of Carey McWilliams*, 75. McWilliams and Klein (using the pen name Clive Belmont) published their initial findings in a series of articles entitled "Factories in the Field," *Pacific Weekly* 4 (March 30, 1936): 165–167; (April 6): 181–182, 188; (April 13): 199–201; (April 27): 231–232; (May 4): 247–249; (May 11): 265–267.

14. McWilliams, *Factories in the Field*, 7, 65, 77, 231; Carey McWilliams, *Ill Fares the Land: Migrants and Migratory Labor in the United States* (Boston: Little, Brown, 1942), 13.

15. McWilliams, *Factories in the Field*, 104; McWilliams, *The Education of Carey McWilliams*, 76–79; McWilliams, "Honorable in All Things," 96–97; Jerold S. Auerbach, *Labor and Liberty: The La Follette Committee and the New Deal* (Indianapolis: Bobbs-Merrill, 1966), 180.

16. Carey McWilliams, foreword to *Factories in the Field: The Story of Migratory Farm Labor in California* (1939; reprint, Santa Barbara: Peregrine Publishers, 1971), xi.

17. Mark Day, *Forty Acres: César Chávez and the Farm Workers* (New York: Praeger Publishers, 1971); John G. Dunne, *Delano: The Story of the California Grape Strike* (New York: Farrar, Straus, & Giroux, 1967); Sam Kushner, *Long Road to Delano* (New York: International Publishers, 1975); Anne Loftis and Dick Meister, *A Long Time Coming: The Struggle to Unionize America's Farm Workers* (New York: Macmillan Publishing Co., 1977); Majka and Majka, *Farm Workers, Agribusiness, and the State;* Ronald B. Taylor, *Chávez and the Farm Workers* (Boston: Beacon Press, 1975).

18. David F. Selvin, "Carey McWilliams: Reformer as Historian," *California Historical Quarterly* 53 (1974): 173–180.

19. Abraham Hoffman, "An Unusual Monument: Paul S. Taylor's *Mexican Labor in the United States* Monographs Series," *Pacific Historical Review* 45 (May 1976): 255–270.

20. Paul S. Taylor and Clark Kerr, "Documentary History of the Strike of the Cotton Pickers in California, 1933," in U.S. Senate, Subcommittee of the Committee on Education and Labor, *Hearings on S. Res. 266, Violations of Free Speech and Rights of Labor,* 74th Cong., 2d sess. (Washington, D.C.: Government Printing

Office, 1939), pt. 54: 19947–20036 (hereafter *La Follette Committee Hearings*); Dorothea Lange and Paul Taylor, *An American Exodus: A Record of Human Erosion* (New York: Reynal & Hitchcock, 1939); Richard Steven Street, "The Economist as Humanist: The Career of Paul S. Taylor," *California History* 58 (Winter 1979–80): 354–356.

21. Testimony of Paul S. Taylor, in *La Follette Committee Hearings*, pt. 47: 17283; Paul S. Taylor, "California Social Scientist" (Regional Oral History Office, Bancroft Library, University of California, Berkeley, 1973), 2:53–63; Street, "The Economist as Humanist," 355–356.

22. Paul S. Taylor, "Factors Which Underlie the Infringement of Civil Rights in Industrialized Agriculture," *La Follette Committee Hearings*, pt. 62, exhibit 9573, p. 22488. While he never published a monograph on the subject, Taylor set forth his ideas in several additional essays: Paul S. Taylor and Tom Vasey, "Historical Background of California Farm Labor," *Rural Sociology* 1 (September 1936): 281–295; Taylor and Vasey, "Contemporary Background of California Farm Labor," *Rural Sociology* 1 (December 1936): 401–419; Taylor, "Migratory Agricultural Workers on the Pacific Coast," *American Sociological Review* 3 (April 1938): 225–232; and Taylor, "Foundations of California Rural Society."

23. Taylor and Vasey, "Historical Background of California Farm Labor," 283.

24. Taylor, "Foundations of California Rural Society," 193; Street, "The Economist as Humanist," 356–359; Mary Ellen Leary, "Paul Taylor: The Power of a Tenacious Man," *The Nation* 219 (October 12, 1974): 333–338; Paul S. Taylor, *Essays on Land, Water, and the Law in California* (New York: Arno Press, 1979).

25. Taylor, "California Social Scientist," 1:162 (emphasis in original).

26. Fuller, "The Supply of Agricultural Labor"; Stuart Marshall Jamieson, *Labor Unionism in American Agriculture*, U.S. Department of Labor, Bureau of Labor Statistics, Bulletin 836 (Washington, D.C.: Government Printing Office, 1945); Walter Goldschmidt, *As You Sow* (Glencoe, Ill.: Free Press, 1947); Stein, *California and the Dust Bowl Migration*.

27. See the Essay on Sources for a full listing, and David Vaught, "Factories in the Field Revisited," *Pacific Historical Review* 66 (May 1997): 149–184, for a more extensive historiographical treatment.

28. Weber, *Dark Sweat, White Gold*, 6.

29. See David Brody, "Reconciling the Old Labor History and the New," *Pacific Historical Review* 62 (February 1993): 1–18, for a provocative analysis that places in historical perspective the tension between presentist and anti-presentist impulses in the new labor history.

30. Daniel, *Bitter Harvest*, 34–39.

31. Mary Neth, *Preserving the Family Farm: Women, Community, and the Foundations of Agribusiness in the Midwest, 1900–1940* (Baltimore: Johns Hopkins University Press, 1995), 2.

Chapter 1: "More Than Manufacturing"

1. *California Fruit Grower*, November 8, 1902.

2. George Robertson, "Statistical Summary of the Production and Resources of California" (1850–1910), in California State Board of Agriculture, *Fifty-eighth Annual*

Report for 1911 (Sacramento: State Printing Office, 1912), 144–152; George Husmann, "The Raisin Industry," U.S. Department of Agriculture, *Bulletin,* no. 349 (Washington, D.C.: Government Printing Office, 1916), 3; "The Grape Growing Industry in the United States," *National Geographic Magazine* 14 (December 1903): 445; M. Theo Kearney, *Fresno County, California, and the Evolution of the Fruitvale Estate* (Fresno: by author, 1903), 16, box 1, M. Theo Kearney Papers, Fresno City and County Historical Society, Fresno (hereafter Kearney Papers — Fresno); Schyler Rehart and William K. Patterson, *M. Theo Kearney — Prince of Fresno: A Biography of Martin Theodore Kearney* (Fresno: Fresno City and County Historical Society, 1988), 18.

3. "Fresno County," in California State Agricultural Society, *Transactions during the Year 1901* (Sacramento: State Printing Office, 1903), 209; *Pacific Rural Press,* January 17 and May 23, 1903; Husmann, "The Raisin Industry," 4; Pierre N. Beringer, "Fresno: The Paradise of the Industrious Man of Small Means," *Overland Monthly* 52 (December 1908): 562–578.

4. *Pacific Rural Press,* August 9, 1902; *Newcastle News,* April 29, 1903.

5. *Pacific Rural Press,* January 7, 1899; August 9, 1902; *Newcastle News,* July 30 and August 13, 1902; "Placer County," in California State Agricultural Society, *Transactions during the Year 1901,* 308–309; Joseph A. McGowan, *History of the Sacramento Valley* (New York: Lewis Historical Publishing Co., 1961), 1:386.

6. *Davisville Enterprise,* December 6, 1901; December 25, 1902; Robertson, "Statistical Summary of the Production and Resources of California," 159; "Yolo County," in California State Agricultural Society, *Transactions during the Year 1901,* 462.

7. *Davisville Enterprise,* March 9, 1900; "Almonds Sold" for 1902 and "Almonds," in George W. Pierce Jr., Account Book, 1897–1910, 119, 121, box 2, Pierce Family Papers, Department of Special Collections, University of California Library, Davis.

8. Caroline M. Olney, "Orchards, Vineyards, and Farms of Yolo County," *Overland Monthly* 40 (May 1902): 171–172, 181–184.

9. *Pacific Rural Press,* June 14, 1901; September 6, 1902; James Jerome Parsons Jr., "The California Hop Industry: Its Eighty Years of Development and Expansion" (M.A. thesis, University of California, Berkeley, 1939), 28, 111.

10. *Pacific Rural Press,* January 17, 1893; *California Fruit Grower,* February 26, 1910; Peter J. Delay, *History of Yuba and Sutter Counties* (Los Angeles: Historic Record Co., 1924), 199, 1187. The other prominent hop regions in California were in Sonoma and Mendocino Counties along the Russian River, and in Sacramento County bordering the American and Sacramento Rivers.

11. *Pacific Rural Press,* August 30, 1902; August 20, 1904; August 11, 1906; *Sacramento Evening Bee,* August 21, 1902; "Immigrant Labor in the Hop Industry," in U.S. Senate, Reports of the Immigration Commission, "Immigrants in Industries," pt. 25, *Japanese and Other Immigrant Races in the Pacific Coast and Rocky Mountain States,* vol. 24, 61st Cong., 2d sess. (Washington, D.C.: Government Printing Office, 1911), 157–158 (hereafter *Dillingham Commission Report*).

12. *Journal of Commerce and Commercial Bulletin* (New York), September 9, 1893, clipping in box 5, Martin Theodore Kearney Correspondence and Papers, Bancroft Library, University of California, Berkeley (hereafter Kearney Papers — Bancroft).

13. *Pacific Rural Press,* June 11, 1904; George Robertson, "The California Fruit In-

dustry," in *Proceedings of the Thirty-eighth Convention of the California State Fruit Growers,* December 6–9, 1910 (Sacramento: State Printing Office, 1910), 88; Paul Rhode, "Learning, Capital Accumulation, and the Transformation of California Agriculture," *Journal of Economic History* 55 (December 1995): 778–779; Gerald D. Nash, "Stages of California's Economic Growth, 1870–1970: An Interpretation," *California Historical Quarterly* 51 (Winter 1972): 315–321.

14. *Pacific Rural Press,* July 15, 1899.

15. William Issel and Robert W. Cherny, *San Francisco, 1865–1932: Politics, Power, and Urban Development* (Berkeley: University of California Press, 1986), 23, 55; Robert Glass Cleland and Osgood Hardy, *March of Industry* (Los Angeles: Powell Publishing Co., 1929), 133–148; Ira B. Cross, *A History of the Labor Movement in California* (Berkeley: University of California Press, 1935), 60–62; William Deverell, *Railroad Crossing: Californians and the Railroad, 1850–1910* (Berkeley: University of California Press, 1994), 22–39.

16. Edward J. Wickson, *The California Fruits and How to Grow Them,* 7th ed. (San Francisco: Pacific Rural Press, 1914), 9–35; Elna Bakker, *An Island Called California: An Ecological Introduction to Its Natural Communities* (Berkeley: University of California Press, 1971), 147–157; Robert W. Hodgson, "The California Fruit Industry," *Economic Geography* 9 (October 1936): 337–344; Lawrence J. Jelinek, *Harvest Empire: A History of California Agriculture,* 2d ed. (San Francisco: Boyd & Fraser, 1982), 1–2; James J. Parsons, "The Uniqueness of California," *American Quarterly* 7 (Spring 1955): 45–55; Ann Foley Scheuring, ed., *A Guidebook to California Agriculture* (Berkeley: University of California Press, 1983), 1–5, 43–64.

17. Charles Howard Shinn, "Early Horticulture in California," *Overland Monthly* 6 (August 1885): 117.

18. Wickson, *The California Fruits and How to Grow Them,* 10.

19. Other prominent specialty crop regions in California at the turn of the century included Monterey County, Oxnard, Chino, Santa Ana, and several other southern California localities (sugar beets); Vacaville-Winters-Suisun (deciduous fruit); Santa Clara (deciduous fruit); the Sacramento–San Joaquin Delta (vegetables); the Florin district (vegetables and berries); Alameda County (vegetables and sugar beets); the Pajaro Valley (apples and berries); Los Angeles, Riverside, and Orange Counties (citrus); and the Imperial Valley (vegetables).

20. *San Francisco Chronicle,* December 14, 1890, reprinted in M. Theo Kearney, *Fresno County, California: The Land of Sunshine, Fruits, and Flowers . . .* (Fresno: by author, 1893), 4, 7, box 1, Kearney Papers—Fresno; N. P. Chipman, "Fruit vs. Wheat: A Discussion of the Relative Importance of Wheat Growing and Fruit Growing in California," in "Transactions of the Sixteenth State Fruit Growers' Convention," November 15–18, 1892, in State Board of Horticulture of the State of California, *Fourth Biennial Report for 1893–1894* (Sacramento: State Printing Office, 1894), 162; George B. Otis, *Reminiscences of Early Days: The Pioneer Days of Selma and Surrounding Country* (Selma, Calif.: Press of the Selma Irrigator, 1911), 15–16, Bancroft Library; Moses J. Church, "Irrigation in the San Joaquin Valley," 7–8, dictation taken May 3, 1883, Bancroft Library; Michael Magliari, "Populism, Steamboats, and the Octopus: Transportation Rates and Monopoly in California's Wheat Regions,

1890–1896," *Pacific Historical Review* 58 (November 1989): 456–460; John A. Shaw, "Railroads, Irrigation, and Economic Growth: The San Joaquin Valley of California," *Explorations in Economic History* 10 (Winter 1973): 211–212.

21. The Central Pacific became the Southern Pacific in 1884 when the former and a number of other lines joined together to form one huge corporation.

22. Paul Gates, *Land and Law in California: Essays on Land Policies* (Ames: Iowa State University Press, 1991), passim; Gerald D. Nash, "Henry George Reexamined: William S. Chapman's Views on Land Speculation in Nineteenth Century California," *Agricultural History* 33 (July 1959): 133–137; Richard J. Orsi, "*The Octopus* Reconsidered: The Southern Pacific and Agricultural Modernization in California, 1865–1915," *California Historical Quarterly* 54 (Fall 1975): 200–201; Donald J. Pisani, "Land Monopoly in Nineteenth-Century California," *Agricultural History* 65 (Fall 1991): 15–23; Wallace Smith, *Garden of the Sun: A History of the San Joaquin Valley* (Los Angeles: Lymanhouse, 1939), 169–202.

23. Pisani, "Land Monopoly in Nineteenth-Century California," 25–27. Riparian rights came with the title to land adjoining streams and lakes; they were tied neither to time nor to use. Prior appropriation, on the other hand, allowed the user to divert water from the natural channel of a stream as long as it was put to good (and continuous) use; the first to use the water held the legal rights.

24. This description of the Fresno agricultural colonies draws from the following: Charles W. Clough and William B. Secrest Jr., *Fresno County — The Pioneer Years: From the Beginning to 1900* (Fresno: Panorama West Books, 1984), 115–120, 143–162; C. E. Grunsky, "Water Appropriation from Kings River," in U.S. Department of Agriculture, *Report of Irrigation Investigations in California,* Office of Experiment Stations Bulletin No. 100 (Washington, D.C.: Government Printing Office, 1901), 259–325; Arthur Maass and Raymond L. Anderson, . . . *and the Desert Shall Rejoice: Conflict, Growth, and Justice in Arid Environments* (Cambridge: MIT Press, 1978), 146–169, 208–214; Virginia E. Thickens, "Pioneer Agricultural Colonies of Fresno County," parts 1 and 2, *California Historical Society Quarterly* 25 (March, June 1946): 17–38, 169–177.

25. *Fresno Daily Evening Expositor,* March 30, 1892, reprinted in William B. Secrest Jr., comp., *Fresno County Scrapbook, 1870–1899* (Fresno: C. W. Clough, 1987), 1:16, Department of Special Collections, Henry Madden Library, California State University, Fresno (hereafter *FCS*).

26. *Fresno Expositor,* January 24, 1877, quoted in Rehart and Patterson, *M. Theo Kearney — Prince of Fresno,* 10.

27. See Thickens, "Pioneer Agricultural Colonies of Fresno County," for sketches of the following colonies: Washington, Nevada, Church, Temperance, Scandinavian, American, Fresno, Easterby, Malaga, Fruit Vale, Perrin, Wolters', West Park, Union, Caledonia, Kutner, Muscatel, Enterprise, Wittram, and Norris.

28. Pacific Coast Land Bureau, *Fresno County, California, and Its Offering for Settlement* (San Francisco: Pacific Coast Land Bureau, 1883), Bancroft Library; Bernhard Marks, *Small Scale Farming in California: The Colonization System of the Great Valley of the San Joaquin in Central California* (San Francisco: H. S. Crocker, 1890), Bancroft Library; Orsi, "*The Octopus* Reconsidered," 208–209.

29. Gustav Eisen, *The Raisin Industry: A Practical Treatise on the Raisin Grapes, Their History, Culture, and Curing* (San Francisco: H. S. Crocker, 1890), 185.

30. *Fresno Weekly Expositor,* October 20, 1879, quoted in Clough and Secrest, *Fresno County—The Pioneer Years,* 147; Charles C. Colby, "The California Raisin Industry: A Study in Geographic Interpretation," *Annals of the Association of American Geographers* 14 (June 1924): 80–83; Ben R. Walker, *The Fresno County Blue Book* (Fresno: Arthur H. Cawston, 1941), 102.

31. C. O. Ziegenfuss, "History of Fresno County, California," in Thomas H. Thompson, *Official Historical Atlas Map of Fresno County* (Tulare, Calif.: Thomas H. Thompson, 1891), 12; Robertson, "Statistical Summary of the Production and Resources of California," 144; Clough and Secrest, *Fresno County—The Pioneer Years,* 146–148; Colby, "The California Raisin Industry," 58.

32. E. Leroy Chaddock, "Fifty Years as a Raisin Packer," typescript, 1943, 40, Department of Special Collections, Henry Madden Library, California State University, Fresno.

33. Eisen, *The Raisin Industry,* preface, 104–132, 213; A. D. Barling, "Culture and Curing," *California, A Journal of Rural Industry* 1 (April 1890): 8–9; "Biography of A. D. Barling," ibid., 9; *Fresno Daily Evening Expositor,* October 10, 1890, FCS, 1:34–35.

34. T. C. White, "The Raisin Grape," in "Proceedings of the Twelfth State Fruit Growers' Convention," November 5–8, 1889, in State Board of Horticulture of the State of California, *Annual Report for 1889* (Sacramento: State Printing Office, 1890), 430–434; White, "Raisin-Drying, Packing, and Preparing for the Market," in Board of State Viticultural Commissioners of California, *Report of the Sixth Annual State Viticultural Convention,* March 7–10, 1888 (Sacramento: State Printing Office, 1888), 17–34; M. F. Austin, "Raisin Making," 1881, reprinted in Clough and Secrest, *Fresno County—The Pioneer Years,* 150; Eisen, *The Raisin Industry,* 106; Eisen, "Raisin Department," *California, A Journal of Rural Industry* 1 (April 1890): 6.

35. "The Raisin Industry of Fresno," *California, A Journal of Rural Industry* 1 (February 1890): 6; Eisen, *The Raisin Industry,* 208–219; "Professor Gustavus A. Eisen," *Fresno Morning Republican,* July 13, 1930, clipping in Ernestine Winchell, "Fresno Memories," 3:21, Bancroft Library; H. M. Butterfield, "The Builders of California's Grape and Raisin Industry," *Blue Anchor* 15 (February 1938): 2–4, 23–25.

36. *Fresno Daily Evening Expositor,* March 30, 1892.

37. Pacific Coast Land Bureau, *Fresno County, California, and Its Offering for Settlement,* 6.

38. Quoted from two promotional pamphlets reprinted in Maass and Anderson, *. . . and the Desert Shall Rejoice,* 166–167; and Marks, *Small Scale Farming in California,* 44. See also *Fresno Daily Evening Expositor,* March 30, 1892; Fresno County Board of Trade, *Climate, Soil, and Water and Their Relation to Homes in Fresno County . . . Facts and Figures* (Fresno: Fresno County Board of Trade, 1888), Bancroft Library; Fresno County Chamber of Commerce, *Fresno County, California* (Fresno: Evening Democrat Print, ca. 1900), 8–12, Bancroft Library; and Eisen, *The Raisin Industry,* 47.

39. Charles Nordhoff, *California for Health, Pleasure, and Residence: A Book for Travelers and Settlers* (1873; reprint, Berkeley: Ten Speed Press, 1973), 180–181; *Fresno Daily Evening Expositor,* March 30, 1892.

40. Ziegenfuss, "History of Fresno County, California," 12; Eisen, *The Raisin Industry,* 125, 208, 210; Hogue, Murray, and Sesnon, *Fresno County, California: Where Can Be Found Climate, Soil, and Water* . . . (Oakland: Pacific Press, ca. 1887), 66, Bancroft Library; "Hedge-Row Vineyard," *Fresno Morning Republican,* May 25, 1930, clipping in Winchell, "Fresno Memories," 3:16; "Miss Lucy Hatch," *Fresno Morning Republican,* June 1, 1930, ibid., 3:17; "Minnie Eshleman," *Fresno Morning Republican,* March 16, 1930, ibid., 3:10; *Fresno Daily Evening Expositor,* June 19, 1891, *FCS,* 1:188–191. Thompson's *Official Historical Atlas Map of Fresno County,* 119–122, provides a good estimate of the number of women "upon 20-acre lots here and there" (in Winchell's words) in Fresno County in 1891: of 304 vineyardists whom he recorded as "patrons," 13 (4 percent) were women.

41. "Immigrant Farmers of Fresno County," in *Dillingham Commission Report,* 24:625–635; *Fresno Morning Republican,* July 6, July 20, and August 3, 1919; Charles Mahakian, "History of the Armenians in California" (M.A. thesis, University of California, Berkeley, 1935), 15, 26–32; Edith Catharine Meyer, "The Development of the Raisin Industry in Fresno County, California" (M.A. thesis, University of California, Berkeley, 1931), 52–61. Easton is quoted from Pacific Coast Land Bureau, *Fresno County, California, and Its Offering for Settlement,* 28.

42. *California Fruit Grower,* December 15, 1888; September 28, 1889 (contains a list of Fresno packers and their eastern agents); D. T. Fowler, "Review of the Raisin Industry," in *Official Report of the Nineteenth Fruit Growers' Convention,* November 5–8, 1895 (Sacramento: State Printing Office, 1896), 64; Edward F. Adams, *The Modern Farmer in His Business Relations* (San Francisco: N. J. Stone Co., 1899), 458–462; Chaddock, "Fifty Years as a Raisin Packer," 42; Eisen, *The Raisin Industry,* 153–168, 205–207; Will Payne, "Cooperation — The Raisin Baron," *Saturday Evening Post,* April 30, 1910, 14–15; Walter V. Woehlke, "In the Service of Quality," *Outlook* 93 (October 23, 1909): 425; Victoria Alice Saker, "Benevolent Monopoly: The Legal Transformation of Agricultural Cooperation, 1890–1943" (Ph.D. diss., University of California, Berkeley, 1990), 178–181.

43. Chaddock, "Fifty Years as a Raisin Packer," 45–52; Franklin P. Nutting, "An Interview with Franklin P. Nutting" (Regional Oral History Office, Bancroft Library, University of California, Berkeley, 1955), 21–25; Fowler, "Review of the Raisin Industry," 65–67; Rehart and Patterson, *M. Theo Kearney — Prince of Fresno,* 26; Saker, "Benevolent Monopoly," 182–184.

44. J. P. Vincent, County Assessor, to M. Theo Kearney, March 17, 1897, box 1, Kearney Papers — Bancroft; *Fresno Daily Evening Expositor,* June 19, 1891, *FCS,* 1:190; Adams, *The Modern Farmer,* 460–462; W. Y. Spence, "Success after Twenty Years," *Sun-Maid Herald* 3 (November 1917): 4–5, 16; Charles W. Clough et al., *Fresno County in the Twentieth Century: From 1900 to the 1980s* (Fresno: Panorama West Books, 1986), 172; Smith, *Garden of the Sun,* 518–521; John Andrew Shaw Jr., "Commercialization in an Agricultural Economy: Fresno County, California, 1856–1900" (Ph.D. diss., Purdue University, 1969), 41; Saker, "Benevolent Monopoly," 188–189.

45. *California Fruit Grower,* November 11, 1899; *Fresno Morning Republican,* June 29, 1919; Payne, "Cooperation—The Raisin Baron," 14; H. E. Erdman, "The Development and Significance of California Cooperatives, 1900–1915," *Agricultural History* 32 (July 1958): 183; Saker, "Benevolent Monopoly," 180, 188–189.

46. T. C. White, "Cooperation among Raisin-Growers," in "Transactions of the Twenty-fifth State Fruit-Growers' Convention," December 4–7, 1900, in State Board of Horticulture of the State of California, *Seventh Biennial Report for 1899–1900* (Sacramento: State Printing Office, 1901), 162; *Fresno Morning Republican,* April 1889, quoted in Kearney, *Evolution of the Fruitvale Estate,* 17; *Pacific Rural Press,* January 17, 1902; Thompson, *Official Historical Atlas Map of Fresno County,* 33; Adams, *The Modern Farmer,* 465; Saker, "Benevolent Monopoly," 188.

47. *Placer Herald,* February 19, 1887; *Placer County Republican,* January 23, 1913; *Sacramento Daily Union,* February 22, 1873; J. F. Madden, *The Resources of the New-castle District . . . Located in the "Warm Gold Belt"* (Sacramento: Goode Brothers, 1887), 11, Bancroft Library; Myron Angell, ed., *History of Placer County, California, with Illustrations and Biographical Sketches of Its Prominent Men and Pioneers* (Oakland: Thompson & West, 1882), 246–248.

48. "Placer County," in California State Agricultural Society, *Transactions during the Year 1887* (Sacramento: State Printing Office, 1888), 147; *Sacramento Daily Record-Union,* July 2, 1887; W. B. Lardner and M. J. Brock, *History of Placer and Nevada Counties* (Los Angeles: Historic Record Co., 1924), 233–234; Leonard M. Davis, *Newcastle, Gem of the Foothills: A Pictorial History of Newcastle, Placer County, California from Its Formative Days to the Present* (Newcastle: Newcastle Community Association, 1993), 15–19.

49. W. B. Gester, "The Placer County Fruit District," in "Transactions of the Fifteenth State Fruit Growers' Convention," November 17–20, 1891, in State Board of Horticulture of the State of California, *Annual Report for 1891* (Sacramento: State Printing Office, 1892), 476–478; *Placer County Republican,* August 13, 1908; *Placer Herald,* October 6 and 20, 1923; *Sacramento Daily Record-Union,* July 2, 1887; Lardner and Brock, *History of Placer and Nevada Counties,* 234, 498–499, 726–727; Samuel Evans Gittings, "The Foundations of Placer County Horticulture, 1850–1900" (M.A. thesis, Sacramento State College, 1959), 45–71, 97–99.

50. H. E. Butler to R. H. Elsworth, June 25, 1927, carton 15, H. E. Erdman Papers, Bancroft Library; *Sacramento Daily Record-Union,* July 2, 1887; *Placer County Republican,* September 8 and 22, 1910; February 6, 1913; Charles E. Uren, *Official Map of Placer County, California* (San Francisco: Britton & Rey, 1887); Ralph D. Robertson and J. W. Nelson, "Irrigation and Soil Conditions in the Sierra Nevada Foothills, California," University of California College of Agriculture, Agricultural Experiment Station, *Bulletin,* no. 253 (May 1915): 353; H. M. Butterfield, "Pioneer Days in California's Peach Industry," *Blue Anchor* 14 (November 1937): 11; Lardner and Brock, *History of Placer and Nevada Counties,* 234.

51. Gittings, "The Foundations of Placer County Horticulture," 105–107; Robert Kelley, *Gold vs. Grain: The Hydraulic Mining Controversy in California's Sacramento Valley* (Glendale, Calif.: Arthur H. Clark Co., 1959), 215–242.

52. *Placer Herald,* March 26 and April 9, 1887; December 29, 1888; *Newcastle News,* January 2, 1889; *Sacramento Daily Record-Union,* July 2, 1887; U.S. Department of Agriculture, *Report of Irrigation Investigations in California,* 136–142; Gittings, "The Foundations of Placer County Horticulture," 109–114.

53. *Placer Herald,* February 19, 1887; *Newcastle News,* April 4, 1888; "Placer County Citrus Colony [Charter]," April 2, 1888, filed under "Leases and Agree-

ments," Book F, 244–252, Placer County Recorder's Office, Auburn, Calif. Subscribers added an additional 2,398 acres the following year, giving the colony a total of 7,563, as noted in Placer County Citrus Colony, *Placer County Citrus Colony, in the Lower Foothills of Placer County, California* (San Francisco: H. S. Crocker, 1889), 20, Bancroft Library.

54. Harry E. Butler, "History of the English Colony," typescript, 1948, 2, Harry Butler Biographical Letter File, California Room, California State Library, Sacramento; R. A. Nicol, "The British Colony in Placer County," *The British-Californian* 5 (May 1899): 9–12; Placer County Citrus Colony, *Placer County Citrus Colony*, 17; Placer County Agricultural Training College, *Prospectus . . . of the Placer County Agricultural Training College, Penryn, Placer County, California* (Penryn: The College, 1894), Bancroft Library.

55. *Placer County Republican*, October 23, 1913; Placer County Citrus Colony, *Placer County Citrus Colony*, 11.

56. *Placer County Republican*, May 24, 1893; Butler, "History of the English Colony," 3–4; *Newcastle News*, December 18, 1889; *Placer Herald*, September 12, 1952; Nicol, "The British Colony in Placer County," 9.

57. *Placer County Republican*, October 27, 1893; *Newcastle News*, November 8 and 29, December 6, 13, and 20, 1893; *Pacific Rural Press*, November 4 and 11, 1893.

58. *Pacific Rural Press*, January 9, 1892; November 25, 1893; P. W. Butler, "Peach Culture," in State Board of Horticulture of the State of California, *Official Report of the Tenth State Fruit Growers' Convention*, November 20–23, 1888 (Sacramento: State Printing Office, 1889), 71–74; *California Fruit Grower*, April 18 and June 13, 1891; E. W. Maslin, "The Sierra Foothills — Soil and Climate and Adaptation to Fruit and Grape Culture," in California State Agricultural Society, *Transactions during the Year 1884* (Sacramento: State Printing Office, 1885), 439–451.

59. *California Fruit Grower*, April 11, 18, and 25, May 2, 1891; *Sacramento Daily Record-Union*, July 2, 1887; P. W. Butler, "Placer County," in State Board of Horticulture of the State of California, *Official Report of the Tenth State Fruit Growers' Convention*, 206–208.

60. *Newcastle News*, January 2 and December 18, 1889; January 13, 1892; February 15, 1893; August 13, 1902; *Pacific Rural Press*, November 25, 1892; *Placer County Republican*, October 23, 1913; Butler to Elsworth, June 25, 1927, Erdman Papers; Harry E. Butler to Mabel R. Gillis, January 25, 1946, Butler Biographical File; May W. Perry, "Stewart's Flat and Penryn," *Placer Nugget*, October 1964, 6–7.

61. *Newcastle News*, January 2 and December 18, 1889; Placer County Land Company, *Placer County: General Information, Facts and Figures* (San Francisco: The Company, 1893), 17, Bancroft Library.

62. *Newcastle News*, November 30, 1887; March 7, July 11, and December 12, 1888; May 20, 1891; May 17, 1893; Lardner and Brock, *History of Placer and Nevada Counties*, 501.

63. *Newcastle News*, January 2 and December 18, 1889; January 8, 1890; *Placer County Republican*, October 23, 1913.

64. *California Fruit Grower*, April 26, 1890.

65. Chaddock, "Fifty Years as a Raisin Packer," 66.

66. William B. Gester, "The Marketing of California Fresh Fruit in the East,"

in "Transactions of the Twenty-fifth State Fruit-Growers' Convention," 100; *California Fruit Grower,* November 24, 1896; July 24, 1897; February 12, 1910; Fred Wilbur Powell, "Co-operative Marketing of California Fresh Fruit," *Quarterly Journal of Economics* 24 (February 1910): 392–418; William A. Taylor, "The Influence of Refrigeration on the Fruit Industry," U.S. Department of Agriculture, *Yearbook, 1900* (Washington, D.C.: Government Printing Office, 1901), 573–575; Erich Kraemer and H. E. Erdman, "History of Cooperation in the Marketing of California Fresh Deciduous Fruits," University of California College of Agriculture, Agricultural Experiment Station, *Bulletin,* no. 557 (September 1933).

67. Fruit could depreciate in value 25 to 50 percent in 24 hours when exposed to the midsummer heat, according to Harris Weinstock's estimate in "Review of Fruit Shipping, 1887," in *Proceedings of the Eighth Fruit Growers' Convention of the State of California,* November 8–11, 1887 (Sacramento: State Printing Office, 1888), 48. See also *Pacific Rural Press,* December 3, 1898; August 9, 1902; *Sacramento Daily Record-Union,* July 2, 1887; *California Fruit Grower,* July 19, 1890; June 13, 1891; Placer County Land Company, *Placer County,* 7–8, 22–25; Placer County Board of Trade, *Placer County, California* (Auburn: Placer County Board of Trade, 1888), 10–11, Bancroft Library; and Placer County Immigration Society, *Placer County, California: Its Resources and Advantages* (Auburn: Placer County Immigration Society, 1886), 13–15, Bancroft Library.

68. *Newcastle News,* December 28, 1887; January 25, 1888; January 2, 1889; March 18, 1895; *California Fruit Grower,* July 19, 1890; February 12, 1910; *Placer Herald,* December 31, 1897; December 16, 1893; *Pacific Rural Press,* December 20, 1902; Erdman, "The Development and Significance of California Cooperatives," 180; Powell, "Co-operative Marketing of California Fresh Fruit," 395–396.

69. *Newcastle News,* August 19, 1891; March 9, 1892; June 27, 1894; *Pacific Rural Press,* November 5, 1893; November 24 and December 1, 1894; *Placer County Republican,* April 5 and 26, 1895; W. B. Gester, "Transportation and Freight Rates of Green and Dry Fruits," in *Official Report of the Eighteenth Fruit Growers' Convention of the State of California,* November 20–23, 1894 (Sacramento: State Printing Office, 1895), 15–16; C. F. Smurr, "Freight Rates," ibid., 63–71; Powell, "Co-operative Marketing of California Fresh Fruit," 398–399.

70. *Newcastle News,* January 2, 1889; C. G. Werner to A. J. Schoendorf, January 21, 1947, printed in A. J. Schoendorf, *Beginnings of Cooperation in the Marketing of California Fresh Deciduous Fruits and History of the California Fruit Exchange* (Sacramento: Inland Press, 1947), 16; T. G. Chamberlain, "Fruit Ranching Conditions in the Placer County Fruit Belt," typescript, June 1916, 4–6, carton 16, Elwood Mead Papers, Bancroft Library; Interview with A. H. Ackermann, Manager, Penryn Fruit Growers' Association, October 30, 1924, carton 15, Erdman Papers; Interview with J. A. Teagarden, President, Auburn Fruit Exchange, October 23, 1924, ibid.

71. *Newcastle News,* June 13, July 4, July 11, and July 18, 1894; March 18, 1895; June 3, June 10, and November 11, 1896; December 28, 1898; *Placer County Republican,* July 6 and 13, 1894; May 29, June 5, June 12, and June 19, 1896; *California Fruit Grower,* February 10, July 7, and July 21, 1894; June 20, 1896; *Pacific Rural Press,* May 4, 1895; July 14, 1894; Werner to Schoendorf, January 21, 1947; Gester, "Transportation and Freight Rates of Green and Dry Fruits," 15–16; Harris Weinstock, "Fruit Marketing,"

in *Official Report of the Eighteenth Fruit Growers' Convention of the State of California*, 16–22; Edward Berwick, "A Fruit Grower's Ideas on Transportation," ibid., 56–57; Thomas R. Bacon, "The Railroad Strike in California," *Yale Review* 3 (November 1894): 241–250.

72. *Newcastle News*, September 28, June 3, June 10, July 1, and December 23, 1896; February 21, 1898; May 24 and July 19, 1899; *Placer County Republican*, May 29, June 5, and June 19, 1896.

73. *California Fruit Grower*, November 28, 1896; July 24, 1897.

74. *Pacific Rural Press*, May 4, 1895; December 16, 1899; *Newcastle News*, July 10, 1895; *California Fruit Grower*, February 12, 1910; Kraemer and Erdman, "History of Cooperation in the Marketing of California Fresh Deciduous Fruits," 29–36; Taylor, "The Influence of Refrigeration on the Fruit Industry," 575–578.

75. *California Fruit Grower*, May 1, May 22, June 26, and July 31, 1897; November 4, 1899; *Newcastle News*, March 18, 1895; June 28, July 5, July 19, July 26, and November 29, 1899.

76. *Newcastle News*, February 27, 1901.

77. Madden, *The Resources of the Newcastle District*, 11, 19; Lardner and Brock, *History of Placer and Nevada Counties*, 233.

78. Information presented here on these settlers, their ranches, and their successors (usually sons) is drawn from *Davisville Enterprise*, January 5, 12, and 19, 1900; Frank T. Gilbert, *The Illustrated Atlas and History of Yolo County* (San Francisco: Depue, 1879), 85, 99, 101, 103; Tom Gregory, *History of Yolo County* (Los Angeles: Historic Record Co., 1913), 229–232, 271, 277–283, 664–667, 691–693, 799–801, 805–806; and Joann Leach Larkey, *Davisville '68: The History and Heritage of the City of Davis, Yolo County, California* (Davis: City of Davis, 1969), 29–31, 154–155, 170, 185–186, 189–190, 194–195, 200–202, 216.

79. Horace Davis, "Wheat in California," *Overland Monthly* 1 (November 1868): 442–452; Alan L. Olmstead and Paul Rhode, "An Overview of California Agricultural Mechanization, 1870–1930," *Agricultural History* 62 (Summer 1988): 86–112.

80. *California Fruit Grower*, October 11, 1890; McGowan, *History of the Sacramento Valley*, 1:217; Nash, "Stages of California's Economic Growth," 317.

81. See, for example, Cleland and Hardy, *March of Industry*, 80–130; Jelinek, *Harvest Empire*, 39–60; Carey McWilliams, *Factories in the Field: The Story of Migratory Farm Labor in California* (Boston: Little, Brown, 1939), 59–65; and Nash, "Stages of California's Economic Growth," 317–319.

82. George W. Pierce Jr., Daily Journals, 1890–1930, entries for January 19, 1893, November 6, 1893, and September 9, 1896, Department of Special Collections, University of California Library, Davis (hereafter Pierce journal); Webster Treat, "Profit in Almonds," *California, A Journal of Rural Industry* 1 (May 1890): 16; State Board of Horticulture of the State of California, *Annual Report for 1892* (Sacramento: State Printing Office, 1892), 317–318.

83. Rhode, "Learning, Capital Accumulation, and the Transformation of California Agriculture," 780–781, 786.

84. *California Fruit Grower*, October 13, 1900.

85. *Pacific Rural Press*, January 21, 1893; *California Fruit Grower*, October 11, 1890; W. G. Klee, "Report of the Inspector of Fruit Pests on the Conditions of Orchards

and Nurseries Visited by Him during the Months of June, July, August, and September, 1886, with Sundry Observations Bearing on the Fruit Industry," in California State Board of Horticulture, *Biennial Report for 1885 and 1886* (Sacramento: State Printing Office, 1887), 352; Webster Treat, "Almond Culture," in "Proceedings of the Thirteenth State Fruit Growers' Convention," March 11–14, 1890, in State Board of Horticulture of the State of California, *Annual Report for 1890* (Sacramento: State Printing Office, 1890), 72–75; N. P. Chipman, "Fruit Growing in California," in California State Agricultural Society, *Transactions during the Year 1887* (Sacramento: State Printing Office, 1888), 209–210.

86. While the evidence does not indicate with certainty that the La Rues were the first to grow almonds on a large scale, their 55-acre orchard, planted in the early 1880s, was one of the earliest and most prominent in the district. See *Pacific Rural Press*, August 27, 1892; *California Fruit Grower*, October 11, 1890; and Larkey, *Davisville '68*, 185–186.

87. Treat, "Almond Culture," 72–73; Treat, "Profit in Almonds," 16; *Pacific Rural Press*, January 21, 1893.

88. *Yolo Weekly Mail*, January 1, 1892.

89. Pierce journal, November 3, 1903; *Davisville Enterprise*, March 30, 1900; *Woodland Democrat*, July 3, 1913.

90. *Pacific Rural Press*, August 27, 1892; Larkey, *Davisville '68*, 185.

91. *Davisville Enterprise*, August 17 and October 26, 1898; November 1, 1900; Larkey, *Davisville '68*, 155, 170, 185, 216.

92. George W. Pierce Jr. to W. L. Morrison, September 21, 1904, box 4, Pierce Family Papers.

93. George W. Pierce, "The Almond," address delivered at the Forty-fourth California State Fruit Growers' Convention, June 5, 1914, in California State Commission of Horticulture, *Monthly Bulletin* 3 (November 1914): 456–460.

94. "Articles of Incorporation of the Oak Shade Fruit Company," February 29, 1876, California State Archives, Office of the Secretary of State, Sacramento; Treat, "Profit in Almonds," 16; Pierce journal, September 9, 1896; *Pacific Rural Press*, January 21, 1893; George W. Pierce, "The Almond Growers' Exchange," in "Proceedings of the Forty-ninth California State Fruit Growers' Convention," November 15–17, 1917, in California State Commission of Horticulture, *Monthly Bulletin* 6 (May 1917): 180; Carl August Scholl, "An Economic Study of the California Almond Growers' Exchange" (Ph.D. diss., University of California, Berkeley, 1927), 3–6.

95. Davisville Almond Growers' Association, Constitution and Minute Book, January 23, 1897, Board of Directors File, Predecessor and Concurrent Organizations, box 1, California Almond Growers' Exchange Records, Sacramento Archives and Museum Collection Center (hereafter DAGA minutes). The charter members of the association and how many tons of almonds each of them produced in 1897 (in order of their signatures in the DAGA minutes) were J. E. La Rue (50), J. W. Anderson (20), J. F. Chiles (6), Charles E. Greene (3), Eli Snider (10), E. W. Shannon (20), L. J. S. Montgomery (not indicated), G. K. Swingle (4), G. W. Sanders (5), W. O. Russell (50), George W. Pierce (12), G. Schmeiser (10), W. H. Marden (10), W. J. Montgomery (14), and W. H. Baker (9). While the minutes do not list their al-

mond acreages, the *California Fruit Grower* (March 6, 1897) reported that the charter members controlled about 600 acres.

96. DAGA minutes, May 8 and July 3, 1897; May 15 and July 15, 1899; July 4, 1900; July 20, 1901; August 9, 1902; *Davisville Enterprise,* May 19, 1899; July 31 and August 14, 1902.

97. DAGA minutes, July 8, 1899; *Pacific Rural Press,* July 22, 1899; July 7, 1900; August 11, 1900; *Davisville Enterprise,* July 14 and December 8, 1899; December 25, 1902; Elizabeth Margaret Riley, "The History of the Almond Industry in California, 1850–1934" (M.A. thesis, University of California, Berkeley, 1948), 28–34.

98. Pierce, "The Almond Growers' Exchange," 181; Olney, "Orchards, Vineyards, and Farms of Yolo County," 181–184; H. E. Erdman and Grace H. Larsen, "The Development of Agricultural Cooperatives in California," California Agricultural Experiment Station, Giannini Foundation of Agricultural Economics, February 20, 1964, filed under Henry E. Erdman, Miscellaneous Publications, Giannini Foundation of Agricultural Economics Library, University of California, Berkeley.

99. *California Fruit Grower,* December 5, 1905; McGowan, *History of the Sacramento Valley,* 2:2.

100. *Wheatland Graphic,* September 5, 1885; *Pacific Rural Press,* July 25, 1891; February 6 and 27, 1892; February 4 and October 28, 1893; February 3 and July 14, 1894; February 19, 1898; *California Fruit Grower,* February 20, 1892; Arthur Amos, "Hop Growing on the Pacific Coast of America," parts 1–4, *Journal of the Board of Agriculture* 19 (May, June, July, August 1912): 89–98, 187–195, 293–300, 378–388; Ninetta Eames, "In Hop-Picking Time," *The Cosmopolitan* 16 (November 1893): 27–35; Daniel Flint, "The Hop Industry in California," in California State Agricultural Society, *Transactions during the Year 1891* (Sacramento: State Printing Office, 1892), 196–198; Flint, *Hop Culture in California,* U.S. Department of Agriculture, Farmers' Bulletin, no. 115 (Washington, D.C.: Government Printing Office, 1900); Flint, "Hops," in California State Agricultural Society, *Report for the Year 1905* (Sacramento: State Printing Office, 1906), 60–62.

101. For example, references to all four terms are found in Eames, "In Hop-Picking Time."

102. *Pacific Rural Press,* April 21, 1894; Hubert H. Parker, *The Hop Industry* (London: P. S. King & Son, 1934), 82.

103. Testimony of E. Clemons Horst, in U.S. Commission on Industrial Relations, *Final Report and Testimony* (Washington, D.C.: Government Printing Office, 1916), 5:4931.

104. *Pacific Rural Press,* July 14, 1877; June 3 and July 8, 1882; March 29, April 26, July 19, and August 2, 1890; May 14, 1892; August 17, 1895; May 19, May 26, June 30, and July 21, 1900; *San Jose Weekly Argus,* July 21, 1877; *Sacramento Record-Union,* August 10, 1886; *Los Angeles Times,* January 29, 1891; *Sacramento Bee,* May 18, 1900.

105. Flint, "Hops," 60; J. V. Tuttle, "Greatest Gamble of the Farm," *Orchard and Farm,* September 1913; Morton Rothstein, "West Coast Farmers and the Tyranny of Distance: Agriculture on the Fringes of the World Market," *Agricultural History* 49 (January 1975): 276.

106. Flint, *Hop Culture in California,* 22; Eames, "In Hop-Picking Time," 33; Parsons, "The California Hop Industry," 112.

107. "Deed," Elizabeth and John Riley to Dr. Daniel Peters Durst, December 7, 1876, and "Records of Deeds Received," December 16, 1915, box 1, Durst Bros. Hop Ranch Papers, Department of Special Collections, Meriam Library, California State University, Chico; J. H. Durst to Jacob Samuels, June 17, 1919, box 2, ibid.; *Wheatland Graphic*, September 6 and 20, 1884; Delay, *History of Yuba and Sutter Counties*, 1187–1188.

108. *Wheatland Graphic*, September 20, 1884; September 5, 1885; *Pacific Rural Press*, April 26, 1890; May 14, 1892; May 19, 1900; Flint, "Hops," 60; Parsons, "The California Hop Industry," 39–40.

109. *Wheatland Graphic*, September 20, 1884.

110. *Pacific Rural Press*, June 17, 1893; June 9, 1900; McGowan, *History of the Sacramento Valley*, 1:226; Kelley, *Gold vs. Grain*, 107–115; Wheatland Historical Society, *The City of Wheatland, California, 1874–1974: The History of Wheatland* (Wheatland: Wheatland Historical Society, 1974), no pagination.

111. *Wheatland Graphic*, August 22, 1885; *Marysville Daily Appeal*, February 26, 1886; *Pacific Rural Press*, August 20, 1892; June 17 and July 8, 1893; *California Orchard and Farm*, August 22, 1895; J. M. Doyle, *Official Map of Yuba County, State of California* (San Francisco: Britton & Rey, 1887); Delay, *History of Yuba and Sutter Counties*, 198–199, 768–769, 1187.

112. W. U. Bowers to Dr. S. Nicholas Jacobs, December 19, 1913, and "Records of Deeds Received," December 16, 1915, box 1, Durst Bros. Hop Ranch Papers; *Pacific Rural Press*, February 4, July 8, and July 22, 1893; July 14, 1894; September 3, 1898; August 12, 1899; March 21, 1903; *California Fruit Grower*, April 15, 1898; Leslie B. Crook, *Official Map of Yuba County, California* (San Francisco: Bashford Smith, 1914); Parsons, "The California Hop Industry," 73.

113. *Pacific Rural Press*, October 28, 1893; January 25, 1896.

114. *Marysville Appeal*, November 15, 1911; "Map of Wheatland, Yuba County, California, 1885," in *California Warehouse Book* (San Pablo, Calif.: Vlak Shkurkin, 1983), 17; Delay, *History of Yuba and Sutter Counties*, 199–200; N. P. Chipman, "The Sacramento Valley: Its Resources and Industries," *Overland Monthly* 37 (April 1901): 923–925; Wheatland Historical Society, *The City of Wheatland, California*.

115. B. M. Lelong, "California Horticulturally," in State Board of Horticulture of the State of California, *Annual Report for 1892*, 38–40.

116. I. N. Hoag, "History of the State Agricultural Society in California," in California State Agricultural Society, *Transactions during the Year 1879* (Sacramento: State Printing Office, 1880), 176–211; Gerald L. Prescott, "Farm Gentry vs. the Grangers: Conflict in Rural America," *California Historical Quarterly* 56 (Winter 1977/78): 329–334; Gerald D. Nash, *State Government and Economic Development: A History of Administrative Policies in California, 1849–1933* (Berkeley: Institute of Government Studies, 1964), 67–69.

117. *Pacific Rural Press*, June 13, 1891; September 5, 1896; June 9, 1900; May 18, 1901; February 8, 1902; Pierce journal, September 2, 1911; Kevin Starr, *Inventing the Dream: California through the Progressive Era* (New York: Oxford University Press, 1985), 137–138.

118. *Hamilton Freeman*, February 16, 1870, quoted in Allan G. Bogue, *From Prairie to Corn Belt: Farming on the Illinois and Iowa Prairies in the Nineteenth Century* (Chicago: University of Chicago Press, 1963), 201.

119. Quoted in Clarence H. Danhof, *Change in Agriculture: The Northern United States, 1820–1870* (Cambridge: Harvard University Press, 1969), 70–71; Bogue, *From Prairie to Corn Belt*, 193–215.

120. Danhof, *Change in Agriculture*, 72.

121. On northern and midwestern farmers' attitudes and values, see Hal S. Barron, *Mixed Harvest: The Second Great Transformation in the Rural North, 1870–1930* (Chapel Hill: University of North Carolina Press, 1997); and Grant McConnell, *The Decline of Agrarian Democracy* (Berkeley: University of California Press, 1953).

122. Hal S. Barron, *Those Who Stayed Behind: Rural Society in Nineteenth-Century New England* (Cambridge: Cambridge University Press, 1984), 31–39.

123. *California Fruit Grower*, March 5, 1892.

124. *Fresno Daily Evening Expositor*, April 19, 1893, reprinted in Kearney, *Evolution of the Fruitvale Estate*, 28.

125. *California Fruit Grower*, August 17, 1889; *Hamilton Freeman*, September 10, 1864, quoted in Bogue, *From Prairie to Corn Belt*, 198; Chipman, "Fruit vs. Wheat," 154.

126. Chipman, "Fruit vs. Wheat," 172; Donald Edgar Walters, "Populism in California, 1889–1900" (Ph.D. diss., University of California, Berkeley, 1952), 75; Orsi, "*The Octopus* Reconsidered," 196–220; Magliari, "Populism, Steamboats, and the Octopus," 449–450.

127. Lawrence Goodwyn, *The Populist Moment: A Short History of the Agrarian Revolt in America* (Oxford: Oxford University Press, 1978), xxiv; James Turner, "Understanding the Populists," *Journal of American History* 67 (September 1980): 354–373; Michael Frederick Magliari, "California Populism, A Case Study: The Farmers' Alliance and People's Party in San Luis Obispo County, 1885–1903" (Ph.D. diss., University of California, Davis, 1992), 33–35, passim.

128. California Fruit Growers' Convention, *Official Report*, December 6, 1881 (San Francisco: Pacific Rural Press, 1882), 1.

129. California State Board of Horticulture, "Minutebook, 1883–1902," November 7, 1887, 50, Records of the Department of Agriculture, California State Archives, Office of the Secretary of State; "Secretary's Report," in State Board of Horticulture of the State of California, *Annual Report for 1890*, 25; California Fruit Growers in Council, *Official Report of the Second State Convention of California Fruit Growers*, November 14–15, 1882 (San Francisco: Pacific Rural Press, 1883), 67; California State Board of Horticulture, *Biennial Report for 1885 and 1886*, 186–188; Ellwood Cooper, "Annual Address," in "Transactions of the Fourteenth State Fruit Growers' Convention," November 18–21, 1890, in State Board of Horticulture of the State of California, *Annual Report for 1891*, 265–269; *Pacific Rural Press*, December 8, 1900; J. W. Jeffrey, "President's Address," in *Official Report of the Thirty-third California Fruit Growers' Convention*, December 3–6, 1907 (Sacramento: State Printing Office, 1907), 11–12.

130. California State Board of Horticulture, "Minutebook," July 18, 1892, 129.

131. "An Act to Create and Establish a State Board of Horticulture, and Appropriate Money for the Expenses Thereof," March 13, 1883, reprinted in State Board of Horticulture of the State of California, *Annual Report* (Sacramento: State Printing Office, 1883), 5–6.

132. Richard C. Sawyer, *To Make a Spotless Orange: Biological Control in California* (Ames: Iowa State University Press, 1996), 23–28; Howard Seftel, "Government

Regulation and the Rise of the California Fruit Industry: The Entrepreneurial Attack on Fruit Pests, 1880–1920," *Business History Review* 59 (Fall 1985): 369–402; Ralph E. Smith et al., "Protecting Plants from Their Enemies," in *California Agriculture,* ed. Claude B. Hutchison (Berkeley: University of California Press, 1946), 239–315; Steven Stoll, "Insects and Institutions: University Science and the Fruit Business in California," *Agricultural History* 69 (Spring 1995): 216–239.

133. *Pacific Rural Press,* August 29, 1902; *California Fruit Grower,* April 9, 1898; Frederick M. Maskew, *A Sketch of the Origin and Evolution of Quarantine Regulations* (Sacramento: California State Association of County Horticultural Commissioners, 1925), 22.

134. State Board of Horticulture of the State of California, *Annual Report* (1883), 13; *Newcastle News,* May 7, 1919; Maskew, *A Sketch of the Origin and Evolution of Quarantine Regulations,* 55–56.

135. Otto L. Bettmann, *The Good Old Days — They Were Terrible!* (New York: Random House, 1974), 109–113; Richard Osborn Cummings, *The American and His Food: A History of Food Habits in the United States* (Chicago: University of Chicago Press, 1941), 43–74, 160; Richard S. Street, "Marketing California Crops at the Turn of the Century," *Southern California Quarterly* 61 (Fall 1979): 239–240.

136. *Placer County Republican,* March 1, 1893; *California Fruit Grower,* September 26, 1896; *Eat California Fruits, By One of the Eaters* (San Francisco: Southern Pacific Company, 1904), 4, Bancroft Library; N. P. Chipman, *Report upon the Fruit Industry of California: Its Growth and Development and Present and Future Importance* (San Francisco: State Board of Trade of California, 1889), 34–35, California Room, California State Library; Hodgson, "The California Fruit Industry," 349–350.

137. Richard J. Orsi, "Selling the Golden State: A Study of Boosterism in Nineteenth-Century California" (Ph.D. diss., University of Wisconsin, 1973), 1–113.

138. *Newcastle News,* December 28, 1887.

139. *Newcastle News,* April 15, May 20, and September 16, 1891; Gittings, "The Foundations of Placer County Horticulture," 154–165; Street, "Marketing California Crops," 251.

140. California State Board of Horticulture, "Minutebook," April 16, 1895, 172.

141. "Placer County Enterprise," *California, A Journal of Rural Industry* 1 (February 1890): 5.

Chapter 2: "This Bugbear of Labor"

1. *Pacific Rural Press,* December 6, 1902; *California Fruit Grower,* December 6, 1902; Eugene Schmitz, "Address of Welcome," in "Transactions of the Twenty-seventh California Fruit Growers' Convention," December 2–5, 1902, in State Board of Horticulture of the State of California, *Eighth Biennial Report for 1901–1902* (Sacramento: State Printing Office, 1902), 245; George W. Pierce Jr., Daily Journals, 1890–1930, entry for December 4, 1902, Department of Special Collections, University of California Library, Davis (hereafter Pierce journal).

2. H. P. Stabler, "The California Fruit-Grower, and the Labor Supply," in "Transactions of the Twenty-seventh California Fruit Growers' Convention," 268–272; G. W. Aiken, "The Labor Question in Vineyards and Orchards," ibid., 392–395;

"Discussion on the Labor Question," ibid., 272–281, 395–398, 415; *Pacific Rural Press,* December 6, 1902.

3. Aiken, "The Labor Question in Vineyards and Orchards," 393; Thomas H. Thompson, *Official Historical Atlas Map of Fresno County* (Tulare, Calif.: Thomas H. Thompson, 1891), 393; George D. Kellogg, "Fruit Packing, Marketing, and Transportation," in "Transactions of the Twenty-seventh California Fruit Growers' Convention," 304–308; "Discussion on the Labor Question," 278; Stabler, "The California Fruit-Grower, and the Labor Supply," 269.

4. On the disjuncture between production time and labor time confronting farm managers, see Max J. Pfeffer, "Social Origins of Three Systems of Farm Production in the United States," *Rural Sociology* 48 (Winter 1983): 540–542. On the subjectivity of American agricultural labor markets, see Gavin Wright, "American Agriculture and the Labor Market: What Ever Happened to Proletarianization?" in *Quantitative Studies in Agrarian History,* ed. Morton Rothstein and Daniel Field (Ames: Iowa State University Press, 1993), 179–206.

5. *Fresno Daily Evening Expositor,* March 30, 1892, reprinted in William B. Secrest Jr., comp., *Fresno County Scrapbook, 1870–1899* (Fresno: C. W. Clough, 1987), 1:16, Department of Special Collections, Henry Madden Library, California State University, Fresno (hereafter *FCS*); *Fresno Daily Evening Expositor,* June 19, 1891, *FCS,* 1:188; *Fresno Weekly Expositor,* July 16, 1879, and April 26, 1882, *FCS,* 1:25, 67; California State Agricultural Society, "Minutes of Meetings," January 24, 1872, 1:2–3, Records of the State Agricultural Society, California State Archives, Office of the Secretary of State, Sacramento; Ben R. Walker, *The Fresno County Blue Book* (Fresno: Arthur H. Cawston, 1941), 102; Wallace Smith, *Garden of the Sun: A History of the San Joaquin Valley* (Los Angeles: Lymanhouse, 1939), 502–503; Charles W. Clough and William B. Secrest Jr., *Fresno County—The Pioneer Years: From the Beginning to 1900* (Fresno: Panorama West Books, 1984), 110.

6. Quoted in Virginia E. Thickens, "Pioneer Agricultural Colonies of Fresno County," *California Historical Society Quarterly* 25 (March 1946): 24.

7. George B. Otis, *Reminiscences of Early Days: The Pioneer Days of Selma and Surrounding Country* (Selma, Calif.: Press of the Selma Irrigator, 1911), 5, Bancroft Library, University of California, Berkeley; *Fresno Weekly Evening Expositor,* March 10, 1888, February 29, 1896, and April 5, 1897, *FCS,* 4:1610–1614; Clough and Secrest, *Fresno County—The Pioneer Years,* 332–333, 335; Charles C. Colby, "The California Raisin Industry: A Study in Geographic Interpretation," *Annals of the Association of American Geographers* 14 (June 1924): 89.

8. *Fresno Weekly Expositor,* October 15, 1879, and July 18, 1883, *FCS,* 1:10, 176; Testimony of H. Madsen of Washington Colony to the Fresno Board of Trade, November 23, 1887, in M. Theo Kearney, *Fresno County, California: The Land of Sunshine, Fruits, and Flowers . . .* (Fresno: by author, 1893), 16, box 1, M. Theo Kearney Papers, Fresno City and County Historical Society, Fresno; Bernhard Marks, *Small Scale Farming in California: The Colonization System of the Great Valley of the San Joaquin in Central California* (San Francisco: H. S. Crocker, 1890), 27–29, Bancroft Library.

9. *Fresno Weekly Expositor,* June 25, 1879, *FCS,* 1:11–12; *Fresno Weekly Evening Expositor,* June 19, 1891, *FCS,* 1:189.

10. *Fresno Weekly Expositor,* August 16, 1882, and June 27, 1883, *FCS,* 1:41, 44; William H. Mills, "Annual Address," in California State Agricultural Society, *Transactions during the Year 1890* (Sacramento: State Printing Office, 1891), 200; Simon W. Hatheway, *The Evolution of the Not-A-Seed Raisin* (Fresno: American Vineyard Company, 1906), no pagination, carton 5, Franklin P. Nutting Correspondence and Papers, Bancroft Library; "Immigrants in Fresno County, California," in U.S. Senate, Reports of the Immigration Commission, "Immigrants in Industries," pt. 25, *Japanese and Other Immigrant Races in the Pacific Coast and Rocky Mountain States,* vol. 24, 61st Cong., 2d sess. (Washington, D.C.: Government Printing Office, 1911), 573–575 (hereafter *Dillingham Commission Report*); Franklin P. Nutting, "An Interview with Franklin P. Nutting" (Regional Oral History Office, Bancroft Library, 1955), 5.

11. A. D. Barling, "Culture and Curing," *California, A Journal of Rural Industry* 1 (April 1890): 8; A. B. Butler, "California and Spain," *California, A Journal of Rural Industry* 1 (March 1890): 6; Otis, *Reminiscences of Early Days,* 22; George Robertson, "Statistical Summary of the Production and Resources of California" (1850–1910), in California State Board of Agriculture, *Fifty-eighth Annual Report for 1911* (Sacramento: State Printing Office, 1912), 26, 144; John Andrew Shaw Jr., "Commercialization in an Agricultural Economy: Fresno County, California, 1856–1900" (Ph.D. diss., Purdue University, 1969), 108–109; Clough and Secrest, *Fresno County—The Pioneer Years,* 148.

12. California State Agricultural Society, *Transactions during the Year 1878* (Sacramento: State Printing Office, 1879), 134; Placer County Immigration Society, *Placer County, California: Its Resources and Advantages* (Auburn: Placer County Immigration Society, 1886), 15–16, Bancroft Library; Myron Angell, ed., *History of Placer County, California, with Illustrations and Biographical Sketches of Its Prominent Men and Pioneers* (Oakland: Thompson & West, 1882), 241; Samuel Evans Gittings, "The Foundations of Placer County Horticulture, 1850–1900" (M.A. thesis, Sacramento State College, 1959), 28–30, 55–56; Paul W. Gates, "California's Embattled Settlers," in *Land and Law in California: Essays on Land Policies* (Ames: Iowa State University Press, 1991), 156.

13. Placer County, "Deeds," Book GG, 206–207, Placer County Recorder's Office, Auburn, Calif.

14. A survey of 55 different growers taken from the following local newspapers, trade journals, and promotional pamphlets reveals that while their orchards averaged about 30 acres, even the most successful growers rarely improved more than half their holdings: *Placer Herald,* April 13 and September 14, 1878; *Newcastle News,* December 28, 1887; January 2, 1889; *Sacramento Daily Record-Union,* July 2, 1887; September 29, 1888; *Pacific Rural Press,* December 25, 1880; *California Fruit Grower,* April 11, April 18, April 25, and May 2, 1891; J. F. Madden, *The Resources of the Newcastle District . . . Located in the "Warm Gold Belt"* (Sacramento: Goode Brothers, 1887), Bancroft Library; Placer County Land Company, *Placer County: General Information, Facts and Figures* (San Francisco: The Company, 1893), Bancroft Library; Placer County Board of Trade, *Placer County, California* (Auburn: Placer County Board of Trade, 1888), Bancroft Library; Placer County Immigration Society, *Placer County, California.*

15. Edward J. Wickson, *The California Fruits and How to Grow Them,* 2d ed. (San Francisco: Dewey, 1891), 85–98; W. G. Gester, "The Placer County Fruit District," in "Transactions of the Fifteenth State Fruit Growers' Convention," November 17–20, 1891, in State Board of Horticulture of the State of California, *Annual Report for 1891* (Sacramento: State Printing Office, 1892), 476–478; Placer County Land Company, *Placer County: General Information, Facts and Figures,* 5–6.

16. Average investment costs for the first six years for a typical Newcastle orchard are estimated in Placer County Land Company, *Placer County: General Information, Facts and Figures,* 14–16. See also Wickson, *The California Fruits and How to Grow Them,* 98, 125–151; P. W. Butler, "Peach Culture," in State Board of Horticulture of the State of California, *Official Report of the Tenth State Fruit Growers' Convention,* November 20–23, 1888 (Sacramento: State Printing Office, 1889), 72; P. W. Butler, "Placer County," ibid., 207–208; and *Pacific Rural Press,* March 13, 1886. Investment costs for "valley" orchards are estimated in *California Fruit Grower,* November 24, 1888; January 30, 1892; N. P. Chipman, *Report upon the Fruit Industry of California: Its Growth and Development and Present and Future Importance* (San Francisco: State Board of Trade of California, 1889), 27, California Room, California State Library, Sacramento; and H. D. H. Connick, "The Use of the Water of Yuba River," in U.S. Department of Agriculture, *Report of Irrigation Investigations in California,* Office of Experiment Stations Bulletin No. 100 (Washington, D.C.: Government Printing Office, 1901), 138.

17. Wickson, *The California Fruits and How to Grow Them,* 152–174, 301–303; Butler, "Peach Culture," 72; "Immigrants in Fresno County, California," 574.

18. George D. Kellogg to P. J. Healey, April 26, 1886, catalogued as a single letter in the Bancroft Library; Statement of J. M. Francis (no. 10), in T. G. Chamberlain, comp., "Statements of Fruit Ranch Owners of Placer County," June 1916, carton 17, Elwood Mead Papers, Bancroft Library (hereafter Chamberlain Survey); "Immigrant Labor in the Deciduous Fruit Industry of the Vaca Valley, California," in *Dillingham Commission Report,* 24:176; R. L. Adams, *Farm Management: A Text-Book for Student, Investigator, and Investor* (New York: McGraw-Hill, 1921), 527.

19. Pierce journal, entries for January and February, 1892–1894.

20. Webster Treat, "Almond Culture," in "Proceedings of the Thirteenth State Fruit Growers' Convention," March 11–14, 1890, in State Board of Horticulture of the State of California, *Annual Report for 1890* (Sacramento: State Printing Office, 1890), 73. The size of Pierce's harvest labor force is calculated from George W. Pierce Jr., Account Book, 1897–1910, box 2, Pierce Family Papers, Department of Special Collections, University of California Library, Davis (hereafter Pierce account book).

21. "Almonds" for 1897 and 1901, in Pierce account book, 118, 120; *Davisville Enterprise,* June 2, June 9, and August 18, 1899; July 25, 1901; December 25, 1902.

22. E. Clemens Horst, "California Leads in Hops," *California Cultivator,* October 15, 1921.

23. *Pacific Rural Press,* February 4 and July 29, 1893; July 14, 1894; Daniel Flint, *Hop Culture in California,* U.S. Department of Agriculture, Farmers' Bulletin, no. 115 (Washington, D.C.: Government Printing Office, 1900), 9–14; Arthur L. Dahl, "Growing Hops in California," *Scientific American Supplement,* no. 2263 (May 17,

1919): 312–313; Hubert H. Parker, *The Hop Industry* (London: P. S. King & Son, 1934), 101–133.

24. A "man-day" is a unit of production equal to the work an average laborer produces in one day. In contrast to hops, pears required 3.8 man-days per acre to harvest; walnuts, 1.0; peas, 8.9; and cotton, 6.4. R. L. Adams, "Seasonal Labor Requirements for California Crops," University of California College of Agriculture, Agricultural Experiment Station, *Bulletin*, no. 623 (July 1938): 5, 15–20; "Immigrant Labor in the Hop Industry," in *Dillingham Commission Report*, 24:155.

25. Adams, *Farm Management*, 525–526.

26. *Wheatland Weekly Graphic*, August 22, August 29, September 5, and September 12, 1885; *Sacramento Weekly Bee*, April 19, 1888; September 30, 1891; August 16, 1893; *Sacramento Daily Record-Union*, August 15, 1893; *Pacific Rural Press*, July 17, 1897; August 6, 1898; September 6, 1902; *California Fruit Grower*, August 31, 1895; California State Bureau of Labor Statistics, *Second Biennial Report for 1885 and 1886* (Sacramento: State Printing Office, 1887), 41; Flint, *Hop Culture in California*, 13–14; Ninetta Eames, "In Hop-Picking Time," *The Cosmopolitan* 16 (November 1893): 27–35; Janet MacDonald, "A California Hop Garden," *Overland Monthly* 45 (April 22, 1905): 325–328.

27. Gustav Eisen, *The Raisin Industry: A Practical Treatise on the Raisin Grapes, Their History, Culture, and Curing* (San Francisco: H. S. Crocker, 1890), 87–91; James Madison, "Raisin History," typescript, July 5, 1914, 2, Ben Walker History Files, Fresno City and County Historical Society; Chester Rowell, "Raisin History," April 28, 1909, Rowell Editorials, carton 2, Chester Rowell Correspondence and Papers, Bancroft Library; H. M. Butterfield, "The Builders of California's Grape and Raisin Industry," *Blue Anchor* 15 (February 1938): 2–3; Smith, *Garden of the Sun*, 486–487.

28. E. Leroy Chaddock, "Fifty Years as a Raisin Packer," typescript, 1943, 35, 37, Department of Special Collections, Henry Madden Library; T. C. White, "The Raisin Grape," in "Proceedings of the Twelfth State Fruit Growers' Convention," November 5–8, 1889, in State Board of Horticulture of the State of California, *Annual Report for 1889* (Sacramento: State Printing Office, 1890), 433; Letter (unsigned) to Gustav Eisen, April 11, 1877, "Miscellaneous Papers" folder, Gustav Eisen Papers, Bancroft Library; Will Payne, "Cooperation—The Raisin Baron," *Saturday Evening Post*, April 30, 1910, 14–15; Edward F. Adams, *The Modern Farmer in His Business Relations* (San Francisco: N. J. Stone Co., 1899), 458; Ann Foley Scheuring, ed., *A Guidebook to California Agriculture* (Berkeley: University of California Press, 1983), 148.

29. D. T. Fowler, "Review of the Raisin Industry," *Official Report of the Nineteenth Fruit Growers' Convention*, November 5–8, 1895 (Sacramento: State Printing Office, 1896), 67.

30. Eisen, *The Raisin Industry*, 116–117; *Fresno Weekly Expositor*, June 27 and July 18, 1883, *FCS*, 1:27, 41.

31. "Interview with T. C. White," *Fresno Weekly Evening Expositor*, May 19, 1892, *FCS*, 1:196–199; Eisen, *The Raisin Industry*, 124–130; Frank H. Ball, "My Work in the Raisin Vineyard," *California, A Journal of Rural Industry* 2 (July 1890): 12 (emphasis in original); "An Interview with Franklin P. Nutting," 7.

32. Eisen, *The Raisin Industry*, 133–149, 185–189; Chaddock, "Fifty Years as a Raisin Packer," 37; White, "The Raisin Grape," 430–433; Ball, "My Work in the

Raisin Vineyard," 12; "Interview with T. C. White"; T. C. White, "Raisin-Drying, Packing, and Preparing for the Market," in Board of State Viticultural Commissioners of California, *Report of the Sixth Annual State Viticultural Convention,* March 7–10, 1888 (Sacramento: State Printing Office, 1888), 17–34; M. F. Austin, "Raisin Making," 1881, reprinted in Clough and Secrest, *Fresno County—The Pioneer Years,* 150; W. B. West, "California Raisins," in California State Agricultural Society, *Transactions during the Year 1880* (Sacramento: State Printing Office, 1880), 185–187; Tucker and Hogue, *Fresno County, California: Its Rapid Development . . .* (Selma, Calif.: Daily Evening Expositor Print, ca. 1890), 6–9, Bancroft Library; Wickson, *The California Fruits and How to Grow Them,* 547–550; *California Fruit Grower,* October 26, 1889; September 19 and October 17, 1891; September 10 and 16, 1892; *Pacific Rural Press,* June 10, 1893.

33. Eisen, *The Raisin Industry,* 153–168, 205–207; Chaddock, "Fifty Years as a Raisin Packer," 36–37; West, "California Raisins," 188–189; White, "The Raisin Grape," 432–434; *California Fruit Grower,* October 26, 1889; September 10, 1892.

34. Kellogg, "Fruit Packing, Marketing, and Transportation," 304; Butler, "Peach Culture," 72–74; *Placer County Republican,* December 15, 1893; *California Fruit Grower,* December 8, 1888; May 16, 1891; June 27, 1891; *Pacific Rural Press,* December 20, 1890; December 30, 1893; N. P. Chipman, "Fruit Growing in California," in California State Agricultural Society, *Transactions during the Year 1887* (Sacramento: State Printing Office, 1888), 202–212; "Immigrant Labor in California Agricultural Industries," in *Dillingham Commission Report,* 24:9–10; Walter V. Woehlke, "In the Service of Quality," *Outlook* 93 (October 23, 1909): 420–423; Willis P. Duruz, "Harvesting and Handling Peaches for Eastern Shipment," University of California College of Agriculture, Agricultural Experiment Station, *Circular,* no. 241 (May 1922): 1–6.

35. Treat, "Almond Culture," 73; *Davisville Enterprise,* July 6, 1898; Wickson, *The California Fruits and How to Grow Them,* 512–517.

36. Warren P. Tufts et al., "The Rich Pattern of California Crops," in *California Agriculture,* ed. Claude B. Hutchison (Berkeley: University of California Press, 1946), 174; Joseph A. McGowan, *History of the Sacramento Valley* (New York: Lewis Historical Publishing Co., 1961), 2:357.

37. Treat, "Almond Culture," 74–75; *Pacific Rural Press,* January 21, 1893; October 31, 1903; *Davis Enterprise,* August 26, 1911; George W. Pierce, "The Almond," address delivered at the Forty-fourth California State Fruit Growers' Convention, June 5, 1914, in California State Commission of Horticulture, *Monthly Bulletin* 3 (November 1914): 462–463; Edward J. Wickson, *The California Fruits and How to Grow Them,* 7th ed. (San Francisco: Pacific Rural Press, 1914), 426–427; R. H. Taylor, "The Almond in California," University of California College of Agriculture, Agricultural Experiment Station, *Bulletin,* no. 297 (August 1918): 40–46.

38. Treat, "Almond Culture," 74–75; *Pacific Rural Press,* January 21, 1893; George E. Colby, "California Walnuts, Almonds, and Chestnuts," in University of California College of Agriculture, *Partial Report of Work of the Agricultural Experiment Stations for the Years 1895–96* (Berkeley: University Press, 1898), 145; *Davisville Enterprise,* August 1, 1901; Taylor, "The Almond in California," 40–45; Pierce journal, July 19, 1897.

39. *Woodland Daily Democrat,* January 28, 1901; *Davisville Enterprise,* July 14, 1899; Pierce, "The Almond," 458, 463–464.

40. Board of State Viticultural Commissioners of California, *Report of the Third Annual State Viticultural Convention,* December 1–3, 1884 (Sacramento: State Printing Office, 1885), 64; Fresno County Board of Trade, *Climate, Soil, and Water and Their Relation to Homes in Fresno County . . . Facts and Figures* (Fresno: Fresno County Board of Trade, 1888), 3, Bancroft Library; Eisen, *The Raisin Industry,* 137; *Fresno Weekly Evening Expositor,* August 19 and October 15, 1891, FCS, 1:163, 167; *California Fruit Grower,* July 6, 1889; June 27, 1891; June 18, 1892; Pierce account book, passim; *Davisville Enterprise,* June 9, 1899; August 15, 1901; Edward J. Wickson, *The Vacaville Early Fruit District of California* (San Francisco: California View Publishing Co., 1888), 127–129; "Immigrant Labor in California Agricultural Industries," 17.

41. See especially Lloyd H. Fisher, *The Harvest Labor Market in California* (Cambridge: Harvard University Press, 1953), 7–19.

42. Eisen, *The Raisin Industry,* 42, 137; "Raisin Department," *California, A Journal of Rural Industry* 1 (April 1890): 7; Adams, *Farm Management,* 554. On Davisville wheat farmers' wage practices, see Pierce account book, passim; the daily journals and account books of George W. Pierce Sr., box 3, Pierce Family Papers, Department of Special Collections, University of California Library, Davis; and Professor Richard Schwab to author, March 15, 1996.

43. *Fresno Weekly Evening Expositor,* quoted in *California, A Journal of Rural Industry* 1 (April 1890): 11.

44. Eisen, *The Raisin Industry,* 185.

45. Board of State Viticultural Commissioners of California, *Report of the Third Annual State Viticultural Convention,* 65.

46. H. Sherwin, "Observations on the Chinese Laborer," *Overland Monthly* 7 (January 1886): 97; *Pacific Rural Press,* October 1, 1881; *California Fruit Grower,* July 6, 1889; Morrison I. Swift, *What a Tramp Learns in California* (San Francisco: Society of American Socialists, 1896), 5–8, California Room, California State Library; John C. Schneider, "Tramping Workers, 1890–1920: A Subcultural View," in *Walking to Work: Tramps in America, 1790– 1935,* ed. Eric H. Monkkonen (Lincoln: University of Nebraska Press, 1984), 212–234; Ira B. Cross, *A History of the Labor Movement in California* (Berkeley: University of California Press, 1935), 60–72; Alvin Averbach, "San Francisco's South of Market District, 1850–1950: The Emergence of a Skid Row," *California Historical Quarterly* 52 (Fall 1973): 202.

47. Pierce journal, January 5 and February 24, 1893; March 31 and May 3, 1897; June 29, 1899; August 24, 1900.

48. Each worked for at least five years; see "Hired Help" for 1897–1903, in Pierce account book, 150–153; and Pierce journal, 1895–1903, passim.

49. Schwab to author, March 15, 1996; David E. Schob, *Hired Hands and Plowboys: Farm Labor in the Midwest, 1815–60* (Urbana: University of Illinois Press, 1975), especially the chapter "Harvesting."

50. Pierce journal, August 2–11, 1900. The wage rate is calculated from "Hired Help" for 1897, in Pierce account book, 150; and Pierce journal, August 31 to September 4, 1897.

51. A. W. Loomis, "How Our Chinamen Are Employed," *Overland Monthly* 2 (March 1869): 231–240; John S. Hittell, "Benefits of Chinese Immigration," *Overland Monthly* 7 (February 1886): 120–124; D. V. DuFault, "The Chinese in the Mining

Camps," *Southern California Quarterly* 41 (1959): 155–170; Sucheng Chan, *This Bitter-sweet Soil: The Chinese in California Agriculture, 1860–1910* (Berkeley: University of California Press, 1986), 37–38, 48–49.

52. *Fresno Weekly Evening Expositor*, December 25, 1895, *FCS*, 1:253–255; *Fresno Weekly Expositor*, May 14, 1873, and March 8, 1876, *FCS*, 1:3–4, 6; Moses J. Church, "Irrigation in the San Joaquin Valley," 7–8, dictation taken May 3, 1883, Bancroft Library; C. E. Grunsky, "Water Appropriation from Kings River," in U.S. Department of Agriculture, *Report of Irrigation Investigations in California*, 259–325; "Immigrants in Fresno County, California," 566, 592–593; Clough and Secrest, *Fresno County— The Pioneer Years*, 121; June English, "Leaves from the Past: Chinese Pioneers of Fresno County," *Ash Tree Echo* 8 (January 1973): 20–37.

53. *Newcastle News*, July 11, 1888; *Pacific Rural Press*, March 13, 1886; March 11, 1893; Harry E. Butler, "History of the English Colony," typescript, 1948, 5, Harry Butler Biographical Letter File, California Room, California State Library; Kellogg to Healey, April 26, 1886; B. M. Lelong, "Secretary's Report," in California State Board of Horticulture, *Biennial Report for 1885 and 1886* (Sacramento: State Printing Office, 1887), 426; Robertson, "Statistical Summary of the Production and Resources of California," 175–176; "Immigrant Labor in the Fruit Industries of the Newcastle District," in *Dillingham Commission Report*, 24:417; Gittings, "The Foundations of Placer County Horticulture," 137–138; May W. Perry, "Stewart's Flat and Penryn," *Placer Nugget*, October 1964, 4–5; Leonard M. Davis, *Newcastle, Gem of the Foothills: A Pictorial History of Newcastle, Placer County, California from Its Formative Days to the Present* (Newcastle: Newcastle Community Association, 1993), 30–32.

54. Board of State Viticultural Commissioners of California, *Report of the Third Annual State Viticultural Convention*, 64; California State Bureau of Labor Statistics, *First Biennial Report for 1883–1884* (Sacramento: State Printing Office, 1884), 167; Adams, *Farm Management*, 540–541; *Fresno Weekly Evening Expositor*, August 19, 1891, *FCS*, 1:163–164; William C. Blackwood, "A Consideration of the Labor Problem," *Overland Monthly* 3 (May 1884): 458; Chan, *This Bittersweet Soil*, 29–31, 327–330, 345.

55. *Fresno Weekly Evening Expositor*, August 19, 1891, *FCS*, 1:163; Davis, *Newcastle, Gem of the Foothills*, 32; Chan, *This Bittersweet Soil*, 122, 328, 344–346; Fisher, *The Harvest Labor Market in California*, 20–24; Levi Varden Fuller, "The Supply of Agricultural Labor as a Factor in the Evolution of Farm Organization in California" (Ph.D. diss., University of California, Berkeley, 1939), 99–100.

56. *Pacific Rural Press*, December 24, 1881; October 8, 1892; *California Fruit Grower*, June 2, 1888; A. W. Loomis, "The Chinese as Agriculturists," *Overland Monthly* 4 (June 1870): 526–532; Chan, *This Bittersweet Soil*, 18–19, 79, 345.

57. Kellogg to Healey, April 26, 1886; Statement of J. M. Frey of Newcastle, Placer County, in "Proceedings of the Fifth Annual State Fruit Growers' Convention," November 17–20, in California State Board of Horticulture, *Biennial Report for 1885 and 1886*, 39.

58. Testimony of C. C. Smith to the Fresno Board of Trade, November 23, 1887, in Kearney, *Fresno County, California*, 15; California State Bureau of Labor Statistics, *Second Biennial Report for 1885 and 1886*, 44–66.

59. *Fresno Weekly Expositor*, September 15, 1875, *FCS*, 4:1518; English, "Leaves

from the Past," 23–31; Davis, *Newcastle, Gem of the Foothills,* 30–32; Clough and Secrest, *Fresno County—The Pioneer Years,* 138–139; Ronald Takaki, *Strangers from a Different Shore: A History of Asian Americans* (New York: Penguin Books, 1989), 100.

60. *Pacific Rural Press,* December 10, 1881, for example.

61. Takaki, *Strangers from a Different Shore,* 99–112; Luther W. Spoehr, "Sambo and the Heathen Chinee: California's Racial Stereotypes in the Late 1870s," *Pacific Historical Review* 42 (May 1973): 185–204.

62. Eisen, *The Raisin Industry,* 186; *Fresno Weekly Expositor,* August 23, 1882, FCS, 1:29; *Fresno Weekly Evening Expositor,* October 12, 1891, FCS, 1:47–50; *Pacific Rural Press,* March 13, 1886; Fuller, "The Supply of Agricultural Labor," 101–105.

63. *Pacific Rural Press,* March 13, 1886; Blackwood, "A Consideration of the Labor Problem," 459–460; Barling, "Culture and Curing," 8; N. P. Chipman, "Annual Address," in California State Agricultural Society, *Transactions during the Year 1886* (Sacramento: State Printing Office, 1887), 188–189, 200–201; Chan, *This Bittersweet Soil,* 374–378; McGowan, *History of the Sacramento Valley,* 1:327–329; Fuller, "The Supply of Agricultural Labor," 109–111.

64. *Fresno Weekly Expositor,* August 23, 1882, FCS, 1:29; *Fresno Weekly Evening Expositor,* October 15, 1891, FCS, 1:167; Madison, "Raisin History," 4; Chaddock, "Fifty Years as a Raisin Packer," 42; Hogue, Murray, and Sesnon, *Fresno County, California: Where Can Be Found Climate, Soil, and Water . . .* (Oakland: Pacific Press, ca. 1887), 66, Bancroft Library; Clough and Secrest, *Fresno County—The Pioneer Years,* 150–151.

65. "An Interview with Franklin P. Nutting," 22–23; Chaddock, "Fifty Years as a Raisin Packer," 41–42; *Fresno Weekly Evening Expositor,* September 28, 1891, FCS, 1:165–167; Eisen, *The Raisin Industry,* 205, 214; Clough and Secrest, *Fresno County—The Pioneer Years,* 342–343.

66. U.S. Department of Commerce, Bureau of the Census, *Chinese and Japanese in the United States, 1910,* Bulletin 127 (Washington, D.C.: Government Printing Office, 1914), 36; *Fresno Weekly Evening Expositor,* August 19, 1891, FCS, 1:163–164.

67. *Fresno Weekly Evening Expositor,* October 15, 1891, FCS, 1:167; Eisen, *The Raisin Industry,* 188–189, 206–207; Chaddock, "Fifty Years as a Raisin Packer," 86; *California Fruit Grower,* January 16, 1897.

68. Kearney, *Fresno County, California,* 8; Eisen, *The Raisin Industry,* 206; Marks, *Small Scale Farming in California,* 29; *Pacific Rural Press,* June 10, 1891.

69. A. B. Butler's unsuccessful "Negro Experiment" was the most concerted effort; see Fuller, "The Supply of Agricultural Labor," 115–117.

70. *California Fruit Grower,* July 6, 1889; September 19, 1891; July 18 and September 10, 1892; *Fresno Weekly Evening Expositor,* September 3, 1891, FCS, 1:164; *Pacific Rural Press,* December 6, 1890; September 5, 1891.

71. *Fresno Weekly Evening Expositor,* August 19, 1891, FCS, 1:163–164.

72. *California Fruit Grower,* October 24, 1889; September 6, 1890; November 7, 1891; September 10, 1892; Fowler, "Review of the Raisin Industry," 64–67; Josiah Flynt, "The American Tramp," *Contemporary Review* 60 (August 1891): 254–255.

73. *California Fruit Grower,* September 12, 1891; June 18, 1892; *California Orchard and Farm,* May 1894; August 22, 1895.

74. *California Fruit Grower,* September 12, 1891; August 26, 1893; *Fresno Weekly*

Evening Expositor, August 15, August 17, August 22, and September 9, 1893, *FCS,* 1:168–171; *Sacramento Daily Record-Union,* August 15, 16, and 21, 1893; *Sacramento Weekly Bee,* August 23, 1893; Clough and Secrest, *Fresno County—The Pioneer Years,* 335–336.

75. *California Fruit Grower,* August 26, 1893; *Pacific Rural Press,* September 1, 1894 (emphasis in original).

76. *California Fruit Grower,* May 30, 1896; *Hanford Sentinel,* quoted in *Pacific Rural Press,* October 5, 1895; *Fresno Weekly Evening Expositor,* September 30, 1895, and August 28, 1897, *FCS,* 1:171, 202; *Fresno Morning Republican,* August 31, 1899, *FCS,* 1:172; E. Hofer, "The Tramp Problem," *Overland Monthly* 23 (June 1894): 628–632; Swift, *What a Tramp Learns in California,* 5–8.

77. Alan L. Olmstead and Paul Rhode, "An Overview of California Agricultural Mechanization, 1870–1930," *Agricultural History* 62 (Summer 1988): 86–88.

78. Chaddock, "Fifty Years as a Raisin Packer," 83–89; Madison, "Raisin History," 6; Payne, "Cooperation—The Raisin Baron," 15; Robertson, "Statistical Summary of the Production and Resources of California," 148–151; *California Fruit Grower,* November 28, 1903; December 17, 1913; *Pacific Rural Press,* May 23, 1903; *Fresno Morning Republican,* August 5, 1907; Edith Catharine Meyer, "The Development of the Raisin Industry in Fresno County, California" (M.A. thesis, University of California, Berkeley, 1931), 71–74.

79. Robertson, "Statistical Summary of the Production and Resources of California," 151.

80. *California Fruit Grower,* September 19, 1891; June 18, 1892; September 16, 1899; *Fresno Weekly Evening Expositor,* August 28 and October 2, 1897, *FCS,* 1:171, 202; *Pacific Rural Press,* September 14, 1901; "Immigrants in Fresno County, California," 584; California State Bureau of Labor Statistics, *Ninth Biennial Report for 1899–1900* (Sacramento: State Printing Office, 1900), 22; "The Grape Growing Industry in the United States," *National Geographic Magazine* 14 (December 1903): 447.

81. Butler, "California and Spain," 6; Eisen, *The Raisin Industry,* 42, 180; Aiken, "The Labor Question in Vineyards and Orchards," 394; "Discussion on the Labor Question," 395; "Immigrants in Fresno County, California," 586.

82. Masakazu Iwata, "The Japanese Immigrants in California Agriculture," *Agricultural History* 36 (Winter 1962): 27.

83. *Pacific Rural Press,* September 1, 1894; *California Fruit Grower,* June 30, 1890; "Japanese in Agriculture," in *Dillingham Commission Report,* 23:67; California State Bureau of Labor Statistics, *Seventh Biennial Report for 1895–1896* (Sacramento: State Printing Office, 1896), 103–104; Yosaburo Yoshida, "Sources and Causes of Japanese Emigration," *Annals of the American Academy of Political and Social Science* 34 (September 1909): 377–387; Kiyoshi K. Kawakami, "The Japanese on Our Farms," *Forum* 50 (July 1913): 82–84; Yamato Ichihashi, *Japanese Immigrants in the United States* (1932; reprint, New York: Arno Press, 1969), 65–82; Masakazu Iwata, *Planted in Good Soil: The History of the Issei in United States Agriculture* (New York: Peter Lang, 1992), 1–26, 71–110; Sandra O. Uyeunten, "Struggle and Survival: The History of Japanese Immigrant Families in California, 1907–1945" (Ph.D. diss., University of California, San Diego, 1988), 1–123.

84. U.S. Department of Commerce, Bureau of the Census, *Chinese and Japanese*

in the United States, 1910, 36; California State Bureau of Labor Statistics, *Seventh Biennial Report for 1895– 1896,* 101–102; Chan, *This Bittersweet Soil,* 386–402.

85. *Fresno Weekly Evening Expositor,* August 28, 1897, *FCS,* 1:202; *Pacific Rural Press,* September 1, 1900; "Immigrants in Fresno County, California," 568; Yuji Ichioka, *The Issei: The World of the First Generation Japanese Immigrants, 1885–1924* (New York: Free Press, 1988), 80–81; Stuart Marshall Jamieson, *Labor Unionism in American Agriculture,* U.S. Department of Labor, Bureau of Labor Statistics, Bulletin 836 (Washington, D.C.: Government Printing Office, 1945), 51–52. Japanese immigration to California increased dramatically after 1898, when the United States annexed Hawaii. Approximately 36,000 contract workers came to California from Hawaii alone over the next seven years; see Uyeunten, "Struggle and Survival," 30.

86. Aiken, "The Labor Question in Vineyards and Orchards," 394; "Discussion on the Labor Question," 396; *Fresno Morning Republican,* August 31, 1899, *FCS,* 1:172; *Fresno Weekly Evening Expositor,* October 26, 1897, *FCS,* 1:202; *California Fruit Grower,* October 7, 1899; "The Grape Growing Industry in the United States," 447; "Call for Convention of Fruit Growers" (poster), January 15, 1901, box 7, Kearney Correspondence and Papers, Bancroft Library; *California Fruit Grower,* March 9 and May 25, 1901.

87. *California Fruit Grower,* January 24, 1903; *Fresno Weekly Democrat,* quoted ibid., August 12, 1899. Other declarations of labor scarcity in Fresno are in *Fresno Morning Republican,* August 31, 1899, *FCS,* 1:172; *California Fruit Grower,* July 20, September 16, and October 7, 1899; June 30, 1900; January 5, 1901; July 12, 1902; and *Pacific Rural Press,* September 1, 1900; September 14, 1901.

88. Aiken, "The Labor Question in Vineyards and Orchards," 392–395; "Discussion on the Labor Question," 395–398.

89. Edward F. Adams, "Recent Progress in Co-operation in California," in "Transactions of the Twenty-seventh California Fruit Growers' Convention," 282–286; "Discussion on Report of Committee on Transportation," ibid., 340–343; "Discussion on Vine Diseases," ibid., 434–435; "Marvels of Fresno County's Wealth," *Orchard and Farm,* March 1904, 24; Aiken, "The Labor Question in Vineyards and Orchards," 394; "Discussion on the Labor Question," 397–398.

90. *Placer Herald,* November 6, 1880; *Pacific Rural Press,* July 28, 1883; Placer County Land Company, *Placer County: General Information, Facts and Figures,* 19; Placer County Board of Trade, *Placer County, California,* 14; R. A. Nicol, "The British Colony in Placer County," *The British-Californian* 5 (May 1899): 9; Placer County Citrus Colony, *Placer County Citrus Colony, in the Lower Foothills of Placer County, California* (San Francisco: Crocker, 1889), 19, Bancroft Library; Gittings, "The Foundations of Placer County Horticulture," 93–95.

91. U.S. Department of the Interior, Census Office, *Tenth Census of the United States: Report on the Productions of Agriculture, 1880* (Washington, D.C.: Government Printing Office, 1883), 106; *Sacramento Daily Record-Union,* July 2, 1887; Placer County Immigration Society, *Placer County, California: Its Resources and Advantages,* 17; Placer County Board of Trade, *Placer County, California,* 17.

92. *Sacramento Daily Record-Union,* September 29, 1888.

93. Gester, "The Placer County Fruit District," 477; W. G. Klee, "Report of the Inspector of Fruit Pests on the Conditions of Orchards and Nurseries Visited by

Him during the Months of June, July, August, and September, 1886, with Sundry Observations Bearing on the Fruit Industry," in California State Board of Horticulture, *Biennial Report for 1885 and 1886*, 367.

94. *Sacramento Weekly Bee*, January 3, 1889.

95. Placer County Board of Trade, *Placer County, California*, 5; Placer County Immigration Society, *Placer County, California: Its Resources and Advantages*, 15, 16; Madden, *The Resources of the Newcastle District*; Placer County Land Company, *Placer County: General Information, Facts and Figures*; *Newcastle News*, December 28, 1887; January 2, 1889; *Sacramento Daily Record-Union*, July 2, 1887; September 29, 1888.

96. P. W. Butler, "Oranges in Northern California," in State Board of Horticulture of the State of California, *Official Report of the Tenth State Fruit Growers' Convention*, 165–166; "The Early Citrus Fruits of Placer County: Its Record at the Citrus and State Fairs of California," in California State Agricultural Society, *Transactions during the Year 1887*, 234–240; *Newcastle News*, January 8, 1890; Madden, *The Resources of the Newcastle District*, 29; Placer County Board of Trade, *Placer County, California: Facts and Figures for the Homeseeker* (Auburn: Placer County Board of Trade, 1891), no pagination, Bancroft Library; Klee, "Report of the Inspector of Fruit Pests," 369; W. B. Lardner and M. J. Brock, *History of Placer and Nevada Counties* (Los Angeles: Historic Record Co., 1924), 228–232; Gittings, "The Foundations of Placer County Horticulture," 145–154; Kevin Starr, *Inventing the Dream: California through the Progressive Era* (New York: Oxford University Press, 1985), 140–147.

97. *Sacramento Daily Record-Union*, July 2, 1887; *Pacific Rural Press*, March 11, 1893.

98. Gittings, "The Foundations of Placer County Horticulture," 153–154.

99. Lawrence J. Jelinek, *Harvest Empire: A History of California Agriculture*, 2d ed. (San Francisco: Boyd & Fraser, 1982), 53. This argument was the central theme of Varden Fuller's 1939 dissertation, "The Supply of Agricultural Labor." Sucheng Chan has questioned his reasoning, claiming that the Chinese were being made the scapegoat not only for land monopolization, but for their own victimization as well; see Chan, *This Bittersweet Soil*, 271–280.

100. *California Fruit Grower*, June 13, 1891; "Immigrant Labor in the Fruit Industries of the Newcastle District," 417.

101. *California Fruit Grower*, June 13, 1891; *Pacific Rural Press*, November 25, 1893; Butler, "Peach Culture," 71; Placer County Land Company, *Placer County: General Information, Facts and Figures*, 7–12; Interview with J. E. Bergtholdt, Newcastle, Calif., November 11, 1924 (no. 40), in Eliot Mears, "102 Interviews with Employers of Farm Workers," box 35, Survey of Race Relations Collection, Hoover Institution Archives, Stanford University, Stanford, Calif.

102. Harry E. Butler, "A History of the First Malaria Mosquito Control Campaign in the United States, at Penryn, California, 1910," typescript, April 15, 1945, 1–3, Harry Butler Biographical Letter File; William B. Herms, *Malaria: Cause and Control* (New York: Macmillan, 1913), 65–67, 89–91, 95–96; Harold Farnsworth Gray and Russel E. Fontaine, "A History of Malaria in California," in California Mosquito Control Association, *Proceedings and Papers of the Twenty-fifth Annual Conference*, June 30, 1957, reprint in the California Room, California State Library.

103. *Pacific Rural Press*, August 1, 1891.

104. Chan, *This Bittersweet Soil*, 90–95. Of 32 fruit growers depicted in Lardner and Brock's "Biographical Sketches," 18 had at one time lived on a midwestern farm (*History of Placer and Nevada Counties*).

105. See, for example, Placer County, "Leases and Agreements," Book D, 299, 406; Book E, 53, 402, 408, Placer County Recorder's Office.

106. Calculated from Placer County, "Lessee-Lessor Index," vol. 1; "Leases and Agreements," Books F and G; "Personal Mortgagee-Mortgagor Index," vol. 1; and "Personal Mortgages," Book E, Placer County Recorder's Office.

107. *California Fruit Grower*, December 12, 1891; R. L. Adams et al., "Land Tenancy in California," in Commonwealth Club of California, *Transactions* 17 (November 1922): 431; Gittings, "The Foundations of Placer County Horticulture," 138.

108. Placer County, "Leases and Agreements," Book F, 351–354, Placer County Recorder's Office; *Placer County Republican*, November 6, 1913; Lardner and Brock, *History of Placer and Nevada Counties*, 815; Madden, *The Resources of the Newcastle District*, 56; Charles E. Uren, *Official Map of Placer County, California* (San Francisco: Britton & Rey, 1887); Chan, *This Bittersweet Soil*, 90–91.

109. Placer County, "Leases and Agreements," Book F, 362–363, 423–425; Book G, 43–45, 56–60, Placer County Recorder's Office; California State Bureau of Labor Statistics, *Fifteenth Biennial Report for 1911–1912* (Sacramento: State Printing Office, 1912), 637; Chan, *This Bittersweet Soil*, 259–262, 422; R. L. Adams, "California Farm Tenancy and Methods of Leasing," University of California College of Agriculture, Agricultural Experiment Station, *Circular*, no. 272 (November 1923): 9; William S. Hallagan, "Labor Contracting in Turn-of-the-Century California Agriculture," *Journal of Economic History* 40 (December 1980): 762–765; Keijiro Otsuka, Hiroyuki Chuma, and Yujiro Hayami, "Land and Labor Contracts in Agrarian Economies: Theories and Facts," *Journal of Economic Literature* 30 (December 1992): 1967–1968.

110. *Newcastle News*, July 29, 1891; August 12, 1891 (reprint of a *San Francisco Post* editorial); October 20, 1892; August 23, 1893 (reprint of a *San Francisco Chronicle* editorial); *Pacific Rural Press*, August 22, 1891; *California Fruit Grower*, December 12, 1891.

111. *Newcastle News*, October 20, 1892; Placer County, "Personal Mortgages," Book E, 169–170, Placer County Recorder's Office.

112. Statement of A. P. Hall, in "The Question Box," *Official Report of the Nineteenth Fruit Growers' Convention*, 89–90; *Newcastle News*, October 31, 1894; January 6, 1897; Placer County, "Leases and Agreements," Book G, 212–215, Placer County Recorder's Office.

113. Placer County, "Personal Mortgages," Books E and 5, passim, Placer County Recorder's Office.

114. *Newcastle News*, May 8, 1893; May 12, 1897; *Placer County Republican*, January 11, 1895; December 10, 1897; March 11, 1903; *California Fruit Grower*, April 7, 1894; March 2, 1895; June 15, 1895; *Pacific Rural Press*, May 22, 1897; Butler, "A History of the First Malaria Mosquito Control Campaign," 3; "Immigrant Labor in the Fruit Industries of the Newcastle District," 416–419; Statement of J. F. Madden (no. 66), Chamberlain Survey; Interview with Lee Tudsbury, Loomis, Calif., November 11,

1924 (no. 40), in Mears, "102 Interviews with Employers of Farm Workers"; Iwata, "The Japanese Immigrants in California Agriculture," 27.

115. *Placer County Republican,* December 1, 1893; November 19, 1897; *Newcastle News,* September 11, 1895; *California Fruit Grower,* June 15 and August 10, 1895; Statement of A. P. Hall, "The Question Box," 89.

116. *Newcastle News,* June 10, 1896; May 12 and 26, 1897; *Pacific Rural Press,* August 7, 1899; June 14 and August 9, 1902; *Oakland Tribune,* May 16, 1901; Statement of E. G. Narramore (no. 56), Chamberlain Survey; "Immigrant Labor in the Fruit Industries of the Newcastle District," 417–418.

117. Calculated from Placer County, "Lessee-Lessor Index," vol. 1; "Leases and Agreements," Book H; "Personal Mortgagee-Mortgagor Index," vols. 1, 1A; and "Personal Mortgages," Books 6–9, Placer County Recorder's Office.

118. Iwata, *Planted in Good Soil,* 193–201; Ichihashi, *Japanese Immigrants in the United States,* 180–182; Kawakami, "The Japanese on Our Farms," 82–83.

119. *Placer County Republican,* March 11, 1903; *Newcastle News,* March 11, 1903.

120. *Pacific Rural Press,* August 16, 1902.

121. *Marysville Daily Appeal,* January 28 and February 26, 1886; *Wheatland Weekly Graphic,* August 22 and 29, 1885; February 20, February 27, March 6, April 10, and June 19, 1886.

122. *Wheatland Weekly Graphic,* August 21, 1886; *Sacramento Weekly Bee,* April 19, 1888; *Wheatland Four Corners,* June 2, 1889; *Wheatland Four Corners,* quoted in *Pacific Rural Press,* August 15 and September 12, 1891; *California Fruit Grower,* August 20, 1892.

123. *Pacific Rural Press,* July 14, 1894; *California Fruit Grower,* August 31, 1895; Eames, "In Hop-Picking Time," 27–28.

124. *Sacramento Weekly Bee,* August 22, 1894; *Wheatland Weekly Graphic,* September 4, 1886; *California Fruit Grower,* September 13, 1890; August 31, 1895; *Pacific Rural Press,* December 12, 1891; Annie Marion MacLean, *Wage-Earning Women* (New York: Macmillan, 1910), 109–111.

125. *Pacific Rural Press,* June 26, July 3, and July 17, 1897; *Davisville Enterprise,* July 30, 1898; *Newcastle News,* July 30, 1902.

126. *Davisville Enterprise,* July 30, 1898; *Pacific Rural Press,* July 3 and August 27, 1897; September 2, 1899; August 30 and September 6, 1902; *San Francisco Chronicle,* August 6, 1913.

127. *California Fruit Grower,* November 30, 1901; *Pacific Rural Press,* August 11, 1900; August 16, 1902; *Marysville Daily Appeal,* August 26, 1900; *Sacramento Evening Bee,* August 31, 1900; James Jerome Parsons Jr., "The California Hop Industry: Its Eighty Years of Development and Expansion" (M.A. thesis, University of California, Berkeley, 1939), 40, 112; Parker, *The Hop Industry,* 309.

128. *Pacific Rural Press,* July 26, 1902.

129. *Marysville Daily Appeal,* August 20, 21, and 23, 1902; *Sacramento Record-Union,* August 20 and 22, 1902; *Sacramento Evening Bee,* August 21, 1902; *Pacific Rural Press,* August 30 and September 6, 1902.

130. Wickson, *The Vacaville Early Fruit District of California,* 23, 46, 127–129; "Immigrant Labor in the Deciduous Fruit Industry of the Vaca Valley," 177–180.

131. *Davisville Enterprise,* August 15, 1901.

132. Pierce journal, August 7–13, 1901; *Davisville Enterprise*, June 9, 1899; August 15, 1901; California State Bureau of Labor Statistics, *Ninth Biennial Report for 1899–1900*, 32.

133. See his advertisement in the *Davisville Enterprise*, November 21, 1901, for example.

134. Pierce journal, August 13–September 13, 1901; August 18–September 18, 1902; "Gathering Almonds, 1901," account at the end of the 1901 volume; "Almonds," in Pierce account book, 121.

135. *Davisville Enterprise*, April 27, 1900; May 8, 1902; *Winters Express*, February 22, 1901; May 8, 1902; *Sacramento Daily Record-Union*, September 11 and 12, 1902; *Pacific Rural Press*, July 13, 1900; July 27, 1901; *California Fruit Grower*, January 5, 1901; July 12, 1902.

136. Pierce journal, August 18, 1902.

137. Stabler, "The California Fruit-Grower, and the Labor Supply," 268–272; Pierce journal, August 7–13, 1901; February 3–March 18, 1903; *Davisville Enterprise*, August 15, 1901; *Iowa Citizen*, quoted in *Davisville Enterprise*, March 14, 1903; "Report of Committee on Farm Labor," in California State Horticultural Commission, *Official Report of the Twenty-eighth California Fruit Growers' Convention*, May 5–8, 1903 (Sacramento: State Printing Office, 1903), 89–91.

138. Pierce, "The Almond," 456.

139. "Discussion on the Labor Supply," 275, 397.

Chapter 3: "Misunderstood and Misrepresented"

1. Levi Varden Fuller, "The Supply of Agricultural Labor as a Factor in the Evolution of Farm Organization in California" (Ph.D. diss., University of California, Berkeley, 1939), 185.

2. *Sacramento Record-Union*, December 22, 1902; *Orchard and Farm*, April 15, 1903; *California Fruit Grower*, December 20, 1902; January 17, January 31, February 7, and July 25, 1903; *Pacific Rural Press*, February 14, 1903; February 14, 1904; *Oakland Tribune*, July 13, 1903; Ellwood Cooper, "President's Annual Address," in California State Horticultural Commission, *Official Report of the Twenty-ninth California Fruit Growers' Convention*, December 8–11, 1903 (Sacramento: State Printing Office, 1903), 7; "Report of Committee on Labor," ibid., 217–221; "Report of the California Employment Committee," in "Proceedings of the Thirtieth Annual Convention of the California State Fruit Growers," December 6–9, 1904, in California Commissioner of Horticulture, *First Biennial Report for 1903–1904* (Sacramento: State Printing Office, 1905), 387–388; Fuller, "The Supply of Agricultural Labor," 177–180.

3. The *Davisville Enterprise* announced "the dropping of the ville" on April 14, 1906.

4. George Robertson, "Statistical Summary of the Production and Resources of California" (1850–1910), in California State Board of Agriculture, *Fifty-eighth Annual Report for 1911* (Sacramento: State Printing Office, 1912), 90–91, 145, 159; "Yolo County," in California State Agricultural Society, *Report for the Year 1910* (Sacramento: State Printing Office, 1911), 203; *Placer County Republican*, November 21, 1912; George Robertson, "The California Fruit Industry," in *Proceedings of the Thirty-eighth Convention of the California State Fruit Growers*, December 6–9, 1910 (Sacra-

mento: State Printing Office, 1910), 88; U.S. Department of Commerce and Labor, Bureau of the Census, *Thirteenth Census of the United States: Agriculture, 1910* (Washington, D.C.: Government Printing Office, 1913), 160; Paul Rhode, "Learning, Capital Accumulation, and the Transformation of California Agriculture," *Journal of Economic History* 55 (December 1995): 773, 778.

5. Alfred D. Chandler Jr., *Scale and Scope: The Dynamics of Industrial Capitalism* (Cambridge: Harvard University Press, 1990), 3–13; H. Vincent Moses, "G. Harold Powell and the Corporate Consolidation of the Modern Citrus Enterprise, 1904–1922," *Business History Review* 69 (Summer 1995): 126.

6. Moses, "G. Harold Powell and the Corporate Consolidation of the Modern Citrus Enterprise," 120; Walter V. Woehlke, "In the Service of Quality," *Outlook* 93 (October 23, 1909): 426.

7. The California Fruit Growers' Exchange (Sunkist) was the major exception. H. E. Erdman, "Possibilities and Limitations of Cooperative Marketing," University of California College of Agriculture, Agricultural Experiment Station, *Circular*, no. 298 (October 1925): 1–2.

8. *Pacific Rural Press*, December 14, 1907.

9. California Development Board, *Twenty-first Annual Report for the Year 1910* (San Francisco: California Development Board, 1911), 65.

10. *California Fruit Grower*, December 19, 1908; Charles H. Bentley to Hiram W. Johnson, March 4, 1910, part 2, box 4, Hiram Johnson Papers, Bancroft Library, University of California, Berkeley; Louis C. Levy, *History of the Co-operative Raisin Industry of California* (Fresno: by author, 1928), 5, Department of Special Collections, Henry Madden Library, California State University, Fresno; James Madison, "Raisin History," typescript, July 5, 1914, 1, Ben Walker History Files, Fresno City and County Historical Society.

11. E. Leroy Chaddock, "Fifty Years as a Raisin Packer," typescript, 1943, 105–107, Department of Special Collections, Henry Madden Library; Will Payne, "Cooperation—The Raisin Baron," *Saturday Evening Post*, April 30, 1910, 14–15; *Fresno Morning Republican*, June 29, 1919; *Fresno Bee*, October 16, 1929; Schyler Rehart and William K. Patterson, *M. Theo Kearney—Prince of Fresno: A Biography of Martin Theodore Kearney* (Fresno: Fresno City and County Historical Society, 1988), 18–22.

12. Chester Rowell, "Autobiography," 18–24, box 3, Chester Rowell Correspondence and Papers, Bancroft Library; Walter V. Woehlke, "Raising the Price of the Raisin: Get Together Pays the Growers," *Country Gentleman* 79 (December 26, 1914): 2058; *California Fruit Grower*, June 9, 1906; Fred K. Howard, "History of Raisin Marketing in California," typescript, ca. 1922, 1–32, University of California Library, Davis; Payne, "Cooperation—The Raisin Baron," 14–15, 44–45; Victoria Alice Saker, "Benevolent Monopoly: The Legal Transformation of Agricultural Cooperation, 1890–1943" (Ph.D. diss., University of California, Berkeley, 1990), 195–199; Rehart and Patterson, *M. Theo Kearney—Prince of Fresno*, 3–42.

13. M. Theodore Kearney, "The Raisin Industry," in *Proceedings of the Twenty-sixth Fruit Growers' Convention*, December 3–6, 1901 (Sacramento: State Printing Office, 1901), 57–58; John Andrew Shaw Jr., "Commercialization in an Agricultural Economy: Fresno County, California, 1856–1900" (Ph.D. diss., Purdue University, 1969), 35.

14. Payne, "Cooperation—The Raisin Baron," 15; Chaddock, "Fifty Years as a Raisin Packer," 114; W. Y. Spence, "Success after Twenty Years," *Sun-Maid Herald* 3 (February 1918): 8; Wallace Smith, *Garden of the Sun: A History of the San Joaquin Valley* (Los Angeles: Lymanhouse, 1939), 521; Saker, "Benevolent Monopoly," 194–200.

15. Payne, "Cooperation—The Raisin Baron," 15, 44; Howard, "History of Raisin Marketing in California," 33–38; Spence, "Success after Twenty Years," *Sun-Maid Herald* 3 (March 1918): 8–9, 12; Saker, "Benevolent Monopoly," 200–209.

16. *Pacific Rural Press,* December 14, 1901; Howard, "History of Raisin Marketing in California," 39–43; Saker, "Benevolent Monopoly," 209–211.

17. Chaddock, "Fifty Years as a Raisin Packer," 106–111; Franklin P. Nutting, "An Interview with Franklin P. Nutting" (Regional Oral History Office, Bancroft Library, 1955), 22–25; *Fresno Morning Republican,* December 25, 1927; Wylie M. Giffen, "Raisin Day—Past, Present, and Future," *Sun-Maid Herald* 1 (May 1916): 1; Erdman, "Possibilities and Limitations of Cooperative Marketing," 14.

18. *Fresno Morning Republican,* December 22, 1920; Chaddock, "Fifty Years as a Raisin Packer," 42, 123–124; W. Y. Spence, "The California Associated Raisin Co.: Organization of the Company," *Sun-Maid Herald* 3 (July 1918): 6–7; Lilbourne Alsip Winchell, *History of Fresno County and the San Joaquin Valley* (Fresno: Arthur H. Cawston, 1933), 279–281; Ben R. Walker, *The Fresno County Blue Book* (Fresno: Arthur H. Cawston, 1941), 109, 370; James Monroe Bragg, "History of Co-operative Marketing in Raisins to 1923" (M.A. thesis, University of California, Berkeley, 1930), 20–30.

19. Chaddock, "Fifty Years as a Raisin Packer," 117.

20. Giffen, "Raisin Day—Past, Present, and Future," 1–2; Spence, "Success after Twenty Years," *Sun-Maid Herald* 3 (November 1917): 5; Walker, *The Fresno County Blue Book,* 524; Charles W. Clough et al., *Fresno County in the Twentieth Century: From 1900 to the 1980s* (Fresno: Panorama West Books, 1986), 175.

21. Giffen, "Raisin Day—Past, Present, and Future," 1–2; *California Fruit Grower,* March 13, April 3, and April 17, 1909; *Fresno Morning Republican,* April 28, 1909; "California Raisins, Their Day," *Sunset* 22 (May 1909): 550; "Raisin Day," *Overland Monthly* 63 (May 1909): 460.

22. Giffen, "Raisin Day—Past, Present, and Future," 1–2; "California Raisins, Their Day," 550; Saker, "Benevolent Monopoly," 180.

23. *Fresno Morning Republican,* April 5, 7, 13, 17, 19, 30, and May 1, 1910; January 30 and February 5, 1911; April 29, April 30, and May 1, 1912; *California Fruit Grower,* April 23, 1910; Giffen, "Raisin Day—Past, Present, and Future," 2; Ralph Palmer Merritt, "After Me Cometh a Builder: The Recollections of Ralph Palmer Merritt" (Regional Oral History Office, Bancroft Library, 1962), 122.

24. *Fresno Morning Republican,* May 1, 1912; March 30, 1913; Spence, "Success after Twenty Years," *Sun-Maid Herald* 3 (June 1918): 7, 30; W. Y. Spence, "The California Associated Raisin Co.: Great Contract and Subscription Campaign," *Sun-Maid Herald* 3 (August 1918): 6–7, 14; Herman Steen, "Story of the California Raisin 'Trust,'" *Hoard's Dairyman* 60 (October 15, 1920): 532–534; Giffen, "Raisin Day—Past, Present, and Future," 1; Woehlke, "Raising the Price of the Raisin," 2057; "James Madison and California Raisins," *Overland Monthly* 64 (September 1914): 320; Fred K. Howard, *History of the Sun-Maid Raisin Growers* (Fresno: by author, 1922), 7–8; Levy, *History of the Co-operative Raisin Industry of California,* 5–6.

25. Steen, "Story of the California Raisin 'Trust,'" 534; Spence, "The California Associated Raisin Co.: Organization of the Company," 6–7, 14; Bragg, "History of Co-operative Marketing in Raisins," 158–162; Saker, "Benevolent Monopoly," 224–232. The CARC's voting-trust agreement, bylaws, and articles of incorporation, as well as several sample contracts, are reprinted in Howard, *History of the Sun-Maid Raisin Growers,* 19–41.

26. *Sacramento Union,* August 15, 1909; F. B. McKevitt, "Marketing of Fruit by California Fruit Distributors," in *Proceedings of the Thirty-eighth Convention of the California State Fruit Growers,* 53; Robert W. Hodgson, "The California Fruit Industry," *Economic Geography* 9 (October 1936): 349–350.

27. Erich Kraemer and H. E. Erdman, "History of Cooperation in the Marketing of California Fresh Deciduous Fruits," University of California College of Agriculture, Agricultural Experiment Station, *Bulletin,* no. 557 (September 1933): 20–22.

28. William B. Gester, "The Marketing of California Fresh Fruit in the East," in "Transactions of the Twenty-fifth State Fruit-Growers' Convention," December 4–7, 1900, in State Board of Horticulture of the State of California, *Seventh Biennial Report for 1899–1900* (Sacramento: State Printing Office, 1901), 96–99; McKevitt, "Marketing of Fruit by California Fruit Distributors," 53–54; *Pacific Rural Press,* December 3, 1898; *California Fruit Grower,* November 19, 1904; February 12, 1910.

29. U.S. Department of the Interior, Census Office, *Eleventh Census of the United States: Agriculture, 1890* (Washington, D.C.: Government Printing Office, 1895), 498–499; U.S. Department of the Interior, Census Office, *Twelfth Census of the United States: Agriculture, 1900,* pt. 2, *Crops and Irrigation* (Washington, D.C.: Government Printing Office, 1902), 604–605, 617.

30. Gester, "The Marketing of California Fresh Fruit in the East," 97; *Sacramento Record-Union,* January 16 and 17, 1901; *California Fruit Grower,* January 19, 1901.

31. *Pacific Rural Press,* January 9, 1901; *Sacramento Record-Union,* January 16, 1901; *Newcastle News,* April 24, 1901; "By-Laws of the Newcastle Fruit Growers' Association of Newcastle, California," April 24, 1901, carton 32, H. E. Erdman Papers, Bancroft Library; J. L. Nagle, "California Fruit Exchange," *Proceedings of the Thirty-eighth Convention of the California State Fruit Growers,* 61; H. E. Erdman, "The Development and Significance of California Cooperatives, 1900–1915," *Agricultural History* 32 (July 1958): 182; Kraemer and Erdman, "History of Cooperation in the Marketing of California Fresh Deciduous Fruits," 41–49, 71–73; Rahno Mabel MacCurdy, *The History of the California Fruit Growers Exchange* (Los Angeles: George Rice & Sons, 1925), 16–35.

32. *Newcastle News,* April 30, 1902; *California Fruit Grower,* May 3, 1902; *Orchard and Farm,* January 1904; "California Fruit Distributors," information card, box 58, Erdman Papers; "Agreement: California Fruit Distributors and Penryn Fruit Company," February 9, 1905, carton 15, Erdman Papers; McKevitt, "Marketing of Fruit by California Fruit Distributors," 55; Kraemer and Erdman, "History of Cooperation in the Marketing of California Fresh Deciduous Fruits," 34, 66–67; Fred Wilbur Powell, "Co-operative Marketing of California Fresh Fruit," *Quarterly Journal of Economics* 24 (February 1910): 404–406.

33. *Placer County Republican,* June 25, 1908; April 13, 1911; *Orchard and Farm,* Jan-

uary 1904; *California Fruit Grower*, May 25, 1907; *Newcastle News*, January 31, 1906; May 18, 1910.

34. *California Fruit Grower*, December 30, 1911; February 12, 1912; *Sacramento Union*, August 15, 1909; *Placer County Republican*, October 7, 1909; McKevitt, "Marketing of Fruit by California Fruit Distributors," 56–58; George D. Kellogg, "Board of Inspection and Control—A Season's Progress and Results in Standardization," in *Proceedings of the Thirty-eighth Convention of the California State Fruit Growers*, 130; U.S. Department of Agriculture, Bureau of Agricultural Economics, *Fruits (Noncitrus): Production, Farm Disposition, Value, and Utilization of Sales, 1889–1944*, Commodity Statistics, no. 27 (Washington, D.C.: Government Printing Office, 1948), 30–45.

35. George D. Kellogg, "Pre-cooling of Fruit with Dry Cold Air for Shipment," in *Proceedings of the Thirty-sixth Convention of the California State Fruit Growers*, December 7–10, 1909 (Sacramento: State Printing Office, 1910), 175; *Placer County Republican*, February 1, 1912.

36. *Placer County Republican*, September 8, 15, 22, and 29, 1910; February 6, 1913; Charles M. Coleman, *P G and E of California: The Centennial Story of Pacific Gas and Electric Company, 1852–1952* (McGraw-Hill: New York, 1952), 94–101.

37. Kellogg, "Pre-cooling of Fruit with Dry Cold Air for Shipment," 175–177; *Newcastle News*, June 22, 1905; June 27, 1906; February 27 and June 12, 1907; June 24, 1908; June 30 and December 22, 1909; *Placer County Republican*, July 4, 1907; October 14 and November 4, 1909; July 21, 1910; *Pacific Rural Press*, August 19, 1905; *California Fruit Grower*, December 25, 1909.

38. *Placer County Republican*, August 11, 1904; November 5, 1908; November 4, 1909; *Newcastle News*, May 2, 1906; Ellwood Cooper, "President's Address," in "Proceedings of the Thirty-second Convention of the California State Fruit Growers," December 4–7, 1906, in California Commissioner of Horticulture, *Second Biennial Report for 1903–1904* (Sacramento: State Printing Office, 1907), 322–323.

39. J. W. Jeffrey to Governor James N. Gillett, January 31, 1908, Records of the Governor's Office, Reports—1907–1910, California State Archives, Office of the Secretary of State, Sacramento; *Placer County Republican*, April 15, 1909; *California Fruit Grower*, December 11, 1909; California Commissioner of Horticulture, *Fourth Biennial Report for 1909–1910* (Sacramento: State Printing Office, 1911), 9; J. W. Jeffrey, "President's Address," in *Proceedings of the Thirty-seventh California State Fruit Growers' Convention*, September 13–14, 1910 (Sacramento: State Printing Office, 1910), 11; Jeffrey, "Fruit Standardization," in *Proceedings of the Thirty-ninth California State Fruit Growers' Convention*, March 7–9, 1911 (Sacramento: State Printing Office, 1911), 113.

40. J. W. Jeffrey to Governor James N. Gillett, [January 1910], Records of the Governor's Office, Reports—1907–1910, California State Archives; *Newcastle News*, September 22 and 29, 1909; Jeffrey, "President's Address," 11; *Placer County Republican*, September 23 and October 7, 1909; *California Fruit Grower*, October 2, 1909.

41. Kellogg, "A Season's Progress and Results in Standardization," 130–133; Jeffrey to Gillett, January 1910; Jeffrey, "Fruit Standardization," 116–117; *Newcastle News*, November 3 and 24, 1909; January 5, January 26, March 30, and May 26, 1910;

Placer County Republican, October 28, 1910; November 4 and 25, 1909; March 31, May 19, and May 26, 1910; November 16, 1911; *California Fruit Grower,* January 8, January 29, and June 25, 1910.

42. Kellogg, "A Season's Progress and Results in Standardization," 133; Jeffrey, "Fruit Standardization," 117, 118; *Newcastle News,* November 23 and December 21, 1910; May 17, November 8, and November 22, 1911; April 12, 1912; April 30, 1913; *Placer County Republican,* October 27, November 17, and November 24, 1910; May 18, July 13, October 12, November 9, November 16, and November 23, 1911; *California Fruit Grower,* June 25 and December 3, 1910; June 3, 1911; April 13 and December 14, 1912; December 13, 1913.

43. *Newcastle News,* March 6, 1912; November 12 and December 10, 1913; January 27, 1915; *Placer County Republican,* October 23, November 6, December 4, and December 11, 1913; February 11, 1915.

44. Davisville Almond Growers' Association, Constitution and Minute Book, November 30, 1901, August 3, 1903, May 5 and 27, 1905, Board of Directors File, Predecessor and Concurrent Organizations, box 1, California Almond Growers' Exchange Records, Sacramento Archives and Museum Collection Center (hereafter DAGA minutes); George W. Pierce Jr., Daily Journals, 1890–1930, entries for June 20, 1903, and September 14, 1907, Department of Special Collections, University of California Library, Davis (hereafter Pierce journal); *Davisville Enterprise,* August 5, 1903; August 20, 1904; *Davis Enterprise,* June 17, 1911; *Pacific Rural Press,* September 16, 1905; July 3, 1909; R. H. Taylor, "Marketing California Almonds," *University of California Journal of Agriculture* 4 (October 1916): 44.

45. DAGA minutes, July 5, 1902; "Manager's Report," May 10, 1917, Board of Directors File, Minutes, box 1, California Almond Growers' Exchange Records (hereafter CAGE minutes); *Davisville Enterprise,* August 5, 1903; *Orchard and Farm,* January 1904; California Almond Growers' Exchange, *California Almond Growers' Exchange* (San Francisco: California Almond Growers' Exchange, 1919), 3, 16, carton 21, Erdman Papers; George W. Pierce, "The Status of the Almond Industry of the Pacific Coast," in *Proceedings of the Thirty-fourth Biennial Meeting of the American Pomological Society,* September 1–3, 1915 (n.p.: The Society, 1916), 79; Taylor, "Marketing California Almonds," 44.

46. *San Francisco Call,* February 13 and 14, 1906; William L. Willis, *History of Sacramento County, California* (Los Angeles: Historic Record Co., 1913), 580–587.

47. California Almond Growers' Exchange, *History of the California Almond Growers' Exchange* (Sacramento: A. N. Bullock, 1913), 3; CAGE minutes, May 6, 1910; J. P. Dargitz, "The Almond Commercially Considered," in *Proceedings of the Thirty-sixth Convention of the California State Fruit Growers,* 64–71; Dargitz, "Report of the California Almond Growers' Exchange," in *Proceedings of the Thirty-eighth Convention of the California State Fruit Growers,* 63–66; *Davis Enterprise,* January 2, 1909; April 30 and May 14, 1910; *Pacific Rural Press,* December 18, 1909; April 16, 1910; *California Fruit Grower,* May 14, 1910.

48. Dargitz, "Report of the California Almond Growers' Exchange," 66; *Pacific Rural Press,* April 16, 1910; *California Fruit Grower,* May 14, 1910; California Almond Growers' Exchange, *By-Laws of the California Almond Growers' Exchange* (Sacramento: A. N. Bullock, 1910), 1–5; Elizabeth Margaret Riley, "The History of the Al-

mond Industry in California, 1850–1934" (M.A. thesis, University of California, Berkeley, 1948), 41–43; Carl August Scholl, "An Economic Study of the California Almond Growers' Exchange" (Ph.D. diss., University of California, Berkeley, 1927), 10–12, 126.

49. Riley, "The History of the Almond Industry in California," 50.

50. J. P. Dargitz, "The California Cured Fruit Exchange," in "Proceedings of the Forty-second California State Fruit Growers' Convention," December 11–13, 1912, in California State Commission of Horticulture, *Monthly Bulletin* 2 (March–April 1913): 474–476; California Almond Growers' Exchange, *By-Laws*, 8; *San Francisco Examiner*, May 2, 1936; Willis, *History of Sacramento County, California*, 583–584; A. J. Schoendorf, *Beginnings of Cooperation in the Marketing of California Fresh Deciduous Fruits and History of the California Fruit Exchange* (Sacramento: Inland Press, 1947), 21.

51. C. D. Hamilton, "Marketing Problems," in "Proceedings of the Fifty-sixth Convention of California Fruit Growers and Farmers," December 6–7, 1923, in California State Department of Agriculture, *Monthly Bulletin* 13 (June 1924): 127; California Almond Growers' Exchange, *Bulletin*, no. 11 (August 13, 1910) (hereafter *CAGE Bulletin*); CAGE minutes, October 14 and November 11, 1910; Pierce, "The Status of the Almond Industry," 81; R. H. Taylor, "The Almond in California," University of California College of Agriculture, Agricultural Experiment Station, *Bulletin*, no. 297 (August 1918): 46–47; Taylor, "Marketing California Almonds," 44–45; Scholl, "An Economic Study of the California Almond Growers' Exchange," 136, 178–179, 186–187, 240.

52. CAGE minutes, December 9, 1910; April 14, 1911; April 19, 1912; *CAGE Bulletin*, no. 9 (July 30, 1910); no. 15 (September 20, 1910); no. 91 (May 27, 1914); no. 93 (April 23, 1914); *Davis Enterprise*, April 6, 1912; May 31, 1913; March 28, 1914; Scholl, "An Economic Study of the California Almond Growers' Exchange," 16, 115, 141–142.

53. "Manager's Report," May 10, 1917, and April 10, 1914, CAGE minutes; Pierce, "The Status of the Almond Industry," 77, 80; *Davis Enterprise*, September 5, 1914; Taylor, "Marketing California Almonds," 44; Scholl, "An Economic Study of the California Almond Growers' Exchange," 116, 259.

54. Erdman, "The Development and Significance of California Cooperatives," 183.

55. *Davisville Enterprise*, June 17, 1911; Dargitz, "The Almond Commercially Considered," 70–71.

56. California Development Board, *California Resources and Possibilities: Twenty-first Annual Report for the Year 1910* (San Francisco: California Development Board, 1912), 4, passim. See also the reports for 1911–15; Richard J. Orsi, "Selling the Golden State: A Study of Boosterism in Nineteenth-Century California" (Ph.D. diss., University of Wisconsin, 1973), 677–683; and William Issel, "'Citizens outside the Government': Business and Urban Policy in San Francisco and Los Angeles, 1890–1932," *Pacific Historical Review* 57 (May 1988): 132.

57. *San Francisco Examiner*, November 2, 1912.

58. Pierce journal, January 14 and August 25, 1911; February 22, 1912; *Davis Enterprise*, November 14 and December 26, 1908; November 5, 1910; July 29 and August 5, 1911.

59. Pierce to State Farm Commission, April 27, 1905, box 4, Pierce Family Pa-

pers, Department of Special Collections, University of California Library, Davis; *Davisville Enterprise*, April 1, May 20, May 27, and December 2, 1905; April 7, 1906; January 24, 1914; Pierce journal, March 24–28, May 17, May 20, August 25, and November 24, 1905; February 16 and 17, 1906; Joann Leach Larkey, *Davisville '68: The History and Heritage of the City of Davis, Yolo County, California* (Davis: City of Davis, 1969), 91–94.

60. California Development Board, *Report for the Year 1910*, 4.

61. Pierce journal, August 26, 1913; George W. Pierce, "The Almond," address delivered at the Forty-fourth California State Fruit Growers' Convention, June 5, 1914, in California State Commission of Horticulture, *Monthly Bulletin* 3 (November 1914): 462.

62. Pierce journal, August 13–September 13, 1903.

63. Pierce journal, August 2, 6, 11, and 29, 1904; Agreement between George W. Pierce and Shi Kubo, August 1904, box 4, Pierce Family Papers; "Almonds" for 1904, in George W. Pierce Jr., Account Book, 1897–1910, 16, box 2, Pierce Family Papers (hereafter Pierce account book).

64. Pierce journal, March 10, 1904; *Davisville Enterprise*, April 9, 1904; "Almonds" for 1904, in Pierce account book, 116; Edward J. Wickson, *The California Fruits and How to Grow Them*, 7th ed. (San Francisco: Pacific Rural Press, 1914), 424; "Review of the Fruit Season," in California State Commission of Horticulture, *Second Biennial Report for 1905–1906* (Sacramento: State Printing Office, 1906), 28–34.

65. "J. Tanaka Account," August 5–31, 1907, box 1, Pierce Family Papers; "Almonds" for 1907, in Pierce account book, 116; Pierce journal, July 21, 1907. For the 1905 harvest, see Pierce journal, August 8–September 16, 1905; and "Hired Help" for 1905, in Pierce account book, 154. For 1906, see Agreement between George W. Pierce and Tom Kujira, July 1906, box 4, Pierce Family Papers; and "Almonds" for 1906, in Pierce account book, 115.

66. "Almonds" for 1908, in Pierce account book, 115; *Davis Enterprise*, April 15, 1908; January 2, 1909; "Review of the Fruit Season," in California State Commission of Horticulture, *Third Biennial Report for 1907–1908* (Sacramento: State Printing Office, 1908), 8–10; *Pacific Rural Press*, July 4, 1908.

67. "The East Indians on the Pacific Coast," in U.S. Senate, Reports of the Immigration Commission, "Immigrants in Industries," pt. 25, *Japanese and Other Immigrant Races in the Pacific Coast and Rocky Mountain States*, vol. 23, 61st Cong., 2d sess. (Washington, D.C.: Government Printing Office, 1911), 323–333 (hereafter *Dillingham Commission Report*); Herman Scheffauer, "The Tide of Turbans," *Forum* 43 (June 1910): 616–618; "The Hindu, the Newest Immigration Problem," *Survey* 26 (October 1, 1910): 2–3; H. A. Millis, "East Indian Immigration to the Pacific Coast," *Survey* 28 (June 1, 1912): 379–386; Joan M. Jensen, *Passage from India: Asian Indian Immigrants in North America* (New Haven: Yale University Press, 1988), 1–41.

68. Pierce journal, May 15–July 29, 1907; "Hired Help" for 1907, in Pierce account book, 155; Jensen, *Passage from India*, 33; Rajani Kanta Das, *Hindustani Workers on the Pacific Coast* (Berlin: Walter De Gruyter, 1923), 6.

69. Pierce journal, January 9, January 10, March 14, May 21, and June 28, 1908; Jensen, *Passage from India*, 9, 33. Because most male Sikhs took the name Singh (meaning "lion" in Punjabi), I refer to them by first name to avoid confusion. In his

journal, Pierce referred to Mousha in a number of ways—"Moushu," "Moushee," "Muchu," etc.—before settling on "Mousha" in 1918.

70. Pierce journal, August 4–September 9, 1908, and "Shaam Singh" account at the end of the volume. On Sikhs and "chain employment," see Bruce La Brack, *The Sikhs of Northern California, 1904–1975* (New York: AMS Press, 1988), 105. While it would be useful to discuss the relation over time between the wage rates Pierce offered his harvest workers and Pierce's own income and other expenses, his surviving records provide only limited information about his wheat crop and other forms of income, and only fragments regarding his nonlabor expenses.

71. Mousha had visited Yuba City earlier in the year; Pierce journal, February 26 and August 6–September 5, 1909.

72. Pierce journal, August 3, 1910.

73. Pierce provides the specifics for each harvest in his daily journals. Wage increases are noted in the account for "Hindu Gang No. 2" at the end of the volume and are calculated from Pierce's Time Book, 1913–19, entries for August 1913, box 4, Pierce Family Papers; and Pierce journal, August 17, 1913. For a more general description of how Sikhs sought to secure employment, see Das, *Hindustani Workers,* 29–36. For evidence suggesting that other DAGA members shared the knockers Mousha procured, see Pierce journal, September 3, 1911; August 27 and 29, 1912; September 5, 1914; September 6, 1916.

74. Pierce journal, December 9, 1913. In 1914, thousands of Indians returned from North America to confront the British; see Jensen, *Passage from India,* 2.

75. Pierce journal, August 1 and 17, 1913; February 4, May 5, June 26, August 8, and December 25, 1914; April 12, July 16, August 16, and December 19, 1915; January 10, March 22, August 6, August 11, and December 26, 1916; September 3, 1917; and the accounts for Indar, Kalla, and Anokh at the end of the volumes for 1914 and 1916.

76. Roger Daniels, *The Politics of Prejudice: The Anti-Japanese Movement in California and the Struggle for Japanese Exclusion* (Berkeley: University of California Press, 1962), 16–78; Yamato Ichihashi, *Japanese Immigrants in the United States* (1932; reprint, New York: Arno Press, 1969), 61–62; Michael Kazin, *Barons of Labor: The San Francisco Building Trades and Union Power in the Progressive Era* (Urbana: University of Illinois Press, 1987), 162–170; H. A. Millis, *The Japanese Problem in the United States* (New York: Macmillan, 1915), 12–18, 120–130, 152–196; Richard B. Rice, William A. Bullough, and Richard J. Orsi, *The Elusive Eden: A New History of California,* 2d ed. (New York: McGraw-Hill, 1996), 369–370.

77. John Higham, *Strangers in the Land: Patterns of American Nativism, 1860–1925* (New York: Atheneum, 1963), 188–189; John F. McClymer, *War and Welfare: Social Engineering in America, 1890–1925* (Westport, Conn.: Greenwood Press, 1980), 88–89.

78. "Immigrant Labor in the Orchards and Vineyards of Fresno County," in *Dillingham Commission Report,* 24:573–600; *Fresno Morning Republican,* September 13, 1910; September 18, 1912; *California Fruit Grower,* May 25, June 29, and August 24, 1907; *Pacific Rural Press,* August 6, 1910; July 29, 1911; Testimony of Koichi Kamikawa, in U.S. House of Representatives, Committee on Immigration and Naturalization, *Japanese Immigration Hearings,* 66th Cong., 2d sess. (Washington, D.C.: Government Printing Office, 1921), 844–847; Yoshino Tajiri Hasegawa and Keith

Boettcher, eds., *Success through Perseverance: Japanese-Americans in the San Joaquin Valley*, vol. 1 (Fresno: San Joaquin Valley Library System, 1980), 16–17, 93, 342, 410, 508–509; Yuji Ichioka, "A Buried Past: Early Issei Socialists and the Japanese Community," *Amerasia Journal* 1 (July 1971): 8–9; Clough et al., *Fresno County in the Twentieth Century*, 169–170.

79. "Immigrant Labor in the Orchards and Vineyards of Fresno County," 598.

80. "Immigrant Labor in the Fruit Industries of the Newcastle District," in *Dillingham Commission Report*, 24:414; William S. Hallagan, "Labor Contracting in Turn-of-the-Century California Agriculture," *Journal of Economic History* 40 (December 1980): 757–776; Robert Higgs, "The Wealth of Japanese Tenant Farmers in California, 1909," *Agricultural History* 53 (April 1979): 488–493.

81. "Immigrant Labor in the Fruit Industries of the Newcastle District," 419–422; *Newcastle News*, August 2, 1899; C. G. Werner to A. J. Schoendorf, January 21, 1947, printed in Schoendorf, *Beginnings of Cooperation*, 16; T. G. Chamberlain, "Fruit Ranching Conditions in the Placer County Fruit Belt," typescript, June 1916, 6, 9, carton 16, Elwood Mead Papers, Bancroft Library; T. G. Chamberlain to Professor Morgan, June 15, 1916, carton 16, Mead Papers; Sucheng Chan, *This Bittersweet Soil: The Chinese in California Agriculture, 1869–1910* (Berkeley: University of California Press, 1986), 262.

82. Calculated from Placer County, "Personal Mortgagee-Mortgagor Index," vols. 1, 1A, Placer County Recorder's Office, Auburn, Calif.

83. "Immigrant Labor in the Fruit Industries of the Newcastle District," 421.

84. Ibid., 427–428; *Sacramento Bee*, April 11, 1905; *Placer County Republican*, January 3 and 31, 1907; *Newcastle News*, January 30, 1907; Statements of S. M. Katzer (no. 6), T. G. Burtcher (no. 11), Jack Hunter (no. 33), Irving Hall (no. 47), and L. Carl (no. 68), all in T. G. Chamberlain, comp., "Statements of Fruit Ranch Owners of Placer County," June 1916, carton 17, Mead Papers (hereafter Chamberlain Survey); Sandra O. Uyeunten, "Struggle and Survival: The History of Japanese Immigrant Families in California, 1907–1945" (Ph.D. diss., University of California, San Diego, 1988), 64–88.

85. Statement of E. G. Narramore (no. 56), Chamberlain Survey; Chamberlain, "Fruit Ranching Conditions in the Placer County Fruit Belt," 11; "Interview with Mr. Yoneda, a Secretary of the Japanese Association of America," December 2, 1924, appendix F in Robert Sinclair Murray, "The Japanese Association in America," typescript, 1924, box 32, Survey of Race Relations Collection, Hoover Institution Archives, Stanford University, Stanford, Calif.; "Immigrant Labor in the Fruit Industries of the Newcastle District," 428; Uyeunten, "Struggle and Survival," 66; Cheryl Lynn Cole, "A History of the Japanese Community in Sacramento, 1883–1972" (M.A. thesis, California State University, Sacramento, 1971), 38–41; Jean C. Gilbert, "Tsuda Grocery: A History," *Sierra Heritage* 8 (May–June 1989): 47–49; Yuji Ichioka, "Japanese Associations and the Japanese Government: A Special Relationship, 1909–1926," *Pacific Historical Review* 46 (August 1977): 414–415.

86. "Immigrant Labor in the Fruit Industries of the Newcastle District," 420, 808–815. County lease and chattel-mortgage documents corroborate the investigators' claim. In 1906, Japanese tenants rented approximately 1,000 acres, and over 3,500 by 1909; calculated from Placer County, "Lessee-Lessor Index," vols. 1, 2;

"Leases and Agreements," Books I, J, K, L; "Personal Mortgagee-Mortgagor Index," vols. 1A, 2; and "Personal Mortgages," Books 11–16, Placer County Recorder's Office. These figures also indicate that about half the leases were unrecorded.

87. Statements of T. L. Herbert (no. 43), J. T. Lesher (no. 46), J. J. Callison (no. 73), and E. S. Birdsall (no. 77), Chamberlain Survey; Chamberlain, "Fruit Ranching Conditions in the Placer County Fruit Belt," 8, 11–13; *Placer County Republican,* March 2, 1911; March 28, 1912; October 9, 1913.

88. H. E. Butler to Editor, *Sacramento Bee,* reprinted in *Pacific Rural Press,* August 12, 1911; *Placer County Republican,* August 24, 1911.

89. Placer County, "Leases and Agreements," Book H, 316–319; Book I, 19–20, 89–91; Book K, 121–122; "Personal Mortgages," Book 9, 144, Placer County Recorder's Office; Statement of Harry Butler (no. 31), Chamberlain Survey; Chamberlain, "Fruit Ranching Conditions in the Placer County Fruit Belt," 13; R. L. Adams and William H. Smith Jr., "Farm Tenancy in California and Methods of Leasing," University of California College of Agriculture, Agricultural Experiment Station, *Bulletin,* no. 655 (October 1941): 26–31; Keijiro Otsuka, Hiroyuki Chuma, and Yujiro Hayami, "Land and Labor Contracts in Agrarian Economies: Theories and Facts," *Journal of Economic Literature* 30 (December 1992): 1967–1976.

90. *Sacramento Bee,* July 24, 1911; *Pacific Rural Press,* August 12, 1911.

91. *Pacific Rural Press,* August 12, 1911; December 26, 1903; Ellwood Cooper, "President's Address," in *Official Report of the Thirty-first California Fruit Growers' Convention,* December 5–8, 1905 (Sacramento: State Printing Office, 1905), 12; J. W. Jeffrey, "Opening Address," in *Proceedings of the Thirty-fifth California Fruit Growers' Convention,* December 1–4, 1908 (Sacramento: State Printing Office, 1908), 37–38.

92. John P. Irish, "Labor in the Rural Industries of California," and G. H. Hecke, "The Pacific Coast Labor Question from the Standpoint of a Horticulturist," both in *Official Report of the Thirty-third California Fruit Growers' Convention,* December 3–6, 1907 (Sacramento: State Printing Office, 1907), 54–66, 67–72; *Pacific Rural Press,* December 14, 1907.

93. *Pacific Rural Press,* January 18, 1908.

94. Cletus E. Daniel, *Bitter Harvest: A History of California Farmworkers, 1870–1941* (Ithaca: Cornell University Press, 1981), 84–86; Melvyn Dubofsky, *We Shall Be All: A History of the Industrial Workers of the World* (New York: Quadrangle, 1969), 184–189; Philip S. Foner, *The Industrial Workers of the World, 1905–1917,* vol. 4 of *History of the Labor Movement in the United States* (New York: International Publishers, 1965), 185–189; Ronald Genini, "Industrial Workers of the World and their Fresno Free Speech Fight, 1910–1911," *California Historical Quarterly* 53 (Summer 1974): 100–114; Hyman Weintraub, "The IWW in California: 1905–1931" (M.A. thesis, University of California, Los Angeles, 1947), 23–32.

95. Foner, *The Industrial Workers of the World,* 261; Genini, "Industrial Workers of the World," 111.

96. Daniel, *Bitter Harvest,* 85–86; Dubofsky, *We Shall Be All,* 188–189; Weintraub, "The IWW in California," 31–32.

97. Dubofsky, *We Shall Be All,* 189.

98. *Industrial Worker,* May 13, May 20, July 15, August 26, September 9, and September 23, 1909; January 22, June 25, and July 23, 1910; Weintraub, "The IWW in

California," 7–14; Daniel Rosenberg, "The IWW and Organization of Asian Workers in Early 20th Century America," *Labor History* 36 (Winter 1995): 77–87; Phil Mellinger, "How the IWW Lost Its Western Heartland: Western Labor History Revisited," *Western Historical Quarterly* 27 (Autumn 1996): 308–316.

99. Ichioka, "A Buried Past," 8–10; Rosenberg, "The IWW and Organization of Asian Workers," 78.

100. Masakazu Iwata, *Planted in Good Soil: The History of the Issei in United States Agriculture* (New York: Peter Lang, 1992), 1–25, 221–259.

101. "Minutes of the Executive Council," California State Federation of Labor, October 8, 1909, carton 5, San Francisco Labor Council Records, Bancroft Library; "Unions Pledged to Assist Organization of Migratory Labor," October 1909, carton 30, ibid.; Paul Scharrenberg to Andrew J. Gallagher, May 4, 1910, carton 5, ibid.; California State Federation of Labor, *Proceedings of the Tenth Annual Convention*, October 4–8, 1909 (San Francisco: Hayden Printing Co., 1909), 45–47; Andrew Furuseth to Samuel Gompers, May 27, 1911, printed on the same day in *San Francisco Bulletin;* "Migratory Workers' Unions," *Survey* 27 (December 16, 1911): 1381; Stuart Marshall Jamieson, *Labor Unionism in American Agriculture*, U.S. Department of Labor, Bureau of Labor Statistics, Bulletin 836 (Washington, D.C.: Government Printing Office, 1945), 57–58.

102. *Fresno Morning Republican*, August 30, September 1, 7, 8, 9, 12, 18, 19, and October 13, 1911; *Pacific Rural Press*, September 9 and 16, 1911; *California Fruit Grower*, September 30, 1911; Jamieson, *Labor Unionism in American Agriculture*, 58.

103. Statement of D. G. Evans (no. 14), Chamberlain Survey.

104. *Sacramento Bee*, February 2 and 8, 1910; *Sacramento Union*, February 5 and 9, 1910; *California Fruit Grower*, February 12, 1910.

105. *Placer County Republican*, April 28, May 5, May 12, and June 30, 1910; *Sacramento Bee*, July 24, 1910; November 11, 1911; *Pacific Rural Press*, May 14, 1910; Testimony of Ivan H. Parker, in U.S. House of Representatives, Committee on Immigration and Naturalization, *Japanese Immigration Hearings*, 322–324.

106. Woehlke, "In the Service of Quality," 425, 427.

107. *Placer County Republican*, January 19, 1911; October 23, 1913; Placer County, "Leases and Agreements," Book H, 309–310, 362–363, and Book K, 198–200; "Personal Mortgages," Book 9, 32, and Book 16, 81, Placer County Recorder's Office; Statement of David Griffith (no. 30), Chamberlain Survey.

108. "Immigration," in Commonwealth Club of California, *Transactions* 8 (May 1913): 155–179; W. F. Stoll, "California's Viticultural Industry: Past, Present, Future," in California State Commission of Horticulture, *Monthly Bulletin* 2 (March–April 1913): 512–513; John T. Bramhall to Chester Rowell, July 19, 1913, box 10, Rowell Papers; *Pacific Rural Press*, January 4, 1908.

109. Irish, "Labor in the Rural Industries of California," 54; Hecke, "The Pacific Coast Labor Question," 72; *Sacramento Union*, February 5, 1910.

110. Chester Rowell to W. M. Giffen, December 10, 1909, box 1, Rowell Papers; Chester H. Rowell, "Chinese and Japanese Immigrants—A Comparison," *Annals of the American Academy of Political and Social Science* 34 (September 1909): 230; Frank W. Van Nuys, "A Progressive Confronts the Race Question: Chester Rowell, the

California Alien Land Act of 1913, and the Contradictions of Early Twentieth-Century Racial Thought," *California History* 73 (Spring 1994): 2–13.

111. *Fresno Morning Republican,* May 30, 1910.

112. Ibid.; Fuller, "The Supply of Agricultural Labor," 174–175.

113. The *Fresno Morning Republican* (May 30, 1910), the *Pacific Rural Press* (June 11, 1910), the *California Fruit Grower* (June 11 and 25, 1910), and numerous other papers published lengthy press releases, however. See also California State Bureau of Labor Statistics, *Fourteenth Biennial Report for 1909–1910* (Sacramento: State Printing Office, 1910), 265–274.

114. M. R. Benedict, "The Economic and Social Structure of California Agriculture," in *California Agriculture,* ed. Claude B. Hutchison (Berkeley: University of California Press, 1946), 421–422.

Chapter 4: "The Intrusion of a Third Party"

1. The most often cited version of Parker's Wheatland report is "A Report to His Excellency Hiram W. Johnson, Governor of California, by the Commission of Immigration and Housing of California on the Causes and All Matters Pertaining to the So-Called Wheatland Hop Fields' Riot and Killing of August 3, 1913, and Containing Certain Recommendations as a Solution for the Problems Disclosed," in Carleton H. Parker, *The Casual Laborer and Other Essays* (New York: Russell & Russell, 1920), app., 171–199 (hereafter *Parker's Wheatland Report*).

2. Carey McWilliams, *Factories in the Field: The Story of Migratory Farm Labor in California* (Boston: Little, Brown, 1939), 154; U.S. Senate, Subcommittee of the Committee on Education and Labor, *Report, Violations of Free Speech and Rights of Labor,* Report No. 1150, 76th Cong., 2d sess. (Washington, D.C.: Government Printing Office, 1942), pt. 3: 245–247. An earlier version of Parker's Wheatland report was entered in U.S. Senate, Subcommittee of the Committee on Education and Labor, *Hearings on S. Res. 266, Violations of Free Speech and Rights of Labor,* 74th Cong., 2d sess. (Washington, D.C.: Government Printing Office, 1939), pt. 54, exhibit 8768, pp. 20069–20073 (hereafter *La Follette Committee Hearings*).

3. Cletus E. Daniel, *Bitter Harvest: A History of California Farmworkers, 1870–1941* (Ithaca: Cornell University Press, 1981), 88–91; Philip S. Foner, *The Industrial Workers of the World, 1905–1917,* vol. 4 of *History of the Labor Movement in the United States* (New York: International Publishers, 1965), 279; Levi Varden Fuller, "The Supply of Agricultural Labor as a Factor in the Evolution of Farm Organization in California" (Ph.D. diss., University of California, Berkeley, 1939), 195–196; Stuart Marshall Jamieson, *Labor Unionism in American Agriculture,* U.S. Department of Labor, Bureau of Labor Statistics, Bulletin 836 (Washington, D.C.: Government Printing Office, 1945), 60–63; Linda C. Majka and Theo J. Majka, *Farm Workers, Agribusiness, and the State* (Philadelphia: Temple University Press, 1982), 52–57; Don Mitchell, *The Lie of the Land: Migrant Workers and the California Landscape* (Minneapolis: University of Minnesota Press, 1996), 36–42, passim; Paul S. Taylor, "Migratory Agricultural Workers on the Pacific Coast," *American Sociological Review* 3 (April 1938): 225; Paul S. Taylor and Clark Kerr, "Documentary History of the Strike of the Cotton Pickers in California, 1933," in *La Follette Committee Hearings,* 19947;

Hyman Weintraub, "The IWW in California: 1905–1931" (M.A. thesis, University of California, Los Angeles, 1947), 68–69.

4. "Immigrant Labor in California Agricultural Industries," in U.S. Senate, Reports of the Immigration Commission, "Immigrants in Industries," pt. 25, *Japanese and Other Immigrant Races in the Pacific Coast and Rocky Mountain States*, vol. 24, 61st Cong., 2d sess. (Washington, D.C.: Government Printing Office, 1911), 3 (hereafter *Dillingham Commission Report*).

5. Donald J. Pisani, *From the Family Farm to Agribusiness: The Irrigation Crusade in California and the West, 1850–1931* (Berkeley: University of California Press, 1984), 250–334.

6. The same can be said for the U.S. Industrial Commission (1901) and the U.S. Commission on Industrial Relations (1914), according to Robert Higgs, *Crisis and Leviathan: Critical Episodes in the Growth of American Government* (New York: Oxford University Press, 1987), 107–113.

7. *California Fruit Grower*, July 30, 1910.

8. "Chronological Guide to Transactions Relative to the Estate of R. H. Durst," 1939, box 2, Durst Bros. Hop Ranch Papers, Department of Special Collections, Meriam Library, California State University, Chico; "Immigrant Labor in the Hop Industry," in *Dillingham Commission Report*, 24:157–159; Yuba County Board of Supervisors, "Report of Commission Investigating Conditions in Hop Fields on and Just Prior to August 3, 1913," July 22, 1914, 46, Government Publications Room, California State Library, Sacramento; *Pacific Rural Press*, July 25, 1903; August 13 and 20, 1904; August 26, 1905; August 11 and 25, 1906; August 15, 1908; August 20, 1910; August 3, 1912; *Marysville Daily Appeal*, February 26, 1911; February 13, 1914; *San Francisco Bulletin*, August 4, 1913; *San Francisco Chronicle*, August 6, 1913; *California Social Democrat*, August 16, 1913.

9. Jonathan H. Durst to Jacob Samuels, June 17, 1918, box 2, Durst Bros. Hop Ranch Papers; *California Fruit Grower*, August 25, September 8, and December 22, 1906; *Pacific Rural Press*, July 30 and August 27, 1904; May 6, 1905; October 20, 1906; *Sacramento Union*, October 18, 1906; Joseph A. McGowan, *History of the Sacramento Valley* (New York: Lewis Historical Publishing Co., 1961), 2:201; James Jerome Parsons Jr., "The California Hop Industry: Its Eighty Years of Development and Expansion" (M.A. thesis, University of California, Berkeley, 1939), 112.

10. Durst to Samuels, June 17, 1918; W. U. Bowers to S. Nicholas Jacobs, December 19, 1913, box 1, Durst Bros. Hop Ranch Papers; *Sacramento Union*, August 15, 1909; *Sacramento Bee*, August 12, 1909; *California Fruit Grower*, December 14, 1907; October 10 and December 19, 1908; December 30, 1911; *Pacific Rural Press*, November 6, 1909; July 6 and August 13, 1912; Arthur Amos, "Hop Growing on the Pacific Coast of America," *Journal of the Board of Agriculture* 19 (May 1912): 91.

11. Durst to Samuels, June 17, 1918; Testimony of E. Clemons Horst, in U.S. Commission on Industrial Relations, *Final Report and Testimony* (Washington, D.C.: Government Printing Office, 1916), 5:4923–4926, 5027; *California Fruit Grower*, April 16, 1904; *Orchard and Farm*, April 1904; George E. Miller, *The Evolution of a Mechanical Hop Picker* (Sacramento: Central Printing Co., 1962), 1, California Room, California State Library.

12. Testimony of E. Clemons Horst, 4924–4925; *Pacific Rural Press*, August 26,

1905; August 13, 1907; *California Fruit Grower,* July 22, 1905; *Davisville Enterprise,* August 4, 1906; Miller, *The Evolution of a Mechanical Hop Picker,* 1.

13. *Marysville Daily Appeal,* August 24, August 31, and September 14, 1905; *Pacific Rural Press,* September 23, 1905; Parsons, "The California Hop Industry," 102–106.

14. *Pacific Rural Press,* September 14, 1907; June 13, August 29, and September 12, 1908; November 16, 1912; *California Fruit Grower,* March 7, 1908; Testimony of E. Clemons Horst, 4926–4927; Amos, "Hop Growing on the Pacific Coast of America," 379–383; Miller, *The Evolution of a Mechanical Hop Picker,* 1–13.

15. *Pacific Rural Press,* March 13, August 14, August 21, and September 11, 1909; *Sacramento Bee,* August 18 and 19, 1909; Miller, *The Evolution of a Mechanical Hop Picker,* 15–16.

16. *Pacific Rural Press,* August 20 and September 10, 1910; May 20 and July 19, 1911; February 17, April 13, August 31, and November 16, 1912; *California Fruit Grower,* August 27 and September 10, 1912; *Marysville Daily Appeal,* August 11, 1910; Miller, *The Evolution of a Mechanical Hop Picker,* 17–21; E. Clemons Horst Co., *Scenes from E. Clemons Horst Company's Hop Ranches . . .* (Sacramento: E. Clemons Horst Co., ca. 1920), no pagination, California Room, California State Library.

17. *Pacific Rural Press,* March 13, 1909; August 9, 1913; "PICK HOPS — DURST HOP YARDS" (poster), 1913, carton 1, Simon J. Lubin Correspondence, Bancroft Library; *San Francisco Chronicle,* August 6, 1913; *Marysville Daily Appeal,* February 13, 1913; *The People of the State of California, Respondent, v. Richard Ford (otherwise known as "Blackie" Ford), and H. D. Suhr, Appellants from the Superior Court of the State of California in and for the County of Yuba,* 1914, 628, Austin Lewis Papers, Bancroft Library (hereafter Ford and Suhr Trial Transcript); Yuba County Board of Supervisors, "Report of Commission Investigating Conditions in Hop Fields," 5–6; George L. Bell, "The Wheatland Hop-Fields' Riot," *Outlook* 107 (May 16, 1914): 120.

18. P. A. Speek, "Report on the Interviews with the Unemployed Migratory Workers in the Streets and Public Parks in San Francisco," October 4, 1914, U.S. Commission on Industrial Relations, 1912–15, Unpublished Records of the Division of Research and Investigations, microfilm (Frederick, Md.: University Publications of America, 1985), reel 6, frames 0317–0322 (hereafter USCIR Records); *Marysville Daily Appeal,* February 13, 1914; Charles B. Barnes, "Unemployment and Public Responsibility," *Survey* 33 (October 10, 1914): 48–50; Ed Delaney, "Wheatland: The Bloody Hop Field," *Industrial Pioneer* 2 (February 1925): 34–36; Arno Dosch, "Self-Help for the Hobo," *Sunset* 36 (January 1916): 19–21, 97–98; J. Edward Morgan, "The Unemployed in San Francisco," *New Review* 2 (April 1914): 193–199; E. Guy Talbott, "The Armies of the Unemployed in California," *Survey* 32 (August 23, 1914): 523–524; Walter V. Woehlke, "The Porterhouse Heaven and the Hobo," *Technical World* 21 (August 1914): 808–813, 938; "Unemployment," in Commonwealth Club of California, *Transactions* 9 (December 1914): 671–714; Alvin Averbach, "San Francisco's South of Market District, 1850–1950: The Emergence of a Skid Row," *California Historical Quarterly* 52 (Fall 1973): 193–228; Udo Sautter, *Three Cheers for the Unemployed: Government and Unemployment before the New Deal* (Cambridge: Cambridge University Press, 1992).

19. *Marysville Daily Appeal,* February 13, 1914; Ford and Suhr Trial Transcript, passim (for work identities of dozens of Wheatland pickers); Yuba County Board of

Supervisors, "Report of Commission Investigating Conditions in Hop Fields," 5–6, 10–11; Stuart Jamieson, "Interview with George Holmes," carton 1, Stuart Jamieson Field Notes Collection, 1941–43, Bancroft Library; *Parker's Wheatland Report,* 179.

20. Ford and Suhr Trial Transcript, 623; Paul F. Brissenden, "A Report on the I. W. W. in California," 1914, USCIR Records, reel 16, frames 0850–0864; Jamieson, "Interview with George Holmes"; Mortimer Downing, "The Case of the Hop Pickers," *International Socialist Review* 14 (October 1913): 210–213; *Parker's Wheatland Report,* 189; Weintraub, "The IWW in California," 67–70.

21. Ford and Suhr Trial Transcript, 558, 561–563, 622, 648, 800–804, 1101, 1314–1316, 1429–1430; Woehlke, "The Porterhouse Heaven and the Hobo," 808–813; Weintraub, "The IWW in California," 73. Few have acknowledged the IWW's strike intentions. The exceptions include Foner, *The Industrial Workers of the World,* 261; William D. Haywood, *The Autobiography of Big Bill Haywood* (New York: International Publishers, 1929), 274–275; and Vincent St. John, *The I.W.W.: Its History, Structure, and Methods,* rev. ed. (Chicago: Industrial Workers of the World, 1919), 30.

22. Ford and Suhr Trial Transcript, 804; Yuba County Board of Supervisors, "Report of Commission Investigating Conditions in Hop Fields," 26, 28–31; *Marysville Daily Appeal,* February 13, 1914. The extent of the bad camp conditions was subject to debate. Compare, for example, the report Inspector Harry Gorman made to the State Board of Health in September 1913—reprinted in *Plotting to Convict Wheatland Hop Pickers* (Oakland: International Press, 1914), 11–12, Bancroft Library—to Yuba County Board of Supervisors, "Report of Commission Investigating Conditions in Hop Fields," 38–46.

23. *San Francisco Bulletin,* August 4, 1913; Bell, "The Wheatland Hop-Fields' Riot," 120–121; Edward B. Stanwood, "The Marysville Case," *Harper's Weekly* 58 (June 20, 1914): 23; *Marysville Daily Appeal,* February 13, 1914; *San Francisco Chronicle,* August 6, 1913.

24. *Los Angeles Times,* August 4, 1913; *San Francisco Chronicle,* August 4, 1913.

25. Cletus E. Daniel, "In Defense of the Wheatland Wobblies: A Critical Analysis of the IWW in California," *Labor History* 19 (Fall 1978): 487; Mitchell, *The Lie of the Land,* 39.

26. *Marysville Daily Appeal,* February 13, 1914.

27. McWilliams, *Factories in the Field,* 159, 163; Melvyn Dubofsky, *We Shall Be All: A History of the Industrial Workers of the World* (New York: Quadrangle, 1969), 296–297.

28. Mitchell, *The Lie of the Land,* 40, passim.

29. Ford and Suhr Trial Transcript, 547–552, 1421–1422, passim; *San Francisco Bulletin,* January 16, 22, 24, 29, 30, and 31, 1914; Testimony of Austin Lewis, in U.S. Commission on Industrial Relations, *Final Report and Testimony,* 4999–5010; Hiram Johnson to Andrew J. Gallagher, December 4, 1913, part 2, box 2, Hiram Johnson Papers, Bancroft Library; Dubofsky, *We Shall Be All,* 296–297.

30. Samuel Gompers, "Labor Camp Life—Its Evils," *American Federationist,* July 1914, 566–570; International Workers' Defense League, "General Financial Statement," 1914, 1915, carton 10, San Francisco Labor Council Records, Bancroft Library; Austin Lewis, "Solidarity—Merely a Word?" *New Review* 3 (July 15, 1915):

127; Lewis, "Potential Solidarity," *New Review* 3 (October 1, 1915): 254–257; Inez Haynes Gillmore, "The Marysville Strike," *Harper's Weekly* 58 (April 4, 1914): 18–20; Philip Taft, *Labor Politics American Style: The California State Federation of Labor* (Cambridge: Harvard University Press, 1968), 37–40; Michael Kazin, "The Great Exception Revisited: Organized Labor and Politics in San Francisco and Los Angeles, 1870–1940," *Pacific Historical Review* 55 (August 1986): 389–398.

31. *Parker's Wheatland Report*, 174–187, 196; Carleton H. Parker, "The Wheatland Hop Field Riot," *California Outlook* 16 (March 14, 1914): 6–7.

32. *Parker's Wheatland Report*, 198; Pauline Jacobson, "Parker, Social Diagnostician," *Miners Magazine* 15 (April 2, 1914): 6–8; Parker, *The Casual Laborer*, 27–59; Samuel Haber, *Efficiency and Uplift: Scientific Management in the Progressive Era, 1890–1920* (Chicago: University of Chicago Press, 1964), 104–106; Mark Perlman, *Labor Union Theories in America: Background and Development* (Evanston, Ill.: Row, Peterson & Co., 1958), 123–128.

33. Simon J. Lubin, "California and the Problems of the Immigrant: A Discussion of the Existing and Future Situation in the State," *California Outlook* 15 (November 15, 1913): 11–12; Carleton H. Parker, "Immediate Program of the Immigration Commission," ibid., 5; "Minutes of Meetings," December 5, 1913, Records of the Department of Industrial Relations, Commission of Immigration and Housing Files, California State Archives, Office of the Secretary of State, Sacramento (hereafter CCIH Files); *Sacramento Bee*, December 7, 1913; Samuel Edgerton Wood, "The California State Commission of Immigration and Housing: A Study of Administrative Organization and the Growth of Function" (Ph.D. diss., University of California, Berkeley, 1942), 76–128.

34. Simon Lubin to David P. Barrows, October 4, 1913, box 4; Carleton Parker to Lubin, December 22, 1913, box 3; Harris Weinstock to Parker, January 10, 1914, box 3; Parker to Weinstock, January 10, 1914, box 4; Lubin to Mary Gibson, February 9, 1914, box 4; Parker to Lubin, March 30, 1914, box 4, all in Lubin Correspondence. Many historians have assumed, inaccurately, that the CCIH was created with the intent of investigating Wheatland and/or that Governor Johnson requested the inquiry. Prior to Weinstock's proposal, the Wheatland issue does not appear in any of the minutes of the commission's meetings, nor was it discussed in members' correspondence or published articles. In a letter to Commissioner Mary Gibson written two days after Weinstock's proposal, Lubin indicated clearly that the Wheatland investigation was Weinstock's idea and that he (Lubin) and Parker had convinced Johnson of its necessity. Lubin to Gibson, January 12, 1914, carton 1, California Department of Industrial Relations, Division of Immigration and Housing Records, Bancroft Library (hereafter CDIR Records).

35. Bell, "The Wheatland Hop-Fields' Riot," 118–123; George L. Bell, "A California Labor Tragedy," *Literary Digest* 48 (May 23, 1914): 1239–1240; Gillmore, "The Marysville Strike," 18–20; Carleton H. Parker, "The Wheatland Riot and What Lay Back of It," *Survey* 31 (March 21, 1914): 768–770; Parker, "The Wheatland Hop Field Riot," 6–7; Woehlke, "The Porterhouse Heaven and the Hobo," 810.

36. *Parker's Wheatland Report*, 193, 196; Parker to Johnson, February 10, 1914, box 3, Lubin Correspondence.

37. Johnson to Parker, February 13, 1914, box 2, Lubin Correspondence.

38. Johnson to Fremont Older, February 28, 1914; Johnson to E. W. Scripps, January 22, 1914, part 2, box 2, Johnson Papers; Dubofsky, *We Shall Be All*, 189–196.

39. Lubin to Gibson, January 12, 1914, box 4; Parker to Lubin, March 24, 1914; Parker to Lubin, February 12, 1914, box 3, Lubin Correspondence; Lubin to Parker, February 13, 1914, carton 1, CDIR Records.

40. Lubin to Parker, February 9, 1914, box 4, Lubin Correspondence. *Organized Labor* (February 21, 1914), the *California Social Democrat* (February 21, 1914), the *California Outlook* (March 14, 1914), and the *Survey* (March 21, 1914) published this first draft in full. This is also the version published in *La Follette Committee Hearings*.

41. *San Francisco Chronicle*, February 9 and 19, 1914; Johnson to Lubin, February 14, 1914, box 2; Lubin to Parker, February 13 and 18, 1914, box 4, Lubin Correspondence.

42. E. Clemons Horst to Lubin, February 12, 1914, box 2, Lubin Correspondence.

43. Lubin to Chester Rowell, February 14, 1914, box 4, Lubin Correspondence.

44. Parker, "The Wheatland Hop Field Riot," 6–7, 17; Parker to Lubin, February 27, 1914, box 3, Lubin Correspondence.

45. George Bell to Lubin, April 4, April 20, and May 6, 1914, carton 1, CDIR Records; "Camp Inspection Register," entries for 1914, CDIR Records; *Davis Enterprise*, June 20, 1914; Commission of Immigration and Housing of California, *First Annual Report* (Sacramento: State Printing Office, 1915), 15–51; Commission of Immigration and Housing of California, *Second Annual Report* (Sacramento: State Printing Office, 1916), 9–40; Hugh S. Hanna, *Labor Laws and Their Administration in the Pacific States*, U.S. Bureau of Labor Statistics, Bulletin, no. 211 (January 1917): 92; Wood, "The California State Commission of Immigration and Housing," 188.

46. J. J. Rosenthal to Lubin, April 27 and May 20, 1914, box 3, Lubin Correspondence; *Wheatland Four Corners*, May 15, 1914; *Parker's Wheatland Report*, 190; Commission of Immigration and Housing of California, *Advisory Pamphlet on Camp Sanitation* (Sacramento: State Printing Office, 1914), Bancroft Library.

47. Bell to Lubin, April 30, 1914, box 1, Lubin Correspondence; *Sacramento Bee*, July 22 and 25, 1914; "Cleaning Camps in California," *California Outlook* 16 (August 8, 1914): 9–10.

48. This was the official version submitted to the USCIR; see "Report on the Wheatland Hop-Fields Riot," USCIR Records, reel 16, frames 0029–0072. See also Parker to Lubin, April 28, 1914, carton 1, CDIR Records.

49. *California Outlook* 16 (July 11, 1914): 5; Johnson to William C. Merill, February 16, 1916, part 2, box 4, Johnson Papers; Commission of Immigration and Housing of California, *Second Annual Report*, 9.

50. The paper was not published, but see *Sacramento Union*, June 2, 1914; *Sacramento Bee*, June 2, 1914; Lubin to Bell, May 2, 1914; Lubin to "Papa," June 4, 1914; Lubin to Ralph Durst, June 11, 1914; and Lubin to Parker, June 14, 1914, all in box 4, Lubin Correspondence.

51. On this point, the daily journals and account books of George W. Pierce Jr. (Pierce Family Papers, Department of Special Collections, University of California Library, Davis) are particularly illuminating. Pierce showed no interest in the hop

pickers' uprising; nor did he ever encounter any union efforts to organize his harvest workers. In addition, the Wheatland incident left little or no trace in the *Pacific Rural Press,* the *California Fruit Grower,* the *Proceedings* of the fruit growers' conventions, or other agricultural publications. See also Ralph Durst to Lubin, June 9, 23, and 28, 1914, box 2; and Lubin to Durst, June 11 and 27, 1914, box 4, Lubin Correspondence.

52. Vincent S. Brown to Katharine W. Treat, May 17, 1927, box 16, Survey of Race Relations Collection, Hoover Institution Archives, Stanford University, Stanford, Calif.

53. Parker to Lubin, March 27, April 2, and October 3, 1914, box 3; Lubin to Parker, March 30, June 26, and September 30, 1914; Lubin to Weinstock, April 1, 1914, box 4, all in Lubin Correspondence; Bell to Lubin, June 24, 1914, carton 1, CDIR Records; *San Francisco Chronicle,* October 10, 1914.

54. This was the version published in Parker, *The Casual Laborer.* See also Lubin to Bell, May 6, 1914, box 4, Lubin Correspondence; and Commission of Immigration and Housing of California, *First Annual Report,* 15.

55. Daniel, *Bitter Harvest,* 88–89.

56. Johnson to Irving Martin, August 14, 1915, part 2, box 4, Johnson Papers.

57. Commission of Immigration and Housing of California, *First Annual Report,* 50.

58. Daniel, *Bitter Harvest,* 98–99; Bruce Nelson, "J. Vance Thompson, the Industrial Workers of the World, and the Mood of Syndicalism, 1914–1921," *Labor's Heritage* 2 (October 1990): 44–65; William Preston Jr., *Aliens and Dissenters: Federal Suppression of Radicals, 1903–1933* (Cambridge: Harvard University Press, 1963), 57–61; Gregory R. Woirol, "Observing the IWW in California, May–July 1914," *Labor History* 25 (Summer 1984): 437–447.

59. Lubin to Members of the Commission of Immigration and Housing of California, June 19, 1923, Executive Officer's Reports, CCIH Files; Wood, "The California State Commission of Immigration and Housing," 130–137.

60. This contrast is the central theme of Spencer C. Olin Jr., "European Immigrant and Oriental Alien: Acceptance and Rejection by the California Legislature of 1913," *Pacific Historical Review* 35 (August 1966): 303–315.

61. "Pacific Coast Opinion of Japanese Immigration and the Desire for Asiatic Laborers," in *Dillingham Commission Report,* 23:173; Alice M. Brown, *The Recrudescence of Japanese Agitation in California* (n.p., 1913), 1, Green Library, Stanford University; *Placer County Republican,* April 24, 1914; Franklin Hichborn, *Story of the Session of the California Legislature of 1913* (San Francisco: James H. Barry Co., 1913), 213–225; Roger Daniels, *The Politics of Prejudice: The Anti-Japanese Movement in California and the Struggle for Japanese Exclusion* (Berkeley: University of California Press, 1962), 46–53; Robert Higgs, "Landless by Law: Japanese Immigrants in California Agriculture to 1941," *Journal of Economic History* 38 (March 1978): 215.

62. W. B. Lardner and M. J. Brock, *History of Placer and Nevada Counties* (Los Angeles: Historic Record Co., 1924), 647–649; Statement of Senator E. S. Birdsall (no. 77), in T. G. Chamberlain, comp., "Statements of Fruit Ranch Owners of Placer County," June 1916, carton 17, Elwood Mead Papers, Bancroft Library (hereafter Chamberlain Survey).

63. *Placer County Republican,* July 24, 1913; John P. Irish to Charles Eliot, May 27, 1913, box 1, John Powell Irish Papers, Special Collections, Green Library, Stanford University; Testimony of Ivan H. Parker, in U.S. House of Representatives, Committee on Immigration and Naturalization, *Japanese Immigration Hearings,* 66th Cong., 2d sess. (Washington, D.C.: Government Printing Office, 1921), 324; J. Soyeda and T. Kamiya, *A Survey of the Japanese Question in California* (n.p., 1913), 6–8, box 7, Survey of Race Relations Collection, Hoover Institution Archives; McWilliams, *Factories in the Field,* 111; Hichborn, *Story of the Session of the California Legislature of 1913,* 225.

64. Hichborn, *Story of the Session of the California Legislature of 1913,* 227–274; H. A. Millis, *The Japanese Problem in the United States* (New York: Macmillan, 1915), 200.

65. Quoted in Richard B. Rice, William A. Bullough, and Richard J. Orsi, *The Elusive Eden: A New History of California,* 2d ed. (New York: McGraw-Hill, 1996), 370.

66. Johnson to Roosevelt, June 21, 1913, printed in Daniels, *The Politics of Prejudice,* 112–117.

67. *Newcastle News,* June 4, July 9, August 21, and December 16, 1913; Millis, *The Japanese Problem in the United States,* 220–221; Eliot Grinnell Mears, *Resident Orientals on the American Pacific Coast: Their Legal and Economic Status* (Chicago: University of Chicago Press, 1928), 254; Higgs, "Landless by Law," 216–220. For examples of leases more than three years long, see Statements of Otto Schnabel (no. 17), L. T. Mursso (no. 27), Louis Perry (no. 29), Irving Hall (no. 47), John Watson (no. 53), E. G. Narramore (no. 56), T. E. Douglas (no. 57), H. Sweesy (no. 67), George Smithen (no. 72), and J. J. Callison (no. 73), Chamberlain Survey.

68. Thomas Forsyth Hunt, "The Motive of the College of Agriculture of the University of California," in "Proceedings of the Forty-second California State Fruit Growers' Convention," December 11–13, 1912, in California State Commission of Horticulture, *Monthly Bulletin* 2 (March–April 1913): 427–439; Hunt, "Some Things the Prospective Settler Should Know," University of California College of Agriculture, Agricultural Experiment Station, *Circular,* no. 121 (October 1914); Hunt, "Some Land Problems in California," in *Proceedings of the Forty-fifth California Fruit Growers' Convention,* November 10–14, 1914 (Sacramento: State Printing Office, 1915), 158–160; Hunt, "Permanent Agriculture and Social Welfare," address delivered before the Farm Management Association, University of California, Berkeley, August 9, 1915, box 23, Records of the College of Agriculture and the Agricultural Experiment Station, University of California Archives, Bancroft Library; Chester Rowell, "Hunt vs. Irish," March 17, 1913, Rowell Editorials, carton 2, Chester Rowell Correspondence and Papers, Bancroft Library; John P. Irish to Editor, *San Francisco Call,* ca. April 1913, box 1, Irish Papers; "State Aid to Agriculture," in Commonwealth Club of California, *Transactions* 6 (November 1911): 407–513; Claude B. Hutchison, "The College of Agriculture, University of California, 1922–1952" (Regional Oral History Office, Bancroft Library, 1961), 63–68; David B. Danbom, *The Resisted Revolution: Urban America and the Industrialization of Agriculture, 1900–1930* (Ames: Iowa State University Press, 1979), chaps. 2–4.

69. Ann Foley Scheuring, *"A Sustaining Comradeship": The Story of University of California Cooperative Extension, 1913–1988* (Berkeley: Division of Agriculture and

Natural Resources, 1988), 7–11; M. R. Benedict, "The Economic and Social Structure of California Agriculture," in *California Agriculture,* ed. Claude B. Hutchison (Berkeley: University of California Press, 1946), 428–430.

70. *Placer County Republican,* December 22, 1904; July 27, 1905; September 6, 1906; January 13 and 20, 1910; *Newcastle News,* February 12, 1902; March 18, 1903; March 29, 1911; *California Fruit Grower,* April 9, 1898; Warren T. Clarke, "The Peach Worm," University of California College of Agriculture, Agricultural Experiment Station, *Bulletin,* no. 144 (September 1902); Gerald Geraldson, "Overworking the Soil," in *Official Report of the Thirty-third California Fruit Growers' Convention,* December 3–6, 1907 (Sacramento: State Printing Office, 1907), 200; Harry E. Butler, "A History of the First Malaria Mosquito Control Campaign in the United States, at Penryn, California, 1910," typescript, April 15, 1945, 1–3, Harry Butler Biographical Letter File, California Room, California State Library.

71. Thomas F. Hunt, *Report of the College of Agriculture and the Agricultural Experiment Station of the University of California from July 1, 1912 to June 30, 1913* (Berkeley: University of California Press, 1913), lxiii–lxx; Claude B. Hutchison, "The College of Agriculture," 63–68; Joann Leach Larkey, *Cooperating Farmers: The 75-Year History of the Yolo County Farm Bureau* (Woodland, Calif.: The Bureau, 1989), 7–8.

72. B. H. Crocheron, "The County Farm Advisor," University of California College of Agriculture, Agricultural Experiment Station, *Circular,* no. 112 (January 1914); Crocheron, "The County Farm Bureau," University of California College of Agriculture, Agricultural Experiment Station, *Circular,* no. 118 (June 1914); Crocheron, "The County Farm Advisor," University of California College of Agriculture, Agricultural Experiment Station, *Circular,* no. 133 (July 1915); Crocheron, "The County Farm Bureau," University of California College of Agriculture, Agricultural Experiment Station, *Circular,* no. 166 (August 1917); Crocheron, "The Function of the Farm Bureau," University of California College of Agriculture, Agricultural Experiment Station, *Circular,* no. 209 (March 1919); Scheuring, *"A Sustaining Comradeship,"* 12–15; Larkey, *Cooperating Farmers,* 8–9.

73. Larkey, *Cooperating Farmers,* 9–23; George W. Pierce Jr., Daily Journals, 1890–1930, entry for March 7, 1914, Department of Special Collections, University of California Library, Davis (hereafter Pierce journal).

74. Frank T. Swett, "California Agricultural Cooperatives" (Regional Oral History Office, Bancroft Library, 1968), 54; Scheuring, *"A Sustaining Comradeship,"* 12–20; *Newcastle News,* October 21 and November 5, 1914; *Placer County Republican,* November 4, 1914; January 7, 1915; Fresno County Farm Bureau, *Serving Agriculture, 50 Years Golden Anniversary: Fresno County Farm Bureau, 1917–1967* (Fresno: Fresno County Farm Bureau, 1967), 7–12.

75. *Pacific Rural Press,* April 29, 1916; Hunt, "Some Things the Prospective Settler Should Know"; A. H. Hendrickson, "Small Fruit Culture in California," University of California College of Agriculture, Agricultural Experiment Station, *Circular,* no. 164 (April 1917); and numerous other Experiment Station circulars published between 1915 and 1918.

76. Swett, "California Agricultural Cooperatives," 49–51; *Placer County Republican,* September 23 and December 30, 1915; January 13, April 7, September 14, September 21, September 28, and October 5, 1915; Testimonies of Frank Lyons of San

Joaquin County (October 6, 1915) and W. H. Hihleman of Glenn County (October 8, 1915), in "Hearings of the California Commission on Land Colonization and Rural Credits," typescript, 279–294, 555–576, carton 19, Mead Papers (hereafter CCLCRC, "Hearings"); Larkey, *Cooperating Farmers*, 15, 69–72.

77. Hunt, "The Motive of the College of Agriculture of the University of California," 427–439; Hunt, "Some Things the Prospective Settler Should Know," 1–15; Hunt, "Some Land Problems in California," 158–160; Hunt, "Permanent Agriculture and Social Welfare," 3–6; Fuller, "The Supply of Agricultural Labor," 191–194.

78. Harris Weinstock to David P. Barrows, September 23, 1914, box 13, Records of the College of Agriculture and the Agricultural Experiment Station; Albert Adelson, *The Unemployment Question Solved: Back to the Land* (San Francisco: California Free State-Wide Colonization, 1915), Bancroft Library; Charles W. Blanpied, *A Humanitarian Study of the Coming Immigration Problem on the Pacific Coast* (San Francisco: Art Press, 1913); O. H. Miller, "Colonizing Northern California," in *Proceedings of the Thirty-eighth Convention of the California State Fruit Growers*, December 6–9, 1910 (Sacramento: State Printing Office, 1910), 179–186; "Immigration," in Commonwealth Club of California, *Transactions* 8 (May 1913): 155–179; California State Bureau of Labor Statistics, *Fifteenth Biennial Report for 1911–1912* (Sacramento: State Printing Office, 1912), 48–49; Commission of Immigration and Housing of California, *Second Annual Report*, 325–327.

79. *San Francisco Examiner, San Francisco Chronicle, San Francisco Bulletin,* January 2, 1914; Morgan, "The Unemployed in San Francisco," 193–194.

80. Johnson to Charles D. Heywood, March 10, 1914, part 2, box 2; Johnson to W. S. Goodrich, March 23, 1914, part 2, box 2; Johnson to Theodore E. Peiser, May 4, 1914, part 2, box 3, Johnson Papers.

81. Johnson to Theodore E. Peiser, May 4, 1914; Weinstock to Barrows, September 23, 1914; Chester Rowell to Mead, December 11, 1914, box 2, Rowell Papers; Walter V. Woehlke, "'Be Sure You're Right, Then Stick!': How Elwood Mead Rose to the Top on This Principle and by Never Fearing to Work beyond the Duties of the Job," *Sunset* 45 (December 1920): 27, 78–88; Elwood Mead, *Helping Men Own Farms: A Practical Discussion of Government Aid in Land Settlement* (New York: Macmillan, 1920), 64–93; Paul K. Conkin, "The Vision of Elwood Mead," *Agricultural History* 34 (April 1960): 88–90; James R. Kluger, *Turning on Water with a Shovel: The Career of Elwood Mead* (Albuquerque: University of New Mexico Press, 1992), 57–73.

82. Johnson to Rowell, March 11, 1915, part 2, box 3, Johnson Papers; "The Land Settlement Bill," in Commonwealth Club of California, *Transactions* 10 (May 1915): 197–238; "Land Settlement in California," in Commonwealth Club of California, *Transactions* 11 (December 1916): 369; Conkin, "The Vision of Elwood Mead," 90; Kluger, *Turning on Water with a Shovel*, 86.

83. Rowell to Johnson, February 17, 1915, part 2, box 29, Johnson Papers; Barrows to Rowell, February 24, 1915, box 9, Rowell Papers; Mead to Members of the Rural Credits Commission, February 11, 1916, carton 16, Mead Papers; Opening Statement of Harris Weinstock, September 29, 1915, in CCLCRC, "Hearings"; Testimony of Edwin Harris, October 6, 1915, ibid.; Elwood Mead, *State Aid in Land Settlement: An Address by Elwood Mead* (Sacramento: State Printing Office, 1915); California Commission on Land Colonization and Rural Credits, *Land Settlement and Rural Cred-*

its: The Need for an Investigation in California (Sacramento: State Printing Office, 1916); *Report of the Commission on Land Colonization and Rural Credits of the State of California* (Sacramento: State Printing Office, 1916), 5–13, passim; Conkin, "The Vision of Elwood Mead," 90; Kluger, *Turning on Water with a Shovel,* 86–87.

84. "The Land Settlement Bill of 1917," in Commonwealth Club of California, *Transactions* 12 (March 1917): 12–16, 24–29, 33–39; Conkin, "The Vision of Elwood Mead," 90.

85. Testimony of C. C. Teague, October 14, 1915, in CCLCRC, "Hearings"; *Fresno Evening Herald,* June 1, 1916.

86. Irish to *Pacific Rural Press,* ca. October 1915, box 1, Irish Papers. See also Swett, "California Agricultural Cooperatives," 51–57.

87. Testimony of Howard C. Rowley, October 23, 1915, in CCLCRC, "Hearings"; *California Fruit News,* October 16, 1915, through February 3, 1917. The journal changed its name from the *California Fruit Grower* in 1915.

88. Weinstock to H. P. Stabler, September 16, 1915, part 2, box 35, Johnson Papers.

89. Weinstock to Johnson, January 18, 1917, box 26, Rowell Papers; Harris Weinstock, "Address on Marketing," in *Proceedings of the Forty-eighth California State Fruit Growers' Convention,* February 18–19, 1916 (Sacramento: State Printing Office, 1916), 63–75; Weinstock, "Scientific Distribution of Fruit," in "Proceedings of the Forty-ninth California State Fruit Growers' Convention," November 15–17, 1916, in California State Commission of Horticulture, *Monthly Bulletin* 6 (May 1917): 159–166; Mead, *Helping Men Own Farms,* 207; Grace H. Larsen, "A Progressive in Agriculture: Harris Weinstock," *Agricultural History* 32 (July 1958): 189–193; Mansel G. Blackford, *The Politics of Business in California, 1890–1920* (Columbus: Ohio State University Press, 1977), 29–38.

90. T. G. Chamberlain, "Fruit Ranching Conditions in the Placer County Fruit Belt," typescript, June 1916, carton 16, Mead Papers; Statements of A. M. Vivier (no. 8), W. R. Fountain (no. 16), Clark J. Reed (no. 19), George Kellogg (no. 23), Harry Butler (no. 31), J. T. Lesher (no. 46), Ed Lardner (no. 54), and E. S. Birdsall (no. 77), Chamberlain Survey; Chamberlain to Professor David N. Morgan, June 22, 1916, carton 16, Mead Papers; *Report of the Commission on Land Colonization and Rural Credits of the State of California,* 60–61; Mead, *Helping Men Own Farms,* 5–7.

91. "The Land Settlement Bill," 209; Mead to Rowell, March 30, 1916, box 20, Rowell Papers.

92. Johnson to Rowell, March 11, 1915, part 2, box 3; Rowell to Johnson, part 2, box 29, Johnson Papers.

93. Rowell to Martin Madsen, May 12, 1917, box 3, Rowell Papers; Swett, "California Agricultural Cooperatives," 54; Elwood Mead, "Government Aid and Direction in Land Settlement," *American Economic Review* 8 (March 1918): 72–78; Conkin, "The Vision of Elwood Mead," 90–91; Kluger, *Turning on Water with a Shovel,* 87–89. On the ultimate failures of the Durham Colony and a similar settlement, see Roy J. Smith, "The California State Land Settlements at Durham and Delhi," *Hilgardia* 15 (October 1943): 399–492.

94. *California Social Democrat,* January 3, 1914; *Pacific Rural Press,* June 13 and March 28, 1914; Edward Berwick, "The Fruit-Grower as a Factor in Politics," in

"Proceedings of the Thirty-second Convention of the California State Fruit Growers," December 4–7, 1906, in California Commissioner of Horticulture, *Second Biennial Report for 1905–1906* (Sacramento: State Printing Office, 1907), 505–512; *Davis Enterprise*, June 6, 1914; *California Fruit Grower*, June 13, 1914; *Farmers' News*, July 1914; Fuller, "The Supply of Agricultural Labor," 200–203.

95. *Placer County Republican*, July 9 and 16, 1914; *Newcastle News*, July 15, 1914; *Pacific Rural Press*, July 25, 1914; *California Fruit Grower*, September 19, 1914; *Farmers' News*, July, November, and December 1914.

96. See virtually any issue of the *Farmers' News*, *Pacific Rural Press*, *California Fruit Grower*, or *California Social Democrat* from June through October 1914; and Ralph Edward Shaffer, "A History of the Socialist Party of California" (M.A. thesis, University of California, Berkeley, 1955), 144–163.

97. *Farmers' News*, August 1914; *Proceedings of the Fifteenth Annual Convention of the California State Federation of Labor*, 1914, 75; California State Federation of Labor, "Minutes of Meeting of Executive Council," July 12, 1914, carton 5, San Francisco Labor Council Records, Bancroft Library; Michael Kazin, *Barons of Labor: The San Francisco Building Trades and Union Power in the Progressive Era* (Urbana: University of Illinois Press, 1987), 151–152.

98. "The Eight Hour Law," in Commonwealth Club of California, *Transactions* 9 (August 1914): 454, passim; *California Fruit Grower*, July 25, 1914; *Farmers' News*, September 1914.

99. *Farmers' News*, September 1914; *California Fruit Grower*, September 19, 1914; "Discussion on Farmers' Protective League," in *Proceedings of the Forty-fifth California Fruit Growers' Convention*, 125–127.

100. *Farmers' News*, October 1914 through April 1915; October 1915; October 1916.

101. The *California Fruit Grower* published both Pierce's and Hecke's papers on September 19, 1914. On the transition from an agricultural to an industrial economy in California at the turn of the century, see Gerald D. Nash, "Stages of California's Economic Growth, 1870–1970: An Interpretation," *California Historical Quarterly* 51 (Winter 1972): 319–324.

102. *California Fruit Grower*, September 19, 1914.

Chapter 5: "Food Will Win the War"

1. *Laton Argus* (Fresno County), June 8, 1916; *Fresno Morning Republican*, August 28 and November 20, 1916; Ralph P. Merritt to S. Parker Frisselle, April 12, 1917, carton 2, Kearney Ranch Papers, Bancroft Library, University of California, Berkeley; Wylie M. Giffen to Ralph P. Merritt, May 21, 1918, box 7, Master Correspondence File, Office of the Federal Food Commissioner, Records of the U.S. Food Administration, California Food Administration (RG 4), National Archives, Pacific Sierra Region, San Bruno, Calif. (hereafter CFA Records, with box numbers referring to the original cataloguing); Ralph P. Merritt, "California Cooperatives Set an Example," *American Review of Reviews* 72 (August 1925): 154; Victoria Alice Saker, "Benevolent Monopoly: The Legal Transformation of Agricultural Cooperation, 1890–1943" (Ph.D. diss., University of California, Berkeley, 1990), 180, 247.

2. *California Fruit News*, December 29, 1917; *Pacific Rural Press*, December 29, 1917; California Development Board, *Twenty-eighth Annual Report for the Year 1917*

(San Francisco: California Development Board, 1918), 23–43; California Development Board, *Twenty-ninth and Thirtieth Annual Reports for the Years 1918 and 1919* (San Francisco: California Development Board, 1920), 35–56; Robert Higgs, *Crisis and Leviathan: Critical Episodes in the Growth of American Government* (New York: Oxford University Press, 1987), 123–124; James H. Shideler, *Farm Crisis: 1919–1923* (Berkeley: University of California Press, 1957), 10–11.

3. Emile J. Bernatche to Frank J. Cunningham, August 23, 1918, carton 63, California Department of Industrial Relations, Division of Immigration and Housing Records, Bancroft Library (hereafter CDIR Records); *Pacific Rural Press,* September 8, 1914; Levi Varden Fuller, "The Supply of Agricultural Labor as a Factor in the Evolution of Farm Organization in California" (Ph.D. diss., University of California, Berkeley, 1939), 194; Melvyn Dubofsky, *The State and Labor in Modern America* (Chapel Hill: University of North Carolina Press, 1994), 61–63.

4. "Minutes of the Meeting of the Executive Committee of the State Council of Defense of California," October 23, 1918, box 31, Master Correspondence File, Office of the Federal Food Commissioner, CFA Records; George Bell to J. H. McBride, May 17, 1917, carton 1, CDIR Records.

5. Edward Krehbiel, "Report of the United States Food Administration for California," typescript, 1919, chap. 8, pp. 1–2, box 1, History File, Speakers Bureau, CFA Records.

6. *Fresno Morning Republican,* August 28 and September 7, 1916; January 31, 1917; *Pacific Rural Press,* July 25, 1914; December 9, 1917; Giffen to Merritt, May 21, 1918; Emma B. Little to John P. McLaughlin, July 27, 1915, box 18, Chester Rowell Correspondence and Papers, Bancroft Library; Testimony of Wylie Giffen, in U.S. Commission on Industrial Relations, *Final Report and Testimony* (Washington: Government Printing Office, 1916), 5:4969–4972; R. L. Adams and T. R. Kelly, "A Study of Farm Labor in California," University of California College of Agriculture, Agricultural Experiment Station, *Circular,* no. 193 (March 1918): 6; Edward J. Wickson, *The California Fruits and How to Grow Them,* 7th ed. (San Francisco: Pacific Rural Press, 1914), 306–311; Charles W. Clough et al., *Fresno County in the Twentieth Century: From 1900 to the 1980s* (Fresno: Panorama West Books, 1986), 169–170, 175; Hans Christian Palmer, "Italian Immigration and the Development of California Agriculture" (Ph.D. diss., University of California, Berkeley, 1965), 149–155, passim.

7. *Fresno Morning Republican,* September 8, November 20, November 24, November 28, and December 7, 1916; *Fresno Labor News,* February 3, 1916; "Report of Keller and Boswell, Fresno," September 17, 1917, box 52, Master Correspondence File, Office of the Federal Food Commissioner, CFA Records; J. Vance Thompson, "Notes on Industrial Conditions in and around Fresno, Stanislaus, San Joaquin, Sacramento, and Yolo Counties," July 23, 1917, carton 1, Simon J. Lubin Correspondence, Bancroft Library; Robert Clark, "The Labor History of Fresno, 1886–1910" (M.A. thesis, California State University, Fresno, 1976), passim. Note that the AWU was not affiliated with the IWW's Agricultural Workers Organization (AWO), as many have assumed.

8. *Fresno Morning Republican,* January 15, January 30, January 31, February 6, February 8, February 10, and February 12, 1917; *Fresno Evening Herald,* February 8, 1917.

9. *Fresno Morning Republican*, February 11, 12, 13, and 14, 1917; *Fresno Evening Herald*, February 12, 13, 1917; W. Flanders Setchel, "Solving Our Labor Problems," *Sun-Maid Herald* 3 (February 1918): 16.

10. *Fresno Morning Republican*, February 17, February 20, February 21, February 22, February 26, March 5, and March 12, 1917; *Pacific Rural Press*, March 17, 1917; Setchel, "Solving Our Labor Problems," 16.

11. Setchel, "Solving Our Labor Problems," 16; W. Flanders Setchel to Frank L. Lathrop, April 6, 1920, in State Board of Control of California, *California and the Oriental: Japanese, Chinese, and Hindus*, rev. ed. (Sacramento: State Board of Control, 1922), 120–121.

12. *Placer County Republican*, August 3, 1916; *Newcastle News*, October 14, 1914; June 30, 1915; H. E. Butler, "Fresh Deciduous Fruit—The Standardization Law as Affecting Marketing," in *Proceedings of the Forty-seventh California State Fruit Growers' Convention*, November 18–20, 1915 (Sacramento: State Printing Office, 1916), 184–188; F. B. McKevitt, "The New Fresh Fruit Standardization Law," ibid., 264–272; Butler, "Practical Application of the California Fresh Fruit Standardization Law with Deciduous Fruits," in "Proceedings of the Forty-ninth California State Fruit Growers' Convention," November 15–17, 1916, in California State Commission of Horticulture, *Monthly Bulletin* 6 (May 1917): 134–137; Mansel G. Blackford, *The Politics of Business in California, 1890–1920* (Columbus: Ohio State University Press, 1977), 24–26.

13. *California Fruit Grower*, October 9, 1915; George W. Pierce, "The Status of the Almond Industry of the Pacific Coast," in *Proceedings of the Thirty-fourth Biennial Meeting of the American Pomological Society*, September 1–3, 1915 (n.p.: The Society, 1916), 78–82; California Almond Growers' Exchange, *Bulletin*, no. 165 (January 10, 1918) (hereafter *CAGE Bulletin*); Thomas W. Murton, "Spain's Almond Production," *CAGE Bulletin*, no. 178 (March 1, 1919); California Almond Growers' Exchange, *Minute Book* 4 (March 1925); R. H. Taylor, "The Almond in California," University of California College of Agriculture, Agricultural Experiment Station, *Bulletin*, no. 297 (August 1918): 46, 64–65; Carl August Scholl, "An Economic Study of the California Almond Growers' Exchange" (Ph.D. diss., University of California, Berkeley, 1927), 17, 95–102, 256; Warren P. Tufts et al., "The Rich Pattern of California Crops," in *California Agriculture*, ed. Claude B. Hutchison (Berkeley: University of California Press, 1946), 172–173.

14. *Newcastle News*, July 5, 1916; Butler, "Fresh Deciduous Fruit," 185.

15. George W. Pierce Jr., Daily Journals, 1890–1930, entries for August 6, August 11, and September 6, 1916, Department of Special Collections, University of California Library, Davis (hereafter Pierce journal); Pierce, Time Book, 1913–19, entries for August and September 1916, box 4, Pierce Family Papers, Department of Special Collections, University of California Library, Davis (hereafter Pierce time book); Pierce, "The Status of the Almond Industry of the Pacific Coast," 80; *Davis Enterprise*, September 23, 1916.

16. *CAGE Bulletin*, no. 163 (November 26, 1917).

17. Quoted in *Farmers' News*, April 1917.

18. *CAGE Bulletin*, no. 168 (April 15, 1918); *California Cultivator*, May 5, 1917; *Pacific Rural Press*, April 14 and May 5, 1917; *Farmers' News*, May 1917.

19. E. M. Cheesewright to Chester H. Rowell, April 20, 1917, box 11; Rowell to W. D. Egilbert, May 18, 1917, box 3, Rowell Papers; *California Fruit News,* May 5, 1917.

20. *Farmers' News,* May 1917.

21. "War Service," in Commonwealth Club of California, *Transactions* 13 (February 1918): 1–34.

22. G. H. Hecke, "Response and Report to the Fiftieth State Fruit Growers' Convention," in "Proceedings of the Fiftieth California State Fruit Growers' Convention," November 21–23, 1917, in California State Commission of Horticulture, *Monthly Bulletin* 7 (January–February 1918): 8.

23. *San Francisco Examiner,* May 16, 1917; Harris Weinstock to Hiram Johnson, April 4, 1917, part 3, box 80, Hiram Johnson Papers, Bancroft Library.

24. *San Francisco Bulletin,* May 13, 1917; *San Jose Mercury Herald,* May 13, 1917.

25. "A Record of War Service of the University of California," typescript, April 25, 1918, 1–2, 15, box 63, Master Correspondence File, Office of the Federal Food Commissioner, CFA Records; *Report of the Activities of the California State Council of Defense from April 6, 1917 to January 1, 1918* (Sacramento: State Printing Office, 1918), 5–8, 20, 49; Thomas Forsyth Hunt, "Some Fundamental Considerations Affecting the Food Supply of the United States," University of California College of Agriculture, Agricultural Experiment Station, *Circular,* no. 163 (April 1917); George E. Mowry, *The California Progressives* (Berkeley: University of California Press, 1951), 278–279.

26. "Minutes of Meetings," State Council of Defense, Committee on Resources and Food Supply, April 10, April 12, April 13, April 18, May 7, May 22, May 26, and May 31, 1917, Bancroft Library (hereafter CRFS minutes).

27. CRFS minutes, April 12 and May 31, 1917; R. L. Adams, "The Farm Labor Situation in California," University of California College of Agriculture, Agricultural Experiment Station, *War Emergency Leaflet,* no. 13 (July 14, 1917): 1–2; Thomas Forsyth Hunt, "Observations on the Recent Agricultural Inquiry in California Made by Direction of the Committee on Resources and Food Supply of the State Council of Defense," University of California College of Agriculture, Agricultural Experiment Station, *Preliminary Circular,* May 1917, 8–10, box 23, Records of the College of Agriculture and the Agricultural Experiment Station, University of California Archives, Bancroft Library; "A Record of War Service of the University of California," 15; *Report of the Activities of the California State Council of Defense,* 20.

28. CRFS minutes, April 12 and May 31, 1917; A. H. Naftzger to Rowell, May 17, 1917, box 10, Rowell Papers.

29. CRFS minutes, April 18, May 7, May 22, May 26, and May 31, 1917; Adams, "The Farm Labor Situation in California," 3–14; Hunt, "Observations on the Recent Agricultural Inquiry in California," 10–19; *Report of the Activities of the California State Council of Defense,* 20–23; *Fresno Morning Republican,* May 12 and 22, 1917; *Newcastle News,* May 16, 1917; *San Francisco Examiner,* May 27 and 28, 1917.

30. *Farmers' News,* May 1917; *Pacific Rural Press,* May 19, 1917; *California Fruit News,* May 19, 1917.

31. California Association of Practical Farmers, "Gleanings from Practical Talks at the Farmers' Convention," June 1, 1917, flyer attached to W. D. Egilbert to Chester Rowell, June 11, 1917, box 12, Rowell Papers; *San Francisco Bulletin,* May 21, 22, and

23, 1917; *San Francisco Examiner,* May 21, 22, and 23, 1917; *San Francisco Chronicle,* May 22, 1917; *Sacramento Bee,* May 22, 1917; *California Fruit News,* June 2, 1917.

32. CRFS minutes, May 31, 1917; *San Francisco Examiner,* May 30, 1917; D. O. Lively to Ralph P. Merritt, September 25, 1917, box 37, Master Correspondence File, Office of the Federal Food Commissioner, CFA Records.

33. *Pacific Rural Press,* May 19, 1917; *California Fruit News,* June 2, 1917; *Farmers' News,* August 1917.

34. CRFS minutes, May 31, 1917.

35. *Fresno Morning Republican,* May 15, June 7, and July 4, 6, 7, 8, 11, 12, and 29, 1917; *Fresno Evening Herald,* July 6, 7, and 28, 1917; *California Fruit News,* July 21, 1917; Mark Reisler, *By the Sweat of Their Brow: Mexican Immigrant Labor in the United States, 1900–1940* (Westport, Conn.: Greenwood Press, 1976), 24–33.

36. *Fresno Morning Republican,* July 11, July 17, July 26, July 29, and August 1, 1917; *Fresno Evening Herald,* July 28, 1917; *Pacific Rural Press,* July 24, 1917; *California Fruit News,* August 4, 1917.

37. *Fresno Evening Herald,* August 7, 1917; *Fresno Morning Republican,* August 7, 1917.

38. *Fresno Morning Republican,* August 6, August 13, August 24, August 25, August 27, September 3, September 13, September 19, September 21, and October 3, 1917; *Fresno Evening Herald,* August 16, August 23, August 28, August 31, and September 25, 1917; W. Flanders Setchel to George Roeding, October 1, 1917, box 54; "Minutes of the Meeting of the Advisory Committee of the United States Food Administration of California, October 2, 1917," box 32, Master Correspondence File, Office of the Federal Food Commissioner, CFA Records; Frank Peltret to Chester Rowell, August 29, 1917, box 22; Rowell to Peltret, August 30, 1917, box 3, Rowell Papers; Adams and Kelly, "A Study of Farm Labor in California," 59–60; *Report of the Activities of the California State Council of Defense,* 22; California State Bureau of Labor Statistics, *Eighteenth Biennial Report for 1917–1918* (Sacramento: State Printing Office, 1918), 19.

39. Pierce journal, July 17 and August 12, 1917; *Fresno Morning Republican,* July 28, 1917; Commonwealth Club of California, "Minutes of Joint Meeting of Committees on Food Production and Labor Conservation," May 15, 1918, box 4, Pierce Family Papers; Adams and Kelly, "A Study of Farm Labor in California," 59.

40. Pierce journal, August 14–25, 1917; Adams, "The Farm Labor Situation in California," 4, 11.

41. Net wages earned, expenses, and total labor costs are calculated from Pierce's time book for August and September 1916; "Anokh Singh" account at the end of his daily journal for 1916; and "Hindu Time" account at the end of his journal for 1917. Only an approximation of Pierce's almond income can be gleaned from surviving documents. For CAGE members overall, gross almond income increased 20 percent from 1917 to 1918; see T. C. Tucker, Manager, "Thirteenth Annual Report on the Finances and Operations of the California Almond Growers' Exchange for the Fiscal Year 1922–1923," April 6, 1923, box 1, Pierce Family Papers. The increased price of flour is not intended to be a precise measurement of inflation, but merely a rough indicator of the reduced purchasing power of Pierce's workers.

42. *Pacific Rural Press*, May 16, June 2, August 4, November 17, and December 29, 1917; *California Fruit News*, November 17 and December 29, 1917; *Fresno Morning Republican*, October 20 and 25, 1917; *Newcastle News*, June 27 and October 10, 1917; *San Francisco Examiner*, June 2, 1917; *Oakland Tribune*, September 11, 1917; J. L. Nagle, "California Fruit Exchange," in "Proceedings of the Fiftieth California State Fruit Growers' Convention," 11–12; Japanese Agricultural Association, *The Japanese Farmers in California* (San Francisco: Japanese Agricultural Association, 1918), 12; R. L. Adams, "Twenty-five Ways to Conserve Labor," University of California College of Agriculture, Agricultural Experiment Station, *Leaflet*, September 1917; Hunt to W. J. Spillman, July 10, 1917, box 13, Records of the College of Agriculture and the Agricultural Experiment Station; W. D. Egilbert to Chester Rowell, June 21, 1917, box 12, Rowell Papers; Setchel to Roeding, October 1, 1917; Lively to Merritt, September 25, 1917.

43. Chester Rowell to Hiram Johnson, June 20, 1917, box 3; Rowell to Martin Madsen, September 17, 1917, box 3; V. S. McClatchy to Ralph Merritt, September 17, 1917, box 20; Rowell to Madsen, November 28, 1917, box 2; John Francis Neylan to William D. Stephens, December 28, 1917, box 21, all in Rowell Papers; Rowell to Johnson, September 12, 1917, part 3, box 69, Johnson Papers.

44. Higgs, *Crisis and Leviathan*, 123–158; Shideler, *Farm Crisis: 1919–1923*, 10–14.

45. Ralph P. Merritt to Rowell, July 25, 1917, box 20, Rowell Papers; Merritt to Herbert Hoover, July 25, 1917, box 31, History File, Speakers Bureau, CFA Records; Ralph Merritt, "The Work of the Food Administration in California," in "Proceedings of the Fiftieth California State Fruit Growers' Convention," 88–94.

46. Hoover to Merritt, July 7, 1917, box 63, Master Correspondence File, Office of the Federal Food Commissioner, CFA Records; *Commercial Bulletin* (Los Angeles), September 7, 1917; Krehbiel, "Report of the United States Food Administration for California," chap. 9, pp. 8–9; Ralph Palmer Merritt, "After Me Cometh a Builder: The Recollections of Ralph Palmer Merritt" (Regional Oral History Office, Bancroft Library, 1962), 22–38.

47. "Mediators' Conference with Growers, San Jose, California, July 30, 1917," transcript, box 52; "Meeting of Cannery Workers at Liberty Hall, August 1, 1917," transcript, box 52; Hoover to Merritt, July 25, 1917, box 27; C. H. Bentley to Merritt, July 25, 1917, box 4; Merritt to Hoover, July 27, 1917, box 27; Merritt and Harris Weinstock to William D. Stephens, July 27, 1917, box 46; The J. H. Flickinger Company et al. to Weinstock and Merritt, July 30, 1917, box 56; Stephens to Weinstock and Merritt, July 31, 1917, box 46; Merritt and Weinstock to Stephens, August 1, 1917, box 46; Merritt to Hoover, August 6, 1917, box 27, all in Master Correspondence File, Office of the Federal Food Commissioner, CFA Records; Hoover to Merritt, July 30, 1917, box 1, Herbert Hoover Correspondence File, Office of the Federal Food Commissioner, CFA Records; Krehbiel, "Report of the United States Food Administration for California," chap. 1, pp. 3–4; *Proceedings of the Eighteenth Annual Convention of the California State Federation of Labor*, 1917, 57–58; Elizabeth Reis, "Cannery Row: The AFL, the IWW, and Bay Area Italian Cannery Workers," *California History* 64 (Summer 1985): 175–191; Jaclyn Greenberg, "Organizing the Great Cannery Strike of 1917," *Harvest Quarterly*, nos. 3–4 (September–December 1976): 5–11.

48. Lively to Merritt, September 25, 1917, box 37, Master Correspondence File, Office of the Federal Food Commissioner, CFA Records; *California Fruit News*, August 25 and September 22, 1917.

49. Krehbiel, "Report of the United States Food Administration for California," chap. 5; "Eat More Fruits," reprint of a U.S. Food Administration poster, purchased from the National Archives, Washington, D.C., in my possession; *California Fruit News*, August 25, 1917; Merritt, "The Work of the Food Administration in California," 88–90; "Summary of the Annual Reports of the Farm Advisors in California for December 1, 1916–December 1, 1917," box 32; V. S. McClatchy to Merritt, September 12, 1917, box 38; Lively to Merritt, September 18, 1917, box 37; Edward A. Dickson to Merritt, September 22, 1917, box 36, all in Master Correspondence File, Office of the Federal Food Commissioner, CFA Records; Merritt to Hoover, December 28, 1917, box 7, History File, Speakers Bureau, CFA Records; Merritt to all County Food Administrators, January 24, 1918, box 1, Correspondence with County Food Administrators File, Office of the Federal Food Commissioner, CFA Records.

50. "Minutes of the Meeting of the Agricultural Production Board, October 5, 1917," box 1, Miscellaneous Records File, Office of the Federal Food Commissioner, CFA Records; Merritt, "The Work of the Food Administration in California," 91; *San Francisco Examiner*, October 6, 1917; *Sacramento Bee*, October 6, 1917; *Los Angeles Times*, October 6, 1917.

51. Merritt to S. Parker Frisselle, April 12, 1917, carton 2, Kearney Ranch Records; Frisselle to Merritt, September 3 and November 1, 1917, box 45; Harris Weinstock to Merritt, September 28, 1917, box 56, Master Correspondence File, Office of the Federal Food Commissioner, CFA Records; Merritt, "After Me Cometh a Builder," 25–26; *California Fruit News*, October 13, 1917; Schyler Rehart and William K. Patterson, *M. Theo Kearney—Prince of Fresno: A Biography of Martin Theodore Kearney* (Fresno: Fresno City and County Historical Society, 1988), 44–45.

52. Merritt to Rowell, July 25, 1917, box 20, Rowell Papers; George F. Porter to A. H. Naftzger, August 22, 1917, box 31; "Minutes of the Meeting of the Advisory Committee of the United States Food Administration of California, October 2, 1917," box 32, Master Correspondence File, Office of the Federal Food Commissioner, CFA Records; Thomas Hunt to Edward Krehbiel, February 7, 1919, box 2, History File, Speakers Bureau, CFA Records; Krehbiel, "Report of the United States Food Administration for California," chap. 1.

53. Thomas F. Hunt, "Report of the Committee on Farm Labor of the Agricultural Production Board," [December 1917], box 11, Press Clippings File, Educational Division, CFA Records.

54. D. O. Lively, "Agricultural Labor Problems during the Past Season," in "Proceedings of the Fiftieth California State Fruit Growers' Convention," 70–73; M. F. Tarpey, "Some Possibilities of the Development of New Labor during the War," ibid., 74–79; A. L. Wisker, "How the Army Draft Affects the Farm Labor Situation," ibid., 79–81; "Discussion," ibid., 81–88; "Resolutions Passed at the Fiftieth Fruit Growers' Convention," ibid., 100–103; "Discussion following the Reading of the Labor Resolution," ibid., 103–109; *Los Angeles Times*, November 24, 1917.

55. *Pacific Rural Press*, May 19, 1917; Lively, "Agricultural Labor Problems during the Past Season," 70; "Discussion," 82, 87.

56. *Fresno Morning Republican,* November 24, 1917; *California Fruit News,* December 1, 1917; *Pacific Rural Press,* December 1 and 8, 1917; *California Cultivator,* December 1 and 8, 1917.

57. *Fresno Morning Republican,* November 24, 1917; *Sacramento Bee,* November 22, 1917; *San Francisco Chronicle,* December 20, 1917; *California Fruit News,* December 22, 1917.

58. *California Fruit News,* December 22, 1917; *California Cultivator,* December 22, 1917; *Davis Enterprise,* December 15, 1917; Merritt, "The Work of the Food Administration in California," 93–94; Pierce journal, December 6, 1917; "Resolution Passed by the Committee on Labor, December 17, 1917," box 4, Pierce Family Papers; Franklin P. Nutting to E. J. Herter & Co., August 21, 1918, carton 3, Franklin P. Nutting Papers, Bancroft Library.

59. "Resolution Passed by the Committee on Labor, December 17, 1917"; "Minutes of the Meeting of the Executive Committee of the State Council of Defense, San Francisco, December 18, 1917," box 31, Master Correspondence File, Office of the Federal Food Commissioner, CFA Records; Pierce journal, December 17, 1917; *Davis Enterprise,* January 5, 1918; *California Fruit News,* November 23, 1918.

60. "Minutes of the Meeting of the Executive Committee of the State Council of Defense, Held in San Francisco on January 8, 1918," box 31; "Minutes of the Meeting of the Executive Committee of the State Council of Defense, Held in San Francisco, January 24, 1918," box 31; "Memo Re Request for Information Concerning Mexican Situation Sent to Washington," January 25, 1918, box 36, Master Correspondence File, Office of the Federal Food Commissioner, CFA Records; R. L. Adams, "Emergency Farm Labor Agencies," University of California College of Agriculture, Agricultural Experiment Station, *Leaflet,* no. 4 (July 1918): 10; Pierce journal, December 21, 28, and 29, 1917; *San Francisco Chronicle,* January 9, 1918; *San Francisco Call,* February 26, 1918; *California Cultivator,* January 26, 1918; *Pacific Rural Press,* January 12 and March 9, 1918; *California Fruit News,* January 12, March 2, March 30, and November 23, 1918.

61. *California Fruit News,* November 23, 1918.

62. Dean Thomas F. Hunt, "Suggested Plan for Handling the Farm Labor Situation in California during 1918," January 26, 1918, box 28; "Report of a Meeting Held by Dean Thomas F. Hunt, in the Conference Room of the United States Food Administration, March 20, 1918," box 46; Frederick H. Ringe to B. T. Bean, January 2, 1918, box 61; Hunt to Merritt, February 4 and 8, 1918, box 46; Hunt to A. H. Naftzger, April 12, 1918, box 38, Master Correspondence File, Office of the Federal Food Commissioner, CFA Records; Merritt to Hoover, March 1, 1918, box 7; Charlotte P. Ebbets, "Women's Land Army of California—Northern Division," 1918, typescript, box 3; "Wanted by Uncle Sam!" poster, box 3; "Farmers—Do You Need Hands?" (San Francisco: Women's Land Army of America, 1918), box 3, History File, Speakers Bureau, CFA Records; State Council of Defense of California, *California in the War: Addresses Delivered at the State War Council,* March 5–6, 1918 (Sacramento: State Printing Office, 1918); *San Francisco Call,* January 26, 1918; *San Francisco Examiner,* February 26 and May 19, 1918; *San Francisco Bulletin,* January 25, 1918; *Fresno Morning Republican,* January 26, 1918; *Stockton Evening Record,* February 18, 1918; *California Cultivator,* April 13 and June 22, 1918; *California Fruit News,* June 15,

1918; E. V. Wilcox, "Plan of the Department of Agriculture for Handling the Farm Labor Problem," *American Economic Review* 8 (March 1918): 170; Krehbiel, "Report of the United States Food Administration for California," chap. 6; George S. Waterman, "An Appeal to the Growers," *Sun-Maid Herald* 3 (July 1918): 3; R. L. Adams, "Farm Labor Situation in California," in Commonwealth Club of California, *Transactions* 13 (May 1918): 74–83; Adams and Kelly, "A Study of Farm Labor in California," 56–70.

63. *California Fruit News,* March 23, March 30, April 20, and April 27, 1918; *Los Angeles Examiner,* January 18, 1918; *San Francisco Call,* January 24, 1918; *San Francisco News,* January 24, 1918; *Fresno Morning Republican,* February 15, 1918; *San Francisco Examiner,* February 5 and May 19, 1918; *Oakland Tribune,* March 17, 1918.

64. "Agreement among Prune Producers," May 29, 1918, box 7; Frisselle to Merritt, January 26, February 7, and April 5, 1918, box 45; C. H. Bentley to Merritt, February 26, 1918, box 54; J. F. Niswander to Merritt, March 13 and April 22, 1918, box 54; H. G. Coykendall to Merritt, April 23, June 4, and June 5, 1918, box 7; Charles Bonner to U.S. Food Administration, April 20, 1918, box 7; Wylie M. Giffen to Merritt, May 21, 1918, box 7; Merritt to Mr. Sims, May 31, 1918, box 7; Frank Buck et al. to Merritt, June 7, 1918, box 7; H. C. Dunlap to Merritt, June 14, 1918, box 7; Merritt to Dunlap, June 17, 1918, box 7; F. H. Wilson to Merritt, June 17 and 28, 1918, box 7; Merritt to W. S. Clayton, June 18, 1918, box 7, all in Master Correspondence File, Office of the Federal Food Commissioner, CFA Records; Herbert Hoover, *Special License Regulations for Distributors of Fresh Fruits and Vegetables* (Washington, D.C.: Government Printing Office, 1918), box 15, Press Clippings File, Educational Division, CFA Records; Frisselle to Edward Krehbiel, January 27, 1919, History File, Speakers Bureau, CFA Records; *Fresno Morning Republican,* February 26 and June 1, 1918; *California Fruit News,* June 1 and July 6, 1918; *San Francisco Chronicle,* June 13, 1918; Krehbiel, "Report of the United States Food Administration for California," chap. 1, pp. 17–18.

65. George W. Pierce, "Farm Labor from an Orchardist's Point of View," in Commonwealth Club of California, *Transactions* 13 (May 1918): 84–97, 118–120; *San Francisco Chronicle,* April 11, 1918.

66. Pierce journal, September 3 and December 31, 1917; February 26, February 27, February 28, March 1, March 5, April 13, April 15, April 22, May 31, June 24, June 27, June 29, and July 28–August 14, 1918; "Hindu Almond Workers' Time" account at the end of the journal for 1918.

67. Frisselle to Merritt, September 15, October 1, and October 4, 1918, box 45; Wylie M. Giffen to Frisselle, August 30, 1918, box 28, Master Correspondence File, Office of the Federal Food Commissioner, CFA Records; "Summary of the Annual Reports of the Farm Advisors of California," University of California College of Agriculture, Agricultural Experiment Station, *Circular,* no. 208 (February 1919): 12; *Fresno Morning Republican,* March 20, April 10, May 17, June 30, July 21, July 25, August 25, September 19, October 4, and October 6, 1918; *Fresno Evening Herald,* May 8, July 17, September 10, and October 3, 1918.

68. *Marysville Daily Appeal,* March 13 and June 26, 1918; *Sutter County Farmer,* March 15 and April 26, 1918; *San Francisco Examiner,* April 24 and May 7, 1918; *California Fruit News,* April 27, 1918; *Sacramento Bee,* May 5 and 7, 1918; *Fresno Morning*

Republican, May 28 and June 21, 1918; *California Cultivator*, May 4 and June 22, 1918; *Sun-Maid Herald*, May, June, and July 1918; Adams, "Emergency Farm Labor Agencies," 8–9.

69. W. T. Boyce to A. H. Naftzger, April 17, 1918, box 38, Master Correspondence File, Office of the Federal Food Commissioner, CFA Records; *San Francisco Examiner*, May 5 and May 10, 1918; *Sacramento Bee*, May 11 and July 6, 1918; *San Francisco Call*, July 25, 1918; *California Cultivator*, August 10, 1918; *Sun-Maid Herald*, July 1918; Adams, "Emergency Farm Labor Agencies," 1–8.

70. Commonwealth Club of California, "Minutes of Joint Meeting of Committees on Food Production and Labor Conservation." See also Pierce's scribbled notes of the meeting on the back of a "Sutter Growers' Association Questionnaire," box 4, Pierce Family Papers.

71. *Fresno Morning Republican*, May 28, May 30, June 21, June 22, and June 27, 1918; Clarke A. Chambers, *California Farm Organizations: A Historical Study of the Grange, the Farm Bureau, and the Associated Farmers, 1929–1941* (Berkeley: University of California Press, 1952), 21–23.

72. R. L. Adams, "The Farm Labor Problem," *University of California Chronicle* 22 (April 1920): 201.

73. Adams and Kelly, "A Study of Farm Labor in California," 9–16; Adams, "Farm Labor Situation in California," 74–83.

74. Alden Anderson to Merritt, June 10, 1918, box 28; R. L. Adams to J. P. Dargitz, June 1, 1918, box 28, Master Correspondence File, Office of the Federal Food Commissioner, CFA Records; *California Cultivator*, May 4 and May 11, 1918; *Davis Enterprise*, May 4, 1918; *Sacramento Bee*, May 7, 1918; *San Francisco Examiner*, May 12, 1918; *Marysville Appeal*, June 26 and June 27, 1918.

75. W. B. Wilson, "Admissions of Agricultural Laborers, U. S. Department of Labor," June 12, 1918, carton 40, CDIR Records; George J. McCarty to the Provost Marshal General, War Department, July 2, 1918, box 27; E. H. Crowder to U.S. Food Administration, July 8, 1918, box 27, Master Correspondence File, Office of the Federal Food Commissioner, CFA Records; Adams, "Emergency Farm Labor Agencies," 12; *San Francisco Examiner*, June 14, June 19, and July 3, 1918; *Marysville Daily Appeal*, June 26 and 27, 1918; *Sacramento Bee*, June 27, 1918; *Fresno Morning Republican*, June 28 and July 1, 1918; *Los Angeles Times*, June 28 and 30, 1918; *Sun-Maid Herald*, August 1918; *California Fruit News*, August 31, 1918.

76. "Minutes of the Meeting of the Executive Committee of the State Council of Defense of California, October 23, 1918," box 31, Master Correspondence File, Office of the Federal Food Commissioner, CFA Records.

77. California State Commission of Horticulture, "Weekly News Letter," September 28, 1918, Records of the Department of Agriculture, Commission of Horticulture files, Confidential Newsletter, 1917–30, California State Archives, Office of the Secretary of State, Sacramento; G. H. Hecke to Ralph P. Merritt, September 30, 1918, box 7, Master Correspondence File, Office of the Federal Food Commissioner, CFA Records; *San Francisco Examiner*, September 13 and October 17, 1918; *California Fruit News*, November 16, 1918; Adams, "The Farm Labor Problem," 203–204.

78. "Minutes of the Meeting of the Committee on Resources and Food Supplies, State Council of Defense, September 25, 1918," box 31; "Proposed Order of

Business, Committee on Resources and Food Supplies, October 15, 1918," box 31; "Minutes of the Committee on Resources and Food Supply, State Council of De: fense, October 15, 1918," box 31; "Minutes of the Meeting of the Committee on Resources and Food Supply, State Council of Defense, October 29, 1918," box 31; "Minutes of the Meeting of the Executive Committee of the State Council of Defense of California, October 23, 1918," box 31; "Minutes of the Meeting of the Executive Committee of the State Council of Defense of California, November 6, 1918," box 31; "Farm Labor Conference Assured," press release, November 4, 1918, box 31; R. L. Adams to U.S. Food Administration for California, October 22, 1918, box 31, all in Master Correspondence File, Office of the Federal Food Commissioner, CFA Records; *California Cultivator,* October 26, 1918.

79. *San Francisco Chronicle,* November 9 and 10, 1918; *San Francisco Examiner,* November 9 and 10, 1918; *San Francisco Bulletin,* November 9, 1918; *Fresno Morning Republican,* November 9, 1918; *California Fruit News,* November 16, 1918.

80. Frank T. Swett, J. P. Dargitz, and R. L. Adams, "Call to Second Farm Labor Conference!" December 7, 1918, box 31, Master Correspondence File, Office of the Federal Food Commissioner, CFA Records.

81. *California Fruit News,* November 22, 1919; George W. Pierce, "Accomplishments and Possibilities of Co-operation," in "Proceedings of the Fifty-second Convention of Fruit Growers and Farmers," November 10–15, 1919, in California State Department of Agriculture, *Monthly Bulletin* 8 (December 1919): 631–635; C. C. Teague, "Work of the Agricultural Legislative Committee," in "Proceedings of the Fifty-third Convention of Fruit Growers and Farmers," November 9–12, 1920, in California State Department of Agriculture, *Monthly Bulletin* 9 (December 1920): 693–696.

82. Frisselle to Edward Krehbiel, January 27, 1919, box 2; Milo L. Rowell to Krehbiel, box 2, History File, Speakers Bureau, CFA Records; Chambers, *California Farm Organizations,* 54–59, passim; Gerald D. Nash, *State Government and Economic Development: A History of Administrative Policies in California, 1849–1933* (Berkeley: Institute of Government Studies, 1964), 240–241; Devra Weber, *Dark Sweat, White Gold: California Farm Workers, Cotton, and the New Deal* (Berkeley: University of California Press, 1994), 30.

83. *Sun-Maid Herald,* October 1918; *California Cultivator,* June 28, 1919; *Fresno Morning Republican,* August 11, 1919; *San Francisco Examiner,* September 30, 1918; *San Jose Mercury Herald,* April 25, 1919; *Mexicans in California: Report of Governor C. C. Young's Mexican Fact-Finding Committee* (Sacramento: State Printing Office, 1930), 18, 25; Reisler, *By the Sweat of Their Brow,* 27–33, 78, 82.

84. Pierce journal, March 26 and July 30–September 29, 1919; *Davis Enterprise,* July 6, 1918; September 26, 1919; Pierce time book, August 1919.

85. Pierce journal, August 28, 1919; July 14 and August 13, 1921; *Davis Enterprise,* September 26, 1919.

86. Pierce journal, March 5, 1921; August 21 and 22, 1928, for example.

87. *Fresno Morning Republican,* July 7, 1921; February 14, 1923; January 24, 1926; *Associated Grower,* March 1921; *Pacific Rural Press,* February 11, 1922; April 18, 1925; Weber, *Dark Sweat, White Gold,* 17–21.

88. S. Parker Frisselle, "The Agricultural Labor Situation," in "Proceedings of

the Sixtieth Convention of California Fruit Growers and Farmers," November 16–17, 1927, in California State Department of Agriculture, *Monthly Bulletin* 17 (February 1928): 75; U.S. Senate, Subcommittee of the Committee on Education and Labor, *Report, Violations of Free Speech and Rights of Labor,* Report No. 1150, 77th Cong., 2d sess. (Washington, D.C., 1942), pt. 4: 498–500; Weber, *Dark Sweat, White Gold,* 37–42.

89. George W. Pierce, "Address" and "Some of Our Legislative Needs," in "Proceedings of the Fifty-third Convention of Fruit Growers and Farmers," 606, 706; Chambers, *California Farm Organizations,* 54, 66, 112, 199.

Conclusion

1. Andrew Alvarado, Herbert O. Mason, and Gary Riley, *The Labor Market in the Central California Raisin Industry: Five Years after IRCA* (Sacramento: Labor Market Information Division, Employment Development Department, 1992); Ann Foley Scheuring, ed., *A Guidebook to California Agriculture* (Berkeley: University of California Press, 1983), 148–149; Hanna Rosin, "Raisin Hell," *New Republic* 211 (November 14, 1994): 15–16.

2. Harry Butler, "A History of the War Exemption Board of Placer County," typescript, May 14, 1919, box 1, Placer County War Committee Records, Bancroft Library, University of California, Berkeley; W. B. Lardner and M. J. Brock, *History of Placer and Nevada Counties* (Los Angeles: Historic Record Co., 1924), 299–305.

3. "Interview with Mr. Yoneda, a Secretary of the Japanese Association of America," December 2, 1924, appendix F in Robert Sinclair Murray, "The Japanese Association in America," typescript, 1924, box 32, Survey of Race Relations Collection, Hoover Institution Archives, Stanford University, Stanford, Calif.; *San Francisco Examiner,* January 29, 1918; *Newcastle News,* January 22, 1919; Toyoji Chiba, "Japanese Farmers' Contribution to California," *Japan Review* 4 (May and July 1920): 212–213, 263–266; Japanese Agricultural Association, *The Japanese Farmers in California* (San Francisco: Japanese Agricultural Association, 1918), passim.

4. Testimony of Ivan H. Parker, in U.S. House of Representatives, Committee on Immigration and Naturalization, *Japanese Immigration Hearings,* 66th Cong., 2d sess. (Washington, D.C.: Government Printing Office, 1921), 322; *Newcastle News,* March 24, 1920; *Sacramento Bee,* March 27, 1958; Leonard M. Davis, *Newcastle, Gem of the Foothills: A Pictorial History of Newcastle, Placer County, California from Its Formative Days to the Present* (Newcastle: Newcastle Community Association, 1993), 41–43, 51–57.

5. Scheuring, *A Guidebook to California Agriculture,* 144–146; Walter Ebeling, *The Fruited Plain: The Story of American Agriculture* (Berkeley: University of California Press, 1979), 369.

6. Testimony of Dr. R. L. Adams, U.S. Senate, Subcommittee of the Committee on Education and Labor, *Hearings on S. Res. 266, Violations of Free Speech and Rights of Labor,* 74th Cong., 2d sess. (Washington, D.C.: Government Printing Office, 1939), pt. 51: 18711; U.S. Senate, Subcommittee of the Committee on Education and Labor, *Report, Violations of Free Speech and Rights of Labor,* Report No. 1150, 77th Cong., 2d sess. (Washington, D.C.: Government Printing Office, 1942), pt. 4: 407–522, 648–664; Levi Varden Fuller, "The Supply of Agricultural Labor as a Fac-

tor in the Evolution of Farm Organization in California" (Ph.D. diss., University of California, Berkeley, 1939), 246–248; Clarke A. Chambers, *California Farm Organizations: A Historical Study of the Grange, the Farm Bureau, and the Associated Farmers, 1929–1941* (Berkeley: University of California Press, 1952), 60–64; Lawrence James Jelinek, "The California Farm Bureau Federation, 1919–1964" (Ph.D. diss., University of California, Los Angeles, 1976), 50–51; Jelinek, *Harvest Empire: A History of California Agriculture,* 2d ed. (San Francisco: Boyd & Fraser, 1982), 71–72.

7. Jelinek, "The California Farm Bureau Federation," viii.

8. Victor Davis Hanson, *Fields without Dreams: Defending the Agrarian Idea* (New York: Free Press Paperbacks, 1996), x, xvii, 25, 46, 76, 102, passim.

9. *San Francisco Examiner,* February 26, 1917; *Pacific Rural Press,* March 3, May 19, and December 29, 1917; *Sacramento Bee,* November 27, 1917; February 9, 1918; *San Francisco Chronicle,* April 1, 1918; *California Cultivator,* June 22, 1918; James Jerome Parsons Jr., "The California Hop Industry: Its Eighty Years of Development and Expansion" (M.A. thesis, University of California, Berkeley, 1939), 82.

10. E. Clemons Horst to Thomas Hunt, June 14, 1917, box 46; Hunt to R. A. Pearson, February 4, 1918, box 46; Horst to State Council of Defense, October 13, 1918, box 46; and Horst's numerous letters to Herbert Hoover, box 35, all in Master Correspondence File, Office of the Federal Food Commissioner, Records of the U.S. Food Administration, California Food Administration (RG 4), National Archives, Pacific Sierra Region, San Bruno, Calif.; *San Francisco Chronicle,* November 22, 1917.

11. *San Francisco Examiner,* August 9, 1921; July 29, 1923; *Yuba-Sutter Appeal-Democrat,* August 2, 1988; Parsons, "The California Hop Industry," 82; Richard Steven Street, "Wheatland," *Sacramento Magazine* 10 (December 1984): 39–40. Details on Durst's estate are in box 4, Durst Bros. Hop Ranch Papers, Department of Special Collections, Meriam Library, California State University, Chico.

12. Carey McWilliams, "Farm Labor Background in California," *Epic News* 3 (July 20, 1936): 4, 11.

Essay on Sources

My objective here is to share with prospective researchers the benefits of my experience. I aim to be informative and suggestive but not comprehensive. A rich body of secondary literature provided factual information and interpretive insights, but the principal sources for this study are primary ones. Growers, farmworkers, state officials, and other historical actors have left behind an abundance of materials that are available in several California archives and libraries. For additional source information, readers should consult the chapter notes. Unless otherwise indicated, all newspapers and periodicals cited are available (usually on microfilm) at either the California State Library in Sacramento or the Doe Library at the University of California, Berkeley.

I began my archival research by reading through the files of California's agricultural periodicals. The *Pacific Rural Press* and the *California Fruit Grower* (*News* after 1915) provide a wealth of information. Every week, growers could find advice on how to plant, prune, water, and harvest their crops, how to control insects and other pests, and how to develop profitable marketing strategies—though only on rare occasions were labor problems discussed. The *Pacific Rural Press*'s "Agricultural Notes" page offers valuable leads to local newspapers from the various specialty crop subregions. Edward J. Wickson's weekly editorials should be supplemented by his *The California Fruits and How to Grow Them* (San Francisco: Pacific Rural Press, nine editions from 1889 to 1921). Equally rewarding are the annual *Proceedings* (sometimes *Transactions* or *Official Report*) of the California state fruit growers' convention, which are conveniently bound together in the Government Publications Room of the California State Library. More obscure (for this study) but still worth consulting are *California, A Journal of Rural Industry; Orchard and*

Farm; the *California Cultivator;* and the *Monthly Bulletin* of the California State Commission of Horticulture. And countless references to contemporary newspapers, periodicals, and other sources can be found in
the Federal Writers' Project on Migratory Labor, the H. E. Erdman Papers, and the Harris Weinstock Scrapbooks—all in the Bancroft Library
at the University of California, Berkeley—and in the California Information File, California Room, California State Library.

Of my four case studies, Fresno has received the most scholarly attention. But most of the books and articles cited in the chapter notes
provide limited insight into the complexities of raisin culture. Fresno's
four daily newspapers—the *Evening Expositor,* the *Morning Republican,*
the *Evening Herald,* and the *Bee*—offer valuable, though scattered, information. Fortunately, there are several clippings collections available:
Fresno County Scrapbook, 1870–1899, compiled by William B. Secrest Jr.
(Fresno: C. W. Clough, 1987), Department of Special Collections,
Henry Madden Library, California State University, Fresno; the Martin
Theodore Kearney Correspondence and Papers, the Franklin P. Nutting
Scrapbooks (in the Nutting Papers), and Ernestine Winchell, "Fresno
Memories," all in the Bancroft Library; and the M. Theo Kearney Pa-
pers, the Sam Naman Scrapbooks Collection, and the Ben Walker His-
tory Files, all at the Fresno City and County Historical Society, Fresno.
The ample correspondence and editorials on raisin affairs by *Fresno
Morning Republican* editor Chester Rowell are contained in his papers at
the Bancroft Library. The rarely examined packers' perspective on both
marketing and labor issues is provided by additional materials in the
Nutting Papers; "An Interview with Franklin P. Nutting" (Regional Oral
History Office, Bancroft Library, 1955); and especially E. Leroy Chaddock, "Fifty Years as a Raisin Packer," typescript, 1943, Department of
Special Collections, Henry Madden Library. Among a number of published contemporary works depicting the labor process, the most revealing is Gustav Eisen, *The Raisin Industry: A Practical Treatise on the
Raisin Grapes, Their History, Culture, and Curing* (San Francisco: H. S.
Crocker, 1890). In addition, several promotional pamphlets cited in the
notes are surprisingly useful. They tend to be overly enthusiastic, to be
sure, but they also contain rich descriptive information often unavailable
elsewhere.

In contrast, Newcastle, despite its early prominence, may be the least
studied subregion of all. Here, too, several promotional pamphlets depict
the development of the fruit belt. The weekly *Newcastle News* catered

first and foremost to fruit growers in that community. The *Placer County Republican* and the *Placer Herald*, weeklies published in nearby Auburn, are well worth reading through as well. The H. E. Erdman Papers contain bylaws and other information from many of the region's local marketing associations. Essays and correspondence in the Harry Butler Biographical Letter File in the California Room, California State Library, reveal this key figure's views on the failed Citrus Colony, Penryn's malaria problem, and other developments. Indispensable to reconstructing the region's labor relations were hundreds of lease records in the Placer County Recorder's Office, Auburn; and T. G. Chamberlain's 77 questionnaires and his report, "Fruit Ranching Conditions in the Placer County Fruit Belt," Elwood Mead Papers, Bancroft Library. Numerous other surveys conducted by Mead's students in 1915 and 1916 for the California Commission on Land Colonization and Rural Credits, as well as the unpublished transcripts of the commission's hearings—also in the Mead Papers—are waiting to be exploited further.

My research of Davis(ville) almond growers, and indeed of horticulture in general, began with the Pierce Family Papers and the George W. Pierce Jr. Daily Journals, both housed at the Department of Special Collections, University of California Library, Davis. The journals and remaining wheat ranch records of George Pierce Sr. await future researchers. The weekly *Davisville Enterprise* (at the UC Davis Library) and, to a lesser extent, the *Yolo Weekly Mail* and the *Woodland Democrat* provide useful supplementary information on the community, other almond growers, and their marketing efforts. The Constitution and Minute Book of the Davisville Almond Growers' Association, complete runs of the California Almond Growers' Exchange *Bulletin* and *Minutebook*, managers' reports, and a vast assortment of other materials are located in the California Almond Growers' Exchange Records at the Sacramento Archives and Museum Collection Center. I also benefited considerably from several contemporary articles, including Caroline M. Olney, "Orchards, Vineyards, and Farms of Yolo County," *Overland Monthly* 40 (May 1902): 171–194; R. H. Taylor, "The Almond in California," University of California College of Agriculture, Agricultural Experiment Station, *Bulletin*, no. 297 (August 1918); and Taylor, "Marketing California Almonds," *University of California Journal of Agriculture* 4 (October 1916): 44–45.

Despite the paramount importance scholars have placed on the 1913 Wheatland hop fields riot, they have all but neglected the history of

Bear River hop culture. My understanding stems primarily from the brief and broken runs of the *Wheatland Weekly Graphic* and the *Four Corners,* the "Wheatland Pick-Ups" and "Wheatland Doings" columns in the *Marysville Daily Appeal* (indexed), and the *Sacramento Record-Union,* as well as from the many contemporary articles cited in the notes. To my knowledge, the only secondary source that even mentions the hop-picking machine, let alone its significance to the Wheatland riot, is James Jerome Parsons Jr., "The California Hop Industry: Its Eighty Years of Development and Expansion" (M.A. thesis, University of California, Berkeley, 1939). This is surprising, because there is extensive coverage of the machine in the *Pacific Rural Press* and brief histories in E. Clemons Horst Co., *Scenes from E. Clemons Horst Company's Hop Ranches . . .* (Sacramento: E. Clemons Horst Co., ca. 1920), and George E. Miller, *The Evolution of a Mechanical Hop Picker* (Sacramento: Central Printing Co., 1962), both in the California Room, California State Library. Also key to my interpretation of the uprising on the Durst ranch are several eyewitness accounts in the rarely cited transcript of the trial of Ford and Suhr, Austin Lewis Papers, Bancroft Library; Yuba County Board of Supervisors, "Report of Commission Investigating Conditions in Hop Fields on and Just Prior to August 3, 1913," July 22, 1914, Government Publications Room, California State Library; accounts in the *San Francisco Bulletin* and the *Marysville Daily Appeal,* found in "Scrapbook of Clippings on the Wheatland Hop Field Riots, Wheatland, California, 1913–1915," Bancroft Library; and several documents in the Durst Bros. Hop Ranch Papers, Department of Special Collections, Meriam Library, California State University, Chico, which otherwise are concerned primarily with the estates of D. P. Durst and his three sons.

An abundance of materials document the inner workings of the California Commission of Immigration and Housing. The most often cited sources are the Simon J. Lubin Correspondence, Bancroft Library; the U.S. Commission on Industrial Relations, 1912–15, Unpublished Records of the Division of Research and Investigations, microfilm (Frederick, Md.: University Publications of America, 1985); and the published annual reports of the commission. Two other archival collections shed additional light: Records of the California Department of Industrial Relations, Division of Immigration and Housing, Bancroft Library (unprocessed), which contain abundant correspondence and inspection files; and Records of the Department of Industrial Relations, Commission of Immigration and Housing files (especially the "Minutes of

Meetings," "Executive Officer's Reports," and "Miscellaneous Correspondence"), California State Archives, Office of the Secretary of State, Sacramento. These should be supplemented by numerous articles published by commission members in the *California Outlook,* the organ of the state's Progressive Party. My understanding of the key role played by the University of California College of Agriculture in grower-state relations stems primarily from correspondence and reports in the Hiram Johnson Papers, the Chester Rowell Papers, and the Records of the College of Agriculture and the Agricultural Experiment Station, University of California Archives—all in the Bancroft Library—as well as from the published articles of Thomas Forsyth Hunt and B. H. Crocheron. For the growers' perspective, the *Farmers' News,* the Farmers' Protective League organ known more for its brief opposition to the IWW, proved very useful.

My interpretation of World War I as a watershed in labor relations is based primarily on the previously unexamined Records of the U.S. Food Administration, California Food Administration (RG 4), National Archives, Pacific Sierra Region, San Bruno, Calif. This rich collection contains extensive correspondence, typescript minutes of numerous committee meetings and farm labor conferences, private memoranda, agreements with grower cooperatives, a massive clippings file, and a useful in-house history. Researchers should be aware that the box numbers cited here refer to the original cataloguing and are subject to change as the collection is processed. Also of considerable value are the "Minutes of Meetings," State Council of Defense, Committee on Resources and Food Supply, 1917, Bancroft Library; Records of the Department of Agriculture, Commission of Horticulture files, California State Archives, Office of the Secretary of State; and Ralph Palmer Merritt's oral history, "After Me Cometh a Builder" (Regional Oral History Office, Bancroft Library, 1962). On the Valley Fruit Growers Association, see W. Flanders Setchel's monthly column in the *Sun-Maid Herald* and the many clippings in the Nutting Scrapbooks.

I benefited from several other government documents, oral histories, and surveys as well. Federal investigators for the Dillingham Commission studied labor conditions in 12 California specialty crop districts between 1907 and 1909, including Fresno, Newcastle, and Wheatland. Their findings—published in U.S. Senate, Reports of the Immigration Commission, "Immigrants in Industries," pt. 25, *Japanese and Other Immigrant Races in the Pacific Coast and Rocky Mountain States,* vol. 24, 61st

Cong., 2d sess. (Washington, D.C.: Government Printing Office, 1911)
—document in detail, if only for a two-year period, how growers pursued a variety of strategies to meet the seasonal requirements of their labor-intensive crops. Relevant crop statistics are conveniently collected in George Robertson, "Statistical Summary of the Production and Resources of California" (1850–1910), in California State Board of Agriculture, *Fifty-eighth Annual Report for 1911* (Sacramento: State Printing Office, 1912); in U.S. Department of Agriculture, Bureau of Agricultural Economics, *Fruits (Noncitrus): Production, Farm Disposition, Value, and Utilization of Sales, 1889–1944*, Commodity Statistics, no. 27 (Washington, D.C.: Government Printing Office, 1948); in the published annual reports of the California Development Board; and in the "annual review" issues of the *California Fruit Grower*. Growers' attitudes on a variety of subjects, including Asian tenant farmers and laborers, are revealed in Eliot Mears, "102 Interviews with Employers of Farm Workers," 1924, box 35, Survey of Race Relations Collection, Hoover Institution Archives, Stanford University. Pear grower Frank T. Swett was not from any of my case studies, but his oral history, "California Agricultural Cooperatives" (Regional Oral History Office, Bancroft Library, 1968), proved valuable nonetheless.

Regarding the secondary literature, the vast majority of our understanding of California agricultural history comes from farm labor studies. Even the more recent works follow the "factories in the field" paradigm established by Carey McWilliams more than half a century ago. Cletus E. Daniel, *Bitter Harvest: A History of California Farmworkers, 1870–1941* (Ithaca: Cornell University Press, 1981), argues that the "erosion of agrarian ideals" and the simultaneous evolution of "industrialized agriculture" in the late nineteenth century provided the foundation for class conflict in the twentieth century. Linda C. and Theo J. Majka's theoretically oriented analysis of farmworker unionism, *Farm Workers, Agribusiness, and the State* (Philadelphia: Temple University Press, 1982), asserts as an article of faith that "large-scale production has dominated California agriculture virtually since statehood." In *This Bittersweet Soil: The Chinese in California Agriculture, 1869–1910* (Berkeley: University of California Press, 1986), Sucheng Chan astutely criticizes scholars who have misrepresented and/or undervalued the role of Chinese farm laborers in the development of California agriculture but does not question the assumption that "factories sprang up in the fields" during the late nineteenth century. Devra Weber, *Dark Sweat, White Gold: California*

Farm Workers, Cotton, and the New Deal (Berkeley: University of California Press, 1994), Gilbert G. González, *Labor and Community: Mexican Citrus Worker Villages in a Southern California County, 1900–1950* (Urbana: University of Illinois Press, 1994), and Camille Guerin-Gonzales, *Mexican Workers and American Dreams: Immigration, Repatriation, and California Farm Labor, 1900–1939* (New Brunswick: Rutgers University Press, 1994) all analyze Mexican farmworkers with deftness and imagination, but for the most part portray their employers in monolithic terms and with minimal documentation.

Other recent histories that stress the agency of farmworkers and provide perfunctory chapters or statements regarding the "industrial" nature of the state's agriculture include Ernesto Galaraza, *Farm Workers and Agri-Business in California, 1947–1960* (Notre Dame, Ind.: University of Notre Dame Press, 1977); James N. Gregory, *American Exodus: The Dust Bowl Migration and Okie Culture in California* (New York: Oxford University Press, 1989); Yuji Ichioka, *The Issei: The World of the First Generation Japanese Immigrants, 1885–1924* (New York: Free Press, 1988); Masakazu Iwata, *Planted in Good Soil: The History of the Issei in United States Agriculture* (New York: Peter Lang, 1992); Mark Reisler, *By the Sweat of Their Brow: Mexican Immigrant Labor in the United States, 1900–1940* (Westport, Conn.: Greenwood Press, 1976); and Vicki L. Ruiz, *Cannery Women, Cannery Lives: Mexican Women, Unionization, and the California Food Processing Industry, 1930–1950* (Albuquerque: University of New Mexico Press, 1987).

There are important exceptions, however. A few recent works challenge, or at least modify, the factories paradigm—albeit indirectly. Gerald L. Prescott examines California wheat growers in their social and cultural contexts in "Farm Gentry vs. the Grangers: Conflict in Rural America," *California Historical Quarterly* 56 (Winter 1977/78): 328–345. Michael Magliari's "California Populism, a Case Study: The Farmers' Alliance and People's Party in San Luis Obispo County, 1885–1903" (Ph.D. diss., University of California, Davis, 1992) demonstrates that wheat growers could be modernizing and wealthy yet so steeped in Jeffersonian values that they joined the Farmers' Alliance. In "Benevolent Monopoly: The Legal Transformation of Agricultural Cooperation, 1890–1943" (Ph.D. diss., University of California, Berkeley, 1990), Victoria Alice Saker challenges conventional wisdom about farm size in California to demonstrate the leverage small growers in the raisin industry held in marketing cooperatives. Steven Stoll emphasizes regional specialization in "The Fruits of Natural Advantage: Horticulture and the Industrial Countryside in California" (Ph.D. diss., Yale University, 1994). Three papers delivered at a 1994 conference on southern California citriculture—Anthea M. Hartig, "'In a World He Has Created': Class Collectivity and the Growers' Landscape of the Southern California Citrus Industry, 1890–1940," *California History* 74 (Spring 1995): 100–111; Grace H. Larson, "The Economics and Structure of the Citrus Industry: Comment on Papers by H. Vincent Moses and Ronald Tobey and Charles Wetherell," ibid., 38–45; and Douglas Cazaux Sackman, "'By Their Fruits Ye Shall Know Them': 'Nature Cross Culture Hybridization' and the California Citrus Industry, 1893–1939," ibid., 82–99 —enhance our understanding of citrus growers by reinvestigating original sources rather than relying on the standard secondary accounts. Kevin Starr's chapter on California's "georgic beginnings" in *Inventing the Dream: California through the Progressive Era* (New York: Oxford University Press, 1985) influenced my thinking considerably.

In addition, the following studies examine Asian farm communities whose economic and cultural complexities bear little resemblance to the industrialized agriculture of McWilliams, Taylor, et al.: James Lukes and Gary Okihiro, *Japanese Legacy: Farming and Community Life in California's Santa Clara Valley* (Cupertino, Calif.: California History Center, 1985); Valerie J. Matsumoto, *Farming the Home Place: A Japanese American Community in California, 1919–1982* (Ithaca: Cornell University Press, 1993); Sally M. Miller, "Changing Faces of the Central Valley: The Ethnic Presence," *California History* 74 (Summer 1995): 165–189; Kesa Noda, *Yamato Colony, 1906–1960: Livingston, California* (Livingston, Calif.: Japanese American Citizens League, 1981); and Sandra O. Uyeunten, "Struggle and Survival: The History of Japanese Immigrant Families in California, 1907–1945" (Ph.D. diss., University of California, San Diego, 1988). Uyeunten's study is particularly illuminating on the unforeseen consequences of the 1907 Gentlemen's Agreement.

Perhaps most suggestive of all is the rich literature on early promoters of modern irrigated agriculture in California. Donald J. Pisani, *From the Family Farm to Agribusiness: The Irrigation Crusade in California and the West, 1850–1931* (Berkeley: University of California Press, 1984), and Donald Worster, *Rivers of Empire: Water, Aridity, and the Growth of the American West* (New York: Oxford University Press, 1985), among others, have demonstrated that William Smythe, William Hammond Hall, and other "crusaders" believed that water could be utilized to promote family farms, break up the state's baronial wheat farms, and still encourage economic development. They saw no contradiction between agrarian ideals and the emerging industrial capitalist order. But irrigation scholars have not examined the worldview of the farmers themselves with the same originality. Pisani, oddly enough, falls back on the agrarian/industrial dichotomy to conclude that nineteenth-century specialty crop growers "saw themselves as businessmen, not community builders." His brief assessment of grower culture stems from a single source—*Factories in the Field.*

Outside of California, the concept of grower culture hardly seems a revelation. Social historians have studied farmers in the Midwest, South, and Northeast with fruitful results. Indeed, "putting the culture back into agriculture" is the core premise of a flourishing subfield, the "new" rural history—everywhere, that is, but in California, where historians in large part remain transfixed by "industrialized agriculture." Four studies in particular have influenced this work. In "Sandy Land and Hogs in the Timber: (Agri)cultural Origins of the Farmers' Alliance in Texas," in *The Countryside in the Age of Capitalist Transformation: Essays in the Social History of Rural America,* ed. Steven Hahn and Jonathan Prude (Chapel Hill: University of North Carolina Press, 1985), 205–229, Robert C. McMath Jr. reminds historians of the double meaning of culture. Pete Daniel's *Breaking the Land: The Transformation of Cotton, Tobacco, and Rice Cultures since 1880* (Urbana: University of Illinois Press, 1985) examines how the contrasting cultures of the South's three staple crops influenced the region's economic and social development. Mary Neth's *Preserving the Family Farm: Women, Community, and the Foundations of Agribusiness in the Midwest, 1900–1940* (Baltimore: Johns Hopkins University Press, 1995) argues that the development of twentieth-century agriculture cannot be fully understood without listening to the voices of farmers themselves. Most recently, Hal S. Barron, in *Mixed Harvest: The Second Great Transformation in the Rural North, 1870–1930* (Chapel Hill: University of North Carolina Press, 1997), analyzes how midwestern and northeastern farmers struggled to come to terms with competing agrarian and capitalist impulses.

Three other studies provided additional insights. Gavin Wright, "American Agriculture and the Labor Market: What Ever Happened to Proletarianization?" in *Quantitative Studies in Agrarian History,* ed. Morton Rothstein and Daniel Field (Ames: Iowa State University Press, 1993), 179–206, examines the relationship between farmers, agricultural workers, and communities in a broader context. Keijiro Otsuka, Hiroyuki Chuma, and Yujiro Hayami survey recent studies of "agricultural contract choice" in developing economies in "Land and Labor Contracts in Agrarian Economies: Theories and Facts," *Journal of Economic Literature* 30 (December 1992): 1965–2018. Risk sharing, the enforceability of contract terms, incentives, supervising concerns, community relations, and a number of other variables, they argue, factor into how farmers assess their particular labor needs. And in the introduction to *The Right to Manage: Industrial Relations Policies of American Business in the 1940s* (Madison: University of Wisconsin Press, 1982), Howell John Harris discusses the dearth of studies of employer culture from an industrial perspective.

Readers interested in cooperative marketing should begin with Saker's "Benevolent Monopoly." Her study is the first to analyze the subject in its legal and social, not just economic, contexts. Previously, scholars relied primarily on the works of agricultural economist H. E. Erdman, cited in the chapter notes. Several other studies were also helpful for my purposes. Edward F. Adams, *The Modern Farmer in His Business Relations* (San Francisco: N. J. Stone Co., 1899), gives a detailed contemporary account of raisin and fruit growers' early cooperative efforts. Mansel G. Blackford, *The Politics of Business in California, 1890–1920* (Columbus: Ohio State University Press, 1977), and Grace H. Larsen, "A Progressive in Agriculture: Harris Weinstock," *Agricultural History* 32 (July 1958): 179–195, clash over the role played by perhaps the most significant nongrower in California's cooperative movement. Blackford also analyzes the standardization movement that began in the Newcastle fruit belt. Carl August Scholl, "An Economic Study of the California Almond Growers' Exchange" (Ph.D. diss., University of California, Berkeley, 1927), remains the only full-length treatment of the subject. A. J. Schoendorf, *Beginnings of Cooperation in the Marketing of California Fresh Deciduous Fruits and History of the California Fruit Exchange* (Sacramento: Inland Press, 1947), explains how the "Newcastle price" worked. And Richard S. Street, "Marketing California Crops at the Turn of the Century," *Southern California Quarterly* 61 (Fall 1979): 239–254 provides an extensively documented overview.

County, local, and regional histories, though often discounted, offer useful biographical, geographical, and community information. Charles W. Clough and William B. Secrest Jr., *Fresno County — The Pioneer Years: From the Beginning to 1900* (Fresno: Panorama West Books, 1984), is particularly valuable for the Fresno colonies. The importance of Raisin Day comes through in Charles W. Clough et al., *Fresno County in the Twentieth Century: From 1900 to the 1980s* (Fresno: Panorama West Books, 1986). Leonard M. Davis, *Newcastle, Gem of the Foothills: A Pictorial History of Newcastle, Placer County, California from Its Formative Days to the Present* (Newcastle: Newcastle Community Association, 1993), describes the development of both "fruit house row" and the Chinese community. Samuel Evans Gittings, "The Foundations of Placer County Horticulture, 1850–1900" (M.A. thesis, Sacramento State College, 1959), is the most comprehensive study available. Joann Leach Larkey describes Putah Creek wheat and almond growers in some detail in *Davisville '68: The History and Heritage of the City of Davis, Yolo County, California* (Davis: City of Davis, 1969). Joseph A. McGowan, *History of the Sacramento Valley*, 3 vols. (New York: Lewis Historical Publishing Co., 1961), surveys many of the region's specialty crop communities, including Davisville, Wheatland, and Newcastle. Wheatland Historical Society, *The City of Wheatland, California, 1874–1974: The History of Wheatland* (Wheatland: Wheatland Historical Society, 1974), reveals that hops were not central to the town's economy or culture.

Few published works explore early-twentieth-century grower-state relations in depth. The standard is Gerald D. Nash, *State Government and Economic Development: A History of Administrative Policies in California, 1849–1933* (Berkeley: Institute of Government Studies, 1964), which takes the grower-state relationship for granted as a natural development in modern society. Daniel's *Bitter Harvest* relies heavily on the notion of a "progressive mentality," and the Majkas' *Farm Workers, Agribusiness, and the State* employs "structuralist" Marxist theory. Neither approach considers how institutional and political imperatives shaped the efforts of individual policymakers. My efforts to explain this complex interaction were informed by Theda Skocpol, *Protecting Soldiers and Mothers: The Political Origins of Social Policy in the United States* (Cambridge: Belknap Press of Harvard University Press, 1992), and Alan Brinkley's review of that book in the *New York Review of Books*, May 26, 1994, 40–43. Two useful "state-centered" California studies are Steven P. Erie, "How the Urban West Was Won: The Local State and Economic Growth in Los Angeles, 1880–1932," *Urban Affairs Quarterly* 27 (June 1992): 519–554; and John Walton, *Western Times and Water Wars: State, Culture, and Rebellion in California* (Berkeley: University of California Press, 1992). I also benefited from analyses of government regulation during the Progressive era and World War I in Melvyn Dubofsky, *The State and Labor in Modern America* (Chapel Hill: University of North Carolina Press, 1994), and Robert Higgs, *Crisis and Leviathan: Critical Episodes in the Growth of American Government* (New York: Oxford University Press, 1987); and from treatments of the county agent system offered by David B. Danbom, *The Resisted Revolution: Urban America and the Industrialization of Agriculture, 1900–1930* (Ames: Iowa State University Press, 1979), and Grant McConnell, *The Decline of Agrarian Democracy* (Berkeley: University of California Press, 1953).

General works on California agriculture from which I have profited include Clarke A. Chambers, *California Farm Organizations: A Historical Study of the Grange, the Farm Bureau, and the Associated Farmers, 1929–1941* (Berkeley: University of California Press, 1952); Robert Glass Cleland and Osgood Hardy, *March of Industry* (Los Angeles: Powell Publishing Co., 1929); Claude B. Hutchison, ed., *California Agriculture* (Berkeley: University of California Press, 1946); Lawrence J. Jelinek, *Harvest Empire: A History of California Agriculture,* 2d ed. (San Francisco: Boyd & Fraser, 1982); and Ann Foley Scheuring, ed., *A Guidebook to California Agriculture* (Berkeley: University of California Press, 1983).

Finally, there are a number of useful bibliographical sources and archival directories available, including Richard J. Orsi, *A List of References for the History of Agriculture in California* (Davis: University of California, Davis, Agricultural History Center, 1974), and its supplement, Mary Davis, Morton Rothstein, and Jean Stratford, *The History of California Agriculture: An Updated Bibliography* (Davis: University of California, Davis, Agricultural History Center, 1991); Richard Steven Street, "Rural California: A Bibliographical Essay," *Southern California Quarterly* 70 (1988): 299–328; Doyce B. Nunis Jr. and Gloria Ricci Lothrop, *A Guide to the History of California* (New York: Greenwood Press, 1989); and Society of California Archivists, *Directory of Archival and Manuscript Repositories in California* (Sacramento: Society of California Archivists, 1994).

Index

Library of Congress Cataloging-in-Publication Data

Vaught, David, 1958–
    Cultivating California : growers, specialty crops, and labor,
1875–1920 / David Vaught.
        p.   cm. — (Revisiting rural America)
    Includes bibliographical references and index.
    ISBN 0-8018-6221-3 (alk. paper)
        1. Agricultural laborers—California—History.   2. Migrant
agricultural laborers—California—History.   3. Industrial relations—
California—History.   4. Cash crops—California—History.
5. Agriculture—Economic aspects—California—History.
6. California—History—1850-1950.   I. Title.   II. Series.
HD1527.C2V38   1999
338.1′09794—dc21   99-30431 CIP

Printed in the United States
6430